CW00434947

Romans

TEACH THE TEXT COMMENTARY SERIES

John H. Walton
Old Testament General Editor

Mark L. Strauss
New Testament General Editor

When complete, the TEACH THE TEXT COMMENTARY SERIES *will include the following volumes:*

Old Testament Volumes

New Testament Volumes

To see which titles are available, visit the series website at www.teachthetextseries.com.

TEACH the TEXT
COMMENTARY SERIES

Romans

C. Marvin Pate

Mark L. Strauss and John H. Walton

GENERAL EDITORS

Rosalie de Rosset

ASSOCIATE EDITOR

BakerBooks

a division of Baker Publishing Group
Grand Rapids, Michigan

© 2013 by C. Marvin Pate

Published by Baker Books
a division of Baker Publishing Group
P.O. Box 6287, Grand Rapids, MI 49516-6287
www.bakerbooks.com

Printed in the United States of America

All rights reserved. No part of this publication may be reproduced, stored in a retrieval system, or transmitted in any form or by any means—for example, electronic, photocopy, recording—without the prior written permission of the publisher. The only exception is brief quotations in printed reviews.

Library of Congress Cataloging-in-Publication Data
Pate, C. Marvin, 1952–
    Romans / C. Marvin Pate.
       p.   cm. — (Teach the text commentary series)
    Includes bibliographical references and index.
    ISBN 978-0-8010-9221-3 (cloth)
    1. Bible N.T. Romans—Commentaries. I. Title.
  BS2665.53.P38 2013
  227′.107—dc23   2012015197

Unless otherwise indicated, Scripture quotations are from the Holy Bible, New International Version®. NIV®. Copyright © 1973, 1978, 1984, 2011 by Biblica, Inc.™ Used by permission of Zondervan. All rights reserved worldwide. www.zondervan.com

Scripture quotations marked ESV are from The Holy Bible, English Standard Version® (ESV®), copyright © 2001 by Crossway, a publishing ministry of Good News Publishers. Used by permission. All rights reserved. ESV Text Edition: 2007.

Scripture quotations marked NRSV are from the New Revised Standard Version of the Bible, copyright © 1989, by the Division of Christian Education of the National Council of Churches of Christ in the United States of America. Used by permission. All rights reserved.

The internet addresses in this book are accurate at the time of publication. They are provided as a resource. Baker Publishing Group does not endorse them or vouch for their content or permanence.

13   14   15   16   17   18   19   7   6   5   4   3   2   1

Interior Design by Brian Brunsting

Contents

Welcome to the Teach the Text Commentary Series

Why another commentary series? That was the question the general editors posed when Baker Books asked us to produce this series. Is there something that we can offer to pastors and teachers that is not currently being offered by other commentary series, or that can be offered in a more helpful way? After carefully researching the needs of pastors who teach the text on a weekly basis, we concluded that yes, more can be done; this commentary is carefully designed to fill an important gap.

The technicality of modern commentaries often overwhelms readers with details that are tangential to the main purpose of the text. Discussions of source and redaction criticism, as well as detailed surveys of secondary literature, seem far removed from preaching and teaching the Word. Rather than wade through technical discussions, pastors often turn to devotional commentaries, which may contain exegetical weaknesses, misuse the Greek and Hebrew languages, and lack hermeneutical sophistication. There is a need for a commentary that utilizes the best of biblical scholarship but also presents the material in a clear, concise, attractive, and user-friendly format.

This commentary is designed for that purpose—to provide a ready reference for the exposition of the biblical text, giving easy access to information that a pastor needs to communicate the text effectively. To that end, the commentary is divided into carefully selected preaching units, each covered in six pages (with carefully regulated word counts both in the passage as a whole and in each subsection). Pastors and teachers engaged in weekly preparation thus know that they will be reading approximately the same amount of material on a week-by-week basis.

Each passage begins with a concise summary of the central message, or "Big Idea," of the passage and a list of its main themes. This is followed by a more detailed interpretation of the text, including the literary context of the passage, historical background material, and interpretive insights. While drawing on the best of biblical scholarship, this material is clear, concise, and to the point. Technical material is kept to a minimum, with endnotes pointing the reader to more detailed discussion and additional resources.

A second major focus of this commentary is on the preaching and teaching process itself. Few commentaries today help the pastor/teacher move from the meaning of the text to its effective communication. Our goal is to bridge this gap. In addition to interpreting the text in the "Understanding the Text" section, each six-page unit contains a "Teaching the Text" section and an "Illustrating the Text" section. The teaching section points to the key theological themes of the passage and ways to communicate these themes to today's audiences. The illustration section provides ideas and examples for retaining the interest of hearers and connecting the message to daily life.

The creative format of this commentary arises from our belief that the Bible is not just a record of God's dealings in the past but is the living Word of God, "alive and active" and "sharper than any double-edged sword" (Heb. 4:12). Our prayer is that this commentary will help to unleash that transforming power for the glory of God.

The General Editors

Introduction to the Teach the Text Commentary Series

This series is designed to provide a ready reference for teaching the biblical text, giving easy access to information that is needed to communicate a passage effectively. To that end, the commentary is carefully divided into units that are faithful to the biblical authors' ideas and of an appropriate length for teaching or preaching.

The following standard sections are offered in each unit.

1. *Big Idea.* For each unit the commentary identifies the primary theme, or "Big Idea," that drives both the passage and the commentary.
2. *Key Themes.* Together with the Big Idea, the commentary addresses in bullet-point fashion the key ideas presented in the passage.
3. *Understanding the Text.* This section focuses on the exegesis of the text and includes several sections.
   a. The Text in Context. Here the author gives a brief explanation of how the unit fits into the flow of the text around it, including refer-

ence to the rhetorical strategy of the book and the unit's contribution to the purpose of the book.
   b. Outline/Structure. For some literary genres (e.g., epistles), a brief exegetical outline may be provided to guide the reader through the structure and flow of the passage.
   c. Historical and Cultural Background. This section addresses historical and cultural background information that may illuminate a verse or passage.
   d. Interpretive Insights. This section provides information needed for a clear understanding of the passage. The intention of the author is to be highly selective and concise rather than exhaustive and expansive.
   e. Theological Insights. In this very brief section the commentary identifies a few carefully selected theological insights about the passage.

4. *Teaching the Text*. Under this second main heading the commentary offers guidance for teaching the text. In this section the author lays out the main themes and applications of the passage. These are linked carefully to the Big Idea and are represented in the Key Themes.

5. *Illustrating the Text*. Here the commentary provides suggestions of where useful illustrations may be found in fields such as literature, entertainment, history, or biography. They are intended to provide general ideas for illustrating the passage's key themes and so serve as a catalyst for effectively illustrating the text.

Preface

It is a joy to be included in Baker's Teach the Text series. I can think of no other biblical book that I would rather write a commentary on than Paul's letter to the Romans, and it is a privilege to be asked to do so. I pray that the reader will thrill to the message of this most important of Paul's writings.

No book is an independent endeavor; certainly not this one. There are numerous people that have helped make my dream of this manuscript become a reality. Here I mention only a few. First, I wish to thank Mark Strauss for extending to me the invitation to participate in this series. Mark is an editor "in whom I am well pleased" (to quote the biblical text)! His expertise, insight, and patience helped me stay the course in this project, and I am deeply grateful to him for it. Next, I am so pleased to have done this work in collaboration with a former colleague of mine, one highly esteemed—Rosalie de Rosset. Dr. de Rosset is an astute professor who has a wonderful grasp of both literature and theology. It is, therefore, an honor for me that she, along with Mark Eckel, has done the sections of each chapter that were illustrative and practical in nature. And, then, as usual it was a pleasure to work with the fine team at Baker, and to once again be impressed by their commitment to the sacred text.

Also, I wish to express my appreciation to my work-study student—Mrs. Jennifer Hill. Jennifer typed much of this manuscript, thereby accomplishing the near-impossible task of reading my handwriting! I am also happy to say that Jennifer and her husband Jason are preparing even now to serve the Lord as international missionaries. Finally, it is a continual blessing to work at such a fine institution as Ouachita Baptist University. The administration, faculty, and especially students deserve many thanks for creating an environment that fosters the love of God and the love of learning. My hope is that this commentary on Romans will reflect those passions.

C. Marvin Pate
Chair of Christian Theology
Pruet School of Christian Studies
Ouachita Baptist University
March 30, 2012

Abbreviations

General

b.	born
ca.	circa
cf.	*confer*, compare
chap(s).	chapter(s)
d.	died
e.g.	*exempli gratia*, for example
esp.	especially
ET	English translation
mg.	margin
s.v.	*sub verbo*, under the word
v(v).	verse(s)

Ancient Text Types and Versions

LXX	Septuagint
MT	Masoretic Text

Modern Versions

ESV	English Standard Version
NASB	New American Standard Bible
NIV	New International Version

Apocrypha and Septuagint

Add. Esth.	Additions to Esther
Bar.	Baruch
Jdt.	Judith
1 Macc.	1 Maccabees
2 Macc.	2 Maccabees
4 Macc.	4 Maccabees
Sir.	Sirach
Tob.	Tobit
Wis.	Wisdom of Solomon

Old Testament Pseudepigrapha

Apoc. Ab.	*Apocalypse of Abraham*
Apoc. Mos.	*Apocalypse of Moses*
2 Bar.	*2 Baruch (Syriac Apocalypse)*
3 Bar.	*3 Baruch (Greek Apocalypse)*
4 Bar.	*4 Baruch (Paraleipomena Jeremiou)*
1 En.	*1 Enoch (Ethiopic Apocalypse)*
2 En.	*2 Enoch (Slavonic Apocalypse)*
Jos. Asen.	*Joseph and Aseneth*
Jub.	*Jubilees*
L.A.B.	*Liber antiquitatum biblicarum (Pseudo-Philo)*
L.A.E.	*Life of Adam and Eve*
Let. Aris.	*Letter of Aristeas*
Pss. Sol.	*Psalms of Solomon*
Sib. Or.	*Sibylline Oracles*
T. Benj.	*Testament of Benjamin*
T. Jud.	*Testament of Judah*
T. Levi	*Testament of Levi*
T. Reub.	*Testament of Reuben*
T. Zeb.	*Testament of Zebulun*

Dead Sea Scrolls

CD	*Damascus Document*
1QH^a	*Hodayot^a*
1QM	*War Scroll*

1QpHab	*Pesher Habakkuk*
1QS	*Rule of the Community*
1QSa	*Rule of the Congregation*
4QMMT	*Halakhic Letter*
4Q171 (4QpPsᵃ)	*Psalms Pesherᵃ*
4Q174 (4QFlor)	*Florilegium*

Mishnah and Talmud

b.	Babylonian Talmud
m.	Mishnah
t.	Tosefta
y.	Jerusalem Talmud

'Abod. Zar.	*'Abodah Zarah*
'Abot	*'Abot*
Hag.	*Hagigah*
Ker.	*Kerithot*
Ned.	*Nedarim*
Shabb.	*Shabbat*
Sanh.	*Sanhedrin*
Yad.	*Yadayim*

Targumic Texts

| *Tg. Neof.* | *Targum Neofiti* |
| *Tg. Yer.* | *Targum Yerushalmi* |

Other Rabbinic Works

Mek.	*Mekilta*
Pesiq. Rab.	*Pesiqta Rabbati*
Rab.	*Rabbah*

Apostolic Fathers

1 Clem.	*1 Clement*
Ign. *Eph.*	Ignatius, *To the Ephesians*
Ign. *Magn.*	Ignatius, *To the Magnesians*
Mart. Pol.	*Martyrdom of Polycarp*

Greek and Latin Works

Aristotle

| *Eth. nic.* | *Nicomachean Ethics (Ethica nicomachea)* |
| *Pol.* | *Politics (Politica)* |

Augustine

Conf.	*Confessions (Confessionum libri XIII)*
Julian	*Against Julian (Contra Julianum)*
Spir. Let.	*The Spirit and the Letter (De spiritu et littera)*

Columella

| *Rust.* | *On Agriculture (De re rustica)* |

Epictetus

| *Disc.* | *Discourses (Dissertationes)* |

Euripides

| *Andr.* | *Andromache* |

Eusebius

| *Hist. eccl.* | *Ecclesiastical History (Historia ecclesiastica)* |

Horace

| *Sat.* | *Satires (Satirae)* |

Irenaeus

| *Haer.* | *Against Heresies (Adversus haereses)* |

John Chrysostom

| *Hom. Rom.* | *Homilies on Paul's Epistle to the Romans* |

Josephus

Ag. Ap.	*Against Apion (Contra Apionem)*
Ant.	*Jewish Antiquities (Antiquitates judaicae)*
J.W.	*Jewish War (Bellum judaicum)*
Life	*The Life (Vita)*

Juvenal

| *Sat.* | *Satires (Satirae)* |

Livy

Hist.	History of Rome (Ab urbe condita libri)

Marcus Aurelius

Medit.	Meditations

Ovid

Cure	The Cure for Love (Remedia amoris)
Metam.	Metamorphoses

Palladius

Insit.	On the Grafting of Trees (De insitione)

Philo

Abraham	On the Life of Abraham (De Abrahamo)
Cherubim	On the Cherubim (De cherubim)
Creation	On the Creation of the World (De opificio mundi)
Decalogue	On the Decalogue (De decalogo)
Embassy	On the Embassy to Gaius (Legatio ad Gaium)
Moses	On the Life of Moses (De vita Mosis)
Posterity	On the Posterity of Cain (De posteritate Caini)
Spec. Laws	On the Special Laws (De specialibus legibus)
Virtues	On the Virtues (De virtutibus)

Plutarch

Mor.	Moralia

Pseudo-Aristotle

Cosmos	On the Cosmos (De mundo)

Pseudo-Lucian

Asin.	Asinus (Lucius, or The Ass)

Seneca

Anger	On Anger (De ira)
Mor. Ep.	Moral Epistles (Epistulae morales)

Suetonius

Claudius	Life of Claudius (Divus Claudius)

Tacitus

Ann.	Annals (Annales)
Hist.	Histories (Historiae)

Xenophon

Cyr.	Cyropaedia

Secondary Sources

ANF	Ante-Nicene Fathers
BDAG	Bauer, W., F. W. Danker, W. F. Arndt, and F. W. Gingrich. Greek-English Lexicon of the New Testament and Other Early Christian Literature. 3rd ed. Chicago, 1999
NPNF¹	Nicene and Post-Necene Fathers, Series 1
PL	Patrologia latina [= Patrologiae cursus completus: Series latina]. Edited by J.-P. Migne. 217 vols. Paris, 1844–64
Str-B	Strack, H. L., and P. Billerbeck. Kommentar zum Neuen Testament aus Talmud und Midrasch. 6 vols. Munich, 1922–61
TDNT	Theological Dictionary of the New Testament. Edited by G. Kittel and G. Friedrich. Translated by G. W. Bromiley. 10 vols. Grand Rapids, 1964–76

Introduction to Romans

Next to Jesus Christ, the apostle Paul is arguably the most important figure in the Christian faith. His life, letters, and theology have indelibly shaped Christianity in the last two millennia. Some of the greatest church leaders have accorded an exalted place to the apostle to the Gentiles: Peter honored him (2 Pet. 3:15–16); Augustine appealed to him; Luther revered him; Wesley found assurance in him; Barth thundered forth because of him; and proponents of the "Old Perspective" and of the "New Perspective" toward Paul alike extol him as their own.[1] And it is no surprise that these people and movements sooner or later based their understanding of Paul on his magnum opus—Romans. Paul and Romans: an unbeatable combination that delivers the knockout punch to any works-oriented righteousness before God; a soothing remedy for the soul that longs for peace with God; and a hopeful proclamation that God has begun to put the world to rights with himself. A commentary on Romans is therefore most fitting. Of course, there are already myriads of works on Romans

going back to the early church fathers, but still, each new generation deserves a fresh hearing of this ancient masterpiece that Paul wrote somewhere between AD 55 and 58. Though daunting, that is the joyous task that this present study attempts to accomplish. Before an introduction to Paul's letter to the Christians at Rome, however, some comments are needed about Paul the man: the contours of his world, the extent of his letters, and the center of his thought.

Paul the Man: His World(s), His Letters, and His Theology

Paul's World(s)

Paul was a product of three worlds: Greco-Roman, Jewish, and Christian. These influences impacted Paul in increasing significance, like concentric circles. At the periphery of Paul's world was the Greco-Roman sphere of influence. Like most travelers in the Roman Empire in the middle of the first century AD, Paul spoke the trade language bequeathed to the masses of his day—Koine (common) Greek. Koine Greek

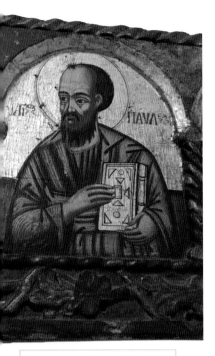

An icon of Paul from a larger piece entitled *Christ and Twelve Apostles* taken from a nineteenth-century AD Orthodox church in the Antalya region of Turkey.

was a mixture of classical Greek dialects and native languages of the conquered peoples in the domain of Alexander the Great (ca. 330 BC). Koine Greek was a standard language used for culture and commerce, much as English is in our day. The influence of Greek culture on Paul is evident also in the way he drew upon ancient classical Greek philosophical traditions such as Platonism, Stoicism, and Epicureanism. Paul also utilized the tools of Greek rhetoric, such as the diatribe, the fool's speech, and the *peristasis* catalogue (a list of afflictions). And, of course, the concept of the *polis* (city) and even democracy had a constant bearing on Paul's daily experiences. Mighty Rome obviously cast its long shadow across the Roman provinces, and Paul made much use of its contributions: *pax Romana* (peace of Rome), brought about by the reign of Caesar Augustus (ca. 31 BC–AD 14) in a world torn by civil war and terrorized by pirates on the sea and bandits on the land; a pervasive and sturdy infrastructure; and a fair-minded jurisprudence system that transcended the petty politics of local towns. Indeed, the last-mentioned amenity ensured Paul an audience with the court of

Rome, where the apostle was bound and determined to visit.

But Paul was born Saul—a Jew by birth and upbringing. Though reared in the Gentile city of Tarsus, Paul probably was taken by his parents as a young person to Jerusalem to be trained as a rabbi (Acts 22:2–3). There he excelled his peers in his grasp of the Torah and the oral tradition of the Pharisees, and in his love for the land of Israel. Indeed, Paul was so zealously Jewish that he devoted himself to stamping out Judaism's newest fringe group, the followers of Jesus. Paul's zeal for Moses, loathing of Gentile influence on Judaism, and hatred of Jesus drove him to the point of violence against the church. He relates his passion for Judaism and contempt for the church especially in Galatians 1:13–14; Philippians 3:4–6; and 1 Timothy 1:13 (cf. Acts 9:1–2).

However, a "funny" thing happened to Paul the Pharisee on his way to Damascus to persecute Christians: he was saved through an encounter with the risen Jesus (Gal. 1:15–16; Phil. 3:7–11; cf. Acts 9:3–18; 22:2–21; 26:4–23). There Paul surrendered to the crucified Jesus, who was none other than the glorious Christ, and, in a divine touché, Paul the Gentile-basher was there and then called to be an apostle to the nations. In a flash, Paul exchanged the law of Moses for faith in Christ, hatred of non-Jews for love of the church, the land of Israel for the kingdom of God, and circumcision and the old covenant for the cross of Calvary. Paul's encounter with the risen Jesus was nothing short of both a conversion and a calling.[2] Indeed, God's setting apart of Paul to preach to the Gentiles the gospel of Jesus Christ was the fulfillment of the end-time conversion of the nations predicted by Old Testament prophets such as Isaiah and Micah.[3]

Paul's Letters

Thirteen New Testament letters are attributed to Paul, and traditionally they are grouped into four categories: early epistles (1–2 Thessalonians); major epistles (Galatians [which some think was Paul's first letter], Romans, 1–2 Corinthians); prison epistles (Philippians, Ephesians, Colossians, Philemon); the Pastoral Epistles (1–2 Timothy, Titus).

The traditional approach to Paul's letters, however, has for the last century or so been vigorously challenged by less conservatively inclined scholars. These scholars attribute only seven of the so-called Pauline Epistles to the apostle himself: Galatians, Romans, 1–2 Corinthians, 1 Thessalonians, Philippians, and Philemon; the rest, they think, were written by Paul's students after the apostle's death in about AD 64. Therefore, it is argued, the latter "pseudonymous" writings are not to be given serious attention in discerning Paul's theology. This wing of Pauline scholarship bases its claim essentially on three arguments. First, the vocabulary of the disputable letters differs from that of the indisputable Pauline Epistles. Second, the history presumed by the Pastoral Epistles matches neither the events of Paul's letters nor the accounts of Paul's travels as recorded in Acts. Third, the theology of the pseudonymous letters is at odds with the undisputed Pauline Epistles.

Since Paul's authorship of Romans is undisputed, a commentary on Romans need not include a full-scale discussion of the issue of how many letters Paul actually wrote, but we should at least note in passing the traditional responses to the foregoing arguments. First, the differences in vocabulary between the disputed and the undisputed letters of Paul can be accounted for by his use of different secretaries for his letters (Rom. 16:22 names Tertius as one of them) and by the differing vocabulary required to address the various circumstances of each church to which he wrote. Second, there is good reason for postulating the theory that Paul was released from his Roman captivity recorded in Acts 28 (ca. AD 62), after which he conducted a mission trip to Spain (see Rom. 15) and perhaps elsewhere, but then was rounded up with Peter and other Christians to be tried by the emperor Nero in Rome. There, reliable tradition tells us, Paul and Peter were martyred for their faith in Christ (ca. AD 64). Indeed, the fact that Luke, Paul's sometime missionary companion and the author

At the foot of the Capitoline Hill, which overlooks the Roman Forum, is a prison built in the seventh to sixth century BC and used until the fourth century AD. Currently located in the lower levels of the church of San Guiseppe dei Falegnami, it is known as the Mamertine Prison. Legend maintains that Paul and Peter were held here while awaiting execution.

of Acts, does not record Paul's death in Acts 28 decidedly points toward this theory. Third, the overall theology of the disputed letters of Paul—the overlapping of the two ages (see below)—is also the driving engine of the undisputed Pauline Epistles, as more than one scholar has noted. And if that is the case for the major theme of Paul's thought, then why should one doubt that it is the same or similar for Paul's minor themes?[4]

Paul's Theology

Four major options have competed as the proposed center of Paul's thought: justification by faith; the Tübingen theory; the history-of-religions approach; and Jewish eschatology. My discussion of these themes proceeds from the assumption that if the key to the apostle Paul's thought can be identified, then therein we find a frame of reference for interpreting his letters.

With the Protestant Reformation, justification by faith became the leading contender to be the center of Paul's theology (at least among non-Catholics), especially when one takes into consideration Galatians, Romans, and Philippians (chap. 3). The thesis of those letters is that the sinner is declared righteous before God through simple faith in Jesus Christ, not by the works of the law of Moses, the Torah. Certainly, justification by faith is a major player in Paul's theology, as we will repeatedly see in the letter to the Romans. However, Pauline scholars of the last century rightly observed that although justification is important to Paul, it is not pervasive in the rest of his writings. Rather, the doctrine of justification by faith seems to have been a teaching that Paul explained and defended

in response to the Judaizers' influence on some, but not all, of the churches to which he wrote. In other words, Paul's apologetic for justification by faith was a polemic against the false teaching of the Judaizers that salvation comes by faith in Christ plus obedience to the Torah. Justification by faith most probably is not, then, the overarching theme driving the Pauline corpus.

The Tübingen theory is named after the university in that German town and was associated with one of that institution's leading theology professors, F. C. Baur.[5] In the mid-nineteenth century, Baur claimed that the key to understanding Paul, and indeed the entire New Testament, is to see that a theological civil war runs throughout its pages: Paul and the message of justification by faith versus Peter and the message of justification by faith plus works of the Torah (the Judaizers). It was left to the anonymous work of Acts in the second century to paint an idyllic portrait of the early church in which Paul and Peter come across as the best of buddies. Although the Tübingen theory enjoyed enormous popularity among New Testament interpreters in Europe during the nineteenth century and the first part of the twentieth century, its influence all but vanished in the second half of the twentieth century thanks to two considerations. First, scholars recognized Baur's theory for what it really was, a foisting upon the New Testament of the dialectic philosophy of Hegel: thesis (Paul's message) versus antithesis (Peter's message) resulting in a synthesis (Acts' reconciliation of the two). In other words, the theology of Paul and the New Testament was distorted by an imposition of philosophical categories upon it. Second, fewer scholars today doubt that Luke wrote Acts and that he did so in the late first century, not the mid- to late second century.

In the first half of the twentieth century another hypothesis concerning the center of Paul's theology arose from the history-of-religions school. Although there were various constructs under the umbrella of this approach, they shared the common idea that Paul gave up his Jewish faith for Hellenistic (Greek) religion, whether Greek mystery religions (so Richard Reitzenstein), Hellenistic mysticism (so Adolf Deissmann), or Platonic gnosticism (so Rudolf Bultmann).[6] Today, the history-of-religions approach is still championed by a few high-profile scholars (e.g., the Jesus Seminar, Elaine Pagels, Bart Ehrman), but most scholars maintain that Paul was true to his Jewish heritage, and that Hellenistic influence was at the periphery, not the center, of his theology. This is so even after we duly note the interpenetration of Hellenism and Judaism in the first century.[7]

The fourth contender for the center of Paul's thought is Jewish eschatology, but in revised form. Albert Schweitzer in the early twentieth century convinced most New Testament scholars that the two-age structure of the writings of Second Temple Judaism (Judaism in the time between the rebuilding of the second

temple in Jerusalem in 519 BC and its destruction by the Romans in AD 70) was the key not only to Jesus' message but also to Paul's theology. Apocalyptic Judaism was a dominant strand of Jewish theology by the time of Jesus, teaching that history divides into two ages: the present age of sin and sorrow caused by Adam's fall, and the coming age of the kingdom of God, a period of unprecedented righteousness and peace; and it would be the Messiah who would establish the latter.[8] Most Pauline scholars today see this as the key to the thought of Jesus, Paul, and indeed the whole of the New Testament.[9] And with this I agree. But there is a significant difference between the ancient Jewish two-age scenario and the New Testament: whereas the former expected that the two ages would be consecutive (when the Messiah comes, he will completely replace this age with the age to come), the latter claims that the two ages are now simultaneous; that is, they overlap. Thus, with the life, death, and resurrection of Jesus Christ the age to come (kingdom of God) broke into

Paul developed his theology under the guidance of the Holy Spirit while living in a polytheistic Roman Empire that was rather tolerant of religion and tended to absorb various belief systems into its own pagan system. As the worship of state gods and goddesses became more ritual observance than religious conviction, several mystery religions sprang up. The one that would rise to prominence toward the end of the first century AD was the cult of Mithras. The meeting places of the followers of Mithraism usually contained an image of Mithras preparing to sacrifice the divine bull, like the one shown here from the second century AD.

this present age but did not end it. This is often labeled "inaugurated eschatology," which holds that with the first coming of Christ the age to come has already dawned, but its completion still awaits the second coming of Christ. The following two charts illustrate the Jewish two-age structure and Jesus' modification of it:

Old Jewish View

The Present Age	The Coming Age (or the Kingdom of God)
The time of Satan Sin, Sickness, and Death Longing for the fullness of the Spirit	The time of God Righteousness, Wholeness, and Eternal Life God's Spirit indwelling all believers

The Christian View

THE END

In-break of Kingdom — Consummation

The Present Age	Between the Times	The Coming Age The time of the Spirit
The time of "the flesh"		

For our purposes, the book of Romans attests to the importance of the overlapping of the two ages for understanding Paul's concept of justification by faith: faith in Jesus Christ apart from the works of the Torah projects end-time justification of the sinner by God into the present age. I will have much more to say on this in the commentary itself; for now, I simply note that inaugurated eschatology (the key to Paul's theology) and justification by faith are kindred spirits in the book of Romans.

With the preceding background in mind, we may now turn to an introduction of Paul's letter to the Romans.

The Letter to the Romans

This introduction to the book of Romans will follow the usual procedure by discussing its importance in church history, composition, date and place of writing, recipients, theme, purpose, and genre/outline. These opening comments, however, will yield some surprising results, especially regarding the last three items mentioned. Hopefully, these new observations will shed considerable light on the letter as a whole.

The Importance of Romans in Church History

The book of Romans, more than almost any other biblical book, has dramatically shaped church history. This is not surprising, since Romans is the most systematic explanation of the gospel of Jesus Christ that the New Testament contains. We may recall here some of the individuals mentioned earlier in this regard whose lives were forever changed by the message of Romans. Augustine (fifth-century church father) at long last found peace with God after reading Romans 13:14: "Clothe yourselves with the Lord Jesus Christ, and do not think about how to gratify the desires of the flesh." Such a challenge was just what the young and restless Augustine needed, and he went on to become perhaps the most important theologian of the church since Paul himself.

Martin Luther in 1517 came to a whole new understanding of the righteousness of God when he meditated on Romans 1:17: "For in the gospel the righteousness of God is revealed—a righteousness that is by faith from first to last, just as it is written: 'The righteous will live by faith.'" Listen to Luther's testimony about his conversion based on this new understanding of divine righteousness as illuminated by this verse:

> Though I lived as a monk without reproach, I felt that I was a sinner before God with an extremely disturbed conscience. I could not believe that he was placated by my satisfaction. I did not love, yes, I hated the righteous God who punishes sinners. . . . At last, by the mercy of God, . . . I began to understand that the righteousness of God is that by which the righteous lives by a gift of God, namely by faith. . . . Here I felt that I was altogether born again and had entered paradise itself through open gates. . . . And I extolled my sweetest word with a love as great as the hatred with which I had before hated the word 'righteousness of God.'[10]

So too did Romans 1:17 change John Wesley, for the mere reading of Luther's commentary on that verse in Aldersgate Chapel on a night in 1738 brought to Wesley an assurance of salvation that had long eluded him. Wesley wrote of that moment,

"My heart was strangely warmed. I felt I did trust Christ; Christ alone for salvation."[11]

Karl Barth's conversion from liberal theology to a more conservative brand of Christianity (known as neoorthodoxy) stemmed from his sermons on the book of Romans. His 1919 commentary on Romans, which declared that change in perspective, was epochmaking. Barth, armed with the message of Romans, singlehandedly brought about the demise of old-line liberal theology.

Besides the spiritual luminaries just mentioned, we can only imagine how large a number of persons have become believers in Jesus Christ by traveling the "Romans road" (Rom. 3:23; 6:23; 10:9–10, 13), the present author included.

Yes, the book of Romans has changed the lives of millions of individuals and governed the very course of church history. It deserves, therefore, our respect and even reverence.

The Composition of Romans

What did Romans look like originally? That is, what did it look like when it left the hands of Paul and his professional scribe, Tertius? Four answers have been given to this question throughout the years.

First, the second-century heretic Marcion said that Romans originally consisted of chapters 1–14. But it is obvious that Marcion had a vested interest in propounding this particular theory. It was the church at Rome that branded Marcion a heretic around AD 150, and Romans 15–16 compliments the Christians there at Rome. Moreover, Marcion was declared a heretic because he argued in favor of the recognition of Paul's letters and a few other

Introduction to Romans

portions of the New Testament as Christian Scripture, but not the Old Testament. Romans 15–16 draws heavily in a positive way on the Old Testament.

A second view is that Romans ended originally at chapter 15, but after Paul's death an editor added chapter 16, thereby redirecting the letter from Rome to Ephesus. Why Ephesus? Because chapter 16 contains greetings to numerous individuals whom Paul knew, but how could Paul know them if he had never been to Rome? It is more likely, so this theory goes, that these are people whom the apostle befriended at Ephesus, a city where he spent three years ministering (Acts 19). But this hypothesis overlooks a key consideration: Paul probably met the folks greeted in Romans 16 during his various missionary travels, and he mentions them here to prepare the way for his imminent arrival at the capital city. In other words, the greetings in chapter 16 point to Rome as the destination of the letter, the composition of which runs from chapter 1 through 16.

Third, the majority opinion today is that Romans originally went from 1:1 to 16:23, thus excluding the doxology in 16:25–27. The many scholars taking this view do so for two reasons: (1) the doxology occurs at different places in the Greek manuscripts of Romans (e.g., after 14:23 or 15:33 or 16:23); (2) the language is liturgical, similar to Ephesians 1:1–14, and many Pauline scholars do not believe that Paul wrote Ephesians. But there are weighty reasons for maintaining that the doxology is original to Romans and occurred at the very end of the letter, where it is found in English translations today. (1) Even though the doxology occurs at different places in some Greek manuscripts, it is found after Romans 16:23 in the majority of the best Greek texts. (2) The theological theme of the doxology—the obedience of the Gentiles—matches the theme of Romans 1:1–7, thus forming an *inclusio* for the letter as a whole and signaling one of the key purposes of the letter (see the discussion to follow and also in the commentary sections on Rom. 1:1–7; 16:25–27). (3) For those like myself who accept the Pauline authorship of Ephesians, it poses no problem that the liturgical style of the doxology in Romans 16:25–27 matches Ephesians 1:1–14 and elsewhere.

Fourth, although it is a minority view, I side with those who argue that Romans looked in the beginning like it looks today in the English text: it started at 1:1 and ended at 16:27.

The Date and Place of the Writing of Romans

There is little debate today concerning the date and the place of the writing of Romans. Most scholars agree that Paul wrote the letter somewhere between AD 55 and 58, on his third missionary trip. This conclusion is based on two considerations: the intersection of two events on Paul's

> Romans was written by Paul and his professional scribe, Tertius (Rom. 16:22). Writing materials during this time period included a stylus for writing on wax tablets, and pen and ink for writing on surfaces such as papyrus, vellum, boards, or pottery. Pictured is a Roman bronze pen and inkpot (first century AD).

second missionary journey with Roman chronology, and the intersection of Paul's comments in Romans with the book of Acts. First, according to Acts 18, which records events from Paul's second missionary trip (which occurred before Paul wrote Romans), Paul appeared before Gallio, Roman proconsul of Corinth (Acts 18:12–17). According to Roman records (the Gallio Inscription in particular), Gallio was proconsul of Corinth in AD 51–52. Note that the Roman emperor Claudius expelled all Jews from Rome in AD 49 (see Suetonius, *Claudius* 25.4; Acts 18:2), but upon the emperor's death in AD 54, Jews were allowed to return to Rome. Indeed, in Romans 16:3 Paul greets Priscilla and Aquila, a Jewish couple who had been expelled from Rome in AD 49, but who now have relocated back in the city, presumably after AD 54. All this is to say that Paul could not have written Romans before AD 52 or before AD 54. Second, Acts 18:23–21:16 records Paul's third missionary journey, including a three-year stay in Ephesus. Most Pauline scholars believe that Paul wrote 1–2 Corinthians from Ephesus, sometime around AD 55. Those two letters speak about Paul's plan

to collect from the church at Corinth and others an offering for the poor saints in Jerusalem (1 Cor. 16:1–4; 2 Cor. 8–9). By the time Paul wrote to the Roman Christians, the churches of the provinces of Macedonia and Achaia (in which Corinth was located) had delivered on their promise to make such a collection (so Rom. 15:25–27). Thus, Romans must have been written after AD 55, the date of the Corinthian letters. From the preceding considerations one arrives at a date for the writing of Romans no sooner than AD 55. But from where do we get the outer date of AD 58 for Romans? The next point provides the answer.

It is commonly agreed that after his stay in Ephesus of approximately two and a half years (see Acts 19:8–10), Paul traveled to Corinth for a three-month stay (Acts 20:1–3), and from there he wrote Romans. Romans 16:1 indicates that Paul was writing from Corinth, since he commends Phoebe, a resident of Cenchreae, which was near Corinth, to the congregations of Rome. Moreover, Paul mentions Erastus in Romans 16:23, the same Erastus who was the director of Corinth's public works. Gaius, who provided lodging for Paul, probably also hailed from Corinth

Most scholars agree that Paul wrote the book of Romans from Corinth between AD 55 and 58 while on his third missionary journey. Shown here are the archaeological remains of the temple of Apollo in ancient Corinth with the Acrocorinth, its acropolis, in the background.

(Rom. 16:23). If indeed Paul was writing the letter of Romans from Corinth, then AD 58 seems established as the outer date for its composition.

The Recipients of Romans

It is clear from Romans itself that the recipients of the letter include both Jewish and Gentile Christians, for both groups are addressed throughout the document (1:1–16; 2:1–3:20; 9–11; 14:1–15:13). The fourth-century church father later called Ambrosiaster no doubt was accurate in saying that the church at Rome was not founded by any apostle (it is obvious that Paul had not visited Rome yet, nor had Peter or any other apostle, for Paul's practice was not to build on any other apostle's foundation [see Rom. 15:20–21]).[12] Most likely, it was founded by Roman Jews who were converted in Jerusalem on the day of Pentecost (Acts 2) and returned home to the synagogues in Rome with their newfound faith in Jesus the Messiah. It is also likely that these Jewish Christians led the Gentile God-fearers who worshiped in their synagogues to Christ. The God-fearers were Gentiles who came to believe in the one God of Israel but did not submit to circumcision or the whole of the law of Moses.[13]

The bust of Emperor Claudius, who ruled the Roman Empire from AD 41 to 54

So somewhere between AD 30 and 55 Christianity became established in Rome, with believers probably meeting in as many as five house and tenement churches (see Rom. 16:5, 10–11, 14–15) and with an attendance of perhaps a few hundred (a large house church could accommodate fifty people for worship). From this we can see how the Roman believers could have become polarized into "weak" (possibly Jewish Christians) and "strong" (possibly Gentile Christians) factions (see Rom. 14:1–15:13), since they met in various locations. Moreover, most scholars today think that the Gentile Christian element in the house churches became dominant when Jews (Jewish Christians included) were expelled from Rome in AD 49 by Claudius. Suetonius (*Claudius* 25.4) reports that the Roman emperor expelled Jews from Rome at that time because they were squabbling over the man Chrestus, whose name probably was a corruption of the Greek *Christos*, meaning "Christ." The early second-century Roman historian no doubt was referring to the controversy between Jewish Christians and non-Christian Jews over whether or not Jesus was the Christ. Since Rome did not distinguish between Jewish Christians and non-Christian Jews, but considered them all Jews, Claudius kicked out the whole lot of them. As noted above, Jews were not allowed to return to Rome until after Claudius's death in AD 54. At that time, Jewish Christians came home to house or tenement churches now dominated by Gentile Christians, making for a tense relationship between the two groups (see Rom. 9–11).

The Theme of Romans

Almost all commentators on Romans look to 1:16–17 as the theme of the letter:

For I am not ashamed of the gospel, because it is the power of God that brings salvation to everyone who believes: first to the Jew, then to the Gentile. For in the gospel the righteousness of God is revealed—a righteousness that is by faith from first to last, just as it is written: "The righteous will live by faith" [Hab. 2:4].

Beyond that, however, there is much debate regarding what these verses actually mean. Three questions perplex scholars: What does Paul mean by "righteousness of God"? What does the phrase "from faith to faith" (NIV: "by faith from first to last") mean? What is Paul's understanding of Habakkuk 2:4? I will deal more at length with Romans 1:16–17 later in the commentary section, but here I tip my hand as to what I think Paul means in these critical verses. Paul is drawing on the theme of the story of Israel.

Very simply put, the story of Israel is fourfold in the Old Testament narrative: (1) God's promised blessing upon Israel if the nation obeyed him; (2) Israel's repeated sins against God; (3) God's response of sending Israel into exile, to Assyria in 722 BC and then to Babylonia in 587/586 BC; (4) God's unwavering promise that Israel will be restored to their land if they repent. In my view, every key word in Romans 1:16–17 is rooted in the fourth point of this story: Israel's promised restoration. Thus, the words "gospel," "power," and "salvation" would have immediately brought to mind Isaiah 40–66 and the promise of the good news that God will restore Israel to their land; this is nothing less than the power of God to save his people, and it will be a demonstration of God's righteousness (e.g., Isa. 46:13; 51:5–8). And when Israel is restored to God and the land, then the

nations of the world will come to believe in Israel's God and stream into Jerusalem to worship him (e.g., Isa. 2:2–4; Mic. 4:1–3). In other words, "first to the Jew" would come restoration/salvation, and "then to the Gentile." In the meantime, however, according to Habakkuk 2:4, the faithful Jew is to wait in faith on the Lord for the day of Israel's restoration by obeying the Torah.

In Romans 1:16–17, however, Paul tweaks or qualifies the way Israel understood this Old Testament story. For the apostle to the Gentiles, the good news of the power of God's salvation and righteousness is not the physical and geographical restoration of Jews to their homeland, but rather the spiritual conversion of sinners precisely because they stop trusting in the works of the law of Moses and place their faith in Jesus Christ alone. Moreover, Paul reverses the order of the restoration of Israel and the conversion of the Gentiles: first comes the conversion of the Gentiles, and then the restoration of Israel (see my comments on, e.g., Rom. 1:1–15; 11:25–27).[14]

The Purpose of Romans

Although the debate continues as to why Paul penned his magnificent letter to the Romans, the apostle himself leaves the reader in no doubt as to his purpose: Paul was divinely called to lead the way in bringing about the end-time conversion of the nations, a mission in which the church at Rome was to play a critical role (see Rom. 1:1–15; 15:14–33; 16:25–27). Thus, Rome was to be the last major stopping point before the apostle launched the final leg of his eschatological mission to Spain, the end of the then-known world (see again Rom. 15:14–33).[15] But to garner the support of the

During the first century AD, the Roman Empire controlled a vast area. It achieved its maximum size around AD 117 under Emperor Trajan. It extended as far north as modern-day Great Britain and as far west as Spain, stretched into parts of North Africa and Egypt to the south, and reached the border of the Parthian Empire and Arabia on the east. Paul desired to preach the gospel to the western end of the then-known world, Spain.

Christians in Rome, the capital city of the Roman Empire, Paul had to accomplish two tasks. First, he had to motivate the Jewish and Gentile Christians in Rome to start getting along again (see esp. Rom. 9–11; 14–15); otherwise the church would not be sufficiently unified to support him financially and spiritually in his Spanish mission. Second, even before that, he had to convince the Roman Christians that he was a legitimate apostle and therefore worthy of their support. Douglas Moo pinpoints this aspect of Romans very well:

> Paul's ultimate destination is Spain. As he clearly hints in 15:24, he is coming to Rome, among other things, to get the Ro-

mans to help him with that mission. But Paul has never been to Rome. Moreover, he is a controversial figure in the early church. As both a faithful Jew and God's "point man" in opening the Gentile mission, he has been constantly under suspicion. Jewish Christians thought he was giving too much of the old tradition away, whereas Gentile Christians thought he was still too Jewish. A lot of false rumors about what he teaches and does swirl around him (cf. 3:8). Paul therefore probably knows he is going to have to clear the air if he expects the Romans to support him. Thus, . . . he writes Romans to clarify just what he believes.[16]

Paul therefore writes Romans to defend his gospel of the grace of God through

Christ by arguing that it is rooted in the Old Testament (Rom. 2–5), providing the disclaimer that it is not antinomian in ethic (God's grace is not a license to sin [so Rom. 6–8]), and holding out a future for Israel (Rom. 9–11). All of these concerns would have helped to allay the fears of Jewish Christians in Rome that Paul was anti-Jewish. But, from the same chapters, the Gentile Christians in Rome would have welcomed Paul's teaching that Gentiles are saved by faith in Christ apart from the law, and that the conversion of the nations is a significant part of God's plan.

In other words, viewing Romans as Paul's official doctrinal statement designed to introduce him to the congregations at Rome for the purpose of gathering their support for the end-time conversion of the nations seems to explain well the contents of the letter. I will keep coming back to this purpose as we move through the commentary.

The Genre/Outline of Romans

The genre or type of literature to which Romans belongs is a hotly contested topic. Is it a letter (as, for convenience, I have repeatedly labeled it so far in this introduction), since it has an epistolary framework (1:1–15; 15:14–16:23)? But if so, why does the bulk of Romans (1:16–15:13) not deal with the specifics of the local congregation in Rome? After all, Paul's other letters do so with their respective churches, and indeed, ancient letters as a whole likewise dealt with the specific situations of their recipients. Is Romans therefore a treatise, since it is a public declaration of Paul's theology of the gospel? This would make it more like ancient public speeches, which presented their sub-

Example of a Hittite Suzerain-Vassal Treaty

Preamble:[a] These are the words of the Sun Mursilis, the great king, the king of Hatti land, the valiant, the favorite of the storm god, the son of Suppiluliumas, the great king, the king of Hatti land.

Historical Prologue: Aziras, your grandfather, Duppi-Tessub, rebelled against my father, but submitted again to my father. . . . When my father became a god (i.e., died), and I seated myself on the throne of my father, Aziras behaved toward me just as he had toward my father. . . . When your father died, in accordance with your father's word I did not drop you. . . .

Stipulations: With my friend you shall be a friend, and with my enemy you shall be an enemy. . . . If you send a man to that enemy and inform him as follows: "An army and charioteers of the Hatti land are on their way, be on your guard!" you act in disregard of your oath. . . . If anyone utters words unfriendly to the king of Hatti land before you, Duppi-Tessub, you shall not withhold his name from the king. . . . If anyone of the deportees from the Nuhassi land or of the deportees from the country of Kinza whom my father removed and myself removed, escapes and comes to you, if you do not seize him and turn him back to the king of the Hatti land . . . you act in disregard of your oath.

Document Clause: (To be placed in the temple)

Appeal to Witnesses: The sun-god of heaven, the sun-goddess of Arinna, the storm-god of Heaven . . . Ishtar of Nineveh, Ishtar of Nineveh, Ishtar of Hattarina. . . . Ninlil, the mountains, the rivers, the springs, the clouds—let these be witnesses to this treaty and to the oath.

Curses and Blessings: The words of the treaty and the oath that are inscribed on this tablet—should Duppi-Tessub not honor them, may these gods of the oath destroy Duppi-Tessub together with his person, his wife, his son, his grandson, his house, his land and together with everything that he owns. But if Duppi-Tessub honors the words of the treaty and the oath that are inscribed on this tablet, may the gods of the oath protect him together with his person, his wife, his son, his grandson, his house, his country.

[a] Treaty can be found in Boadt, *Reading the Old Testament*, 179.

ject matter for a broader audience. But why, then, use the private/epistolary framework of Romans relating it to the congregations in Rome? Perhaps Romans is a rhetorical speech patterned after the ancient rhetorical handbooks. But if so, which rhetorical pattern is it: demonstrative, or deliberative, or persuasive? The fact that no consensus has emerged among those categorizing Romans as rhetorical speech does not bode well, it seems, for that approach to identifying the genre of Romans.

I suggest that there is a genre closer to hand for understanding the type of literature to which Romans belongs: the covenant structure/format that is pervasive in the Old Testament and is especially clear in the book of Deuteronomy (upon which Paul draws some ten times in Romans). It has long been recognized that the book of Deuteronomy matches perfectly the ancient Hittite suzerain-vassal treaty, and a close look at that background can help illumine the covenant structure built into Deuteronomy and drawn on by Paul in Romans. The Hittite suzerain-vassal treaty takes us back in history to the second millennium BC. At that time, in what is modern-day eastern Turkey, the Hittite Empire ruled the Levant (ancient Syria and Israel) in the years 1400–1200 BC. That civilization was uncovered in 1906 by archaeologists who discovered, among other things, numerous examples of a contract between the Hittite king and his people, now known as the Hittite suzerain-vassal treaty. In these contract documents between the king and his empire, six components can be identified. The first was the "preamble,"

Most Hittite suzerain-vassal treaties share the same basic components. Pictured is the treaty between Suppluluiuma and Hukkana from the thirteenth century BC. It contains a preamble, stipulations, divine witnesses, and curses and blessings.

a statement identifying the name of the Hittite king. Second came the "historical prologue," which contained a summary description of the king's relationship to his people, usually his past protection of them. Third, there followed the "stipulations" of the covenant, especially what the king expected of his people if they were to continue to enjoy his provision and protection. Fourth, a fascinating component, the "blessings and curses," followed, whereby the contract or treaty pronounced blessings on the people if they obeyed the king's stipulations but curses upon them if they did not. Fifth, the "document clause" was a statement notifying the interested parties that a copy of the document would be placed in a public setting for all to see, usually a temple. Sixth, the king of the Hittite treaty appealed to his gods to ratify, or testify to, the treaty; in other words, the gods were "witnesses" of the treaty. Though their order might vary, these components were fairly fixed (see sidebar for an example).[17]

From the 1950s onward, scholars have demonstrated that the six components of the Hittite suzerain-vassal treaty match the book of Deuteronomy (see table 1):

1. *Preamble* (Deut. 1:1–5), which accentuates the most intimate name of God: Yahweh.

2. *Historical Prologue* (Deut. 1:6–3:29), which provides a wonderful description of Yahweh's saving acts on behalf of Israel.

3. *Stipulations* (Deut. 4–26), which are divided into two classifications: the Ten Commandments (Deut. 4–11) and those general commandments specified in terms of Israel's relationship with God and others (chaps. 12–26).

4. *Curses and Blessings* (Deut. 27–30), the former pronounced by the Levites on Mount Ebal should Israel prove to be disobedient to Yahweh's stipulations, and the latter pronounced by priests on Mount Gerizim should Israel prove to be obedient. The blessings and curses alternate like an antiphonal chorus, culminating in Deuteronomy 30:15–20, which presents the "two ways" tradition: the way of obedience and covenantal blessings, and the way of disobedience and covenantal curses.

5. *Document Clause* (Deut. 31:9, 24–26), which specifies that the law on the tablets of stone be placed inside the ark of the covenant for safekeeping. Indeed, Joshua 24 reminds Israelites in the days of Joshua that the law of Moses, now in a book, is to be remembered by setting up a stone of public witness.

6. *Appeal to Witnesses* (Deut. 31:26–32:47), where Yahweh appeals not to pagan deities, since he alone is God, but rather to history, which is a witness to God's faithfulness to his covenant with Israel.

My contention in this commentary is that the book of Romans amazingly follows the covenant form of Deuteronomy (which in turn is based closely on the Hittite

Table 1: The Hittite-Treaty Structure of Deuteronomy

Hittite Treaty	Deuteronomy
1. Preamble	1:1–5
2. Historical Prologue	1:6–3:29
3. Stipulations	4:1–26:19
4. Curses/Blessings	27:1–30:20
5. Document Clause	31:9, 24–26
6. Appeal to Witnesses	31:26–32:47

suzerain-vassal treaty/covenant format), except that Paul qualifies the old covenant of Moses and replaces it with the new covenant in Christ. Table 2, showing the covenant-treaty structure in Romans as the old covenant is replaced by the new, will serve as our basic outline of Romans, which will be unpacked in more detail as we move through the text itself.

Table 2: Old Covenant Replaced by the New Covenant in Romans

Old Covenant of Israel	New Covenant in Romans
1. Preamble	Romans 1:1–15 (Christ the Son of God and the conversion of Gentiles before the restoration of Israel)
2. Historical Prologue	Romans 1:16–17 (spiritual, not physical or geographical, restoration in Christ)
3. Stipulations	Romans 1:18–4:25 (by faith in Christ, not the law of Moses)
4. Blessings	Romans 5–8 (blessings on believing Gentiles)
5. Curses	Romans 9–11 (curses on unbelieving Israel)
6. Appeal to Witnesses	Romans 12:1–15:13 (renewal of the covenant ceremony)
7. Document Clause	Romans 15:14–16:27 (on a letter, not on stone)

The Gospel of God in Christ through Paul

Big Idea *Paul, the apostle to the Gentiles, was divinely chosen to preach the gospel of God in Christ, the end-time fulfillment of the twofold Old Testament promise of the restoration of Israel and the conversion of the Gentiles.*

Understanding the Text

The Text in Context

Romans 1:1–7 forms the first half of Paul's introduction to Romans (1:8–15 is the second half). The introduction, or prescript, to ancient letters consisted of three parts: identification of the author, identification of the recipients, and a salutation or greeting to the recipients. Thus, these are the three parts for Romans 1:1–7:

1. Sender: Paul (1:1–6)
2. Recipient: To those in Rome (1:7a)
3. Greeting: Grace and peace (1:7b)

The sender/author component in 1:1–6 is probably so extensive because Paul is introducing himself to the Christians at Rome for the first time.

There is an *inclusio*—an opening idea of a text that is stated, developed, and then returned to at the conclusion—for the whole book of Romans centering on the "gospel" (compare 1:1, 2, 9, 15 with 15:16, 19;

16:25–27). Indeed, "gospel" receives pride of place, occurring in the letter's thematic statement in 1:16–17. Thus, Paul from the beginning alerts the readers to the letter's theme: the gospel of God through Jesus Christ.

Finally, 1:1–7, along with 1:8–15, corresponds with the preamble section of the covenant format that is so visible in Deuteronomy. The preamble section of the Old Testament covenant structure introduced Yahweh as Israel's covenant-keeping God. So does 1:1–15, except that Paul equates Jesus Christ with God, whose new-covenant gospel now impacts not only Jews but also Gentiles.

The following outline will guide the examination of Romans 1:1–7:

1. Paul is called to be an apostle of the gospel of God in Christ, which is the fulfillment of the twofold Old Testament end-time promise (1:1)
2. The restoration of Israel (1:2–4)
3. The conversion of Gentiles (1:5–7)

Historical and Cultural Background

1. Ancient Greek letters contained three parts: introduction, body, and conclusion. The New Testament letters, including Paul's, do the same.

2. The "Holy Scriptures" that Paul refers to in 1:2 are the Old Testament, which, in its Hebrew form, is divided into three sections: Torah (Law), Nebiim (Prophets), and Ketubim (Writings). That Paul and the other New Testament authors followed this threefold division of the Old Testament is clear (see Luke 24:27, 44; cf. in other ancient Jewish literature the prologue of Sirach; *4 Ezra* 14.37–48; Josephus, *Ag. Ap.* 1.37–42).

3. Although the primary source for Paul's gospel is the Old Testament, his Roman audience would not have missed that the word "gospel" conjured up praise for Caesar Augustus and the *pax Romana*, the peace that his rule brought to the Mediterranean world. This study of Romans will show that just as Paul shows the inadequacy of the Old Testament law for salvation, so does he undermine any misplaced confidence in Caesar. Indeed, if Paul has his way, his upcoming mission to Spain at the hands of Roman Christianity will result in the second coming of Christ and the overthrow of the Roman Empire!

4. In 1:1–7 Paul seems to cast himself in the role of the Suffering Servant from the

Key Themes of Romans 1:1–7

- Paul has been called by God to be an apostle, especially to the Gentiles (1:1, 5–7).
- Paul's message is the gospel of God in Christ, which is the end-time fulfillment of the twofold Old Testament promise of the restoration of Israel (1:2–4) and the conversion of the Gentiles (1:5–7).
- But Paul reverses the order: first comes the conversion of the Gentiles, and then the restoration of Israel (compare 1:1–7 with 11:25–27).
- Paul utilizes the preamble section of the Old Testament covenant format.

book of Isaiah. Note the following possible connections:

> Paul is a servant (compare 1:1 with Isa. 42:1–9; 49:1–13; 50:4–11; 52:13–53:12).
>
> Paul is called (compare 1:1, 6–7 with Isa. 41:9; 42:6; 43:1; 45:3–4; 48:12, 15; 49:1; 51:2).
>
> Paul is an apostle, a sent one (compare 1:1 with Isa. 6:8).
>
> Paul is sent to share good news (compare 1:1–7 with Isa. 40:9).
>
> Paul is sent to the Gentiles (compare 1:5–7 with Isa. 42:6–7).

This is a letter written between AD 97 and 103, which was found in the remains of a Roman fort at ancient Vindolanda (modern Chesterholm, Northumberland, England). Written on a thin piece of wood, it starts, "Claudia Severa [sender] to her Lepidina [recipient] greetings." The body of the letter is an invitation to a birthday celebration, and it ends with the greeting section, "Give my greetings to your Cerialis. My Aelius and my little son send him their greetings. I shall expect you, sister. Farewell, sister, my dearest soul, as I hope to prosper, and hail" (Klauck, *Ancient Letter*, 107). Two different styles of handwriting are evident, indicating that the majority of the letter was dictated to a scribe and the last two lines were penned by the sender herself.

Interpretive Insights

1:1 *Paul, a servant . . . an apostle . . . set apart for the gospel of God.* Paul provides three descriptions of himself. First, he is a servant or slave (*doulos*) of Jesus Christ. Besides the demeaning connotation of *doulos*, Paul also may have intended a positive allusion to the Old Testament "servant of Yahweh" tradition that was applied to Israel (Neh. 1:6; Isa. 43:10), the prophets (2 Kings 9:7; 17:23), Moses (Josh. 14:7; 2 Kings 18:12), Joshua (Josh. 24:29), and especially the Suffering Servant in Isaiah (Isa. 42:1–9; 49:1–13; 50:4–11; 52:13–53:12). Paul's usage of the less common title "Christ Jesus," instead of the more common "Jesus Christ," may allude to his mystic encounter with the risen Jesus on the road to Damascus. Paul tends to use "Christ Jesus" when alluding to his dramatic conversion experience. Second, Paul is called to be an apostle, which means that he has been accorded the same status as the original twelve disciples. This is true even if Paul never knew the historical Jesus. What mattered was that Paul had met the resurrected Jesus (e.g., Gal. 1:15–18; 1 Cor. 15:8). Third, Paul was set apart for the gospel of God. "Set apart" probably refers to Paul's divine call from birth to be an apostle of Christ, a call that was actualized on the Damascus road (see Gal. 1:15–18). As noted earlier, the term "gospel" has its taproot in the promise of the good news of the end-time restoration of Israel (see esp. Isa. 40:9; 52:7; 61:1 [cf. Luke 4:18]; also Isa. 60:6; Joel 2:32; Nah. 1:15). Such a message of good news also included the conversion of the Gentiles (see Isa. 2:2–4; Mic. 4:1–3; Rom. 9:25–27; 15:16–33). This is the gospel of "God" in Christ because

it originated in the Old Testament as the divine promise to Israel and is fulfilled in Jesus Christ.

1:2 *the gospel he promised beforehand through his prophets.* Commentators agree that "prophets" here refers to the whole of the Old Testament. Thus, Paul is saying that the Old Testament prophetically witnesses to the gospel of God. This can be seen already in Genesis 12:1–3, where God promises to bless Abraham's descendants (Jews) as well as the nations of the world (Gentiles). Indeed, this is how Paul read Genesis 12:1–3 (see Rom. 4:9–12; cf. Gal. 3:6–9). And that twofold promise of God's blessing on Jews (the restoration of Israel) and Gentiles (conversion of the nations) receives eschatological status in Isaiah 40–66. This twofold promise is spelled out in Romans 1:3–4 concerning Israel and in 1:5–7 concerning Gentiles. Jesus Christ is the one ordained by God to bring about the fulfillment of those promises.

1:3–4 *descendant of David . . . Son of God.* First, many interpreters believe that these two verses consist of a pre-Pauline hymn or creed about Jesus because of the un-Pauline words here ("descendant/seed of David," "Spirit of holiness") and the parallelism inherent in the verses. The parallelism, seen more clearly in the Greek text, is as follows:

who has come	who was appointed[1]
from the seed of David	Son of God in power
according to the flesh	according to the Spirit of holiness (from the resurrection of the dead)

Second, the key to interpreting 1:3–4 is to grasp the meaning of the contrast of "flesh"

(NIV mg.) versus "Spirit of holiness." Although the issue is debated, the best view interprets flesh/Spirit as the contrast between the present age and the age to come. To the former belongs the flesh, in this case Jesus, the human descendant of David; to the latter pertains the age to come, the age of the Spirit. Paul later will make clear that Jesus' humanity is only in the likeness of sinful flesh (Rom. 8:3). Although the meaning of the phrase "Spirit of holiness" is uncertain (it appears only here in the New Testament), the Greek phrase most likely reflects a Semitic construction referring to the Holy Spirit.

Third, in light of the first two points, we may conclude that "Son" / "Son of God" in 1:3–4 forms an *inclusio*, signifying that the eternal, preexistent Son of God became human in the form of the seed of David, and, at his resurrection, the Son (Jesus Christ) was raised to a new status: the powerfully exalted, heavenly Son of God.

Fourth, the message of this christological piece is that in Jesus Christ the promised restoration of Israel is beginning to be fulfilled. Note the following four connections between 1:3–4 and the promise in the Old Testament and Second Temple Jewish literature of the restoration of Israel, laid out in table 1.[2]

Table 1: Jesus Christ in Romans 1:3–4 and the Restoration of Israel

Restoration of Israel	Romans 1:3–4: Jesus is the . . .
The good news of the restoration of Israel (Isa. 40–66)	"gospel" (Rom. 1:1–7)
The Davidic Messiah will restore Israel in the age to come (2 Sam. 7:12–16; Isa. 11:1, 10; Jer. 23:5–6; 30:9; 33:14–18; Ezek. 34:23–24; 37:24–25; *Pss. Sol.* 17.21; 4Q174)	Davidic Messiah (compare Rom. 1:3 with Matt. 1:1–16; Luke 1:27, 32, 69; 2 Tim. 2:8; Rev. 5:5; 22:16)
Israel is the Son of God (Exod. 4:22–23; Jer. 31:9; Hos. 11:1; Wis. 9:7; 18:13; *Jub.* 1.24–25; *Pss. Sol.* 17.30; 18.4)	Son of God, the true/restored Israel (compare Rom. 1:3–4 with Matt. 4:1–11; Luke 4:1–13)
The future restoration of Israel is likened to the resurrection of the dead (Isa. 26:19; Ezek. 37:1–14)	one raised from the dead (Rom. 1:4)

1:5 *Through him we received grace and apostleship . . . obedience that comes from faith.* Paul's description of his calling as that of "grace and apostleship" suggests that his encounter on the Damascus road with the risen Jesus was both his conversion to Christ and his call to be the apostle to the Gentiles. We should not eliminate the former of these from the equation, as some interpreters do. The meaning of the phrase "obedience of faith" or "obedience that comes from faith" (NIV) is debated and may mean that obedience is the expression of faith ("obedience that is faith"), or that obedience results from faith. In either case, this faith/obedience refers to the Old Testament end-time promise that Gentiles will convert to the true God upon the restoration of Israel (see Isa. 2:2–4; Mic. 4:1–3; Rom. 9:25–27; 15:16–33), except that Paul reverses that order in Romans 11:24–27. Indeed, the eschatological conversion of the Gentiles is the theme of 1:5–7 as a whole.

1:6 *And you also.* Paul implies two things here. First, Gentile Christians are the dominant group over the minority Jewish Christians in the Roman congregations; hence, this is his comment to them (cf. 11:11–24). Second, they are under Paul's apostolic authority as the premier apostle to the Gentiles.

1:7 *To all in Rome.* Although the words "in Rome" are absent from a few ancient manuscripts, certainly they belong to the original text, providing the name of the recipients of the letter. Paul applies three Old Testament labels for Israel to the Gentile Christians at Rome: "called" (cf. Deut. 4:37; 10:15; Isa. 41:9; 48:12), "beloved" (cf. Deut. 4:37; 10:15; see also Deut. 7:8; 23:5), and "saints" (cf. Exod. 19:5–6; Lev. 19:2; Deut. 7:6). The apostle to the Gentiles thereby communicates that they are as much a part of the people of God as is Israel.

Too much should not be made of the fact that Paul does not address the Christians in Rome as "the church in Rome," since he omits that title in the greeting of some of his other letters (Philippians, Colossians, Ephesians).

Paul offers the Christian salutation to the Roman church: "grace" and "peace." "Grace" (*charis*) is an adaptation of the typical Greek greeting (which uses the verb *chairō*), in that Paul roots God's grace in Christ, and "peace" is an adaptation of the Jewish greeting *shalom*, and also comes from Christ.

Theological Insights

At least four theological insights surface in Romans 1:1–7: (1) The themes of promise and fulfillment undergird these opening verses and, for that matter, the whole letter. (2) Paul is careful to suggest that there is only one people of God: believing Jews and believing Gentiles. (3) Paul reads his Old Testament messianically (as did the other New Testament authors): Christ is its climax. (4) Later church creeds about the two natures of Jesus Christ and the Trinity are implicit here.

Teaching the Text

Three applications regarding the gospel for all audiences emerge from Romans 1:1–7. First, the theological orientation of the gospel is the Old Testament. Thus, the gospel is rooted in the Old Testament, fulfilled in Jesus Christ the promised Messiah, and articulated by Paul the Jewish Christian. To lose this orientation is to follow the path of the heretic Marcion, who claimed that the Bible presents two different gods, the Old Testament god of wrath and the New Testament god of love. One of my professors used to say that to be a strong Christian, one had to know the Old Testament. He was right. The Old Testament demonstrates the one God's love and justice, while the New Testament does the same.

Second, the personal benefits of the gospel are breathtaking: peace, love, and holiness from God through Christ. Romans will fill out the details regarding these blessings, but suffice it to say here that the love of God in Christ provides sinners with peace with God when they accept by faith that Christ died for their sins and arose for their justification.

Third, the evangelistic scope of the gospel is cosmic. Jesus, the Messiah of Israel, is Savior of the world and Lord of the universe. The message of Jesus Christ knows no boundaries. It spread from Jerusalem to Judea to Samaria to the uttermost parts of the world, thanks to the ministries of the thirteen apostles, including the apostle Paul.

Illustrating the Text

The theological orientation of the gospel is the Old Testament.

Education: A number of years ago, a Harvard faculty committee declared that "the aim of a liberal education" was "to unsettle presumptions, to defamiliarize the familiar, to reveal what is going on beneath and behind appearances, to disorient young people and to help them to find ways to reorient themselves." This implied a holistic way of living that emphasized independent thinking with a certain amount of skepticism for what has been done before, including one's upbringing. Such a perspective is in keeping with modern individualistic culture with its focus on questioning, self-discovery, and personal satisfaction. A more traditional approach to living is discussed in a book called *On Thinking Institutionally*, by the political scientist Hugh Heclo, who emphasizes not what we want from life but what it wants from us. Heclo writes, "institutionalists see themselves as debtors who owe something, not creditors to whom something is owed."[3]

The scope of the gospel is universal, reaching out to Jews and Gentiles.

Hymn Text: "All Hail the Power of Jesus' Name," by Edward Perronet. Particularly relevant in this text by Perronet (1726–92) are "Ye chosen seed of Israel's race, / Ye ransomed from the fall, / Hail Him who saves you by his grace, / And crown Him Lord of all" (stanza 2); "Let every kindred, every tribe / On this terrestrial ball, / To Him all majesty ascribe" (stanza 4); and "Extol the Stem of Jesse's Rod" (stanza 5).

Obedience of faith means justification and sanctification should not be separated.

Apologetics: *All of Grace*, by Charles Haddon Spurgeon. In this work (1894), Spurgeon illustrates the concept of obedience of faith by noting that justification without sanctification is not salvation at all. "It would call the leper clean and leave him to die of his disease; it would forgive the rebellion and allow the rebel to remain an enemy to his king. . . . It would stop the stream for a time but leave an open fountain of defilement which would sooner or later break forth with increased power."[4]

Quote: Seneca. The Roman philosopher Seneca (ca. AD 4–65), whose life coincided with Paul's, said that all people were looking toward salvation. What we need, he said, is "a hand let down to lift us up."[5]

Bust of Seneca, one side of a double-headed herm (first to third century AD)

The Obedience
of Faith of the Gentiles

Big Idea *Paul expands upon his conviction that God called him to bring about the end-time conversion of the Gentiles—that is, the obedience of faith of the nations. Moreover, Paul also hints that God will reverse the order of the twofold Old Testament promise of the future restoration of Israel and the conversion of the Gentiles.*

Understanding the Text

The Text in Context

Romans 1:8–15 is the second part of the introduction to Romans, consisting of the proem—a thanksgiving and a prayer. Thus, 1:8 is Paul's thanksgiving for the Roman Christians, while 1:9–15 is his prayer for them.

The theme of the obedience of the faith of the Gentiles[1] forms an *inclusio* framing the whole book of Romans, occurring in 1:5 (cf. 1:8, 12, 16; 15:18) and concluding the letter in 16:25–27. Here in 1:8–15 the obedience of the faith of the Gentiles unfolds in three stages: east of Rome (1:8), Rome itself (compare 1:8 with 1:9–10, 13–15), and ultimately in Spain (1:11–12).

I also suggest that 1:8–15 continues the "preamble" section of the covenant structure that began with 1:1.

Historical and Cultural Background

An ancient map of the Roman Empire preserved in a thirteenth-century copy known as the *Tabula Peutingeriana* reveals the eschatological genius behind Paul's plan to visit Spain for the purpose of preaching the gospel. That map shows that the ancients believed that Illyricum was a key stopping point on the way to Rome and that Rome was halfway to Spain, the end of the then-known world. If we compare this map with Romans 1:8–15 and 15:19–29, we arrive at the logic behind Paul's passion to go to Spain: having just evangelized Illyricum (the area of modern Albania and former Yugoslavia), Paul now needed the Roman Christians' support to conduct his mission to Spain and thereby bring about the conversion of the remaining Gentiles. This was to bring in "the fullness of the Gentiles" right before the restoration of Israel (11:25–27). Robert Jewett puts it this way: "[Paul's] calling is to extend the gospel to the 'rest of the Gentiles,' a stunningly sweeping scope whose rationale becomes clear when one realizes that Spain marked the end of the known world, the end of the 'circle' (Rom 15:19) of the known world that ran from Jerusalem through Illyricum and Rome to the Pillars of Hercules [Strait of Gibraltar]."[2]

Interpretive Insights

1:8 *your faith is being reported all over the world.* The Roman Christians' faith in and obedience to Christ was noteworthy: people in the capital city of the world at that time had been converted to Christianity! In other words, Gentiles in Rome as well as Gentiles east of Rome who had heard the gospel from Paul (see 15:17–22) were now included in the category of "the obedience of faith." Paul will have more to say on Roman Christianity in 1:9–10, 13–15.

1:9 *the gospel of his Son.* The gospel is the twofold end-time promise of the Old Testament regarding the restoration of Israel and the conversion of the Gentiles.

1:11 *I may impart to you some spiritual gift.* The "spiritual gift" that Paul mentions here does not refer to the gifts of the Spirit (see 1 Cor. 12–14; Eph. 4:11–12); he will

Key Themes of Romans 1:8–15

- The obedience of the faith—the end-time conversion of the Gentiles—is occurring now in three stages: the evangelization of Gentiles to the east of Rome (1:8), in Rome (compare 1:8 with 1:9–10, 13–15), and to the west of Rome in Spain, the end of the then-known world (1:11–12).

- This is nothing less than the reversal of the twofold Old Testament promise of the restoration of Israel followed by conversion of Gentiles. First will come conversion of Gentiles, which will be the catalyst for the restoration of Israel (compare 1:13 with 11:25–27).

The *Tabula Peutingeriana* is an ancient map that reveals the logic behind Paul's passion to preach the gospel in Spain. Rome and Spain were strategically important for the conversion of the Gentiles because Rome was the capital of the ancient world and Spain marked the end of the then-known world. The map shows the Roman road network with place names and stopping places with accommodations, and labels seas, rivers, mountains, and forests. It is a complicated map to read for modern readers because it is distorted in its compass orientation and not to scale. The portion shown here shows the region of Illyricum as the topmost landmass separated from Rome by the Adriatic Sea. (Detail, copy of the Roman original, French, 1265 [vellum])

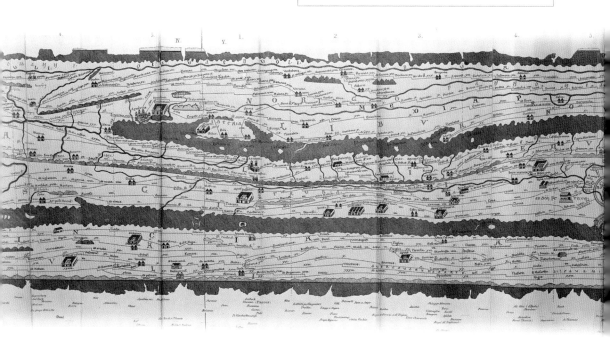

This funerary monument shows several classes in the Roman social hierarchy. The large figures shown in deep relief are a family of freedmen and freedwomen. The smaller figures in shallow relief are the slaves that belong to the family. The visual contrast highlights the difference in social status, a divide overcome by the gospel. (Thessaloniki, ca. 50 BC)

touch upon that topic in 12:3–8. More likely, Paul has in mind in 1:11–12 spiritual blessings or spiritual insight. Such spiritual encouragement will be reciprocal: Paul will bless the Roman congregations, and they will bless him. One is distinctly reminded by this of 15:23–29, where Paul encourages Gentile Christians to financially support their poorer Jewish Christian brothers and sisters (back in Jerusalem) because the latter have supported the former spiritually in that they brought to the Gentiles the gospel. Indeed, the word "harvest" (*karpos*) in 1:13 is the same word that Paul uses in 15:28 of the Gentiles' collection for the Jerusalem Christians. Such reciprocity of ministry in 15:23–29 and in 1:11–12 has a specific intention: Paul knew that unity between Jewish and Gentile Christians in Rome was vital to the apostle's mission to Spain. He needed them to be reconciled to each other (see chaps. 11; 14–15) so that,

among other reasons, they could provide a unified front from which Paul could launch his mission to Spain.

1:13 *I do not want you to be unaware . . . I planned many times to come to you.* Since Rome was the capital of the empire, Roman Christians may have asked more than once why Paul had not yet visited them. Paul's answer is that he has been so busy evangelizing Gentiles east of Rome (cf. 1:8) that he has not yet had the time to visit Rome itself (1:10, 13–15; see again 15:19–29). Indeed, the world of the Gentiles was Paul's apostolic domain—civilized (Greek/wise) and uncivilized (barbarian/foolish). Jewett is more precise here, arguing that Spain was occupied by only the "barbarian/foolish."[3]

Verse 13 begins with the same disclosure formula that introduces 11:25–27: "I do not want you to be unaware, brothers and sisters." Since the latter usage of the formula equates the knowledge that Paul is about to reveal to the Roman Christians with God's "mystery" that the order of the twofold eschatological Old Testament promise of the restoration of Israel and the conversion of the Gentiles is now reversed, we are justified in anticipating that meaning here in 1:13. Thus, Paul is hinting now at what he will make more lucid later: as the apostle to the Gentiles, he is evangelizing the nations because their conversion will precede, even spark, the conversion of Israel to their rightful Messiah.

Theological Insights

A number of theological insights emerge from Romans 1:8–15. First, we learn from Paul that no Christian is an island but rather is a part of the whole, the body of Christ. Even the great Paul, so forceful in personality and fearless in preaching the gospel, needed other believers to help him in the quest to advance the kingdom of God on earth. The same is true for us. Second, the gospel of Jesus Christ is inclusive in nature; it is good news for all. There should never be even a hint in our message that the gospel is otherwise. Jew and Gentile, male and female, rich and poor, powerful and weak, and any of the other divides that people use to categorize this world are not in play with the gospel. Third, the gospel is also exclusive in nature; there is no name under heaven whereby humans can be reconciled to God other than that of Jesus

The Parousia

The term "parousia" is the transliteration of a Greek word meaning "coming" or "presence." In New Testament studies, the term "parousia" is used to refer to the second coming of Jesus Christ at the end of history. Interestingly enough, "parousia" was a term used of a Roman general or of Caesar himself. As the general or emperor approached a city, the moment of his appearance on the horizon was called the "parousia." In using this term for Jesus, the early church may have been replacing Caesar with Christ.

Christ (Acts 4:12). Thus the "obedience of faith" that Paul talks about in 1:8–15 confirms that all the world will one day bow before Christ the Lord to honor him. This will happen either because the nations willingly accept Christ now as Savior and Lord or because they will be required to do so at his return (cf. Phil. 2:9–11). Fourth, it must be acknowledged that Paul's intensive campaign to evangelize the Gentiles as the catalyst for the parousia (see the sidebar) did not bring it about in Paul's lifetime. Yet, according to Jesus himself, the gospel will indeed go to all the world just before he returns (Matt. 24:14). Thus, Paul's message was correct even though the timing of the parousia has been delayed. But the delay of the parousia did not seem to bother the early church all that much, for it realized that the first coming of Christ had set in motion the age to come. That assurance sustained the early Christians and so should govern our perspective as well (see further discussion of this under Rom. 13:8–14).

Teaching the Text

At least four themes in Romans 1:8–15 can be used as sermons or lessons. First, taking verses 8–15 with verses 1–7 makes it clear that there is but one people of God: those whose faith is in Jesus Christ. This applies to both Jew and Gentile. There is no room here for a "two covenant" approach to the people of God whereby Gentiles are saved by faith in Jesus while Jews are saved by being the Old Testament people of God and by following the law of Moses. Paul will correct any such notion in 1:18–11:36.

Second, the "obedience of faith" means that justification and sanctification should never be separated. As 1:16–5:21 indicates, justification before God is based solely on faith in Jesus Christ minus human effort of any kind, but as 6:1–8:15 indicates, genuine faith in Christ results in a holy life. That is to say, faith leads to obedience.

Third, a secondary theme that is nonetheless highly significant for this discussion of 1:8–15 is that the gospel is both theological and social in orientation. Faith in Jesus Christ will result in meeting the social needs of people. Thus it is that Paul urged the Roman Christians to minister to the poor Jerusalem Christians (compare 1:11–12 with 15:14–22). There is no room here for pitting the "true" gospel (theology) against the "social" gospel (meeting the tangible needs of humankind). The latter is the platform for and entailment of the former.

Fourth, the Great Commission (Matt. 28:19–20) has not been rescinded. So it was that Paul was committed to reaching the world with the gospel, and so it should be for the modern church. If the church lets go of its petty disagreements, thereby freeing up its energy and resources, then it really can propagate the gospel worldwide. And who knows? Maybe that effort will bring about the final sign of the time before Christ returns.

Illustrating the Text

The gospel is theological and social in orientation.

Quote: **"I Have a Dream," by Martin Luther King Jr.** "I have a dream that my four little children will one day live in a nation where they will not be judged by the color of their skin but by the content of their character." That dream above all should be fulfilled in the church, where there is neither slave or free, male or female, Jew or Gentile (Gal. 3:28).

Both Old and New Testament believers were saved by faith.

Quote: **"Preface to the Complete Edition of Luther's Latin Writings," by Martin Luther.** "I greatly longed to understand Paul's Epistle to the Romans, and nothing stood in the way but that one expression, 'the righteousness of God,' because I took it to mean that righteousness whereby God is righteous and deals righteously in punishing the unrighteous. . . . Night and day I pondered until . . . I grasped the truth that the righteousness of God is that righteousness whereby, through grace and sheer mercy, he justifies us by faith. Thereupon I felt myself to be reborn and to have gone through open doors into paradise. The whole of Scripture took on a new meaning, and whereas before 'the righteousness of God' had filled me with hate, now it became to me inexpressibly sweet in greater love. This passage of Paul became to me a gateway to heaven."[4]

Leaders and laypeople must encourage each other's faith in prayer and humility.

Story: **"The Time in the City," by Walter Wangerin.** Wangerin (b. 1944), an award-winning American writer who is white, once served as pastor of an all-black congregation in Evansville, Indiana. He has since become a novelist, poet, essayist, and author of practical theology who writes unforgettable stories that are eminently usable in preaching or teaching. In this story based on his experience in the church in Evansville, Wangerin talks about the experience of being ordained and the purity that he felt in his calling. He felt that his "education had come to a climax; [his] knowledge was being validated."[5] He felt the Spirit was with him even though he was in a small parish with a homely office. He began preaching with a certain power. Then, through members of his congregation he began to learn to listen, to pay attention to what they were trying to teach him. He says then, "Earn your right to be heard by The City. . . . It comes of a very specific labor. It comes when you—to your own sacrifice—commit your ways to the people."[6]

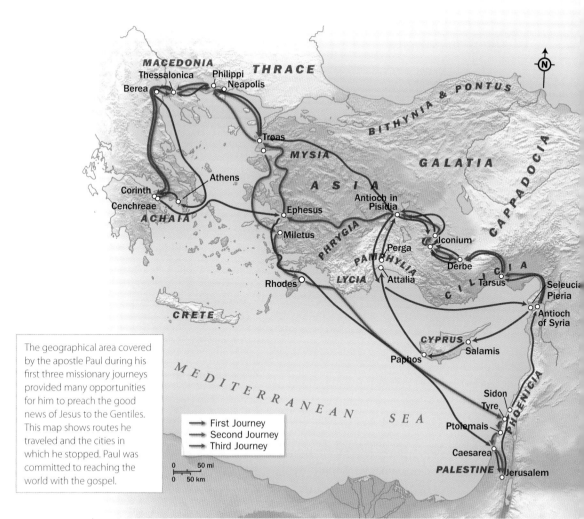

The geographical area covered by the apostle Paul during his first three missionary journeys provided many opportunities for him to preach the good news of Jesus to the Gentiles. This map shows routes he traveled and the cities in which he stopped. Paul was committed to reaching the world with the gospel.

Romans 1:8–15

The Gospel of Deliverance

Big Idea *The gospel of Jesus Christ is the final stage of salvation history, the ultimate fulfillment of the twofold Old Testament promise of the restoration of Israel and the conversion of the Gentiles.*

Understanding the Text

The Text in Context

In 1:15 Paul expressed his deep desire to preach the gospel in Rome. Now, in 1:16–17, he spells out the nature of that gospel. In so doing, 1:16–17 forms the theme of the letter to the Romans: the gospel of Jesus Christ. As Thomas Schreiner points out, it is this theme that integrates the other key ideas in 1:16–17 and, indeed, in the entire letter: salvation, justification by faith, and the order of salvation (Jew first, then Gentile). Schreiner catches the ensuing logic of 1:15–17: Paul is eager to preach at Rome (1:15) because he is not ashamed of the gospel (1:16a), and he is not ashamed of the gospel because it is God's power for salvation (1:16b), and the gospel is God's power of salvation because it conveys the righteousness of God to all who believe (1:17a).[1] All of this is rooted in Habakkuk 2:4 (and in the story of Israel's restoration as proclaimed by other prophets, such as Isaiah).

My contention is that the Old Testament covenant structure informs Romans. We saw above that 1:1–15 fits nicely with the pre-amble component of the covenant format. Now I suggest that 1:16–17 corresponds to the historical prologue component of the covenant structure. The historical prologue section (see, e.g., Deut. 1:6–3:29) rehearses God's intervention on behalf of ancient Israel, often recalling the exodus and the conquest of Canaan as well as the return of Israel to their homeland after exile in Babylonia (587/586 BC). These events theologians call "salvation history"—that is, God's acts of salvation on behalf of Israel. Romans 1:16–17 is doing much the same, except that it conveys the conviction that God's greatest act of deliverance on behalf of Israel is now happening in Jesus Christ because of his death and resurrection (cf. 1:3–4), and that it includes the salvation of Gentiles (cf. 1:5–15).

Historical and Cultural Background

1. Besides the Old Testament covenant structure, a key point in the historical background of Romans 1:16–17 is the story of Israel. That story unfolds in the Old Testament in three stages: Israel's sin of idolatry against Yahweh; Israel's rejec-

tion of the prophets of Yahweh who called Israel to repentance and God's subsequent sending of Israel away into exile, first into Assyria in 721 BC and then to Babylonia in 587/586 BC; and the promise of Israel's return/restoration to their homeland if they repent by turning back to God. It is this third stage that weighs so heavily in the meaning of Romans 1:16–17. I will call attention to these three components of the story of Israel repeatedly in my treatment of Romans.

2. Another key reference point for appreciating Romans 1:16–17 is to relate its message to the culture of the day, especially the mindset of the capital city of Rome. Paul declares in 1:15–16 that he is not ashamed of the gospel, for it is the power of God unto salvation. Such a bold assertion by the apostle came in the face of Rome's execution of Jesus by way of crucifixion. Indeed, the cross of Christ had already become a laughingstock in the Greco-Roman world, as 1 Corinthians 1:18–28 makes clear. Not long after Paul, graffiti was found in Rome mocking the cross of Christ. A drawing on a plaster wall near the Circus Maximus depicts a man worshiping the crucified Christ, who is portrayed as a donkey on a cross.[2] The implication of the drawing is obvious: to worship a crucified king is asinine! To the contrary, however, Paul knows that the gospel of the crucified Christ is the most powerful message in the world.

> God sent Israel into exile because of their sin of idolatry, but in keeping with his covenant promises, God later restored Israel to their homeland. The Israelite city of Lachish was destroyed by the Assyrians under Sennacherib in 701 BC and then again by the Babylonians under Nebuchadnezzar in 587/586 BC. Sennacherib tells the story of his conquest in large wall reliefs that were excavated from his palace in Nineveh. The section shown here shows Israelite families leaving the city as exiles.

Key Themes of Romans 1:16–17

- The gospel of Jesus Christ is the last and greatest divine act of salvation and deliverance on behalf of Israel and, for that matter, the entire world.
- The gospel is for the Jew first and then the Gentile (compare 1:16 with 2:1–3:20; 9–11; 14–15), which means that the twofold end-time Old Testament promise of the restoration of Jews and the conversion of Gentiles is now being fulfilled in Jesus Christ.
- It is by faith in Christ alone that anyone can receive the gospel of deliverance.

See the "Historical and Cultural Background" section of Romans 16:25–27 (a passage that corresponds closely with 1:16–17) below for a further discussion of the themes of anti-imperialism, emperor worship, and Paul's use of "gospel" language.

Interpretive Insights

1:16–17 *I am not ashamed of the gospel . . . "The righteous will live by faith."* Three major interpretive insights emerge from these theologically dense and much-debated

verses. First, a growing chorus of scholars roots the major key terms in 1:16–17 in the Old Testament promise of the restoration of Israel, especially as presented by Isaiah.[3] Note the connections laid out in table 1.

Table 1: Romans 1:16–17 and the Restoration of Israel

Romans 1:16–17	The Restoration of Israel, Especially as Recorded in Isaiah
"not ashamed" (compare 1:16 with 9:33; 10:16)	one who trusts in the Lord will not be disappointed—that is, they will participate in Israel's restoration (Isa. 28:16)
"gospel"	the good news of Israel's return to their land (Isa. 40:9; 52:7; 61:1; Nah. 1:15; see also Isa. 60:6; Joel 2:32)
"power"	God's saving action at the exodus, a motif applied to the return of Israel from exile (Isa. 43:2, 16–19; 52:10–12; see also Exod. 9:16; Pss. 77:14–15; 140:7)
"salvation"	God's deliverance of Israel from the exile (Isa. 12:2; 25:9; 46:13; 49:6; 52:7, 10)
"righteousness"	God's faithfulness to his covenant by restoring Israel to himself (Isa. 46:13; 51:5, 6, 8; Mic. 6:5; 7:9)
"revealed"	the restoration of Israel will reveal God's righteousness and his faithfulness to his covenant (Isa. 22:14; 40:5; 43:12; 53:1; 56:1; 65:1)
"faith"	the righteous one is the one who trusts in the Lord to bring Israel out of exile and back to their homeland (Hab. 2:4)

Second, the theme of the restoration of Israel found in 1:16–17 takes on two nuances in Romans: (1) The restoration of Israel will witness the establishment of a new covenant (compare Rom. 11:27 with Isa. 27:9; 59:20–21; and Rom. 2:14–15; 2:29;

8:1; 9:4 with Jer. 31:31–33; Ezek. 36:24–3). (2) The restoration of Israel will include the conversion of the Gentiles (Isa. 2:2–4; 52:15; 61:9–11; 65:1; Mic. 4:1–3).

Third, uncovering the story of Israel, especially the restoration of Israel, as the immediate background to 1:16–17 helps to resolve three critical issues therein: the meaning of the phrase "righteousness of God"; the meaning of the words "faith to faith"; and how 1:17 relates to Habakkuk 2:4. These concerns will now be addressed briefly, with the story of Israel's restoration in mind.

1. Much ink has been spilled over the phrase "righteousness of God," with essentially two interpretations ruling the day: the forensic view and the transformative view.[4] The forensic view understands the righteousness of God to be God's legal declaration that the believer in Jesus is righteous before God; that is, God's righteousness is imputed to the sinner's standing before God. The primary support for such a perspective is found in Paul's emphasis in Romans on faith as the sole means of acquiring God's righteousness (cf. 1:17; 3:21–22; 4:3, 5–6, 9, 11, 13, 22; 9:30–31; 10:3, 4, 6, 10; see also Gal. 2:20–21; 3:6, 21–22; 5:5; Phil. 3:9). To be sure, Paul refers to faith as the basis of receiving God's righteousness three times in Romans 1:16–17 alone.

The transformative view of the phrase "righteousness of God" understands the action of God as transforming the sinner. In support of this view one could point to the apostle's words in 1:16: the gospel is the saving power of God. Moreover, as mentioned before, all the key terms in Romans 1:16–17, including "righteousness," are essentially rooted in Isaiah's good news that God is faithful to his covenant people Israel and will restore them to himself. Many modern commentators are reticent to choose between these two options because both are grounded in Romans 1:16–17 and its Old Testament moorings. Thus, the righteousness of God is God's saving act of fulfilling his promise to restore Israel and convert Gentiles based exclusively on faith in Jesus Christ. With this conclusion I agree.

2. What does the phrase "from faith to faith" (NIV: "by faith from first to last") mean? Various explanations have been offered: from the faith of the Old Testament to the faith of the New Testament; from the faith of the law to the faith of the gospel; from the faithfulness of God to the faith of human beings; from beginning to end, salvation is by faith. The last-mentioned possibility is the one most defended today because of the emphasis in Romans 1:16–17 on faith and believing. I agree with this conclusion and would add one important detail: for the Old Testament covenant, keeping the law of Moses was the way to ensure that the Israelite remained in a right relationship with God,[5] but according to Paul, one receives the righteousness of God by believing in Jesus Christ, not by obeying the Torah. Moreover, the restoration of Israel is no longer geographical in orientation or exclusive in membership; rather, it is spiritual in nature and encompasses all the nations.

3. Three questions await the reader of Habakkuk 2:4 as quoted by Paul in Romans 1:17. First, why does Paul omit the personal pronoun "my" from the Greek text (LXX) of Habakkuk 2:4: "But the righteous shall live by *my* [God's] faithfulness" (contrast the Hebrew text [MT]: "But the righteous by *his* [the Israelite's]

faith/faithfulness shall live")? The answer seems to be that Paul wants to make it clear that it is the faith of the individual that he has in mind (so the MT, not the LXX). Second, what does "by faith" modify: "the just/righteous by faith shall live" or "the righteous shall live by faith"? The former seems to be correct, since Romans 1:18–4:25 highlights faith as the means to justification, and Romans 5–8 seems to emphasize eternal life as the gift of justification. Third, are Habakkuk and Paul at odds with each other? That is, does Habakkuk 2:4 affirm that obeying the law is the way to stay in covenant with God? There does seem to be tension between Habakkuk and Paul here. For Habakkuk, obedience to the law is the means to being faithful to God; for Paul, faith in Christ is the means to be justified. But this is no real contradiction, since both inspired authors emphasize that faith resulting in faithfulness is the means to receiving God's approval (cf. Rom. 3:21–22).

We see in all of this that Romans 1:16–17 nicely corresponds to the historical prologue section of the covenant format: God in Christ has been faithful to his Old Testament promises to Israel and Gentiles, but based on faith and not on the law.

Theological Insights

The reader of Romans 1:16–17 encounters several theological truths. First, the gospel is still the power of God to deliver sinners. Second, God is faithful to his covenant promise: he sent the Messiah to save his people and beyond. Third, there is no room for anti-Semitism, certainly not in the Christian community; but neither is the law of Moses a covenant marker any longer for the people of God by faith. Fourth, faith in Jesus Christ is the end-all means to receiving the righteousness of God.

Teaching the Text

The following themes can be the bases for sermons or lessons regarding Romans 1:16–17: First, a message entitled "Saved by Faith" could make the point that both Old Testament and New Testament believers were saved by faith. This is in contrast to past generations of interpreters who argued that salvation in the Old Testament was based on obeying the law while salvation in the New Testament is by faith in Christ. The content of salvation may have changed between the two Testaments—God's revelation through Moses and God's revelation in Christ—but the method of receiving that revelation leading to salvation in both cases was based on faith.

Second, a message entitled "Not Ashamed of the Gospel" could dwell on the scandal and paradox of the cross: the crucifixion of Jesus Christ for the sin of the world is an abhorrent thought to most moderns but is nonetheless the power and wisdom of God for salvation. As Martin Luther proclaimed, the cross is *Deus absconditus* (God hidden); that is, behind the weakness, foolishness, and sinfulness of the cross is divine power, wisdom, and righteousness.

Third, still another sermon/lesson based on Romans 1:16–17 is "The Reverse of the Curse," dealing with the fact that the sin/curse of the law was poured out on Jesus on the cross, while his resurrection dispenses the blessing/restoration of the covenant to all who believe.

Fourth, the message "The Just by Faith Shall Live" could explore how Paul highlights "by faith" in Romans 1:18–4:25 and "shall live" in Romans 5–8. The goal of such a message or lesson would be to show that Paul first makes it clear in the former section that justification before God is based on faith in Christ alone, while the latter section expounds on the life that results from justification.

Illustrating the Text

While abhorrent to many, the crucifixion is God's power and wisdom for salvation.

Art/History: Alexamenos Graffito. The Alexamenos Graffito, also known as the *Graffito Blasphemo*, is an inscription carved in plaster on a wall near the Palatine Hill in Rome, close to the Circus Maximus. It depicts a humanlike figure attached to a cross and having the head of a donkey. The date for this inscription is most likely the beginning of the third century. The inscription is thought by most scholars to be a mocking description of a Christian. Justin Martyr, a Christian apologist, summarized the view of Christ by the people of the time. They considered it a joke that a crucified man would be made equal to the eternal creator God. A person like that could only be treated with disdain or contempt; he must be a lunatic.

Quote: *The Passion of the Christ.* In this film (2004), a powerful and graphic portrayal of the suffering and death of Jesus, one of the criminals to be crucified with Jesus asks him, "Why do you embrace your cross, you fool?"

Song: "Scandalon," by Michael Card. This is a powerful, contemporary lyric that addresses the scandal of the cross.

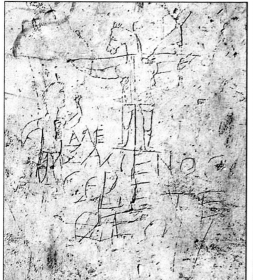

The Alexamenos Graffito. The Greek inscription on the graffito reads, "Alexamenos worships [his] god."

Song: "Sovereign Lord," by Phil Mehrens. This is another contemporary lyric that posits the great paradox taught here.

The just (those made righteous by faith) will live.

Film: *Martin Luther.* This classic film (1953), produced in black and white, stars Niall MacGinnis as Luther. It was filmed in what was then West Germany in studios in Wiesbaden in collaboration with the Lutheran Church. The acting is memorable and raw, and the scene where Luther discovers the meaning and dimension of the doctrine that the just will live by faith reveals the power of that Scripture passage. It is a careful and faithful portrayal of Luther's story; the research was done by, among others, Theodore Tappert, a scholar of the Reformation, and Jaroslav Pelikan, a scholar of church history and the history of theology. A more recent version, *Luther* (2003), has useful scenes but is, finally, less faithful, more of a biopic.

The Story of Israel and the Story of Gentiles

Big Idea *There is plenty of condemnation to go around for Jews as well as Gentiles. In this passage the story of Israel is reflected in the story of Gentiles—sin and judgment for both. But this bad news is designed to drive both to the gospel, the ultimate restoration of the Jews and conversion of the Gentiles.*

Understanding the Text

The Text in Context

Romans 1:18–4:25 is the unit of Romans that corresponds to the stipulation component of the Old Testament covenant formula. According to Paul, the stipulation for receiving the gospel of the righteousness of God—the true restoration of Israel and conversion of the nations—is faith in Jesus Christ, not the law of Moses or natural law. On the contrary, rather than bringing about obedience to God, these legal stipulations actually stir up disobedience within the human heart (see 1:32 regarding the natural law, and 3:19–20 regarding the Torah). With that in mind, 1:18–32 focuses on Gentiles' disobedience of natural law (though Jews also come under the purview of Paul's condemnation there), while 2:1–3:8 focuses on Jews' disobedience of the Torah. Consequently, all fall woefully short of God's righteousness (3:9–20). But this bad news predisposes all humans to accept the good news that faith in Jesus Christ is the only way to become right with God (3:21–4:25).

Romans 1:18 is the key theme governing 1:19–3:20: the wrath of God falls on those who break his law (those who commit ungodliness and wickedness), whether they be Gentiles who disobey natural law (1:19–32) or Jews who disobey the Torah (2:1–3:8). Romans 1:19–32 divides into two parts: verses 19–21 are a general statement of Gentile disobedience of God's natural law (but also with Jews and the Torah in mind); verses 22–32 are a detailed analysis of Gentile disobedience to God (but also concerning Jewish disregard for the Torah). This last section further divides into three subsections (vv. 22–24, 25–27, 28–32), each centering on the ominous phrase "God handed them over."

As Jews read about the sin and judgment of Gentiles as spelled out in these paragraphs, they would have heard echoes of their own story of sin and judgment/exile.

The four points of comparison between the Gentiles and Israel would have impressed themselves on Jewish (and Gentile) readers of Romans 1:18–32.

1. The various synonyms for "truth" and phrases to describe it throughout 1:18–32—"truth" (1:18); "what may be known" (1:19); "is manifest among them" (1:19; NIV: "is plain to them"); God's attributes of deity and power perceived in creation (1:20); "knew God" but did not "glorify him" (1:21); "exchanged the truth about God for a lie" (1:25); "natural" (1:26); "knowledge" (1:28); know God's "righteous decree" (1:32)—allude to both a Gentile Stoic concept (a Greek philosophy that taught that conscience is the divine standard resident in all humans) and a Jewish concept, the Noahic commandments that God prescribed for the world to follow after the flood (compare this to Gen. 9:1–17; *Jub.* 7.20; Acts 15:20–21, 29). This Noahic covenant with the world mirrors God's covenant with Israel and even overlaps with it as natural law overlaps with the Mosaic law.

2. Thus, just as Israel must keep the law of Moses in order to maintain their covenant with God, so must the Gentiles keep the Noahic law (natural law) if they want to remain in sync with God's covenant with creation. Therefore, both covenants contained stipulations.

The major theme is Paul's indictment of pagan Gentiles, but also of Jews. The stories of Gentiles/Adam and of Israel have four points of comparison:

- Various synonyms for "truth" allude to the Stoic concept of harmony with the divine being as well as to the commandments God prescribed for the world in his covenant with Noah.
- Just as Israel must keep the stipulations of the Mosaic law to remain in covenant with God, so Gentiles must keep the Noahic law to remain in God's covenant with creation.
- But neither Israel nor the nations have kept God's stipulations; rather, Gentiles followed Adam and Eve's idolatry, and Israel fell into idolatry with the golden calf.
- Consequently, God "handed over" the Gentiles to reap the results of their idolatry, just as God handed over Israel to their enemies for worshiping foreign gods.

3. But, in point of fact, neither Israel nor the nations kept God's respective stipulations for them. Rather, beginning with the fall of Adam (compare Gen. 1–3 with Rom. 1:18–32) and continuing after Noah, Gentiles continued in the idolatry of the first couple, and Israel (which fancied itself as God's replacement of Adam) fared no better, falling into idolatry at the incident of the golden calf (Exod. 32; cf. Ps. 106:20; Jer. 2:11). In other words, the sin component of the story of Israel and the sin component of the story of Gentiles, both rooted in idolatry, overlap or mirror one another.

4. Consequently, God "handed over" the Gentiles to the results of their idolatry (1:24, 26, 28), just as God handed over Israel to its enemies in judgment and exile (compare Rom. 1:22–32 with Exod. 23:31;

Zeno of Citium (ca. 333–262 BC), whose bust is shown here, was the father of Stoicism. The Stoics believed that one could develop a natural perception of God by observing the beauty and harmony of the world. They would have agreed with Paul's statement in Romans 1:20 that God's "eternal power and divine nature" could be understood from observing his creation.

Romans 1:18–32

Deut. 7:23; "handed over" is a stereotypical formula depicting God handing over Israel to enemies). Thus, the judgment/exile component of the story of Gentiles (Adam was judged and expelled from Eden) and of the story of Israel (Jews were judged/expelled from their homeland to Assyria and Babylonia) would have impressed itself upon the reader of Romans 1:18–32.

Historical and Cultural Background

1. Genesis 1–3, especially Adam's fall, informs Paul's indictment of Gentiles in Romans 1:18–32.

2. Both the Old Testament and the literature of Second Temple Judaism pointed toward Israel as God's intended replacement of Adam,[1] but, alas, Israel's idolatrous act of worshiping the golden calf (Exod. 32) constituted its own Adam-like fall. In other words, Israel, instead of being the remedy for Adam's sin, was now also marred by it.[2] Paul agrees with this in Romans 1:18–32.

3. It is commonly thought that the content of the "righteous decree" and its synonyms throughout Romans 1:18–32 tap into the Jewish fusion of the traditions of Stoic natural law and the Noahic laws. The former is alluded to in 1:19–20 (God's "invisible/visible"

Twice in Romans 1:18–32, Paul refers to the wickedness of idolatry. In 1:23 he talks about people exchanging "the glory of the immortal God for images made to look like a mortal human being and birds and animals and reptiles." In 1:25, they "worshiped and served created things rather than the Creator." Here is a statuette of a god standing on a bull where the bull functions as a pedestal for the deity. It is from the second half of the second millennium BC.

[aorata/kathoratai] attributes [see Pseudo-Aristotle, Cosmos 399b.14] and his "divinity" [theiotēs] [see Plutarch, Mor. 98A; 665A]) and in 1:26–27 ("natural" is related to "nature" [physis], a term pervasive in Stoicism, referring to living in harmony with the natural order by allowing reason to rule the person).[3] The latter concept, Noahic covenant/law, was well known in Paul's day to refer to the divine standard to which Gentiles would be held accountable before God—avoiding idolatry, immorality, and eating meat without the blood drained from it (cf. Gen. 9:1–7; Jub. 7.20–21; Sib. Or. 4.24–39; Acts 15:20–21, 29). Romans 1:18–32 highlights the abhorrence of idolatry and immorality.

Interpretive Insights

1:18 *The wrath of God . . . against all the godlessness and wickedness of people, who suppress the truth.* God's wrath is personal, not an impersonal cause and effect built into the universe to correct wrong behavior. God's wrath is just and can lead the sinner to the mercy of repentance. Moreover, God's wrath is eschatological: it is already but not yet. It is already here in that divine wrath has broken into history with the first coming of Christ, such that how people respond to God's revelation now (1:18) is how judgment will go for them on the last day (2:5, 8; 3:5; 5:9; cf. 1 Thess. 1:10; 5:9).

The truth that Gentiles suppress is natural law adopted in Judaism as the Noahic law/covenant. One can hear in this the story of Israel as reflected in the story of the Gentiles—sin and judgment. The nations sinned against God, and so he handed them over to the disastrous consequences of their idolatry. In the same way, God handed

Israel over to their enemies in payment for their idolatry.

1:21–24 *God gave them over in the sinful desires of their hearts.* Three times in 1:22–32 Paul says that God gave the Gentiles over/up to judgment. In 1:21–24 there is an implied connection between idolatry and immorality. The bottom line for Paul is that God's wrath upon those who reject him as the Creator often takes the form of letting people suffer the consequences of getting what they want. To put it another way, we become like that which we worship.

1:26–27 *God gave them over to shameful lusts . . . due penalty for their error.* For a second time Paul says that God gave over/up the Gentiles to judgment, this time with reference to sexual perversion—homosexuality and lesbianism. The apostle to the Gentiles minces no words concerning homosexual behavior; it is the product of the wrath of God. It may be that we are to see a connection between the general immorality mentioned in 1:24 and same-sex relations detailed in 1:26–27; the continual abandoning of oneself to immorality in general can be a slippery slope to more perverse sexual activities. And, for Paul, all of this starts with idolatry: to exchange worship of the Creator for worship of the creature is to invite the exchange of normal sexual relations for unnatural ones.

1:28–32 *God gave them over to a depraved mind . . . Although they know God's righteous decree.* For the third and final time Paul says that God gave the Gentiles over/up to his wrath, and in 1:29–32 he details their offenses in the form of a vice list. Catalogs of vice were well known in the ancient world, particularly among the Stoics. They were also adopted in Judaism (e.g., Wis. 14:25–26; 4 Macc. 1:26–27; 2:15; 1QS 4.9–11) and in early Christianity (e.g., Mark 7:21–22; 1 Cor. 5:10–11; 6:9–10; Gal. 5:19–21).[4] As Douglas Moo notes, the vices in Romans 1:29–32 fall into a threefold structure: (1) the first four are general in scope ("wickedness, evil, greed, depravity"); (2) the next five revolve around envy ("envy, murder, strife, deceit, malice"); (3) the last twelve begin with two depicting slander ("gossips, slanderers"), move on to four focusing on arrogance ("God-haters, insolent, arrogant, boastful"), and conclude with six that are less closely related ("inventors of evil, disobedient to parents, senseless, faithless, heartless, ruthless"). Most of the sins in this vice list are societal in nature and threaten to undo the fabric of civilization.[5] The "righteous decree" is not the Torah referred to in 2:26 and 8:4 but rather natural law / Noahic law. Nevertheless, it overlaps with the law of Moses. Thus, the Jewish reader would have heard echoes of the story of Israel here in the story of the Gentiles in Romans 1:18–32.

Theological Insights

Powerful theological insights confront the reader of Romans 1:18–32. First, God is both loving and just. Without the former, God would be harsh; without the latter, God would be doting. According to Romans 3:26, at the cross of Christ God's love and justice were ultimately reconciled. Second, for centuries Protestants and Catholics have debated whether humans can know God in a saving way based only on the witness of creation and the conscience. Catholics have tended to say yes, while Protestants have tended to say no. The former position is called "natural theology," and the latter "natural revelation." It is clear that Paul does not believe in natural theology, since he argues in 1:18–32 that humankind consistently and without excuse rejects the message of creation that God is, and that he is powerful and therefore deserves our worship. Third, Paul also is clear in 1:18–32 that he does not condone same-sex relations; in fact, the apostle to the Gentiles condemns the practice. Moreover, Paul seems to say that the behavior is itself the judgment of God upon those who exchange the worship of him for the worship of the creature. But does Paul hold no hope out for those involved in this lifestyle? That perspective goes beyond Paul's warning. It is more likely the case that Paul hopes that those caught up in such living will grow weary of its consequences and turn to God for forgiveness and healing.

The Romans had a full pantheon of gods to whom they offered sacrifices and worship. Here is a bust of Minerva, goddess of wisdom, an image "made to look like a mortal human being" (Romans 1:23), dated between AD 50 and 150.

ance God's wrath with his love. But at the end of the day, Paul and the Bible as a whole do not shy away from preaching the holiness and wrath of God against sin.

Second, another controversial sermon topic based on 1:18–32 is "Same-Sex Marriage and Paul." Although Paul does not specifically refer to same-sex marriage in this passage, his injunction here against lesbian and homosexual relationships is clear. And if Paul lived in the twenty-first century, he undoubtedly would apply that prohibition to same-sex marriage as well.

Third, related to the debate over natural theology relative to 1:18–32, one could preach or teach on the topic "Are the Heathen Lost?" Those religious traditions in favor of natural theology would be inclined to answer no to that question. Thus, a famous Jesuit theologian, Karl Rahner, argued in the last century that even a person who only acknowledges an inner divine transcendence is accepted by God. Such a person Rahner labeled an "anonymous Christian." But those who reject natural theology argue instead that one is accepted by God only by receiving his Son as savior.

Fourth, on a little more pluralistic note, a sermon entitled "Common Ground: Universal Ethics and Romans 1:18–32" might be appealing for postmodern audiences. The goal here might be to identify moral

Teaching the Text

Several sermon titles/ideas easily present themselves in Romans 1:18–32. First, "Sinners in the Hands of an Angry God" is a sermon topic sure to elicit anything but a neutral response from listeners. I well remember reading Jonathan Edwards's famous sermon for the first time in a high school English class. Talking about God holding sinners over the fires of hell like one roasting an insect over a flame certainly got my attention! But the image is, in reality, a caricature, because Edwards's theology was much broader than that one sermon, encompassing the love of God as well, and because the metaphor fails to bal-

commonalities among the major religions of the world in the hope of establishing a broad base of rules by which various societies can get along. Romans 1:18–32 spells out such ethics in the negative.

Illustrating the Text

God is both loving and just.

Classic Sermon: "Sinners in the Hands of an Angry God," by Jonathan Edwards. One could put this famous sermon (1741) on display in the church, have members of the congregation read the entire sermon (easily available online) in advance of the Sunday on which this text is preached, read or have members of the congregation read selected portions aloud during the sermon (these could also be made available in the bulletin), and ask if this is what Paul has in mind in Romans 1:18–32 when he talks about the wrath of God.

Film: *No Country for Old Men*; *A Serious Man*. It might be useful to present the audience with clips from either of these movies (2007, 2009) by Ethan and Joel Coen, in which the absence of God is palpably seen through random violence that goes unpunished. In the case of *A Serious Man*, the protagonist, Larry, suffers tremendous doubts about the goodness of God in the face of increasing loss. Larry cannot comprehend why he has been targeted for misfortunes that grow in intensity. The rabbi has no answer, and when there is finally evidence of transcendence, it comes in the form of a tornado bearing down on the house, what looks like a final judgment. After introducing your congregation to the premise, you could show or describe a film clip, and the audience could be prompted to defend Paul's statement.

Paul does not condone same-sex relations.

Chart: Comparing Romans to Modern Laws. While one must be prepared for what follows because it may be provocative, one could create a chart setting Romans 1:18–32 beside those state laws approving same-sex marriages and ask the audience to react to the difference between the two.

Humans do not heed creation's message that God is powerful and deserves worship.

Literature: *The Last Battle*, by C. S. Lewis. This final book (1956) of The Chronicles of Narnia series depicts a scene in which the pagan Emeth encounters Lord Aslan. Emeth discovers that his service to the god Tash has actually been service to the true God. The audience could be asked: Is this a form of natural theology? If so, do you agree or disagree with Lewis's perspective? To fill out Lewis's perspective, it would be useful to refer to *The Abolition of Man*, in which Lewis takes up the same subject.

The Story of Israel Now and Later

Big Idea *Paul makes explicit the story of Israel. Obedience to God's law was required for Israel to remain in covenantal relationship with God. But Israel repeatedly broke the law, and consequently divine judgment fell on Jews. Moreover, God's judgment will fall on individual Jews on the final day of reckoning if they do not repent by accepting Jesus as the Messiah.*

Understanding the Text

The Text in Context

In placing Romans 2:1–11 in its literary context, we focus in from the big picture of 1:18–3:20, which condemns all of humanity, to Paul's condemnation of one people group, the Jews.

The theme of Romans 1:18–3:20, as noted previously, is that the wrath of God (1:18) is upon Gentiles for breaking the stipulations of the Noahic covenant (1:19–32) and upon Jews for breaking the stipulations of the Mosaic covenant (2:1–3:8). So there is no doubt that 3:9–20 indicts all of humankind because it fails to keep covenant with God.

Romans 2 fills out the details of Paul's condemnation of Jews in his day. They disobey the Torah, the stipulation of the Mosaic covenant (2:1–16), which cancels out the very validity of their circumcision, which is the ultimate sign of the covenant with God (2:17–29).

Romans 2:1–16 focuses on the Jews' breaking of the Torah. These verses divide into three paragraphs:

1. Israel is not exempt from the wrath of God, since it disobeys the Torah (2:1–5).
2. God is impartial and will judge both Gentile and Jew according to truth—that is, according to their works (2:6–11).
3. Gentiles are not exempt from the wrath of God, since they disobey natural law / Noahic law (2:12–16).

Romans 2:1–11 has a number of connections with the Old Testament covenant:

1. "The day of God's wrath" (2:5; cf. 2:16) draws on the "day of the Lord" tradition so prevalent in the Old Testament, especially the idea in the prophets that because of Israel's sin against the covenant, the purported coming day of the Lord's might on behalf of his people would be turned against them (e.g., Isa. 2:11, 17, 20; Joel 1:15; 2:2; Amos 5:18; 8:9; Zeph. 1:15, 18 ["the day of the LORD's wrath"]). The punishment associated with the

day of the Lord's wrath upon Israel is the actualization of the covenantal curses (see Deut. 28–30).

2. The stark contrast in 2:1–11 between divine wrath on those who disobey the Torah and eternal life for those who obey the Torah is rooted in the blessings/curses component of the covenant first articulated in Deuteronomy 27–30, with Deuteronomy 30:15–20 encapsulating those contrasting destinies.

3. The terms "kindness" (2:4) and "stubbornness" (2:5) take one back to the covenant: the first refers to God's faithfulness to his covenant with Israel (e.g., Wis. 15:1),[1] while the second refers to Old Testament Israel's repeated hardness of heart toward the stipulations of its covenant with God (beginning in Deut. 9:27).

4. "Storing up wrath against yourself" (2:5) reverses the Jewish concept that obeying the Torah stored up for oneself and other Israelites a treasury of merits (e.g., Tob. 4:9–10; *Pss. Sol.* 9.3–5; *4 Ezra* 6.5; 7.77; *2 Bar.* 14.12) by asserting quite to the contrary that attempting to attain merit before God by obeying the Torah actually reserves wrath for a person in the future. James Dunn puts this well: "The pious interlocutor assumes that by his faithfulness to the covenant he is laying up treasure in heaven; but by his failure to recognize the need for a more radical repentance he is actually storing up not 'good,' not 'life,' but wrath."[2]

5. These covenant connections illumine what Paul means in 2:1, 3 when

- There is no partiality with God, no double standard in the way God judges both Gentiles and Jews, which is according to works.
- Several important connections with the Old Testament covenant emerge in Paul's argument about God's judgment.

he accuses Jews of committing the "same things" as Gentiles: the same sins of idolatry (1:19–27) and social injustice (1:28–32) that the nations are guilty of are also perpetrated by the Jews. And when one remembers that the Old Testament prophets consistently thundered forth against Israel for committing the two sins of idolatry and injustice and thus breaking the stipulations of the covenant (e.g., Isaiah, Amos, Micah), one can better appreciate the nature of the sins of Israel here pointed out by Paul.

Historical and Cultural Background

The major historical and cultural background of Romans 2:1–11 is the story of Israel as reflected in the Old Testament and in

The Roman occupation of the land of Israel was considered by many Jews to be part of God's judgment. Marcus Antonius Felix was the Roman procurator of the province of Judea from AD 52 to 59. He was a less-than-effective administrator governing at a time when discontent and rebellion were increasing in the Roman-controlled area of Palestine. He was accused of arranging for the murder of the high priest in Jerusalem and used Roman troops when necessary to quell more organized uprisings. These coins were minted during his time in power.

Romans 2:1–11

Second Temple Judaism, especially the sin and judgment/exile components (though the restoration aspect is implicit in 2:4 and later explicit in 11:25–27). Three nuances in Romans 2:1–11 echo this story.

1. As noted above, the twofold sin of Israel against the covenant with God was idolatry and injustice. Micah provides a classic illustration of how the prophets railed against Israel for doing these. In Micah 1:1–7 that prophet warns that the Lord will come to judge Israel because of their transgressions, notably idolatry: "All her idols will be broken to pieces; . . . I will destroy her images" (1:7). And Micah 6:8 states that the other stipulation of Israel's covenant with God is social justice: "He has shown you, O mortal, what is good. And what does the LORD require of you? To act justly and to love mercy and to walk humbly with your God." Then, in Micah 6:9–7:7, the prophet spells out the acts of social injustice on the part of Israel against fellow Jews that annulled their covenant with God.

2. In the Old Testament, many in Israel labored under the assumption that their election as God's chosen people exempted them from divine judgment even if they sinned, a notion with which the prophets begged to disagree (e.g., Isa. 2:6–4:1; Jer. 2–35; Ezek. 1–24). Yet, even after the Assyrian and Babylonian exiles, the notion of Israel's inviolability persisted. One of the most famous expressions of this, and one that many commentators believe is alluded to by Paul in Romans 2:4, is Wisdom of Solomon 15:1–2: "But you, our God, are kind and true, patient, and ruling all things in mercy. For even if we sin we are yours." It is just such a notion that Paul rejects in Romans 2:1–11.

3. Romans 2:4–5 announces a "double whammy" on Jews: the wrath of God has already fallen on Israel in history through past exiles (Assyrian and Babylonian) and present exile (Roman occupation) (a view reflected in, e.g., the Dead Sea Scrolls, Baruch, Tobit, Sirach, 2 Maccabees, *Psalms of Solomon*),[3] and the wrath of God will also fall upon Jews on the final day of judgment because they do not believe in Jesus the Messiah, who provides the true restoration to God.

Built during the reign of Nebuchadnezzar (605–562 BC) in the city of Babylon, the Ishtar Gate with its beautiful and elaborate decoration represented the power of the Babylonian gods and their king. The Babylonians were God's instrument of judgment on the Israelites with two mass deportations of the residents of Judah. The first occurred in 597 BC and the second after the destruction of Jerusalem in 587/586 BC.

Interpretive Insights

2:1–3 *You, therefore, have no excuse . . . you who pass judgment do the same things.* Although some commentators think that Paul now addresses "moral" Gentiles in 2:1–11 in contrast to "pagan" Gentiles in 1:18–32, most believe instead that Paul is turning his attention to the Jews (cf. 2:17). There are several reasons for this position. First, the sense of entitlement to divine mercy referred to in 2:4 is more characteristic of Jews than Gentiles (recall my earlier comments on Wis. 15:1–2 relative to Rom. 2:4). Second, indeed there are notable points of contact between Romans 2 and Wisdom of Solomon 12–15 that confirm a Jewish mindset here in 2:1–11. Third, Paul's direct appeal to "the Jew" in 2:17 does not indicate that he is there introducing a new audience.

The key to understanding Romans 2:1–5 is to see the two components of the story of Israel at play there. The first is that Israel has sinned against the stipulations of the Torah, in terms of both idolatry and injustice. These sins are the "same things" (referred to three times in 2:1–3) that the Gentiles commit. And, since Israel commits the same sins that Gentiles commit, Israel too will be held accountable before God, who judges all humankind by the same standard of truth.

2:4–5 *you show contempt for the riches of his kindness . . . storing up wrath against yourself.* These two verses tap into the second component of the story of Israel: God's judgment upon and exile of Israel for not repenting of their idolatry and injustice. Verse 4 recalls the "already" aspect of that judgment, Israel's past and present exiles (Assyrian, Babylonian, Roman), while verse 5 warns of the "not yet" aspect, Israel's future judgment and ultimate exile at the judgment bar of God on the last day. But there is hope for Israel: if they will repent, they will experience a restored relationship with God (implied, if Israel accepts Jesus as the Messiah [see 11:25–27]).

2:6–11 *God "will repay each person according to what they have done."* Romans 2:6–11 forms a chiasm:

> A God will judge everyone equitably (v. 6).
> > B Those who do good will attain eternal life (v. 7).
> > > C Those who do evil will suffer wrath and anger (v. 8).
> > > C′ Those who do evil will suffer trouble and distress (v. 9).
> > B′ Those who do good will receive glory, honor, peace (v. 10).
> A′ God judges impartially (v. 11).[4]

It becomes clear from this structure that Paul's message is simple: God is fair and will judge Jew and Gentile alike according to their works. Those who live a life of good works will enter into eternal life, but those who live a life of evil will enter into divine judgment. As noted earlier, this powerful and yet simple contrast in destinies recalls Deuteronomy 27–30, especially 30:15–20 and the "two ways" tradition specified there: if Israel obeys the stipulations of the Torah, they will experience the blessing of the covenant, which is life, but if they disregard the Torah, they will experience the curse of the covenant, which is wrath in the form of exile (cf. 30:4–5).

But does the teaching in Romans 2:6–11 contradict Paul's gospel that justification before God at the final judgment depends solely on faith and not on works (so Rom. 1:16–17)? Not when one keeps in mind the overarching purpose of Romans 1:18–3:20, which is that Paul wants to show that acceptance before a righteous God is based on *perfectly* following his law, which, in fact, no one can do, not even Jews. Coming to grips with that reality, Paul hopes, will drive the sinner into the arms of God's grace and mercy in Jesus Christ (see Rom. 3:21–4:25).

Theological Insights

A number of insights meet us in Romans 2:1–11. First, profession without practice does not impress God. Neither does it convince those who observe the lifestyles of religious people. If we profess to be believers, we must back up that profession with how we live; otherwise we rightly earn for ourselves the name "hypocrite." Second, it is comforting to know that on the final day of reckoning, truth will win out. All inconsistency, duplicity, and hypocrisy will not dupe Almighty God. Third, God's goodness can nevertheless overtake one's duplicitous ways. Such grace can bring about within us true repentance and result in a consistent Christian walk.

Teaching the Text

At least two attention-getting sermon/lesson titles surface in Romans 2:1–11: first, "The Hypocrisy of Humanity and the Impartiality of God"; second, "The Goodness of God Leads Us to Repentance." With regard to the first sermonic idea, Paul is exercised about those Jews who point out sins in

Gentiles that those very Jews themselves are committing. One is reminded here of Jesus' excoriation of the Pharisees in the Gospels who did not live up to the Mosaic code that they expected their compatriots to follow. And in modern society some well-known preachers in the recent past lambasted their congregations over sins that turned out to be the very sins those preachers themselves were committing. News reporters call such hypocrisy "preaching against one's own demons." The point that Paul wants to make here is that no one can live up to the perfect standards of the law, and it is duplicitous to expect others to do what the religious leaders cannot do.

Regarding the second sermonic idea, the ancient Jews misinterpreted God's lack of immediate judgment upon them as meaning that God was not going to judge them at all because they were the people of God. But in reality the Jews in Paul's day were experiencing the proverbial calm before the storm. Part of the reason for that calm before judgment fell stemmed from God's mercy and grace. He was giving his Old Testament people time to repent. I had a barber in Chicago who lived a wild life despite being married and having children. He was a party-going, pill-popping hipster. But one morning he told me of an amazing experience that he recently had. He said that suddenly the sense of God's blessings on his life overwhelmed him—a faithful wife, lovely children, financial security. The barber felt so convicted by the goodness of God to him that he fell to his knees and repented of his wild lifestyle. There and then he committed himself to God and his family. The mercy of God led him to repentance.

Illustrating the Text

Unlike humans, God judges everyone impartially in truth.

Bible: One could refer to 2 Samuel 12:1–7, where Nathan uses a parable to expose David's sordid sins, and Amos 1–2, in which the Lord delineates the sins of the Gentile world and then turns to also censure Judah and Israel. Both of these provide famous "gotcha" stories reminiscent of Romans 2:1–11.

Television: *24.* An innovative and acclaimed drama on television, starring Kiefer Sutherland, this suspenseful series has been nominated for a total of sixty-eight Emmy Awards, winning for outstanding drama series in 2006. During the seventh season, the character Allison Taylor is inaugurated as president of the United States and presides over the ensuing episodes. During this season, her daughter, who has been one of her chiefs of staff, later takes the law into her own hands against her mother's wishes and engineers the murder of another character (Jonas) to avenge her brother's death. Although she loves her daughter, the president will not make allowances for her and proceeds to uphold the law and have her arrested. The president's husband, reeling from grief over the loss of both children, disagrees with her, and in the culminating episode he leaves her. Here is a moving story of a political figure who has acted without partiality.

The goodness of God leads us to repentance.

Film: *The Mission.* This enduring, award-winning film (1986) stars Jeremy Irons and Robert De Niro and features lush, Oscar-winning cinematography. It also includes one of the great cinematic scenes of repentance and forgiveness. The story examines the events surrounding the Treaty of Madrid in 1750, when Spain ceded part of South America to Portugal. Two European forces win the South American natives over to imperialist ways. The plunderers want to extract riches and slaves from the New World; the missionaries want to convert the indigenous peoples to Christianity and win over their souls. Mendoza (played by De Niro) is an exploiter dabbling in the slave trade. After he kills his brother in a fit of rage—a Cain and Abel story—he languishes depressed in jail until a local priest, Father Gabriel (played by Irons), reaches out to him in his cell. Eventually broken and wanting to do penance, Mendoza repeatedly climbs up the Iguazu Falls with a heavy bag on his back weighted down with symbols of his past—armor, sword, and so on. The indigenous Guarani people, watching him from above the falls where they live, at first want to kill him, but then they finally cut his burden loose and show him utter forgiveness. Mendoza, completely overcome by the goodness of God that he sees in this act, weeps and then goes to live with them. Later, he defends them, at the expense of his life, against those who would do what he had previously done. The film clip of his climb up the falls is worth showing.

The Story of the Gentiles Now and Later

Big Idea *Gentiles, like Israelites, are a part of the story. They sin against natural law and consequently are subject to judgment now in an accusing conscience and later at the great day of reckoning. More particularly, just as Gentiles occasionally obey the Torah as it overlaps with natural law but are condemned for not obeying all God's revelation, so Jews who obey the Torah only occasionally are condemned before God.*

Understanding the Text

The Text in Context

The reader will recall that Romans 2:1–16 is divided into three paragraphs: verses 1–5, 6–11, 12–16. Verses 6–11 made the point that because God is impartial, he will judge both Jew and Gentile according to their works. But verses 1–5 made the case that Jews are guilty before God because they do not keep the Torah, and therefore judgment has set in on the nation of Israel (this is the story of Israel). Now, verses 12–16 will make a similar case against Gentiles. Because they do not keep the natural law even as it intersects with the Torah, divine judgment has set in on the Gentiles (this is the story of Gentiles).

Historical and Cultural Background

Two Greek influences are apparent in Romans 2:12–16: the usage of the dia-tribe and the employment of the term "conscience."

1. Commentators have long noted the influence of the debating style known as "diatribe" on Romans 2:1–3:8. Ancient Greeks used diatribe in debating. In this style of argumentation, the proponent of a position anticipated opponents' criticisms by raising those points before they did, either in the form of outright objections or as questions placed on the lips of an interlocutor. In anticipating and then answering the criticisms and arguments of opponents, the proponent was able to head them off at the pass, so to speak. The diatribe consisted of three parts: explicitly or implicitly addressing opponents, raising their criticisms, and then answering those criticisms.[1] Paul employs the diatribe technique against Jews who have rejected Jesus as Messiah in Romans 2:1–3:20 at three places: 2:1–11; 2:17–24; 3:1–8. Those oc-

casions can be summarized in chart form, as shown in table 1.

It is interesting, by way of contrast, that Paul does not use the diatribe style when dealing with the subject of the sinful status of Gentiles in 1:19–32, here in 2:12–16, and in 2:25–29, presumably because his arguments therein would not precipitate any protest from Gentiles. That is, what Paul says about the lost condition of Gentiles in the above three passages apparently would occasion little shock on their part in contrast to the Jews' vociferous reaction to Paul's indictment of them in 2:1–11; 2:17–24; 3:1–8.

2. "Conscience" (*syneidēsis* [2:15]) was a Greek concept, especially the Stoic idea that the conscience is the moral mechanism within humans that convicts them of bad actions (e.g., Seneca, *Anger* 3.36.1; *Mor. Ep.* 28.10). Hellenistic Judaism adopted this nuance in its usage of the term (e.g., Wis. 17:11; Philo, *Spec. Laws* 2.49; *Virtues* 134; Josephus, *Ant.* 16.103). Paul refers to this negative aspect of conscience here in Romans 2:15 and also in 1 Corinthians 8:7, 10, 12; 1 Timothy 4:2; Titus 1:15; but note the positive role that the conscience plays

Key Themes of Romans 2:12–16

- The law (of Moses) is mentioned for the first time in Romans.
- Natural law / Noahic law and Torah overlap (an intersection similar to what theologians call "common grace"). That is, God's natural revelation in creation and conscience is consistent with God's special revelation—Old and New Testaments—but far less definitive.
- Gentiles sometimes obey God's natural law, but not always. Therefore they are condemned (a conclusion with which Jews in Paul's day would have agreed). But neither are Jews justified by God unless they perfectly keep all 613 commandments of the Torah (a conclusion that would have horrified Paul's Jewish readers).

The diatribe was a teaching technique used by Paul as he addressed the arguments of Jewish unbelievers in Romans 2 and 3. It was a debating style inherited from the philosophers and sophists of ancient Greece. Teachers would gather a group of students, often instructing them in a public setting such as a stoa, gymnasium, or marketplace. Here are the archaeological remains of the Forum of Caesar in Rome. Built around 46 BC, it was destroyed by fire and reconstructed several times through the third century AD. The columns typically supported a roofed portico area providing a place for public and private discourse.

Table 1: Paul's Use of Diatribe in Romans 2–3

Diatribe components	Romans 2:1–11	Romans 2:17–24	Romans 3:1–8
Interlocutor Paul addresses	2:1–2 (implied): Jewish unbeliever	2:17 (explicit): Jewish unbeliever	3:1 (explicit): Jewish unbeliever
Arguments by the opponents	2:3–4 (raised by Paul): You think that you are exempt from the judgment of God.	2:17–20 (raised by Paul): You boast about your covenant relationship with God as making you superior to Gentiles.	3:1–3 (raised directly by the interlocutor): According to you, Paul, there is no advantage in being Jewish, and therefore God has broken his promises to Israel, his chosen people.
Answers by Paul	2:5–6: But to delay repentance now is to store up wrath for the future.	2:24: But you hypocritically commit the same sins as do Gentiles and thereby invalidate your circumcision, the Old Testament sign of the covenant.	3:4–8: But God is true and faithful.

elsewhere for Paul, in Romans 9:1; 2 Corinthians 1:12; 1 Timothy 1:5, 19; 3:9; 2 Timothy 1:3.

Interpretive Insights

2:12–14 *All who sin apart from the law will also perish apart from the law.* The theme of 2:12–16 is the story of the Gentiles, which is a mirror image of the story of Israel: sin against God's revelation and subsequent judgment. The Gentiles' sin is treated by Paul in 2:12–14, and their judgment is covered in 2:15–16. Paul's point in 2:12 is that because God is impartial, both Gentiles and Jews will be judged based on the amount of revelation to which they have access: for Gentiles, natural law (though that overlaps with the Torah [see 2:14]); for Jews, the Torah. The criterion of divine judgment is obeying/doing God's revelation, not just hearing it (2:13). We may anticipate in 2:13 Paul's statements, made later in 3:20; 4:14–15; 7:5 and also in 3:23; 10:5, that obeying/doing the law means following it perfectly—something that no

human can do, if for no other reason than that the law stirs up the individual to sin. Indeed, 1:19–32 has already placed the Gentiles under indictment for disobeying the light that they have in creation, and 2:1–11 did the same for Jews because they did not live up to the light of the law of Moses.

The majority view of 2:14–15 is that Paul is dealing with non-Christian Gentiles who, though occasionally obeying the Torah as it intersects with natural law / Noahic law as revealed in creation and in the conscience, do not obey the entirety of God's special revelation in the Torah and, therefore, are still lost (a conclusion with which most Jews would have agreed). A vocal minority of commentators, however, maintains that the Gentiles in 2:12–16 are Christian Gentiles who by virtue of faith in Jesus and the indwelling Spirit are participants in the new covenant.[2] Table 2 lays out these two views, highlighting the clash between them regarding the specific issues in 2:14–15.

In my view, the reading that sees Paul having non-Christian Gentiles in mind has

Table 2: Non-Christian or Christian Gentiles in Romans 2:14–15

Non-Christian Gentiles	Christian Gentiles
Verses 14–15 go with verse 12a = non-Christian Gentiles who sin without the law (Torah).	Verses 14–15 go with verse 13 = Christian Gentiles who obey the law of Moses from the heart, the promised new covenant (compare v. 15 with Jer. 31:31–33; cf. Ezek. 36:24–28), because of their faith in Jesus and the indwelling of the Holy Spirit.
In verse 14 *physei* ("by nature") belongs with the verb "do" (*poiōsin*): "do by nature things required by the law." This refers to non-Christian Gentiles who occasionally obey the Torah as it intersects with natural law ("a law unto themselves") but still are not justified, since they do not follow that revelation perfectly.	In verse 14 *physei* ("by nature") belongs with the verb "do not have" (*mē echonta*): "by nature do not have the law." This refers to Christian Gentiles who, by race, do not have the Torah but nevertheless obey the Torah by believing in Jesus and walking in the Spirit.
Law is natural law overlapping with the law of Moses.	Law is only the law of Moses, not natural law.
The emphasis is on the divine judgment of non-Christian Gentiles, whose consciences mostly convict them of disobeying natural law, a foretaste of the coming day of reckoning.	The emphasis is on the divine justification of Gentile Christians, whose faith in Jesus and walking in the Spirit fulfill the intent of the Mosaic code.

a much better argument than its rival view. This is confirmed by something apparently not noted in many commentaries: a chiastic arrangement governing 2:14 that distinguishes two laws, Torah and natural law.

A Gentiles do not have the law (Torah)
   B they do by nature things required (natural law)
   B′ they are a law (natural law) unto themselves
A′ they do not have the law (Torah)

2:15–16 *the requirements of the law are written on their hearts.* Verses 15–16 announce divine judgment on non-Christian Gentiles, who only occasionally obey the Torah as natural law intersects with it. Verse 15 declares that such judgment occurs now in history every time a Gentile is convicted by conscience of doing wrong, though the conscience will approve the Gentile's actions when they are right, however

occasionally that may happen. And verse 16 provides the foreboding announcement that non-Christian Gentiles also will face final judgment on the day of divine reckoning. In table 3, we see how the story of Gentiles mirrors the story of Israel.

Table 3: The Story of Gentiles and the Story of Israel

Story of Israel in Romans 2:1–11	Story of Gentiles in Romans 2:12–16
Verses 1–3, 6–11: Non-Christian Jews sin in that they do not fully comply with the Torah.	Verses 12–14: Non-Christian Gentiles sin in that they do not fully comply with the Torah and, for that matter, not even with natural law.
Verses 4–5: Non-Christian Jews are being judged now in history via Roman occupation of the land of Israel (cf. the earlier Assyrian and Babylonian exiles) and will be finally judged at the day of reckoning.	Verses 15–16: Non-Christian Gentiles are judged now in history via their consciences and will be finally judged at the day of reckoning.

Romans 2:12–16

In light of 2:12–16a, one wonders how in 2:16b Paul could call such news "gospel." The answer will unfold in the course of his argument in 2:17–3:31: the bad news of judgment upon sin that rests on the whole human race is designed by God to drive people to the good news of justification by faith in Christ alone.

Theological Insights

A number of theological truths emerge in Romans 2:12–16. First, all people have a witness from God: Jews in the Torah, and Gentiles in natural law (creation says that there is a God and that he is powerful, and the conscience bespeaks the holiness of God, the sense of "oughtness" in every heart). Second, the criterion for being justified before God is perfection, both in respect to natural law and even regarding the Torah. Third, the real challenge to obeying the law is the human condition—depravity of the heart, as Paul will later expound upon in 3:9–20. Fourth, judgment day is coming; it is as sure as God himself. And on that day all wrongs will be righted as all the world is silent before the judge over all of reality. Fifth, it does seem that there will be degrees of judgment and reward in heaven, because the works of every individual will be evaluated in the light of what amount of truth he or she possessed.

Teaching the Text

At least two topics of preaching/teaching surface for the reader of Romans 2:12–16. The first might be entitled "A Law unto Themselves: Common Grace as God's Witness in the World." The message here is that God has spoken to all people groups of the world through his natural law in creation and in the human conscience. Therefore, all are without excuse before God. The idea of common grace, on a more positive note, also accounts for the good in the world that humans do because they are created in the image of God and therefore have some knowledge of him. This came home to me as an undergraduate student in a large secular university. I was intimidated by the brilliance and graciousness of my non-Christian professors; their knowledge and kindness put me to shame even as a Christian. But one day I realized that these individuals, though not religious, were nevertheless created in the image of God and endowed with common grace. I could therefore appreciate their gifts as a service to humankind, even as God intended.

Second, an ominous topic of discussion or preaching inspired by 2:12–16 would be entitled "All or Nothing! God's Law and Judgment Day." The foreboding message here is that anyone who hopes to be accepted by God on judgment day based on obedience to his law had better make sure to follow it perfectly because that is the only standard that God accepts. But the eminently easier way to be justified before God is to receive by faith the perfect righteousness of Jesus Christ, who alone fulfilled the law of Moses (see Rom. 10:4). A colleague of mine in teaching tried to illustrate this principle by offering his students enrolled in a course on Romans a choice for their final exam: they could choose either to take the test (a very difficult one!) or to accept as a gift from the professor a grade of "A." The professor was shocked that most of the students did not want the gift; rather, they wanted to do it the "old-fashioned way"—earn it! There seems to be something about us human beings that impels us to want to earn our standing before God instead of accepting it as a gift in Christ.

Illustrating the Text

God speaks to all people through natural law in creation and in their conscience.

Ethics: One could place side by side the various ethics that major religions of the world espouse to see if there is commonality among them. Those values found perhaps could serve as a common ethic to live by for a world diverse in religious perspectives.

Philosophy: Immanuel Kant. One could find in Kant's "categorical imperative" a practical defense of the idea that there is a sense of oughtness/conscience within every human.

Apologetics: *Mere Christianity*, **by C. S. Lewis.** In book 1 of this renowned work (1952) Lewis uses vivid analogies to illustrate the principle of natural law.

Theological Book: *Eternity in Their Hearts*, **by Don Richardson.** The basic premise of this book (1981) is that God, in his mercy, has permitted every culture in the world to retain a portion of the truth.

Judgment day, on which the works of each individual will be judged, is coming.

Literature: *The Inferno*, **by Dante Alighieri.** To show the power of judgment, it might be good to find a pictorial illustration of Dante's *Inferno*, such as Gustave Doré's classic engravings illustrating the nine circles of hell. Dante's poem begins on the night before Good Friday in the year 1300. Dante is lost in a dark wood (often interpreted as sin) and is unable to find the right way to salvation (symbolized by the sun behind the mountain). Virgil comes to his aid and guides him on a journey to the underworld. There he sees that individual sins are punished in ways symbolically appropriate to their nature. Fortune-tellers, for instance, have to walk with their heads on backwards, blind to what is ahead, because of their preoccupation in life with knowing the future.

Art: *The Last Judgment*, **by Hieronymus Bosch.** Bosch's painting, created sometime after 1482, is a triptych whose middle panel reflects a vivid view of people suffering from the horrors of hell. Another work that exhibits a similar theme is the sculpture *The Gates of Hell*, **by Auguste Rodin,** inspired in part by Dante's *Inferno*.

The Gates of Hell, sculpted by Auguste Rodin (1880–1917)

Romans 2:12–16

Paul Reinterprets the Story of Israel

Big Idea *Paul reverses the role that the law played as the stipulation of the old covenant. He argues that the very attempt to obey the law is keeping Israel in bondage. This is because obsession with the Torah derailed Jews from accepting Jesus as the Messiah and from seeing that the law was fulfilled in him and finished at the cross.*

Understanding the Text

The Text in Context

Romans 2:17–24, together with 2:25–29, focuses on the twin themes of the law of Moses as the stipulation of the Old Testament covenant and circumcision as the sign of that covenant. We can divide 2:17–24 into three points. The theme of Israel's disobedience regarding the law in 2:21a, 23 forms an *inclusio* for 2:21–23.

1. Israel's boasts in the law of Moses (2:17–20)
   a. It is the stipulation of Israel's covenant with God (2:17)
   b. It provides divine instruction for Israel (2:18)
   c. It makes Israel the Gentiles' teacher (2:19–20)
2. Israel's flagrant disobedience of the Decalogue (2:21–23)
   a. Theft (2:21)
   b. Adultery (2:22a)
   c. Idolatry (2:22b)
3. Israel's exile (2:24)

Historical and Cultural Background

1. Paul resumes the diatribe style of argumentation in Romans 2:17–24, which focuses on the disingenuousness of the Jewish boast in the Torah. It is interesting that Stoic usage of the diatribe could also point out hypocritical boasts of fellow Stoics who were not actually following acceptable Stoic principles (see Epictetus, *Disc.* 2.19–20; 3.7, 17).[1]

2. As mentioned in the "Key Theme" and discussed further in the sidebar, "covenantal nomism" probably is an accurate label for the perspective toward the covenant and law that one finds in Second Temple Jewish literature, whether in theocratic, apocalyptic, Hellenistic Jewish, or even sectarian circles.[2] And yet it seems to me that Paul thoroughly believed that covenantal nomism (the idea that Jews entered the cov-

enant with Yahweh by faith but stayed in the covenant by doing the Torah) was still legalistic. More specifically, Paul seems to have felt that covenantal nomism was synergistic—humans cooperate with God in their salvation—and therefore legalistic. Thus, staying in the covenant by adhering to the Torah is attempting to be accepted by God on the basis of one's merit.[3]

Interpretive Insights

2:17–20 *if you call yourself a Jew; if you rely on the law and boast in God.* These verses make the first of three points of Paul's argument in 2:17–24 (the first point being Israel's disobedience to the law). Verses 17–20 also offer three comments regarding the law of Moses. First, in 2:17 the "Jew" boasted of being in possession of the law as the stipulation of Israel's covenant with God. "Jew" (*Jehuda*) is a play on the word "praise" (*judah*) to God (cf. 2:29) and is connected in 2:17 with "boast," but in an ironic way—Jews ("praise to God") "boast" in their possession of the law but do not obey it. More specifically, Jews bragged

- Romans 2:17–29 is dominated by the law of Moses as the stipulation of the old covenant (vv. 17–24) and circumcision as the sign of that covenant (vv. 25–29). These twin themes of law and circumcision informed ancient Israel's understanding of their covenant with Yahweh in that, while Israel believed that they became the people of God by faith and thereby entered into that covenant, it was their obedience to the Torah that kept Jews in that relationship with God. Biblical scholars call this dynamic "covenantal nomism" (see sidebar). However, Paul disagrees with this perspective.

about possessing the Torah as the sign that they were the chosen people of God; that is, they enjoyed a covenant relationship with God. But Paul's use of the word "boast" for Israel's possession of the law does not bode well for their spirituality, for elsewhere "boast" is a pejorative term in Romans when it pertains to persons parading their merit before God to earn his favor (3:27; 4:2; 11:18).[4] Here, then, is clear indication that ancient Israel thought of its relationship with God as that of covenantal nomism (cf. Rom. 9:4). Second, the law of Moses instructed Israel in its relationship with God. Note the terms used for the law to that end: "his will," "what is superior," "instructed by the law" (2:18). Third, Israel's

This is the first of four excavated bronze tables known as *Lex Ursonensis* found in ancient Urso, Spain. Originally part of a larger work known as the *Law of Colonia Genetiva Julia*, it was the charter for the Roman settlement of Urso in Spain, 47–44 BC. Like a constitution, it describes how the government should operate. Of interest to readers of Romans is paragraph 72, which deals with money brought to the temples as a sacred offering. It decrees that this money should not be used for any other purpose even if there is a surplus. Even Roman law showed concern for "stealing" from the temple (cf. Rom. 2:22).

privileged possession of the law made Israel the teacher of Gentiles and therefore superior to the nations. Verses 19–20 draw upon the prevalent notion in early Judaism that the wisdom that the Gentiles longed for was to be found in the Torah (e.g., Sirach, Baruch, Dead Sea Scrolls, *4 Ezra*, *2 Baruch*, 4 Maccabees).

2:21–23 *You who boast in the law, do you dishonor God by breaking the law?* The problem of inconsistency between profession and practice forms an *inclusio* for 2:21–23: "You, then, who teach others, do you not teach yourself?" (v. 21a) and "You who boast in the law, do you dishonor God by breaking the law?" (v. 23). In between verse 21a and verse 23 are listed three specific sins that Paul accuses his compatriots of hypocritically committing: theft, adultery, and idolatry. The first sin clearly is literal. The second sin likewise seems to be literal, though some think that Paul here refers to the spiritual adultery of idolatry of which the Old Testament prophets accused Israel. But this seems unlikely in light of the sin of idolatry mentioned next.

The nature of the third sin is debated: how could "robbing temples" be an act of idolatry? Three possibilities are suggested by commentators. First, robbing temples could be literal. Thus, there is some evidence, though slim, that ancient Jews robbed pagan temples for the money. Related to this is the theory that Jews at this time were relaxing the strictures against using the precious metals from idolatrous articles (cf. Deut. 7:26). If so, Paul would then be saying that such a practice contradicted Jewish abhorrence of idolatry. Second, Paul could be pointing out the hypocrisy of some Jews who failed to pay the annual Jerusalem temple tax (see *Pss. Sol.* 8.11–13; *T. Levi* 14.5). Third, "robbing temples" could be a symbolic way to refer to the sacrilege of turning the law itself into an idolatrous practice. As Don Garlington says, "[temple robbing] is Israel's idolatrous attachment to the law itself . . . its tenacious insistence that the Torah is God's definitive provision for eternal life and, therefore, its clinging to the law as an object of trust to the exclusion of Christ."[5] I am inclined to follow this last suggestion, especially in light of the irony that pervades 2:17–29 (see below).

2:24 *As it is written: "God's name is blasphemed among the Gentiles because of you."* Paul here quotes Isaiah 52:5 LXX, which points a finger of guilt at Israel because their sin against God resulting in their exile in Babylonia caused the nations to bad-mouth God. This is clear indication that the story of Israel—their sin and exile—is front and center in Paul's argument in Romans 2. But there is also potent irony in 2:24, as there is throughout 2:17–29, which strongly supports my reading of these verses.

With that in mind, we look here at six instances of irony in 2:17–29 that combine to give the impression that Paul thought that Israel was still in exile precisely because they tried to keep the Torah.

> A temple tax of a half-shekel was levied every year on Jewish males twenty years old and older no matter where they lived. The shekel of Tyre, shown here, is from the first century AD and was the main silver coin used to pay the temple tax.

1. Although Jews boasted in the law, they were no better than Gentiles, since the Jews hypocritically/ironically sinned against that very law (2:17–24).
2. Consequently, the "Jew," whose name means "praise to God" and whose mission was to convert Gentiles to the worship of the one true God, conversely brought dishonor to God in the eyes of the nations (2:24).
3. Even though Israel had returned to their land, they were still in exile, being under Roman occupation and, worse, alienated from God himself (2:24).
4. (Christian) Gentiles (see discussion of 2:25–29 below) are participants of the new covenant, while (non-Christian) Jews remain in the old, ineffective covenant.
5. The aforementioned suggestion, which I support, that robbing temples was the sacrilege of obsessing over the Torah so that it itself became idolatrous (2:22) is obviously ironic. Such irony would be heightened for Paul's readers because the ancient rabbis claimed that Israel had forsaken idolatry since returning home from the Babylonian exile.
6. Many commentators puzzle over why Paul accuses all Jews of committing such sins as theft, adultery, and idolatry when surely not all Jews did.[6] But, I submit, the issue here is not frequency or pervasiveness of sins committed but rather the flagrancy of the three sins committed. For, next to murder, these three sins against the Decalogue (Ten Commandments) would have been considered by any Jew as most serious. And herein lies the irony of it all: it is

Covenantal Nomism

E. P. Sanders first coined the term "covenantal nomism" in his book *Paul and Palestinian Judaism.* There he argued that Pauline scholars had misinterpreted ancient Judaism as "legalistic"—salvation by works—and that in fact both the Old Testament and early Judaism taught that Israel entered into the covenant with God by faith but remained in that covenant by observing the Torah. Entering into the covenant by faith was connected to three key celebrations: Passover, when all Jews viewed themselves as saved by God at the exodus; circumcision, when the Jewish male was circumcised; and the *bar mitzvah* or *bat mitzvah,* when the Jewish male and female (respectively) placed themselves under the authority of the Torah. Sanders's view is the basis of the New Perspective on Paul, which sees Paul as contrasting a nationalistic confidence in the possession of the law with obeying the law by faith. The critical phrase in this debate is "the works of the law" (see further the commentary on Rom. 3:9–20).

precisely the law of Moses that stirred up Jews to commit such flagrant sins.

All combined, the six ironies suggest that Paul believed that Israel was still in exile not because they disobeyed the Torah, but precisely because they tried to obey it. This was truly a subversive reading of the story of Israel regarding the stipulation of the law of Moses.

Theological Insights

A number of theological insights surface in Romans 2:17–24. First, when it comes to one's spirituality, much humility is needed to convey that spirituality. Otherwise, one can come across as a "holier than thou" individual. Moreover, related to that is the need for one's practice to match one's profession. One is reminded in this of the sage advice given by Francis of Assisi: continuously preach the gospel through loving deeds of kindness and, when necessary, through words. Second, even God's inspired word—the Bible—can become an object of idolatry if we worship it instead of its divine author. Third, sin is so devious that it can use the holy commandments of God to stir up disobedience within a person (compare 2:17–24 with 7:7–14).

Teaching the Text

Several key teaching points for lessons or sermons can be drawn out of Romans 2:17–24. First is "Thy Word Is a Light and a Lamp." The inspired and instructional nature of the Old Testament, for Christians as well as Jews, is an important message to be gleaned from these verses. It must be said that Paul is no Marcionite. He loves the Jewish Scriptures (= the Old Testament) and respects them as God's Word. But for Paul, the Word of the Lord is dialectical: it convicts so that it might drive sinners to the gospel. One is reminded here of Martin Luther's three famous metaphors for the law. The law is a mirror that shows sinners who they really are before God. The law is a hammer that crushes human arrogance when humans see who they are before God. But the law is also a mask: behind this mask is the mercy of God, to which the law drives the sinner and the saint.

A second sermon, "Sin, Human Nature, and the Law: The Evil Triumvirate," could communicate the idea that not even the Torah can prevent sin from using the law itself to stir up human nature to sin against God. At the end of the day, this is Paul's perspective concerning the law: ultimately, it is not the law's fault that we sin; rather, it is our own sinful nature that flouts God's commands.

Third, at this point in Paul's argument in Romans a sermon might be fitting with the title "Christ and the Story of Israel: How Jesus the Messiah Embraced Our Sin and Exile So That We Might Be Restored to God." Such a message would serve to remind the audience that Israel's failure before God was nevertheless a part of God's plan for salvation because Israel's sin moved salvation history along to the arrival of Jesus the Messiah, whose death has fulfilled the Old Testament commands and clothes the sinner with the righteousness of God.

Modern Jews read from a Torah scroll at the Western Wall of the temple mount in Jerusalem, showing their love and respect for Jewish Scriptures (the Old Testament).

Illustrating the Text

Judgment is based on breaking the law; Jews are not spared by being Jewish.

Personal Stories: Bill Hybels, senior pastor of Willow Creek Community Church near Chicago, Illinois, once began a sermon on the Ten Commandments by walking onto the church stage and silently staring at the Decalogue posted for all to see. (The Decalogue could also be printed on a bulletin insert.) Then he confessed, "Yes, in my heart I have broken every one of the Ten Commandments!" The shock of the audience that day would have matched the shock of Paul's Jewish audience in this passage.

Song: "Harper Valley P. T. A.," by Tom T. Hall. You could use the lyrics to this "oldie-but-goodie" song, which points out the hypocrisy of accusing others of the very same sins that you yourself are committing.

The Torah cannot keep sin from using the law to stir up human nature against God.

Literature: *The Pilgrim's Progress*, **by John Bunyan.** Early in *The Pilgrim's Progress* (1678), in the section entitled "The Interpreter's House," Christian receives his theological instruction before he lays his burden at the cross. The instruction consists of seven scenes, five of teaching, two of judgment. In one of the teaching scenes Christian is led by the Interpreter, his guide and teacher, into a parlor filled with dust. The Interpreter calls for a man to come and sweep, but when he does so, the dust just flies about thickly, choking Christian. The Interpreter then calls to a woman standing by to bring water, with which she sprinkles and washes the room, after which it is cleansed and pleasant. The Interpreter then explains to Christian that the dust-filled room is the human heart, where the law (the sweeper) has raised the dust of original sin and inward corruption that defiles the soul and spirit. Only the water of grace can subdue that dust, but the dust must be raised in order to bring about awareness of personal uncleanness.

It is idolatrous to worship the Bible and not God.

Theological Reference: **Karl Barth.** On this matter one could supply a few choice quotes from Barth. G. K. Beale supplies just such a listing in his 2008 book *The Erosion of Inerrancy in Evangelicalism: Responding to New Challenges to Biblical Authority*, though it must be added that Beale disagrees with Barth.

Human Metaphors: It has been said that worshiping the Bible and not God is like loving a marriage license instead of one's spouse, like loving a birth certificate instead of one's child.

Literature: "The Birthmark," by Nathaniel Hawthorne. This noted American author (1804–64) tells the story of a scientist who marries a beautiful woman whose beauty is marred, he believes, by a birthmark, shaped like a hand, on her cheek. He is obsessed with removing the birthmark, trying to concoct a chemical that will do so. He succeeds and, putting the woman to sleep, administers the solution. In the end, the mark is gone, but she has died. He has worshiped at the altar of perfection instead of loving his wife.

The Gentiles and the Restoration of Israel

Big Idea *If in 2:1–24 Paul argued that Israel's attempt to keep the Torah results in continued sin and exile, in these verses the apostle to the Gentiles offends all Jewish sensitivities by asserting that (Christian) Gentiles are part of the new-covenant people whose conversion to Christ constitutes a part of the long-awaited restoration of Israel.*

Understanding the Text

The Text in Context

In Romans 2:17–29 Paul criticizes the two hallmarks of Israel's covenant relationship with God: the law as the stipulation of the covenant, and circumcision as the sign of that covenant. We looked at the first of these in the last unit (2:17–24), and now we turn in 2:25–29 to Paul's unusual criticism of circumcision. Since Gentiles come more clearly into view in 2:25–29, we should not be surprised that Paul no longer uses the diatribe style of argumentation. He uses that style when addressing his main debating partner, the unbelieving Jew. Thus, Paul's diatribe will resume in 3:1–8 against that target group.

The best way to outline 2:25–29 is to put in chart form the running contrasts that Paul makes therein between unbelieving Jews and Christian Gentiles (see table 1).

Table 1: Unbelieving Jews and Christian Gentiles

Unbelieving Jews	Christian Gentiles
Break the law of Moses (v. 25)	Fulfill the intent of the law of Moses (vv. 26–27)
Exterior, physical circumcision (vv. 25, 27–28)	Interior, circumcision of the heart (vv. 26, 29)
Letter/law (v. 29)	Spirit/intent of the law (v. 29)
Think that they will judge Gentiles on the last day (v. 27)	Will judge Jews on the last day (v. 27)
Will not be justified by God on the last day—covenant curses (v. 27)	Will be justified by God on the last day—covenant blessings (v. 27)
Do not live up to their name, which means "praise God" (v. 25)	Will praise God (v. 29)
Consequence: Physical Israel is no longer the covenant people of God because, ironically, they try to keep the law.	Result: Christian Gentiles are part of the new-covenant people of God because of their faith in Christ and the indwelling Spirit.

Historical and Cultural Background

1. Circumcision was instituted by God as the sign of his covenant with Israel, beginning in Genesis 17:9–14 and continuing throughout the Old Testament and beyond.

2. "Circumcision of the heart" is a phrase used in the Old Testament to express the longing that one day Israel will obey God from the heart; that is, they will inscribe the commandments on stone into their life (Deut. 10:16; 30:6; Jer. 4:4; 9:25–26; Ezek. 44:9; see also 1QpHab 11.13; 1QS 5.5; *Jub.* 1.23). Such a hope was connected with the arrival of the Holy Spirit and the attendant new covenant (Jer. 31:31–34; Ezek. 36:26–27).

3. There were two types of Gentiles in Paul's day who embraced Israel's God: the proselyte and the God-fearer. The first was a Gentile who became Jewish by being circumcised and baptized. By doing so, such a Gentile submitted to the entirety of the Mosaic law.[1] The second kind of Gentile who embraced the one true God was the God-fearer or God-worshiper (see Acts 10:2, 22; 13:16, 26; 16:14; 18:7), who probably represented a significant part of the church in Rome at the time of Paul's letter to the Romans. This group did not accept circumcision, and consequently they submitted to only the Noahic commandments (see the discussion of Rom. 2:12–16). These folk could attend the synagogue services but were required to sit in a separate space and were not considered to be Jews.

Interpretive Insights

2:25–29 *a person is a Jew who is one inwardly.* In Romans 2:25–29 we meet with six major contrasts, really reversals of roles,

- Israel's failure to keep the whole law of Moses negates circumcision, the sign of the Jews' covenantal relationship with God.
- Christian Gentiles' fulfillment of the (implied) intent of the Torah by faith in Jesus Christ and through the indwelling of the Holy Spirit makes them God's new-covenant people, a part of the true restoration of Israel.

between unbelieving Jews and Christian Gentiles:

First, the unbelieving Jew continues to break the law of Moses (2:25) while the Christian Gentile, ironically, fulfills the (implied) intent of the law of Moses through faith in Jesus Christ and the indwelling of the Holy Spirit (2:26–27). For Paul, the Jew breaks the Torah by failing to follow it perfectly (recall my earlier comments regarding Rom. 2:12–16). Moreover, in insisting on following the law since the coming of the Messiah, the Jew also misses the temporary nature of the Torah, which was to prepare the world for the arrival of the Messiah (see Rom. 3:21–31; 9:30–10:4; cf. Gal. 3:19–25). That the "uncircumcised" (*akrobystia* = "foreskin" [2:26]) refers to Gentiles is clear from Jewish texts such as 1 Maccabees 1:15; *Jubilees* 15.33–34, and no doubt it is a derogatory label. Paul intends the reader to equate these Gentiles with Christians (as opposed to the non-Christian Gentiles back in 2:12–16). This is made relatively clear because Paul applies the language of the new covenant to them: "circumcision of the heart" (2:29); indwelt by the Holy "Spirit" (2:29); they fulfill the "righteous requirements of the law" (*ta dikaiōmata tou nomou* [2:26]; cf. "obeys the law" [2:27]), which matches the description of Christians in Romans 8:4 who, now that Christ has replaced the law, fulfill the intent of the law through faith in Jesus the Messiah and through the power of the resident Holy Spirit. That these Gentiles are Christians is confirmed further by Paul's usage of *logisthēsetai* ("regarded" or "reckoned") of them (2:26), which anticipates Paul's later usage of the term *logizomai* for those who are regarded as justified by God based on faith (3:28; 4:3–6, 8–11, 22–24; 9:8).

Second, Paul characterizes unbelieving Jews as being circumcised only in the flesh; that is, they are Jews only outwardly (2:25, 27–28). Israel's disobedience to the law (and to the gospel) has rendered their most sacred rite, circumcision, invalid; it is as if they are uncircumcised. Such an accusation by Paul would have brought to mind the decree by the Syrian ruler Antiochus IV Epiphanes that Jews cease the practice of circumcision. Paul's criticism of circumcision would have also brought to mind those Jews who went so far as to have their foreskin surgically replaced (a procedure called *epispasmos*) so that Gentiles would not ridicule them (see again 1 Macc. 1:15; *Jub.* 15.33–34). Needless to say, Paul's labeling here of Jews as "uncircumcised" would

have been fighting words to the nation of Israel. This was tantamount to saying that Israel was no longer the covenant people of God. Furthermore, Paul had the audacity to label Christian Gentiles as "circumcised in the heart" (2:29 [cf. 2:26]). This was the same as saying that Christian Gentiles were now participants in the new covenant (recall Jer. 31:31–34; Ezek. 36:26–27).

Third, Paul further contrasts Jewish disobedience of the law with Gentile obedience of the intent of the law by labeling the former as the "letter" and the latter as the "Spirit." Three views have emerged among Pauline scholars regarding the identification of the contrast between "letter" (*gramma*) and "spirit" (*pneuma*). (1) An older view is that Paul is referring to a distinction between reading the Old Testament literally (the "letter") and reading it allegorically ("spirit"). But such a view is misguided, for Paul here is talking about justification, not hermeneutics. (2) A more recent view—the New Perspective on Paul—is that Paul is contrasting a nationalistic confidence in the possession

The temple complex in Jerusalem was perhaps the focal point for the Jewish concern with keeping the law. Jews traveled here to celebrate the festivals and bring the offerings prescribed by the law. The teachers of the law gathered here to teach the law and to debate what behaviors were necessary to "keep the law." The temple that was in operation from the time of Jesus until its destruction in AD 70 was built by Herod the Great. This photo shows Herod's temple and a portion of its northern court as part of a reconstruction of the first-century AD city of Jerusalem on display at the Israel Museum in Jerusalem.

of the law with a Spirit-led observance of the Torah. But this rendering fails on the fact that for Paul, the phrase "works of the law" refers not to the Jewish national covenant markers of circumcision, Sabbath keeping, and observing the kosher categories, but rather to the works of the Torah in total (see the discussion of Rom. 3:20). (3) Most interpreters of Romans 2:29 rightly see in this verse a contrast between the totality of the Torah (the "letter") and the indwelling of the Holy Spirit and entrance into the new covenant through faith in Christ ("the Spirit"). With this I agree.

Fourth, it was a commonplace expectation within Second Temple Judaism that Jews would judge the unrighteous nations at the final day of reckoning (Wis. 3:8; *1 En.* 91.12; 98.12; *Apoc. Ab.* 29.19–21), but Paul stands that expectation on its head, claiming instead that righteous Gentiles (made so by faith in Christ) will judge non-Christian Jews on the last day.

Fifth, and flowing from the previous contrast, non-Christian Jews will suffer the curses of the covenant on judgment day, whereas Christian Gentiles will enjoy the blessings of the covenant.[2]

Sixth, the unbelieving "Jew" (2:17, 25)—the term is a play on the word "praise" (2:29)—has brought anything but praise to God among the Gentiles (recall my earlier comments on 2:24), whereas the Christian Gentile has both received praise from God and (implied) has caused God's name to be praised among the Gentiles (2:29). Here we have an allusion to the end-time conversion of the Gentiles promised in the Old Testament and now being fulfilled in Christ and his new covenant.

The upshot of the preceding six contrasts between unbelieving Jews and Christian Gentiles is that, for Paul, the former are still in sin and exile because they attempt to obey the law, while the latter now enjoy the new covenant/true restoration of Israel because their faith is in Christ. Ironically, the latter group fulfills the intent of the law through the power of the indwelling Holy Spirit. These are the ones whom Paul earlier referred to as constituting the obedience/faith of the Gentiles, the end-time conversion of the nations to Christ before the restoration of Israel (see again Rom. 1:1–16). Indeed, Paul seems to imply that converted Gentiles (and Jews) represent the true restoration of Israel in advance of that nation's conversion to Christ (see Rom. 11:1–27).

Before concluding my interpretive comments on Romans 2:25–29, I offer a suggestion as to why Paul deals with both non-Christian Gentiles (in 2:12–16) and Christian Gentiles (in 2:25–29): both categories are needed to mirror the story of Israel. On the one hand, non-Christian Gentiles, who follow parts of the Torah in that they obey parts of the natural law/Noahic law but nevertheless are lost, mirror Israel's sin and exile before God due to their failure to follow the Torah perfectly (2:12–16). But, on the other hand, Christian Gentiles, who by faith in Jesus the Messiah and in the power of the resident Spirit end up obeying all that the law envisioned in the first place (even though it is finished since the coming of Christ), mirror the restoration part of the story of Israel (2:25–29). This suggestion seems to be confirmed by the very structure of Romans 2:

Romans 2:1–16	Romans 2:17–29
2:1–11: Unbelieving Jews are in sin and exile.	2:17–24: Unbelieving Jews are in sin and exile (= no restoration).
2:12–16: Unbelieving Gentiles mirror Israel's sin and exile.	2:25–29: Believing Gentiles are the true restoration in Christ.

Theological Insights

Three theological truths from Romans 2:25–29 impress the reader. First, there is no room in this text or elsewhere in Paul's letters for the "two-covenant theory," which teaches that Jews are, and continue to be, saved by practicing the law, while Gentiles are saved by faith in Christ.[3] Paul surely argues in 2:25–29, as he will throughout Romans, that there is only one covenant relationship with God, and it is based exclusively on faith in Jesus Christ. The new covenant in Christ has permanently replaced the old covenant, whose stipulation is the law of Moses. Second, faith in Christ and the indwelling Holy Spirit fulfill the requirements for which the Torah was first given. Paul will confirm this statement in Romans 8:4; 10:4, and he will specify what he means by "requirements of the law" (2:26) in Romans 13:8–10: loving one's neighbor and loving God supremely (cf. Lev. 19:18; Matt. 5:43–48; 19:19; 22:34–40; Mark 12:28–33; Luke 10:25–28; Gal. 5:14; James 2:8). Third, the new covenant has been instituted by Christ (compare Rom. 2:25–29 with 2 Cor. 3:1–4:6). The Old Testament promise to Israel of the coming restoration and new covenant has now been fulfilled in Christ.

Teaching the Text

The best way to preach or teach Romans 2:25–29 is to entitle the presentation something like "The Gentiles and the Restoration of Israel" and use the contrasts between unbelieving Jews and Christian Gentiles in table 1 as the basis of the sermon or lesson. Thus, (1) ironically, Jews do not keep the law, while Christian Gentiles fulfill the intent of the law without being enslaved to it; (2) circumcision, so important to the religion of Jews, is inferior to circumcision of the heart (obedience) that describes Gentile believers; (3) that antithesis corresponds to the contrast between letter/law (Jews) and Spirit/intent of the law (Christian Gentiles); (4) rather than Jews judging Gentiles on judgment day, the reverse will occur; (5) so also will non-Christian Jews receive the covenant curses on judgment day, while believing Gentiles will receive the covenant

Obedience to God from the heart was Paul's exhortation to the Roman believers, who were living in a very secular and pagan city. Temples to Roman gods were abundant. Here are the remains of the temple to Saturn located at the western end of the Roman forum.

blessings; (6) Gentile Christians live to the praise of God, while the Jew (= "praise to God") who rejects Christ will not. All of these contrasts add up to the ironic fact that non-believing Jews are no longer God's covenant people, whereas Christian Gentiles are part of God's new-covenant people. But it must be noted here, and Paul will say this later in Romans, that these contrasts should not be misconstrued to mean that the apostle is anti-Semitic in his remarks. Paul's strictures against his kin of the flesh are no different from the scathing critiques delivered by the Old Testament prophets against ancient Israel for mistakenly assuming that Jews were the people of God based on nationality rather than on obedience to God from the heart.

Illustrating the Text

There is only one covenant relationship with God, based on faith in Jesus.

Bible: The Parable of the Prodigal Son (Luke 15:11–32). In this parable the lost son could represent the repentant Gentile, and the older, Pharisaic-like brother could stand for the unbelieving Jew.

Bible: The Parable of the Vineyard Workers (Matt. 20:1–16). This parable nicely illustrates the reversal of values and rewards that will be meted out on judgment day. Those who worked all day received no more reward than those who started work at the end of the day, for divine evaluation is based on grace, not works. Jesus summarizes this great reversal in Matthew 20:16: the last will be first (believing Gentiles in Rom. 2:25–29), and the first will be last (unbelieving Jews in Rom. 2:25–29).

Bible: Philippians 3:4–9. Paul's own testimony in this text bears out the truth of this passage in Romans. Before his conversion, Paul was a Pharisee who trusted in the works of the law (compare Phil. 3:4–6 with unbelieving Jews in Rom. 2:25–29), but after his conversion to Christ, Paul relied solely on the grace of God in Christ (compare Phil. 3:7–9 with Christian Gentiles in Rom. 2:25–29).

Real religion that comes from God is manifest in inward and outward obedience.

Literature: *To Kill a Mockingbird*, by Harper Lee. This book (1960), widely known by the general public and further popularized by the film version (1962), is set in the fictional town of Maycomb, Alabama, in the 1950s and is based on the author's experiences. It is, some critics believe, the most widely read book on race in America. The central narrative is pertinent to Romans 2:25–29, as it tells the story of a very kind black man, Tom Robinson, who has been falsely accused of raping a poor, abused white girl, whom he has helped and who attempted to seduce him because of her loneliness. Although Tom's innocence is evident after his defense, and his accuser is the town drunk, a white jury convicts Tom, and he is to be hanged. Through the voice of the protagonist, Tom's lawyer, Atticus Finch, who defends Tom eloquently, Harper Lee challenges every authority in Maycomb: the school and its teachers, the criminal justice system, and the religious establishments, all of which are closed, ingrown, and rigid. Maycomb embraces racism and still tries sincerely to remain a decent society—a contradiction in terms.

The Faithfulness of God and the Covenantal Curses on Israel

Big Idea *God's faithfulness is actually demonstrated through the covenantal curses on Israel.*

Understanding the Text

The Text in Context

In Romans 2 Paul showed that Israel's attempt to obey the law is, ironically, the reason that they are still in exile and under divine judgment. Romans 3:1–8 therefore anticipates, in diatribe fashion, three Jewish objections to that notion: (1) there is no advantage to having the law, (2) God has broken his promise, and (3) God is unfair to punish Israel (see table 1).

Historical and Cultural Background

Besides the diatribe style (see discussion under Rom. 2:12–16), the main background pertaining to Romans 3:1–8 is the common Jewish notion that God is holy and therefore the righteous judge over the world (e.g., Gen. 18:25; Deut. 32:4; Job 34:10–12; Ezra 9:15; Neh. 9:32–33; Lam. 1:18; Dan. 9:14; *Pss. Sol.* 2.15–18; cf. Rom. 2:5; 2 Thess. 1:5–6). Another idea impinging upon Romans 3:1–8 is antinomianism and the notion that we should sin so that grace may abound (see the sidebar and commentary on Rom. 6:1).

Interpretive Insights

The best way to cover Romans 3:1–8 is to follow the diatribe style that governs these verses, especially the three Jewish objections that Paul answers regarding his thesis in Romans 2 that Israel's attempt to keep the law is the very reason that they are still in exile and under divine judgment.

3:1–2 *What advantage, then, is there in being a Jew . . . ? Much in every way!* The Jewish interlocutor's protest in 3:1 makes sense if Paul has been arguing since chapter 2 that Israel's very attempt to obey the Torah is the reason that they are still in exile and under divine judgment. On that reading, the question of the advantage of being a Jew with the law as the stipulation of the covenant and circumcision as the sign of the covenant as opposed to being a Gentile makes perfect sense. But Paul's response to such a protest is surprising, for the reader rather would have expected the apostle to answer, "There is no advantage in being a Jew!" Instead, Paul answers that there most definitely is an advantage to being a Jew and not a Gentile: Jews are privy to the oracles (*logia*) of God. The "oracles of God," as Douglas Moo observes, refers to the Old Testament revelation as a whole and to the promises of God to Israel in the law in particular (Num. 24:4, 16; Deut. 4:8; Ps. 147:19–20; cf. Rom. 9:4–5).[1] The LXX of Numbers 24:4, 16 is interesting in this regard because there the oracle of Balaam, who once tried to curse ancient Israel but was divinely overruled such that he blessed Israel, is called the "oracles [*logia*] of God." That the oracles of God include the blessings of the covenant is also signaled by Romans 3:4, where Paul quotes Psalm 51:4, the record of David's repentance and subsequent restoration to God, as the antidote to Israel's sin and exile detailed in Psalm 50 (see comments below on Rom. 3:4).

3:3–4 *Will their unfaithfulness nullify God's faithfulness? Not at all!* Paul's detractor counters that Israel is experiencing anything but the blessings of the covenant; rather, they are encountering the curses of the covenant. And if they are

Key Themes of Romans 3:1–8

- Israel does indeed have an advantage over the Gentiles: they have the revelation of God, especially the promise of the covenantal blessings.
- The covenantal curses upon Israel demonstrate God's faithfulness in that they are a part of God's promise to Israel in the event that they disobey him.
- Even though the covenantal curses demonstrate the faithfulness of God, because God is the righteous judge, he still must punish Israel's sin.

undergoing the covenantal curses, then has not God canceled his covenant with Israel and thereby broken his promise to them? Paul's reaction to such a question is emphatic: *mē genoito* ("May it never be!"). Paul then goes on to say that rather than the covenantal curses canceling God's covenant with Israel and thereby breaking his promise with them, those very same curses prove that God is faithful to his promise to Israel precisely because not only did God promise to bless Israel if they

As recorded in Deuteronomy 27:13, the tribes of Reuben, Gad, Asher, Zebulun, Dan, and Naphtali were to stand on Mt. Ebal, where the Levites would pronounce the covenantal curses. Here is a view of Mt. Ebal from Mt. Gerezim.

Table 1: Jewish Objections in Romans 3:1–8 and Paul's Answers

Interlocutor's Objection	Paul's Answer
1. There is no advantage to our having the law as the stipulation of the covenant and circumcision as the sign of the covenant (3:1).	Yes, there is an advantage in being Jewish: Jews have the oracles/revelation of God, especially the promised blessings of the covenantal relationship with him (3:2).
2. If our attempt to keep the law is bringing about the covenantal curses rather than the covenantal blessings, then God must have broken his promise to maintain his covenant with us, and he is unfaithful (3:3).	No, because the covenantal curses serve two purposes: (1) they prove that God is faithful to his promises to Israel, even if by way of enforcing the covenantal curses; (2) they are designed to bring Israel to repentance (implied) so that they will be weaned from trusting the law and learn to trust Christ (3:4).
3. But if Israel's covenantal curses/unrighteousness, lies, and evil accentuate God's righteousness, truth, and goodness, then God is unfair to punish Israel (3:5–8). In other words, why not sin so that God's holiness will look good (= antinomianism [cf. Rom. 6:1])?	No, because God is holy by nature as the judge over the world and must therefore punish sin (3:6–8).

obeyed the Torah, but also God promised to discipline Israel if they broke the divine law. Either way, blessing or curse, God kept his promise to the Jews regarding the covenant.

But there is something more in Paul's reply in 3:4 that commentators seem to overlook: in quoting Psalm 51:4—David's confession that God is just in judging his sin, in a psalm that follows the story of Israel's sin and exile in Psalm 50—Paul finds in King David the recipe for the restoration of Israel. That is, David responds to his sin the way Israel should respond to their sin and exile, which is to repent and thereby be restored to Yahweh. This background leads one to the conclusion that Romans 3:4 taps into the biblical tradition that holds out restoration to Israel if they repent by turning back to God. To put it another way, one of the reasons why God sends the covenantal curses upon Israel is to motivate them to turn back to him.

Another reason is covered later by Paul in Romans 11:11–24: while Israel is under the covenantal curses, the door is open to Gentiles to turn to God.

3:5–8 *God is unjust in bringing his wrath on us? . . . Certainly not!* In 3:5–8 Paul answers the final volley of protests from his Jewish sparring partner, though Paul probably crafts the objection himself, as he did in 3:1–4. The objection proceeds as follows: if Israel's unrighteousness, lies, and evil (all synonymous for sins against the covenant) make God's righteousness, truth, and goodness look good, then God is unfair to judge Israel. This complaint is tantamount to antinomianism (i.e., let us sin so that grace may abound [cf. Rom. 6:1]). Paul's emphatic answer in 3:6 (*mē genoito* ["May it never be!"; NIV: "Certainly not!"]) takes offense at the very notion that God would condone sin. Rather, God is the righteous judge of the world and must punish sin even if it supposedly makes him look good by way of contrast.

Theological Insights

Three theological insights emerge from this text. First, God is holy and must judge sin even if, by way of contrast, human sin accentuates God's righteousness. Second, humans therefore are responsible for their sin. Third, from those to whom much is given much is required. This principle applies both to ancient Israel and to modern Western society, with blessings such as freedom, material wealth, and abundant access to and study of God's Word.

Teaching the Text

Paul's three answers to the three objections posed in Romans 3:1–8 make for powerful sermons/lessons. First, from 3:1–2 we learn, as noted above, that God holds accountable those who have been blessed with much—from ancient Israel to the modern West. Related to this principle, three areas regarding Western Christians in particular require change. (1) Involvement in the church in the Western world is treated much too casually, even to the point of believers not attending services at all. This sad state of affairs might be redressed if Christians became informed about church involvement among those believers living under totalitarian regimes who gladly place themselves in harm's way to worship God. (2) Neither does Bible reading receive the attention that it deserves, even in the so-called Bible Belt in the United States. Modern believers would do well to study how costly it has been

Antinomianism

Antinomianism is based on two Greek words—*anti* ("against") and *nomos* ("law"). It essentially means that since a person is under grace they are not obligated to live by law or morality. It is clear that some of the Jewish audience of Romans accused Paul's gospel of being antinomian. In other words, Paul's message supposedly was that the Christian is no longer under the constraints of morality. But Paul himself decries such a label (see Rom. 3:1–8; 6:1). And, in a positive way, the apostle draws favorably on the Ten Commandments as a rule for life (see Rom. 13:8–10). The real issue in this debate, according to Paul, is what best induces a holy lifestyle—grace and the power of the Spirit or the Torah? For Paul, it is grace. We might add that some interpreters of Paul were apparently parading his gospel as antinomian in the congregations of James, the half brother of Jesus (at least, that is how some theologians understand James 2:14–26).

for Christians in the past to translate and pass on our sacred text, cost measured in the shedding of their blood. (3) Since God obviously has blessed Western Christianity financially, it is incumbent on us in this part of the world to give to missions to the point of sacrifice.

Second, from 3:3–4 we learn that God disciplines those whom he loves, whether the Old Testament people of God or the New Testament people of God. God is the originator of "tough love" when it comes to his children. Such discipline demonstrates God's concern for us much like parents' discipline of their sons and daughters shows their love for them.

Third, from 3:5–8 we learn that the divine judge over the world is coming to execute his righteousness. It behooves us all therefore to prepare to meet our God. And the best way to prepare to meet God is to be clothed with the righteousness of Christ, which is received by faith in his atoning death on the cross.

Illustrating the Text

God holds accountable those who have been blessed with much.

Biography/Autobiography: *God Runs My Business*, by Albert W. Lorimer; *Mover of Men and Mountains*, by R. G. LeTourneau. In these two books (1941, 1960) we learn about LeTourneau (1888–1969), who became the greatest builder of earthmoving machines in history, producing 70 percent of the army's earthmoving machinery during World War II. He spoke of God as being the chairman of his board. He was also the founder of LeTourneau University. Most important, he shunned the high life, giving 90 percent of his income to God. He said that he could not "outgive God."

Literature: *Great Expectations*, by Charles Dickens. In this novel (1861), one of Dickens's most accessible works, the protagonist, Pip, born into poverty, inherits a large sum of money from an unknown benefactor, leading him to a comfortable life. He becomes proud and indolent, dismissive of his roots, until two events occur. First, he discovers that his

These are the limited archaeological remains of the Basilica Julia located at the southwestern end of the Roman Forum. Paul may have received his death sentence in this building. All that can be seen today are a few brick walls, the steps of the podium, and the building's basic floor plan marked by column bases. Its construction began in 54 BC under Julius Caesar and was completed during the reign of Augustus (12 BC–AD 12). It was a large public building designed with a central three-story roofed hall and vaulted porticoes. It served as a meeting place, contained government offices, and housed shops and perhaps most importantly the civil law courts.

benefactor is a convict whom he unwittingly helped years before. Ashamed of the source of his wealth, Pip is, nevertheless, led to humility and generosity through the example of the convict's faithfulness and gratitude. Second, his sister's husband, Joe, a picture of kindness and goodness, who has been rejected by Pip when he becomes successful, nurses Pip back to health during a serious illness, asking nothing in return, not even his friendship. Pip, then, learns the lessons of accountability. Several movies and television versions of the novel exist. Two television versions, the miniseries featuring Anthony Hopkins (1989) and the *Masterpiece Theatre* version (2011), contain clips of these scenes.

God disciplines his people, whom he loves—in both the Old and the New Testaments.

Literature: *The Wise Woman*, **by George MacDonald.** This powerful children's story (1875) is a classic and quotable portrait of a righteous, disciplining God written by MacDonald (1824–1905), the nineteenth-century innovator of modern fantasy whose work would influence C. S. Lewis. In this tale two children have been spoiled in different ways by unwise parents. Into the midst of both lives comes the wise woman (a portrait of God—omniscient, omnipresent, possessing supernatural powers), who whisks them both away and puts each one through a rigorous regime of discipline, tailor-made so that the child might be redeemed from a deformity of soul. Caring more for their moral development than their comfort, the wise woman loves the children but allows them much suffering. In their discipline, the wise woman knows, is their potential purification. Both must be saved from self-absorption, the one from her demanding behavior, the other from her conceit.

Film: *The Miracle Worker*. In this well-known and beloved film (1962), which won both of the principal actresses Academy Awards, Anne Sullivan (played by Anne Bancroft) uses tough love to break through to the deaf and blind Helen Keller (played unforgettably by Patty Duke). In what has been called "The Breakfast Scene," Anne Sullivan understands the necessity of bringing Keller, who has been allowed to behave wildly and violently, under control and into a civilized way of life. Over and over Sullivan must overcome Keller's wild behavior until she is brought into the submission of eating properly. It is a contest of wills; the stubborn will must be taught.

The Whole World Is under the Curses of the Covenant

Big Idea *Israel fares no better than the Gentiles in being enslaved to sin, because sin stirs up disobedience through the law. In other words, both Jew and Gentile are under the curses of the covenant.*

Understanding the Text

The Text in Context

Romans 3:9–20 is the climax of Paul's argument in 1:18–3:8, concluding that both Jew and Gentile are under sin (implied) because they try to keep the old-covenant stipulation of the law (Jews by way of the Torah, Gentiles by way of the overlapping of natural law / Noahic law with the Torah). Both Jew and Gentile, however, are guilty before God because they are enslaved to sin.

In Romans 3:9–20 Paul portrays the world as on trial before God in the heavenly courtroom. The following outline unfolds the dramatic scene:

1. The Charge: All are under sin (3:9).
2. The Evidence: The total depravity of humanity (3:10–18). The evidence is cited from a number of Old Testament texts that describe the wicked (Jew or Gentile) persecuting the righteous Jew.
   a. Psalm 14:1–3 (3:10–12)
   b. Psalm 5:9 (3:13a)
   c. Psalm 140:3b (3:13b)
   d. Psalm 10:7 (3:14–16)
   e. Isaiah 59:7–8a (3:17)
   f. Psalm 36:1b (3:18)
3. The Verdict: All are guilty before God. No one will be justified by the works of the law (Paul implies that this is because the law itself is under sin and therefore motivates disobedience rather than obedience) (3:19–20).

Historical and Cultural Background

Several historical-cultural considerations are key here because, although Romans 3:9–20 may seem clear enough to the reader, recent theologians have questioned its more traditional interpretation.

1. The label "total depravity" is not defined the same by all Christian traditions. Some understand the idea to mean that humankind is sinful to the core of its being and unable therefore to do good. Others argue that total depravity means that humans have a propensity to sin, but they also have

a conscience that can steer them in the right direction; it is not automatic that a human being will sin. Furthermore, this approach appeals to the fact that the image of God and common grace reside in everyone and can enable one to resist sin.

2. Related to the preceding discussion, particularly as it informs Romans 3:9–20, Second Temple Judaism held to the doctrine of good and bad inclinations (cf. 4 Macc. 2:21–23; *4 Ezra* 3.20–27; 7.70–74). That is, within every human being are two equally powerful inclinations: one to obey God (*yetzer hatob*) and one to disobey God (*yetzer hara*). But according to Jewish theologians roughly at the time of Paul, meditating on the Torah resulted in the individual siding with the good inclination. In a tour de force, Paul argues just the opposite in Romans 3:9–20 and elsewhere (see Rom. 4:14–15; 7:5, 7–12; 1 Cor. 15:56; Gal. 2:16; 3:10–13, 22; 4:3, 8–11, 21–31; 5:1–12): to rely on the Torah is to stir up the bad inclination. This is why, says Paul in Romans 3:19–20, no one will be justified at the final judgment before God by the works of the law, because, as good and well intentioned as the Torah is, it only stirs up sin within the individual, not obedience. And this is because the law itself is under the power of sin.

- Both Jew and Gentile are under the power of sin.
- Sin distorts every aspect of what it means to be human. In short, sin has brought about "total depravity" in the human race.
- Sin has even distorted the holy law of God, the Torah, so that it is a catalyst to disobeying God in that it stirs up the flesh to say no to the divine commands. That is to say, the law is itself under the sway of sin.

3. Paul's all-important phrase in Romans 3:20, "by the works of the law" (*ex ergōn nomou* [cf. Rom. 3:28; Gal. 2:16; 3:2, 5, 10]), takes the reader into a minefield of interpretation, with two leading views contending for acceptance among New Testament scholars. The old view of this phrase, championed by the likes of Augustine, Luther, and Calvin, was that by "works of law" Paul means the law of Moses in its entirety and that no one is able to keep all the Torah in order to be justified before God on the last day. But with a groundbreaking article in 1963 by Krister Stendahl, "The Apostle Paul and the Introspective Conscience of the West," a new interpretation of Paul's view of the law began to emerge: before and after becoming a Christian Paul maintained a positive view of the Torah. It was only Lutheran exegesis that gave the false impression that Paul had a negative view of the law. Three scholars in particular

Shown here are the remains of the fourth-century AD synagogue at Hammath Tiberias with its beautiful mosaic floor. Jewish ritual objects, the ark, lampstands, censers (incense pans), shofars, and *arbah minim* (associated with the Feast of Tabernacles) depicted in the mosaic are reminders of the activities that took place at the temple in Jerusalem, as the Jews attempted to follow the law of Moses. However, Romans 3:20 points out that "no one will be declared righteous in God's sight by the works of the law."

Table 1: Three Scholars from the New Perspective on Paul

New Perspective Scholar	New Perspective Slogan	New Perspective Position	Old/Traditional Perspective Critique
E. P. Sanders	Covenantal Nomism	Second Temple Judaism was not legalistic, but rather taught that Jews entered the covenant by faith and remained in it by keeping the works of the law.	This is still legalism because it synergistically combines grace (entering the covenant by faith) with works (remaining in the covenant by the law).
J. D. G. Dunn	Works of the Law (focus on the Jewish national markers of circumcision, dietary laws, and Sabbath keeping)	Paul is not criticizing the law per se but rather the law being used by Jews to separate themselves from Gentiles by the national/covenant markers.	All occurrences of "works of the law" in Paul equate that phrase with the entirety of the Torah, and therefore Paul critiques not national markers but rather individual attempts to be accepted by God based on personal merit.
N. T. Wright	Righteousness of God	For Paul, the righteousness of God is God's faithfulness to his covenant, which the people of God receive by faith, not so much the justification of the individual before God on the last day.	It is impossible to avoid the justification of the individual in Paul's usage of the phrase "righteousness of God" (see Rom. 1:16–17; 3:5, 21, 22, 25, 26; 10:3; 2 Cor. 5:21).

followed Stendahl's path of interpretation of Paul, and the New Perspective on Paul was born. I list those three scholars in table 1, which consists of their respective slogans and positions, plus the traditional/old perspective's recent critique of those positions.[1] Space constraints permit no further elaboration, except to say, with Moo, "I think, however, that properly nuanced, the traditional viewpoint remains the best explanation of the Pauline polemic."[2]

Interpretive Insights

3:9 *Jews and Gentiles alike are all under the power of sin.* Verse 9 begins Paul's conclusion to his argumentation in 1:18–3:8 to the effect that the Jew's advantage over the non-Christian Gentile is to no avail because, just like the pagan Gentile, the Jew

disobeys God, even the special revelation of the Torah. This is because both are under the sway of sin.

3:10–18 *"There is no one righteous, not even one."* Here we meet the classic statement of "total depravity," the conviction that every aspect of humans is impacted by sin: their minds (vv. 10a–11); their actions (v. 12); their words (vv. 13–14a); their relationships (vv. 14b–17); their attitude toward God (v. 18). The outline above, listing Paul's quotations of Psalms and Isaiah, shows the Old Testament substructure of 3:10–18, which decries the evil actions of the enemies of God toward the righteous. But in 3:10–18 all humans are categorized as wicked, and none are classified as righteous, so all-encompassing is sin.

3:19 *so that every mouth may be silenced.* The first use of the word "law" in 3:19

probably indicates the Old Testament revelation, since its antecedent is the collection of verses from Psalms and Isaiah that Paul has just quoted in 3:10–18. Paul can use "law" with reference to the Old Testament canon itself (see 1 Cor. 9:8, 9; 14:21, 34; Gal. 4:21b). But the second use of "law" in 3:19 no doubt refers to the law of Moses. Combining the two nuances of law in 3:19, Paul says that the Old Testament revelation of God has already announced that all—Jew and Gentile alike—have broken the stipulation of the old covenant. Or, as Douglas Moo puts it, Paul supplies in 3:19 a "greater to lesser" argument (see the discussion of *qal waḥomer* below under the "Historical and Cultural Background" of Rom. 4:1–8): if Jews, God's chosen people, cannot be excluded from the scope of sin's tyranny, then certainly neither can Gentiles.[3] We should also note that the phrase "under the law" in 3:19 is parallel with "under sin" in 3:9, strongly implying that the two are in tandem in stimulating humans to sin. Paul makes this connection more specific in 3:20.

3:20 *through the law we become conscious of our sin.* Here is where Paul's argument has been leading since 1:18: no one can keep the law perfectly enough (not Gentile regarding the natural law / Noahic law, not Jew concerning the Torah) such that one's obedience will merit favor before God. This is because the law reveals the sinful heart of each individual and shows how far short each one falls of the divine righteousness (see Rom. 3:23). More than that, according to verses such as Romans 7:5 ("the sinful passions [are] aroused by the law"), the law of God actually motivates people to defy God's commands. All of this is, of course, very bad news. But this bad

news, as Romans 3:21–31 will go on to say, is designed to drive the sinner to the gospel of the grace of God in Christ. In other words, the stipulation of the new covenant is not the law of Moses, but rather faith in Jesus Christ. This is wonderful news for both Jew and Gentile, and Paul will develop this in Romans 3:21–4:25.

We might pause to speculate as to why Paul came to this shocking conclusion about the law. Theologians have offered two suggestions. First, perhaps Paul's conversion as wrought by God caused him to realize that he had hurt, maybe even had killed, innocent people (the Jerusalem Christians whom the pre-Christian Paul persecuted) in the name of the law (see Acts 8:1–3). Second, even more shocking, Paul, upon his conversion, might have come to see that the law unjustly punished Jesus Christ on the cross (see Gal. 3:10–13).

Theological Insights

Three theological insights surface in Romans 3:9–20. First, total depravity does seem to be a biblical doctrine, based on the Old Testament and developed by Paul (see again Paul's use of Psalms and Isaiah texts in 3:10–18). This does not rule out, however, the common grace of God accomplishing wonderful things through sinful humanity. Second, to be under the law is to be under sin. Or, as I put it in my treatment of Romans 2:1–3:20, for Israel to even attempt to keep the law engenders sin against the covenant and therefore keeps them in exile and awaiting God's judgment. Third, all of this bad news is intended by Paul to motivate Jew and Gentile alike to exchange their "good works" for the gospel of Christ.

Teaching the Text

An arresting sermon or lesson title based on Romans 3:9–20 is "Let's Have a Little Respect for Depravity!" In that sermon/lesson one could first eliminate some of the more popular reasons as to why the world is in such a mess—capitalism (so argued by socialists), socialism (so argued by capitalists), impeded evolutionary development (wrong actions are thought to be simply the residual effect of animal behavior that humans eventually will outgrow), the misfiring of brain chemistry (so argued by some neuroscientists), dogmatism (especially on the part of religious extremists; so argued by secularists)—and then present the biblical explanation: the heart of the problem is the problem of the heart. That is, starting with the disobedience of Adam and Eve to the divine command in the garden of Eden the sinful nature has been bequeathed to the human race. This latent propensity within all of us to flout God's law is at the core of all sin and evil.

A second sermon rooted in Romans 3:9–20 could be a more exegetical one: "Not by the Works of the Law." This message could put aside the more recent explanations of Paul's phrase in Romans 3:20—"covenantal nomism," "national markers," "corporate righteousness"—arguing instead for the traditional view that "works of the law" is the entirety of the Mosaic system (if the presenter happens to agree with the traditional view on Paul and the law). The reader will recall that covenantal nomism, as described by Sanders, claims that Second Temple Judaism was not a legalistic religion but rather based on grace—grace to enter the covenant with God, and works to stay in that relationship. Related to this, Dunn's theory is that Paul in Romans and Galatians is not criticizing the law of Moses per se, but only the national markers of circumcision, the

Adam and Eve try to hide behind fig leaves after they succumb to temptation, in this relief on the sarcophagus of Junius Bassus (d. AD 359). As a result of Adam and Eve's disobedience to God's command in the garden of Eden, the human race is endowed with a sin nature.

dietary laws, and Sabbath keeping. Such a perspective is exclusivist, barring Gentiles from entering the Jewish covenant with God. Wright's corporate view of justification says that justification by faith is what the people of God experience, not so much the individual sinner coming into a right relationship with God. But surely these three views born out of the New Perspective on Paul do not do justice to the apostle's phrase "works of the law." The more straightforward meaning of this phrase indicates the law of Moses in its totality. Paul thereby refutes a synergistic/legalistic approach to justification that was pervasive in Second Temple Judaism.

Illustrating the Text

The heart of all humankind is depraved.

Literature: *Lord of the Flies*, by William Golding. Written by a Nobel Prize–winning British author, this novel (1954) is sometimes seen as an allegory or fable. A group of British schoolboys is stranded, with no adults, on a tropical island after their plane crashes. Left alone in a paradisiacal place, far from modern civilization, these well-educated children regress to a primitive state. Two of the boys attempt to set up a democratic system of rule in order to survive. However, another boy becomes obsessed with other pursuits and loses sight of the democratic vision. Soon, these "normal" children become corrupted and capable of great destruction, even murder. Some critics have suggested that the story is a response to other works of that time in which authors showed belief in the inherent goodness of human nature. Depravity, Golding seems to suggest, is part of humankind's composition, manifesting itself even in children. There are two film versions (1963, 1990), from which key scenes could be shown. A similar work is the short story "The Destructors," by Graham Greene, in which children living in post–World War II London pervert the gift of creation to destroy.

Sin causes alienation from God, oneself, and others.

Visual: Using concentric circles to illustrate, beginning with a small circle, draw a chart to show that humans are alienated from God, causing spiritual problems. This then alienates humans from themselves, causing psychological problems. Next they are alienated from other individuals, causing local problems, and groups are alienated from other groups, causing societal problems. Finally, humans in one society are alienated from those in other societies, causing global problems.

Literature: *The Lion, the Witch and the Wardrobe*, by C. S. Lewis. In the fourth chapter of this book (1950), one sees the downward movement of Edmund after he has followed his wicked heart and come under the White Witch's power. He becomes progressively self-focused in his lust for the Turkish Delight. He spirals out of control, finally becoming indiscreet, vain, antisocial, and alienated from everyone, including his own siblings, whom, in his self-focus, he betrays and endangers. In short, he can think of nothing but his addiction to self and instant gratification. This is an excellent study in the alienating power of sin. There is also a 2005 film version of the book.

God's Saving Righteousness and the Restoration of Israel

Big Idea *Paul anticipates here in verses 21–26 Martin Luther's famous question, "How can I, a sinner, stand before a holy God?" The apostle's answer is that at the cross of Jesus Christ, the judging righteousness of God (his holiness) is reconciled to God's saving righteousness (his mercy) such that God is at once both just and the justifier of him whose faith is in Jesus.*

Understanding the Text

The Text in Context

Romans 1:17–18 signaled two aspects of divine righteousness: saving righteousness and judging righteousness. Paul has dealt with the latter in 1:19–3:20, demonstrating that even attempting to obey the law brings about divine wrath and spiritual exile. Now Paul intends to show that God's saving righteousness has been manifested in the death of Jesus and is to be received by faith alone; at the cross God's judging righteousness (3:25–26) and saving righteousness (3:21–24) were reconciled.

Paul draws upon a series of contrasts between God's judging and saving righteousness, shown in table 1.

Historical and Cultural Background

A number of considerations provide the reader with the needed background to bet-

Table 1: Contrasts in God's Righteousness

Judging Righteousness	Saving Righteousness
Old covenant (3:21)	New covenant (3:21)
Law as the stipulation (3:21)	Faith as the stipulation (3:21–22)
For unbelieving Israel (3:23–24)	For all (3:23–24)
Old Testament sacrificial system obsolete and ineffective (3:25–26)	Christ's sacrifice permanent and effective (3:25–26)

ter interpret this passage. Only the first is mentioned here; the other, more technical considerations appear in the "Additional Insights" at the end of this unit.

"The Law and the Prophets" (3:21) was a characteristic way to refer to the twofold division of the Old Testament in Second Temple Judaism, if not to all three divisions: Law, Prophets, and Writings[1] (see 2 Macc. 2:2–3, 13; 15:9; the prologue to Sirach; 4 Macc. 18:10; 4QMMT 95–96; Matt. 11:13 // Luke 16:16; Matt. 5:17; 7:12; 22:40;

Luke 24:44; John 1:45; Acts 13:15; 24:14; 28:23). Only here does Paul refer to the Old Testament in this way. Elsewhere he has other designations (e.g., "law," "prophets," "Scripture").

Interpretive Insights

3:21 *But now apart from the law the righteousness of God has been made known.* "But now" marks the eschatological shift between this age and the age to come; between the old covenant and the new covenant; between the old era of the domination of sin and the new era in Christ of salvation that began at the cross (cf. Eph. 2:13; Col. 1:22).

"Righteousness of God" (3:21) is the key theological term in 3:21–26. The noun "righteousness" (*dikaiosynē*) occurs four times (vv. 21, 22, 25, 26), the verb "to make righteous" (*dikaioō*) twice (vv. 24, 26), and the adjective "righteous" (*dikaios*) once (v. 26). As mentioned earlier, there are two aspects of divine righteousness in these verses: God's saving righteousness (3:21–24) and his judging righteousness (3:25–26). In verse 21 we have the first contrast between God's judging and saving righteousness: the old covenant belongs to the former, while the new covenant belongs to the latter. But Paul's statement that, in effect, God's saving righteousness was also attested in the Old Testa-

Once Christ's blood was shed on the cross, there was no more need for the Old Testament sacrificial system, which required altars such as this one found and reconstructed at Beersheba, Israel. As part of the ritual connected with the sin offering, blood was sprinkled on the horns of the altar.

Key Themes of Romans 3:21–26

- The new-covenant restoration of Israel is superior to the old covenant.
- This new covenant has as its stipulation faith in Christ, not the law of Moses.
- The new-covenant restoration of Israel includes Gentiles, who even outnumber Jews.
- Even though the Old Testament sacrificial system served God's purpose in the Old Testament, it has become obsolete and ineffective in light of the atoning sacrifice of Christ on the cross.
- The law is powerless to effect obedience and bring about salvation, leaving sinners to face the judging righteousness of God, but in Jesus Christ God's power for salvation has been made known, revealing the saving righteousness of God.

ment warns against the notion (later embraced by Marcion) that only God's wrath was manifested in the Old Testament and only his love was shown in the New Testament. On the righteousness from God apart from the Torah that is witnessed to in "the Law and the Prophets," see further the commentary on Romans 3:27–31.

3:22 *righteousness is given through faith in Jesus Christ to all who believe . . . Jew and Gentile.* One of the two contrasts that

Paul touches upon is that whereas the stipulation of the old covenant was the law of Moses (3:21), the stipulation of the new covenant is faith in Jesus Christ (3:22). The second contrast is that the old covenant pertained only to Jews, but the new covenant includes Gentiles (3:23–24). But

Paul seems to dig deeper when he makes the two contrasts: the new covenant does not include the old covenant (contrary to the Old Testament, which seems to have anticipated the incorporating of the old covenant in the new covenant), and the conversion of the Gentiles precedes the restoration of Israel, even replaces it to some extent. (Though, as Rom. 11 will make clear, Jewish Christians represent a partial restoration of Israel in the present, yet it is also clear that the remnant in Paul's day did not constitute the majority of the church, as the Gentile believers did.) Yet we see here how fair God is in all of this: all have sinned before him, but all can be saved through faith in Christ (see sidebar).

3:23 *for all have sinned and fall short of the glory of God.* Two pieces of Paul's Adam theology surface here. First, the aorist tense of the verb *hēmarton* ("have sinned") no doubt alludes to Adam and Eve's fall in the garden of Eden (see Rom. 5:12–21; cf. 1:18–32). Thus, in some mysterious way all of humanity has been impacted by Adam's sin (see the commentary on Rom. 5:12–14).

> In Romans 3:24, Paul says, "all are justified freely by his grace through the redemption that came by Christ Jesus." The Greek word translated "redemption" was used to describe the process by which slaves could purchase their freedom. In Roman culture, slaves could be freed in several ways. They could be freed directly by their masters, or they could earn money (the equivalent of their purchase price) to eventually buy their freedom. Free men might purchase the freedom of female slaves in order to marry them. Freed slaves then had the status of *libertus* (freedman) or *liberta* (freedwoman). This first-century AD inscription from Thessaloniki is a memorial to the freeing of a female slave by her mistress.

Second, Paul's reference to all of humanity falling (*hysterountai* ["fall short"] is a present tense used in gnomic fashion, indicating something that is constantly going on) probably alludes to the first couple's loss of divine glory upon their sin in paradise (see Gen. 1:26–28; Ps. 8:4–8; *Apoc. Mos.* 21.6; *3 Bar.* 4.16; 1QS 4.22–23; CD 3.19–20; 4Q171 3.1–2) as well as the eschatological hope of the restoration of that glory.[2]

3:25–26 *God presented Christ as a sacrifice of atonement [propitiation] . . . to demonstrate his righteousness.* The death of Jesus reconciled God's judging and saving righteousness (see "The Text in Context" section above and table 1). According to Paul, the Old Testament sacrificial system (in this case, the Day of Atonement) was temporary and insufficient to fully pay for the sins of Israel (and even more so the sins of Gentiles, who did not have access to the Old Testament sacrificial system as did Jews). But this was according to the divine plan. The sacrifices of the old covenant simply anticipated the full and final atonement of Jesus. God therefore could look beyond the Old Testament sacrificial system to the cross. To put it another way, the complete forgiveness of the sins of ancient Israel depended on the coming sacrifice of Christ. Herein is the final contrast in 3:21–26: the judging aspect of God's righteousness under the old covenant (in that Israel's sins were not fully forgiven) finds its counterpart in the saving aspect of God's righteousness at the cross (where sin is fully forgiven). Thus, the death of Jesus demonstrates that God is both just (judging righteousness) and justifier (saving righteousness).

Theological Insights

A number of truths confront us in Romans 3:21–26. First, God is just and justifier, holy and loving. The cross demonstrates this to be so. Second, God is fair: if all have sinned and fall short of his righteousness, then through faith in Jesus Christ all can be saved. As the old saying goes, "The ground at the foot of the cross is level." Third, the major theological point that Paul makes here is that the promised restoration of Israel is now occurring in Christ. Various notions make that clear: God's righteousness is his faithfulness to

Faith in/of Jesus Christ

How should the phrase *dia pisteōs Iēsou Christou* in Romans 3:22 be translated? If the genitive *Iēsou Christou* is objective (with Christ as the object of faith), then the translation is "faith in Jesus Christ." This is the majority view.

A more recent view is that the genitive is subjective (with Christ as the subject of faith), thus requiring the translation "the faith/faithfulness of Jesus Christ."[a] The difference is significant because with "faith *of* Jesus Christ," the emphasis in 3:22 is on Christ's work on the cross, whereas "faith *in* Jesus Christ" involves personal faith in Christ. Since the Greek genitive could have either meaning here, the arguments for the subjective reading can be reduced to two: (1) if "faith in Jesus Christ" is what Paul meant, it would make the following words, "for all those who believe," redundant, but "faith of Jesus Christ" would not; (2) how can it be said that the righteousness of God is manifested in human faith?

But these two arguments are not persuasive. Regarding the first, the emphasis in "for all those who believe" is not on "believe" but rather on "all"—that is, the universal opportunity for all to believe. The second argument unduly pits the manifestation of God's righteousness at the cross of Christ against the individual's reception of that message. In light of these responses, it seems that the better translation in 3:22 is "faith in Jesus Christ." Added to these arguments is the fact that Romans and Galatians are filled with references to the believer's faith in Christ, but there is no unambiguous reference in Paul's letters to the "faith of Christ."[b]

[a] Richard Hays has popularized the "faith of Jesus Christ" view; see his *Faith of Jesus Christ*.

[b] See Schreiner, *Romans*, 185, for a list of references. For a penetrating critique of Hays's position, see Dunn, "Once More, *Pistis Christou*," which has convinced many.

the covenant with Israel; redemption from exile and judgment is now available in Christ; the anticipation in the law and the prophets of Israel's deliverance is here, and with it the new covenant. Yet Paul reveals some surprises regarding the restoration of Israel. The long-awaited new covenant means a break with the old covenant. The restoration of Israel is based on faith in Jesus Christ, not on the law of Moses and its sacrificial system. The restoration of Israel includes Gentiles; indeed, from Paul's day until ours it is composed largely of Gentiles. Finally, Jews who do not believe in Christ remain under the judgment aspect of the righteousness of God.

Teaching the Text

A couple of sermons/lessons come to mind in contemplating Romans 3:21–26. One is a sermon entitled "Is Christianity a Slaughterhouse Religion?" I well remember hearing just such a sermon when I was a teenager. The preacher captured the loathing that many moderns feel about the cross of Christ. And yet, Paul would be the first to say, "No blood, no forgiveness." Today, however, even some evangelicals are calling Christ's sacrificial death a case of "cosmic child abuse." Related to this criticism, C. H. Dodd rejected the term "propitiation" as an appropriate term for Jesus' death because he felt that such a concept presented God as fickle and bloodthirsty, stemming from the portrayal of the ancient Greek gods. Instead, Dodd preferred the word "expiation" or "forgiveness" for Jesus' atonement because that seemed more humane and palatable to modern readers.[3] But in the face of all of this criticism, the Scriptures do not cower away from presenting Jesus' death as violent and sacrificial, nor should Christians. Christ's death was his voluntary choice, not something forced upon him. In this regard he was much like a soldier who volunteers to be put in harm's way to protect the homeland. And as that soldier who is killed in action pays the supreme cost for the good of others, so Jesus paid the ultimate sacrifice for the sake of others' relationship with God. Jesus' death on the cross also is a stark reminder that the holiness of God is not to be taken lightly. All of us will have to face this righteous God one day, and the only way to find acceptance in him is to embrace God's Son, who was willing to be forsaken by God on the cross so that we never will have to face that foreboding reality.

Another sermon from this text is "The Fairness of God: All Are Lost, and All Can Be Found." This sermon makes the point that salvation by grace through faith in Jesus' atoning death is the only fair way for all of humankind to find peace with God. God does not discriminate in this most important matter: if the observance of the Torah were the only avenue to salvation, then the Gentiles would be disqualified from the get-go. And, despite Jewish possession of the law of Moses, that people group does not actually match up to the perfect standard of the Old Testament law, and thereby fall short of God's righteousness as well. So Paul's

> "God presented Christ as a sacrifice of atonement, through the shedding of his blood—to be received by faith" (Rom. 3:25).

point is that God offers justification equitably to all. Therefore all must acknowledge that they do not keep the divine revelation given them and humbly bow before God and by faith accept his offer of forgiveness of sin and justification through the finished work of Christ on the cross.

Illustrating the Text

God is just and justifier, holy and loving, as seen through the cross.

Church History: One idea is to talk about the second-century heretic Marcion, his aversion to the Old Testament, and his splitting of God into two deities: the Old Testament god of wrath and the New Testament god of love. One could contrast this with Romans 3:21–26. As suggested above, a sermon could be preached entitled "Is Christianity a Slaughterhouse Religion?" Marcion observed a vast difference between the God represented in the Old Testament and the God of Jesus in the New Testament. His answer was to reject the God of the Old Testament, seeing him as the creator of an evil world. Marcion then constructed the first recorded listing of New Testament texts, basically his personal canon. He excluded the entire Old Testament, and from the New Testament he retained only Paul's letters and Luke's Gospel. In addition, he excluded parts of Paul's letters that refer to the Old Testament (Marcion claimed that these had been tampered with by the Jews) and references to hell and/or judgment (e.g., 2 Thess. 1:6–8). This is the unorthodox canon that led the church fathers to begin naming the "accepted" documents. Marcion's influence was significant enough for his teaching to be refuted by several church fathers, including Justin, Irenaeus, Clement of Alexandria, Origen, and Tertullian.

Bible: One could tell the story of the Day of Atonement as found in Leviticus 16: on one day each year the high priest spread the blood of a slain goat on the mercy seat in the holy of holies and then sent a second goat, associated with Israel's sin, into the wilderness, never to be seen again. The scapegoat symbolized forgiveness of the sins of the whole nation for a year. The imagery graphically informs the death of Christ.

Because God is fair, all who are lost can be found.

Literature: *Cry, the Beloved Country* and *Too Late the Phalarope*, by Alan Paton. In *Cry, the Beloved Country* (1948), a novel about the unjust social structures in South Africa, Theophilus Msimangu, a priest, says, "The tragedy is not that things are broken. The tragedy is that they are not mended again." In *Too Late the Phalarope* (1953), likewise set in South Africa, the protagonist, Pieter van Vlaanderen, is a gifted, handsome, young police officer who is tormented by internal darkness and sexual temptation brought about through the breakdown of his relationship with his father. He cannot find mercy in the face of God. One Sunday at church, the minister preaches a powerful sermon, arguing for hope for all, a sermon that deeply affects the tormented Pieter. This appears in chapter 10 and can be read aloud, as it is short.

Apologetics: *Mere Christianity*, by C. S. Lewis. In chapter 5 of book 1 of this renowned work (1952) Lewis approaches the problem of the lost and has some quotable things to say about God's character. All of book 1 is useful.

Sacrifice | Redemption | Paul's Use of Traditional Material

First, an important tradition informing Paul's language of sacrifice in Romans 3:25–26, especially his choice of the word *hilastērion* in 3:25, is the Day of Atonement. Some seventy-five years ago C. H. Dodd disagreed that *hilastērion* referred to the mercy seat, the cover over the ark of the covenant where Yahweh accepted the high priest's sacrifice on the Day of Atonement for Israel's sins (see Lev. 16:2 LXX; also Heb. 9:5).[1] Leon Morris, however, has convinced many against Dodd.[2] Dodd argued that *hilastērion* should not be translated "propitiation" because that conveys the idea that God was like the Greek gods, bloodthirsty and capricious. Rather, it should be rendered as "expiation," a more general term for forgiveness. Morris demonstrated, to the contrary, that in the Old Testament *hilastērion* does indeed convey the idea of the appeasement of God's wrath through animal sacrifice and should therefore be translated "propitiation."[3] Moreover, Morris showed that Dodd overlooked the fact that Romans 3:25–26 indicates that it was God who initiated the process of forgiveness, something completely different from the deities of Greek religion.

Second, the Greek word *apolytrōsis* ("redemption") in Romans 3:24 harks back in the LXX to Israel's liberation from Egypt (e.g., Deut. 7:8; 9:26; 15:15; 24:18) as well as to Israel's release from the Babylonian exile (Isa. 41:14; 43:1, 14; 44:22–24; 51:11; 52:3; 62:12; 63:9).[4] In other words, "redemption" could be a synonym for Israel's restoration, which is no doubt how Paul uses the term in Romans 3:24. An issue with the word "redemption" is whether it involves a ransom price. Thomas Schreiner offers two decisive arguments that it does: (1) Paul does say that we are justified "freely" by God's grace through the redemption that is in Christ (3:24), which implies a price paid freely for the sinner—the death of Jesus; (2) the sacrificial language in 3:25–26 invokes the offering of an animal (paying a price with its life's blood), to which Paul compares the death of Christ (compare Rom. 3:24–26 with Eph. 1:7; see also Acts 20:28; 1 Cor. 6:20; 7:23). These considerations lead to the conclusion that Christ's death was the price paid to satisfy the righteous wrath of God for sin. However, in accepting this conclusion, one need not subscribe to the patristic theory that the ransom that Christ paid was to Satan.[5] It is clear in Romans 3:24–26 that redemption starts and ends with God, not some dualistic force.

Third, the reader of Romans 3:21–26 needs to be aware of the debate during the last generation as to whether Paul is here drawing upon traditional material. This is the case for 1:3–4, where Paul shows his agreement with the Christology of the early church by quoting an early Christian hymn. Is it also the situation for 3:21–26? The theory is that 3:21–24 is Pauline, but 3:25–26a is pre-Pauline. Those who support this view point to two "un-Pauline" ideas in these verses: (1) the sacrificial language of 3:25, especially "faith in his blood"; (2) God overlooked past sins committed in the Old Testament. The upshot of these arguments is that Paul corrects a hymn that emphasized God's making sinners right with himself by introducing the notion that the death of Christ did more than that: it appeased the wrath of God toward humankind.[6] The crux of the matter is that Paul introduces the judging aspect of divine righteousness into a creed that emphasized only the saving aspect of God's righteousness. These arguments appear to be valid, but if one accepts Ephesians 1:7 as Pauline and the report of Acts 20:28 as reliable, then referring to Jesus' death as a "bloody" sacrifice is not un-Pauline at all. Furthermore, the fact that only once in his letters does Paul mention God's passing over the sins of the past need not preclude this mention as being from Paul. But most important, already in Romans 1:17–18 (which no one thinks is pre-Pauline) we see Paul juxtaposing God's saving and judging righteousness. Actually, for Paul, both are needed to present the character of God, who is both holy and loving (so 3:26b). There is no need, therefore, to resort to the theory of Romans 3:25–26a being pre-Pauline.

Boasting in the Law versus Justification by Faith

Big Idea *These verses contain three contrasts between boasting in the law of Moses and justification by faith in Christ alone: boasting in individual legalism versus justification by faith and acceptance before God; boasting in national exclusivism versus justification by faith and monotheism; boasting in the old covenant versus justification by faith and the new covenant.*

Understanding the Text

The Text in Context

Romans 3:27–31 is a transitional passage. It points backward to Paul's argumentation in 1:18–3:26, reiterating that justification before God is conditioned on faith in Christ and not on the works of the law. And it looks forward to Paul's argumentation in 4:1–23 that Abraham, the founding father of the Jews, was accepted by God on the basis of faith some four hundred years before the advent of the law of Moses.

The theme of Romans 3:27–31 is that boasting in the law is antithetical to justification by faith. Three contrasts drive that message home:

1. Boasting in individual legalism versus justification by faith and acceptance before God (3:27–28)
   a. Law (3:27a)
   b. Faith (3:27b)
   b′. Faith (3:28a)
   a′. Law (3:28b)
2. Boasting in (Jewish) national exclusivism versus justification by faith and monotheism (3:29–30)
3. Boasting in the old covenant versus justification by faith and the new covenant (3:31)

Historical and Cultural Background

1. As Simon Gathercole has perceptively demonstrated with regard to Romans 3:27–31, against the New Perspective on Paul, the literature of Second Temple Judaism is filled with individual boasting before God based on observing the whole Torah—boasting, no less, in anticipation of judgment day (e.g., 2 Maccabees, *Testament of Job*, *Sibylline Oracles*, *Psalms of Solomon*, *4 Ezra*, *2 Baruch*, Dead Sea Scrolls). In other words, boasting in the Judaism of Paul's day went well beyond

Jewish national pride in the three covenant markers (circumcision, Sabbath, diet). And it is individual boasting in the entirety of the Torah that Paul condemns in Romans 3:27–28.[1]

2. Romans 3:29–30 draws on the fundamental tenet of Judaism: God is one—monotheism. Thus, Jews recited the Shema (Hebrew for "hear," the first word of Deut. 6:4) every day: "Hear, O Israel: The LORD [Yahweh] our God, the LORD is one . . ." (Deut. 6:4–5).

3. Two covenants are at work in Romans 3:27–31; 4:1–23: the Abrahamic covenant and the Mosaic covenant. For Paul, these two are in tension, and the former anticipates the gospel, the new covenant (see table 1).

Table 1: The Abrahamic Covenant and the Mosaic Covenant

Abrahamic Covenant (Gen. 12–50)	Mosaic Covenant (Exod. 20; Deuteronomy; Josh. 24)
Based on the faith of the individual	Based on the law of Moses
Rooted in God's grace	Rooted in an individual's works
Unconditional (God promised to keep his covenant with Abraham regardless of human response)	Conditional (Israel's response determined whether the nation would experience the covenant blessings)

Key Themes of Romans 3:27–31

- Paul has in mind three nuances with regard to *nomos*: "principle," "law of Moses," and "covenant."
- Paul attacks both individual boasting before God based on obedience to the Torah (3:27–28) and national exclusivism based on circumcision, Sabbath keeping, and dietary laws (3:29–31). The basis of Israel's national boasting that Paul criticizes is not just the three covenant markers but the entire Torah.

Interpretive Insights

3:27–28 *Where, then, is boasting? It is excluded. Because of what law* [nomos]? *The law that requires works? No, because of the law* [nomos] *that requires faith . . . a person is justified by faith apart from works of the law* [nomos].[2] These verses point out that boasting in individual legalism is antithetical to justification by faith. This is seen in the chiasm that these verses form:

> A Law (of Moses) (v. 27a)
>   B Faith (in Jesus Christ) (v. 27b)
>   B′ Faith (in Jesus Christ) (v. 28a)
> A′ Law (of Moses) (v. 28b)

There are two standard opinions on the meaning of *nomos* ("law" or "principle") in 3:27–31 (v. 27 [2x], v. 28, v. 31 [2x]). Some think that "law" in verses 27, 28, 31

Jebel Musa in the mountains of Sinai is the traditional location where Moses received the law from God. Paul warns his Jewish audience that they cannot boast in their observance of the law.

refers to the law of Moses.[3] Others think that two different nuances of law are intended: "law of Moses" (v. 27 [the first instance], v. 28, v. 31 [both times]) and "principle" (v. 27 [the second occurrence]).[4] I suggest instead that *nomos*, both times in 3:27, means "principle," but two different principles: the principle of obeying the works of the Torah (v. 27a) versus the principle of justification by faith (v. 27b). Many commentators who take *nomos* here either as the law of Moses (v. 27a) and the principle of faith (v. 27b) or as the law of Moses in both cases miss the antithetical parallelism and the double meaning of *nomos* in 3:27:

> Verse 27a: principle (*nomos*) of works (of the Torah) (cf. v. 28b)
>
> *versus*
>
> Verse 27b: principle (*nomos*) of faith (cf. v. 28a)

On this reading, in 3:27–28 Paul is summarizing his argument in 1:18–3:26: no individual can boast before God regarding obedience to the law of Moses because no one can ever follow the law perfectly enough to be accepted by God on judgment day. More than that, the law stirs up disobedience, not obedience, to God in the first place. Verses 27–28 add one more vital detail to Paul's argument: the law itself stirs up individual pride before God and others. Rather, it is only by faith in Christ that anyone will be justified before God.

3:29–30 *Or is God the God of Jews only? Is he not the God of Gentiles too?* Here Paul turns his attention to criticizing Jewish national exclusivism.[5] Jews fancied themselves to be better than Gentiles because they worshiped the one true God and possessed his law. In 3:29–30 Paul turns this argument on its head: monotheism means that the one true God is uniting all humankind (Jew [circumcised] and Gentile [uncircumcised]) on the basis of justification by faith in Christ (see Paul's extensive argument in Rom. 4:1–25). In other words, for Paul, justification by faith is rooted in monotheism. In this scenario there is no longer any room for the law of Moses. It divided humankind, but justification by faith unites humankind. This is because all can have faith in Jesus, whereas only one nation (Israel) can lay claim to the law of Moses.

3:31 *Do we, then, nullify the law* [nomos] *by this faith? Not at all! Rather, we uphold the law* [nomos]. This verse has generated three major interpretations, to which I will add a fourth. First, the more traditional perspective on Paul sees a problem with his statement here about faith establishing the law of Moses. Up until now in Romans the apostle has said next to nothing positive regarding the Torah, but now suddenly he seems to assert that faith establishes the law. How so? This view answers that Paul is talking not about the law of Moses per se but rather about the intent or commands of the Torah. In light of Romans 2:25–29; 8:4; 13:8–10 (which seem to say something similar: faith in Christ and the indwelling of the Spirit empower the Christian to do even better than the Torah, namely, to fulfill the divine intent behind the Torah in the first place without getting bogged down in its 613 specific laws), this may well be the case. A second traditional view is that Paul is not making a positive comment about the law in 3:31 but rather is saying that the purpose of the Torah is strictly negative: to bring all humanity up short of the righteousness of

God and thereby drive all people to the gospel (cf. Rom. 3:19–26; Gal. 3:1–4:7). This, too, is quite possible. Third, the New Perspective argues that *nomos* is the law of Moses throughout 3:27–31, and Paul is criticizing not the law but rather the improper usage of it whereby Jewish covenant markers are used to marginalize Gentiles in their relationship with God. This view seems to me off base in that it does not recognize that Paul is using *nomos* in more than one way in these verses, and that in 3:27–28 he is attacking individual boasting before God, not just national exclusivism.

A fourth view of 3:31 is reflected in my suggested translation: "Do we then nullify the old covenant [*nomos*] by faith? May it never be! [Implied: faith did not need to nullify the old covenant because the law of Moses itself already did that by stirring up humans to sin against God.] Rather, we establish the new covenant [*nomos*] by faith." Here, *nomos* means "covenant," and, as in 3:27, Paul is using *nomos* in antithetical parallelism and with a double meaning:

> Verse 31a: we do not nullify the old covenant (*nomos*) by faith
>
> (implied: the law of Moses itself did that by stirring up sin)
>
> Verse 31b: rather, we establish the new covenant (*nomos*) by faith

Paul uses the Jewish belief in one God to present his case for justification by faith. Both of these concepts would have been contrary to the Roman way of thinking. The Romans worshiped many gods, and it was proper ritual that gained the favor of the gods, not good behavior or correct belief. Here is a relief of Jupiter (AD 100–150), the chief god of the Roman pantheon. The inscription has been translated, "Jupiter, the best and greatest, the foremost and the most excellent."

Several factors lead me to this translation. (1) The law was the stipulation of the covenant for Israel; the two ideas went hand in hand. Indeed, the New Perspective assumes that Paul is talking about the "covenant" markers in 3:29–30. (2) My suspicion that Paul is continuing to think about the covenant in 3:31 seems confirmed by his choice of the word "establish" (*histēmi*), which is used in the LXX for establishing the covenant (Deut. 28:69 [29:1 ET]; 1 Sam. 15:13; 2 Chron. 35:19a), including the new covenant (Jer. 42:14, 16 [35:14, 16 ET]). In other words, for Paul to say in 3:31 that faith establishes the covenant would have reminded his Jewish readers of the Old Testament phrase "the law establishes the covenant." (3) Here the antithetical parallelism surfaces in 3:31: the other word that Paul uses of *nomos* in 3:31

Romans 3:27–31

(besides "establish") is "nullify" (*katargeō*), which in 2 Corinthians 3:1–4:6 Paul uses four times regarding the demise of the old covenant in light of the arrival of the new covenant in Christ (2 Cor. 3:7, 11, 13, 14). Thus, it appears that Paul signals by the two words "nullify" and "establish" the antithesis between the old and new covenants. (4) Immediately following 3:31 is Paul's discussion of the contrast between the Abrahamic and Mosaic covenants. (5) Since Paul uses the word *nomos* in two different ways in 3:27–28 ("principle" [2x in v. 27] and "Torah" [v. 28]), it would not be surprising that he would continue to offer another nuance of the word in 3:31 ("covenant"). This to say that Paul provides a play on the word *nomos* throughout 3:27–31: "principle" (v. 27), "Torah" (v. 28), and "covenant" (v. 31). (6) The verb *katargeō* is also used in Romans 4:14 of the promise to Abraham—the Abrahamic covenant—as being void if that promise/covenant is based on the law of Moses. (7) This proposed reading would mean that Paul is perfectly consistent with his negative presentation of the law of Moses throughout Romans 1:18–3:31. These seven considerations combine to suggest that 3:31 contains a third contrast between boasting in the law and justification by faith: the former is not appropriate since the old covenant has passed away; only the latter is the avenue to the new covenant.

Theological Insights

Even though it is a short passage, Romans 3:27–31 is full of profound theological truths. First, individual boasting before God because of one's supposed good works is a dead-end street spiritually. Such arrogance only distances a person from God because trying to match one's righteousness with God's is a hopeless endeavor. Second, boasting in one's supposed national superiority over others can also lead to a quagmire in relationships. Patriotism is not wrong, but it can go awry and bring about disastrous results. What we can learn from these two theological insights is that humility before God and others is the best way to go through life. Third, the divine plan for salvation is based on faith, beginning with the Old Testament and continuing to the New Testament. The Abrahamic covenant (compare Rom. 3:29–30 with Rom. 4) revealed that acceptance before God is based on faith; indeed, the true children of Abraham are those who are saved by faith, not by the law of Moses. Why, then, did God give the Torah to Israel? Ultimately, it was to drive both Jew and Gentile to belief in Jesus (compare Rom. 1:18–4:25 with Gal. 3:1–4:7). Fourth, the overarching argument that Paul makes in Romans 1:18–3:31 is that the stipulation of the new covenant is faith in Jesus Christ, not the law of Moses.

Teaching the Text

The best way to preach or teach Romans 3:27–31 is to title the message something like "No Boasting before God" and then simply to explain the three contrasts between boasting in the law of Moses and justification by faith. First, individual legalism constitutes a roadblock to justification by faith because most people in this category are religious by nature and therefore assume that their good works—church/synagogue/mosque attendance, helping others, living a morally upstanding life, and so on—will earn them salvation. Indeed, Christian evangelism exposes such a baseless assumption when a person is asked, "If you stood before God today and he asked you why he should let you enter heaven, what would you say?" Most folk in the category of individual legalism will point out the good works in their lives as grounds for their justification on judgment day. The challenge of the Christian evangelist is to wean such persons from trusting in their own merits before a perfect God.

Second, millions of people trust in their national identity to be justified by God. One thinks especially of Americans who claim that their country is a Christian nation and therefore they have inherited the blessings of that faith, including acceptance before God. But Paul and Jesus vociferously denied that one is born a believer by being born in Israel (compare Rom. 3:29–30 with John 1:11–13), and the same argument can be made for America.

Third, Paul contrasts the old covenant with the new covenant in 3:31. Since the law and the old covenant failed to justify humans before God, the new covenant received by faith in Christ alone is the only legitimate way to be accepted by God.

Illustrating the Text

Boasting before God because of one's supposed good works is a dead-end street.

Literature: *The Wind in the Willows*, by Kenneth Grahame. This British children's classic (1908) features four colorful characters, Beaver, Rat, Mole, and Toad. Toad is a proud, self-obsessed character who brags about himself incessantly, inventing good works

that he has done, even composing songs to his glory, and making self-destructive decisions. The book is funny and wise and full of camaraderie as the friends try to rescue Toad from himself. A passage from this book could be read to either children or adults during the service, especially for a children's sermon.

Humility before God and others is the way to go through life.

Theological Book: *A Little Exercise for Young Theologians*, by Helmut Thielicke. Thielicke (1908–86), a German theologian and pastor who served as a professor of systematic theology at the University of Hamburg, talks directly to young theologians about the inherent dangers at their stage of life. Of the importance of humility he writes,

> Truth seduces us very easily into a kind of joy of possession: I have comprehended this and that, learned it, understood it. Knowledge is power. I am therefore more than the other man who does not know this and that. I have greater possibilities and temptations. Anyone who deals with the truth . . . succumbs all too easily to the psychology of the possessor. But love is the opposite of the will to possess. It is self-giving. It boasteth not itself, but humbleth itself.[6]

Poetry: "The Apologist's Evening Prayer," by C. S. Lewis. In this poem Lewis asks to be delivered from all his "lame defeats," from all his "victories," from his "cleverness," things that make audiences "laugh" and angels "weep." He also asks to be delivered from all his proofs of God's divinity and to be set free from trusting in himself, from his thoughts, and from his "trumpery."

Faith and Law in Paul

Related to the issue of the meaning of *nomos* and the differing approaches between the old and new perspectives toward Paul is the challenge of explaining the relationship between faith and law in Romans 3:27–31 (cf. 3:21) and, indeed, in all of Paul's letters. The question is this: are they positively related or not? The literature on the subject is vast and vexing, but we can identify some six constructs regarding the relationship between faith and law. Space permits only, in table form, a list of the options and my own view (see table 1).[1]

Table 1: Six Constructs on the Relationship between Faith and Law

Name of the Construct	Explanation of the Construct	Weakness of the Construct
Traditional (Old Dispensationalism)	Old Testament legalism (salvation by the works of the law) versus New Testament grace (justification by faith in Christ alone).	But Paul says that the Old Testament teaches salvation by faith apart from legalism (see Rom. 3:21; 4:1–23).
Covenantal Nomism	The Old Testament does not teach legalism; rather, it teaches that one entered the covenant by faith and remained in the covenant by obeying the law.	But Paul declares that the old covenant / Mosaic system was based on legalism (see Rom. 2:1–3:20; 7:1–13; 8:1–4; 9:30–10:5). And covenantal nomism is still legalistic because it is synergistic.
Two-Covenant Theory	Paul taught that Jews should continue to be saved by obeying the Torah like the Old Testament says, but that Gentiles are saved by faith in Christ apart from the Torah.	But Romans 1:18–3:26; 9:30–10:5, for example, make it clear that Paul believes that both Jews and Gentiles can be justified before God only by faith in Christ alone apart from works of the law.
Modified Judaizing Theory	Paul taught that Jews are saved by obeying the whole of the Torah, while Gentiles are saved by obeying the moral summary of the Torah/Noahic laws.[a]	But we have seen that Romans 1:18–3:20 makes precisely the opposite point: Jews are not saved by obeying the Torah, and Gentiles are not saved by obeying the Noahic commandments. Both Jew and Gentile are saved by trusting in Christ alone.

[a] So Nanos, *Mystery of Romans*. Nanos believes that this is what Paul means by the "obedience of the Gentiles" in Romans. However, I have argued that Paul says nothing of the kind: the "obedience of the Gentiles" signifies Gentiles who believe in Jesus Christ apart from both the Torah and the Noahic laws, as my exegesis of Romans 1:18–3:26 consistently demonstrated.

Name of the Construct	Explanation of the Construct	Weakness of the Construct
Law/Gospel	Luther's famous law/gospel hermeneutic claims that the Bible conveys two basic words from God: law = conviction, and gospel = grace, with the one dialectically driving the reader to the other. This twofold message occurs throughout both Testaments.	This venerable approach to the Bible has much to commend it, but it does not ultimately explain why Paul does not explicitly attribute grace to the Torah and law to the gospel, which one would expect if the two are in a dialectical relationship.
Abrahamic Covenant versus Mosaic Covenant	Paul reads the Scriptures (= the Old Testament) as conveying two different approaches to salvation: according to the Abrahamic covenant, acceptance before God is based on faith in God's grace, but according to the Mosaic covenant, salvation is based on the works of the law. The former takes precedence over the latter, while the latter serves the divine purpose of driving sinners to the gospel (see Rom. 4:1–23; Gal. 3:6–29).	I see no weakness in this construct; indeed, it seems to be a better approach than the traditional and new perspectives on Paul. It is better than the traditional perspective on Paul because that approach sees only law/works in the Old Testament, not grace, whereas my approach sees grace/faith in the Old Testament (= Abrahamic covenant). My approach also is better than the New Perspective on Paul because that approach sees only grace in the Old Testament, not legalism, whereas my approach (which, of course, I did not originate) sees legalism in the Old Testament (= Mosaic covenant).

Faith and Law in Paul

The Story of Abraham versus the Story of Israel

Big Idea *Unlike the Mosaic covenant, based on obeying the Torah, the Abrahamic covenant is based on faith. Abraham becomes Paul's star witness that justification is by faith alone. Paul marshals five arguments to refute the commonly held view that Abraham was justified by his good works: theological (4:1–5), hermeneutical (4:6–8), historical (4:9–12), logical (4:13–17a), and experiential (4:17b–25).*

Understanding the Text

The Text in Context

The general context of Romans 4 is that it continues the discussion of 3:27–31: the latter states that justification is by faith, while the former illustrates that principle from the life of Abraham. We may correlate these two passages in this way:

1. Justification is by faith (3:27–28; 4:1–8)
2. Justification by faith is for Jews and Gentiles (3:29–30; 4:9–17)

Text	Faith	Works
3:31	New covenant (compare 3:31 with 4:24–25)	Old covenant
4:1–25	Abrahamic covenant (4:1–23)	Mosaic covenant

More specifically, Romans 4:1–8 unfolds the first two of Paul's arguments that Abraham was accepted by God by faith:

1. Theological argument (4:1–5)
   a. Negatively, Abraham had no merit before God (4:1–2)
   b. Positively, Abraham was reckoned righteous by God's grace (4:3–5)
2. Hermeneutical argument—*gezerah shawah* (4:6–8)
   a. Genesis 15:6 (4:6 [cf. 4:3, 5])
   b. Psalm 32:1–2 (4:7–8)

Historical and Cultural Background

Two key items inform Romans 4: the high estimation of Abraham in the Old Testament and in Second Temple Judaism, and Rabbi Hillel's rules for interpreting the Scriptures.

1. Three points about Abraham are indispensable for interpreting Romans 4. (a) Abraham was revered by Jews as the father of the Jewish people (Gen. 12–22; Ps. 105:6; Isa. 41:8). (b) Abraham was thought to have obeyed the Torah in advance and

thereby to have been justified by his good works (e.g., Sir. 44:19–20; 1 Macc. 2:52; *Jub.* 19.8–9; 23.9–10; CD 3.2–4). (c) In a number of ancient Jewish texts, Genesis 15:6 (Abraham believed God's promise to give him innumerable seed, and therefore God reckoned that Abraham was righteous) was interpreted through the lens of Genesis 17 (Abraham's institution of circumcision as an act of obedience to God) or Genesis 22 (Abraham's offering of Isaac) to show that Abraham was declared righteous because he obeyed the Torah in advance.[1] In Romans 4 Paul begs to differ with the second and third points. Thus, Paul denies that Abraham was justified by his works, and he gives priority to Genesis 15:6 over both Genesis 17 and Genesis 22.

2. Rabbis such as Paul were taught seven rules developed by Hillel, a leading rabbi of the first century BC, for interpreting the Scriptures (see sidebar). In Romans Paul uses two of these rules: *qal wahomer* (what applies in a less important case will certainly apply in a more important case) and *gezerah shawah* (where the same words are applied to two separate cases, it follows that the same considerations apply to both).

Interpretive Insights

4:1–2 *If . . . Abraham was justified by works, he had something to boast about— but not before God.* Romans 4:1–8 presents the first two arguments of Paul's five in chapter 4 that Abraham was justified by faith and not by works. Verses 1–5 contain the theological argument, while verses 6–8 develop the hermeneutical argument. Regarding the theological argument, there are two competing views as to what Paul is

Key Themes of Romans 4:1–8

- Abraham was justified by faith. This is so theologically, in the sense of articulating Abraham's spiritual understanding of faith, and hermeneutically, in terms of how one should interpret Paul's combination of Old Testament verses.

- The Abrahamic covenant is in contrast to the Mosaic covenant: the former is based on faith and for all nations, whereas the latter is based on works and is exclusive to Israel.

- The Abrahamic covenant is in continuity with the gospel of the new covenant in that the two are based on faith and provide blessings for all nations.

decrying in 4:1–5, especially concerning the phrase "justified by works."

The traditional view is that Paul is stating, in contrast to the prevailing view in Second Temple Judaism, that God's declaration of Abraham as righteous was not based on the patriarch's good works. In other words, the apostle is taking issue with individual legalism as the means of acceptance before God, even as he did in 3:27–31. But the New Perspective on Paul argues to the contrary that "works" in 4:2 are Israel's covenant markers that manifest an exclusivity toward Gentiles. This school of thought bases its case on two points: (1) since Paul is talking about Abraham in 4:1–23, beginning with 4:1–8, he must be attacking Jewish nationalism, not individual legalism; (2) Paul's discussion of circumcision in 4:9–17 indicates that the works are neither good works in general nor the entirety of the Torah but rather the three covenant markers of circumcision, Sabbath, and diet.[2]

The traditional perspective counters these two arguments as follows. First, in 4:1–5 Paul is not so much popping the balloon of Jewish pride in Abraham as the source of their superiority over the Gentiles but rather jettisoning individual merit on the part of Abraham before God. And if Abraham, the father of the Jewish people, cannot be justified by works, then neither can his descendants. Both can be accepted by God only on the basis of his grace and the sinner's faith. Second, the works in 4:2, and for that matter throughout Romans 4, have nothing to do with the Torah. The issue of works instead pertains to Abraham, who lived four hundred years before the giving of the Torah (compare 4:1–5 with 4:9–17), and to David's confession of his sin (lack of works [4:6–8]). Moreover, only circumcision is mentioned in Romans 4 and not Sabbath keeping or dietary laws. Therefore, I believe that the traditional view here is correct. To recap 4:1–2: on the negative side, Abraham had no merit before God.

4:3–5 *"Abraham believed God, and it was credited to him as righteousness."* Here we have the positive side of Paul's theological argument regarding Abraham: he was justified before

God by faith. In other words, Abraham could not save himself (4:1–2), but God could save him (4:3–5). Verse 3 quotes Genesis 15:6, a text drawn on thereafter in every section of Romans 4 (vv. 3–8, 9–12, 13–23). The Greek word *logizomai* is also pervasive in Romans 4 (vv. 3, 4, 5, 6, 8, 9, 10, 11, 22, 23, 24). That term (variously translated in Rom. 4 as "credited," "reckoned," "counted," "imputed," "declared," all of which are essentially the same) was used in commercial language to refer to payment to a person for service rendered (e.g., Thucydides, 2.40.4; *4 Ezra* 8.31–36). Paul's point in 4:4, then, is that if Abraham had performed exemplary religious service to God, then God would be obligated to

Abraham was declared righteous not by his works but by his faith. This sixth-century Byzantine mosaic depicts, on the left, Abraham showing hospitality to the three visitors who bring God's message that Sarah will bear a son and, on the right, Abraham's sacrifice of Isaac.

remunerate him by saving him. But quite to the contrary, says Paul, Abraham performed no such service; rather, he was reckoned to be righteous simply by believing God's promise to make of him a great nation (Gen. 15:6; Rom. 4:3).

In 4:5 Paul amplifies the theological argument of 4:1–4 (no one, not even Abraham, has lived a good enough life to obligate God to save them) by stating what was unthinkable to the Jewish mind: God justifies the ungodly (for the canon of Jewish justice that God does not justify the ungodly, see Exod. 23:7; Prov. 17:15; 24:24; Isa. 5:23; Sir. 42:2; CD 1.19; for the Old Testament conviction that sinners are outside the covenant with God, see Pss. 1:1, 5; 36:34 LXX [37:34 ET]; Prov. 11:31; 12:12–13; Ezek. 33:8–11; cf. Sir. 7:16–17; 9:11–12; 41:5–8).[3] And, if Paul's audacious assertion that God justifies the ungodly by faith was not revolting enough, the apostle goes on to indicate that Abraham himself was ungodly and thus had no hope of obligating God to save him; his only hope was to be reckoned by God to be righteous by faith.[4] Thus, Paul's theological point in 4:1–5 is that Abraham was a sinner, and so God was not obliged to justify him; instead, God saved the father of the Jewish people solely because of divine grace, which Abraham received by faith apart from any good work.

4:6–8 *"Blessed is the one whose sin the Lord will never count against them."* In 4:6–8 Paul the rabbi utilizes Rabbi Hillel's hermeneutical rule known as *gezerah shawah* to make the controversial point that Abraham was a sinner and therefore could be justified before God only by faith. According to *gezerah shawah*, if the same key word occurs in two Old Testament texts, even

Hillel's Seven Rules of Biblical Interpretation

1. *Qal wahomer*—what applies in a less important case will certainly apply in a more important case, or stated another way, if the greater argument is true then how much more so is the lesser argument true (though note that Paul can reverse this order to heavy/greater to light/lesser, as he does in Romans 5 and 11; see my comments there).
2. *Gezerah shawah*—verbal analogy from one verse to another: where the same words are applied to two separate cases, it follows that the same considerations apply to both.
3. *Binyan ab mikathub 'ehad*—building up a family from a single text: when the same phrase is found in a number of passages, then a consideration found in one of them applies to all of them.
4. *Binyan ab mishene kethubim*—building up a family from two texts: a principle is established by relating two texts together; the principle can then be applied to other passages.
5. *Kelal upherat*—the general and the particular: a general principle may be restricted by a particularization of it in another verse; or, conversely, a particular rule may be extended into a general principle.
6. *Kayoze bo bemaqom 'aher*—as is found in another place: a difficulty in one text may be solved by comparing it with another that has points of general (though not necessarily verbal) similarity.
7. *Dabar halamed me'inyano*—a meaning established by its context.[a]

[a] See Bowker, *Targums and Rabbinic Literature*, 315.

if far removed from each other contextually (often the particular word occurred in the Pentateuch and in the Writings, as is the case here in Rom. 4:6–8 [Gen. 15:6; Ps. 32:1–2]), then those two texts should be read as mutually interpretive:

> Genesis 15:6 LXX: "Abraham believed God, and it was credited [*logizomai*] to him as righteousness" (Rom. 4:6 [cf. 4:3, 5])
> Psalm 31:1–2 LXX (32:1–2 ET): "Blessed is the one whose sin the Lord will never count [*logizomai*] against him" (Rom. 4:7–8)

Since the key word, *logizomai*, occurs in both Genesis 15:6 and Psalm 32:1–2, Paul, using the principle of *gezerah shawah*, interprets Genesis 15:6 through the lens of Psalm 32:1–2 thus: Abraham being credited/counted righteous before God (Gen. 15:6) means that God did not credit/count against Abraham his sin (Ps. 32:1–2, referring to God's forgiveness of David's sins of adultery and murder [see 2 Sam. 11]). All this to say that Abraham was justified before God by faith, not by works. Indeed, Abraham was a sinner whose only hope was God's grace received through faith. Thus, Paul's hermeneutical argument in 4:6–8 reinforces his theological argument in 4:1–5.

Theological Insights

Several theological insights jump out at the reader of Romans 4:1–8. First, God is no one's debtor. In other words, no one can live a life exemplary enough to force God's hand to save them: not Abraham, not David, not Paul, not anyone. Rather, God offers his salvation in Christ freely to all who will receive it as a gift. Second, related to the previous point, faith is not a work. It is, rather, receiving God's righteousness as an unearned gift. Third, Paul's term *logizomai* indicates that God declares, not makes, a person righteous who receives Christ as Savior. Technically speaking, justifica-

tion is God crediting to the "account" of the sinner the righteousness of Christ; it is not yet sanctification, whereby God makes the sinner righteous through the lifelong process of spiritual transformation (Rom. 6:1–8:16 discusses sanctification, as we will see later). Fourth, except for the sin of rejecting Christ, there is no sin that God cannot forgive through Christ, not even adultery and murder, as David testifies to in Psalm 32:1–2.

Teaching the Text

Two sermon ideas impress me from Romans 4:1–8. "No One's Debtor" (based on 4:1–5) could make the powerful, but elusive, point that salvation is based not on human works,

This ivory book cover shows David dictating the Psalms (tenth to eleventh century AD). Paul quotes David from Psalm 32 to make the point that God graciously forgives sins in Christ: "Blessed are those whose transgressions are forgiven, whose sins are covered. Blessed is the one whose sin the Lord will never count against them" (Rom. 4:7–8).

but solely on the grace of God received by faith. Surveys have been taken in which passersby are asked if they know that they are going to heaven and why. The results usually are discouraging; many answer by listing their religious works as the basis for salvation. Another sermon that could be delivered from Romans 4:1–8 is "No Sin Too Great: Romans 4:6–8," with reference to God forgiving David his detestable acts of adultery and murder. David, of course, still had to pay the consequences of his sins (loss of a baby, rebellion and death of another son, rebellion in his kingdom), yet God forgave David, whom God saw as "a man after his own heart" (1 Sam. 13:14).

Illustrating the Text

Like Abraham, we receive God's righteousness as an unearned gift through faith.

Lyrics: Both the children's song **"Father Abraham"** and the great hymn **"My Faith Has Found a Resting Place"** illustrate the theme of justification by faith and could be used to reach all elements of the congregation. Particularly appropriate is the first verse of the hymn: "My faith has found a resting place, / not in device nor creed. / I trust the ever-living One, / his wounds for me shall plead."

Biography: Scottish writer J. M. Barrie, author of *Peter Pan*, told a story about another Scottish writer, Robert Louis Stevenson, author of *Treasure Island*. When Stevenson moved to the island of Samoa toward the end of his life, he built a small hut before he moved into a larger house. On the first night he spent at the larger house, he was feeling very tired and regretful that he had not had the forethought to ask his servant to bring him coffee and tobacco. At about that time, the servant came in with a tray carrying the coffee and tobacco. Stevenson said to him in his native language, "Great is your forethought." The boy corrected him, "Great is the love."[5]

There is no sin that God cannot forgive through Christ.

Film: *The Silence of the Lambs*; *No Country for Old Men*; *The Dark Knight*. It seems useful, in the interest of freshness, to illustrate this point by describing the lead characters in these well-known films (or others like them) and then ask the audience if they think that Christ could forgive a cannibal (*The Silence of the Lambs* [1991]), a psychopathic killer (*No Country for Old Men* [2007]), a human being relentlessly bent on destruction (*The Dark Knight* [2008]). In these films (widely viewed by young people, especially *The Dark Knight*) the lead characters are purely evil. The much earlier one, *The Silence of the Lambs*, is included because of the public's widespread knowledge of the gruesome character Hannibal Lecter. Too often films like these get caricatured or treated too lightly. In fact, college students have had look-alike contests in which an award is given for the best *Dark Knight* costume. It would be good to arouse thoughtfulness about the reality of human evil and Christ's ability to forgive.

The Abrahamic Covenant versus the Mosaic Covenant

Big Idea *Paul's historical argument: Abraham was reckoned righteous before his circumcision (which in Judaism became the sign of the Mosaic law), so he is the father of all believers, apart from the law. Paul's logical argument: The means for actualizing God's promise to Abraham are based not on the law but solely on faith. The Abrahamic covenant is therefore superior to the Mosaic covenant.*

Understanding the Text

The Text in Context

In general, Romans 4:9–17a continues Paul's argumentation that Abraham was justified by faith, adding two more pieces of evidence: the historical argument (vv. 9–12) and the logical argument (vv. 13–17a). The flip side is that Romans 4 offers four contrasts between the covenant with Abraham and its counterpart, the covenant with Moses, as seen in table 1.

More specifically, Romans 4:9–17a provides historical and logical arguments that Abraham was justified by faith. The historical argument (4:9–12) can be outlined thus:

1. The biblical basis (4:9)
2. The historical priority (4:10–11a)
3. The spiritual principle (4:11b–12)

The logical argument (4:13–17a) can be outlined thus:

1. The promise to Abraham defined (4:13a)
2. The promise to Abraham was not by the law (4:13b–15)
3. The promise to Abraham was by faith (4:16–17a)

Historical and Cultural Background

1. The traditional view (especially in the Pentateuch and in Second Temple Judaism) was that Abraham was the father of those committed to the Torah; that is, Abraham kept the Torah in advance by obediently submitting to the divine command to be circumcised (Gen. 17), and so should all Jews.[1] Moreover, Judaism could readily embrace the thought of Abraham as the father of Gentiles if they became proselytes by being circumcised.[2] All of this carried into the future restoration of Israel. With the Old Testament prophets, however, a new view

of the Abrahamic and Mosaic covenants began to emerge: the latter coming to signify Israel's sin and exile, the former being recognized as the ground for Israel's hope for restoration and the attendant conversion of the Gentiles (see, e.g., 2 Kings 13:23; Dan. 7–9, where Daniel portrays the sin-exile-restoration of Israel in terms of the cosmic story of the nations to the effect that the fulfillment of the Abrahamic promise will be carried out by the new Adam, the heavenly Son of Man).[3] Paul aligns himself with the prophets.

2. Paul's statement of the promise that Abraham would be the heir of the world (in Rom. 4:13) conflates three guarantees God gave to Abraham in Genesis 12:1–3: his descendants would be a great nation; they would inherit the land (of Israel); and Abraham would be a blessing to all peoples. Later in the Old Testament it is indicated that Israel will inherit not only its own land but also the world (e.g., Isa. 55:3–5). This was seen in ancient Judaism as the fulfillment of Genesis 1:26–28 and God's command to Adam to subdue the earth.[4]

Key Themes of Romans 4:9–17a

- Paul pits the covenant of Abraham against the covenant of Moses.
- Those Jews and Gentiles whose faith is in Christ are the true seed or descendants of Abraham.
- The law of Moses stirs up the heart to disobedience, whereas the promise engenders faith and obedience (for the former, see 4:13–15; for the latter, see 4:17b–25).
- God's promise to Abraham is a main theme in this passage. Paul addresses it in three steps: the definition of that promise; a negative point about the Torah and the Abrahamic promise; a positive point concerning faith and that promise.

Interpretive Insights

4:9 *Is this blessedness only for the circumcised . . . ?* In 4:9–12 Paul presents the historical argument that Abraham was justified by faith. The argument consists of three parts (as outlined above): the biblical basis (v. 9), the historical priority (vv. 10–11a), and the spiritual principle (vv. 11b–12). Verse 9a piggybacks on 4:6–8 and David's statement quoted there that God forgives sins. One rabbinic interpretation of Psalm 32:1–2 was that such forgiveness applied only to Israel (*Pesiq. Rab.* 45.185b), a view probably held in Paul's day.[5] But 4:9b refers

Table 1: The Abrahamic and Mosaic Covenants in Romans 4

Romans 4	Abrahamic Covenant	Mosaic Covenant
4:1–5	Abraham was justified by faith.	The individual is saved by the works of the Torah.
4:6–8	Paul separates Genesis 15 from Genesis 17 and/or Genesis 22.	The Pentateuch and Second Temple Judaism combine Genesis 15 with Genesis 17 and/or Genesis 22.
4:9–12	Paul (like the Old Testament prophets) maintains there is discontinuity between the divine promise that Abraham will be the father of many nations and the divine command that Abraham be circumcised.	The Pentateuch and Second Temple Judaism maintained there is continuity between the divine promise that Abraham will be the father of many nations and the divine command that Abraham be circumcised.
4:13–25	According to Paul, the law of Moses stirs up disobedience (vv. 13–17a), whereas the promise engenders faith and obedience (vv. 17b–25).	The law engenders obedience to God, the basis of the divine promise to Abraham.

back to Genesis 15:6, reminding the reader that Abraham was reckoned righteous by faith. Romans 4:9, then, is the second half of Paul's usage of *gezerah shawah*, with Genesis 15:6 casting light on Psalm 32:1–2, even as Psalm 32:1–2 in Romans 4:6–8 cast light on Genesis 15:6 in Romans 4:3, 5, 6. Thus, Psalm 32:1–2 and the blessedness of forgiveness (4:9a) are interpreted through the lens of Genesis 15:6 (4:9b) to say that the blessedness of being credited righteous by faith (= forgiveness of sin) applies to both Jew and Gentile (like Abraham's faith [Rom. 4:10–12] and against the rabbinic restriction of that faith to Jews).

4:10–11a *was it credited . . . after he was circumcised, or before?* Romans 4:10–11a is the heart of Paul's historical argument that Abraham was justified by faith and not by the works of the law. Verse 10 makes it clear that Abraham was reckoned righteous by faith (Gen. 15:6) before (twenty-nine years before, on Jewish reckoning) the giving of the rite of circumcision (Gen. 17; later recognized as the sign of the Mosaic covenant, a connection made in 1–2 Macc.).[6] For Paul, circumcision is a sign that Abraham earlier had been justified by faith, not a sign that he kept the Torah (4:11a). Paul thus introduces a discontinuity between faith and circumcision (in the sense that circumcision was not the basis of faith but rather the later sign that faith had already occurred and that before circumcision), the likes of which was known only by the Old Testament prophets (see Jer. 4:4; 9:25; cf. already in Deut. 10:16; 30:6). All

other expressions of Judaism maintained continuity between Abraham's faith and circumcision, between the covenants of Abraham and Moses, beginning with Deuteronomy 10:16; 30:6. But Paul asserts in 4:10–11a that the chronological priority of faith over circumcision dismisses the notion that Abraham kept the Torah in advance by submitting to circumcision. In other words, the apostle to the Gentiles continues the prophetic tradition of pitting the Abrahamic covenant against the Mosaic covenant.

4:11b–12 *he is the father of all who believe.* Paul spells out in 4:11b–12 the spiritual principle driving the story of Abraham: faith, not the works of the law. Because Abraham was credited as righteous before God by faith alone, all people who have faith (in Christ), Jew and Gentile alike, are the children of Abraham. Note the parallel between 4:11b and 4:12: both the uncircumcised/Gentile Christians and the circumcised/Jewish Christians are children of Abraham by faith, meaning that righteousness is credited to them by faith.[7]

4:13a *the promise that he would be heir of the world.* Romans 4:13–17a provides the logical argument for Paul's case that Abraham was justified by

Abraham is revered by Jews, Christians, and Muslims. His burial place was a pilgrimage site for these three faiths. Even today tourists visit the Tomb of the Patriarchs, where they can see Abraham's cenotaph. This empty tomb functions as a monument to Abraham and dates from the ninth century AD.

faith. Verse 13a defines the promise God gave to Abraham: God was going to make Abraham the heir of the world. The noun "promise" (*epangelia*) occurs four times in 4:13–22 (vv. 13, 14, 16, 20; cf. v. 21), signaling the main theme of those verses. As we noted earlier, the promise that Abraham would be the heir of the world is a conflation of the foundational guarantees that God made to Abraham in Genesis 12:1–3. Moreover, Genesis 12 implies that Adam's dominion over the world has now devolved onto Abraham. Paul interprets this to mean that Abraham is the father of those who have faith in Christ; that is, Christians, both Jews and Gentiles all across the world, are Abraham's descendants. Moreover, the physical land of Israel is replaced by the kingdom of God in the hearts of his people (see Rom. 14:17). Not Jews ruling Gentiles, but the two together reigning in Christ, fulfill God's promise to Abraham that he would inherit the earth.

4:13b–15 *if those who depend on the law are heirs, . . . the promise is worthless.* The negative aspect of Paul's logical argument appears here. If righteousness is by the works of the law, then righteousness by faith is made of no effect, and the promise is rendered null because the law stirs up wrath and therefore transgression. The word that Paul uses here of making void (NIV: "worthless") the promise (covenant of Abraham) is *katargeō*, which, I suggested earlier, Paul applies to the old covenant in Romans 3:31. Here Paul implies that the new covenant would be rendered void by the law of Moses, if it were indeed the way of salvation. Surely it is wrong to interpret these verses as no more than Paul's criticism of Jewish nationalism.[8] True, Paul is against

Covenants and Their Signs

There are a number of covenants in the Bible, each having its respective sign (see chart below). Three issues of interpretation emerge with these covenants.

(1) Are these covenants different in nature? Some dispensationalists tend to say yes. The Mosaic/Sinaitic covenant, it is argued, is based on salvation by works, while the other covenants are based on faith. Reformed theologians and the New Perspective on Paul say no, all of the covenants of the Bible are but different nuances of the same covenant of faith.

(2) Which of the covenants are unconditional (humans need not obey the stipulation of the covenant, since God keeps the covenant unilaterally), and which are conditional (humans must obey in order to maintain the covenant)? This question is controversial, and I suggest the following:

Covenant	Sign	Conditions
Noahic (Gen. 9:8–17)	Rainbow	Unconditional
Abrahamic (Gen. 12:1–3; 15:9–21; 17:1–22)	Circumcision	Unconditional
Mosaic/Sinaitic (Exod. 19–24)	Sabbath/ circumcision	Conditional
Davidic (2 Sam. 7:5–16)	Eternal descendant	Unconditional
New Covenant (Jer. 31:31–34; Ezek. 36:24–32; the New Testament)	Baptism in the New Testament (see Col. 2:11–12)	Unconditional

(3) What is the relationship of the sign to the covenant? This issue centers on the new covenant and baptism: whether baptism is sacramental. That is, does the sign (baptism) participate in the reality that it represents (new covenant / salvation)? Christian traditions are divided over this question. For his part, Paul emphasizes faith as the precondition of baptism (see Rom. 6:1–14).

the Jewish exclusion of Gentiles from the Abrahamic covenant, but Jews exclude Gentiles precisely because they demand adherence to the entire Torah. Thus, Paul is decrying both exclusivism and legalism (cf. 3:27–31).

4:16–17a *Therefore, the promise comes by faith.* Paul here presents the positive aspect of his logical argument. Since the promise to Abraham is based on faith and grace, both Jew and Gentile can have the righteousness of God. Though this is debated, the words "not only to those who are of the law but also to those who are of the faith of Abraham" probably mean that the seed of Abraham is not merely the Jew ("not only to those who are of the law") but the Jew whose faith is in Christ ("but also to those who are of the faith of Abraham"; cf. 4:12). Furthermore, the words "faith of Abraham . . . father of us all" certainly include Christian Gentiles as Abraham's spiritual offspring (cf. 4:11). Simply put, God's promise to make Abraham a father of many nations (Rom. 4:17a; Gen. 17:5) has failed if it is rooted in the law of Moses, since no one can obey the Torah; indeed, the law stirs the heart to disobedience. Therefore, the promise has failed and is totally illogical. But if the promise to Abraham is based on faith, then all can participate in it. This is only logical.

Theological Insights

At least two powerful truths are embedded in Romans 4:9–17a. First, for Paul the Abrahamic covenant, not the Mosaic covenant, contains the most realistic hope for the restoration of Israel and the conversion of the Gentiles. This is because the divine promise to Abraham is based on faith, not works, and therefore is the legitimate foreshadowing of the new covenant. Second, Romans 4:9–17a (cf. Gal. 3:6–29) reveals that the gospel of Christ was anticipated in God's covenant with Abraham in that it is based on faith and is inclusive. This is in contrast to the Mosaic covenant, which is legalistic and exclusivistic. If the Abrahamic covenant conveys God's promise of

grace to both Jew and Gentile, what, then, is the purpose of the Mosaic/Sinaitic covenant? The law of Moses was given by God to convict humankind of its sin and thereby drive people to the gospel of God's grace in Christ. The Reformer Martin Luther recognized this long ago.

Teaching the Text

A couple of sermons come to mind for Romans 4:9–17a. The first, based on 4:9–12, could cover the historical argument. It would follow the outline above for that section: the biblical basis (v. 9), the historical priority (vv. 10–11a), and the spiritual principle (vv. 11b–12). The first point finishes Paul's connection of Genesis 15:6 and Psalm 32:1–2 and shows that Jew and Gentile are saved by faith. The second point calculates that salvation by faith came twenty-nine years before circumcision. The third point demonstrates that people of faith are the true children of Abraham.

Second, a sermon based on Romans 4:13–17 could cover the three points of the outline followed above: the promise to Abraham defined (v. 13a); the promise to Abraham was not by the law (vv. 13b–15); the promise to Abraham was by faith (vv. 16–17a). The message might be entitled "Give Me That Old-Time Religion." The first point suggests that Christians—those whose faith is in Christ alone for salvation—are the fulfillment of the promise God made to Abraham. And yet, nowhere is the church more divided than on Sunday morning. Messianic Jews and Gentile Christians meet in separate locations, as do whites and people of color, not to mention the wealthy and the poor. Christians of every race, background, and status need to actualize God's fulfilled promise to Abraham by uniting in their worship. The second and third points combine to make it clear that not only is nationalism out of place in the fulfillment of the Abrahamic promise, but so also is legalism. Abraham's faith preceded the law and therefore trumps it in the plan of God. It is important for Jewish believers in particular to be vigilant regarding their own venerable religious heritage. They rightfully remain Jewish and may well celebrate, for example, the Old Testament feasts of the Lord such as Passover, but from a perspective of faith in Christ as the fulfillment of the Torah. Moreover, Jewish believers will want to be sensitive to their Gentile siblings in the faith and careful not to impose on them Jewish culture.

Illustrating the Text

Many religions say Abraham is their father, but only Christians are his true seed.

News Story: Ann Holmes Redding, ordained as an Episcopal priest in 1984, made a profession of faith in Islam in 2006, and she claims to be both a Christian and a Muslim. Because of her decision, she was deposed as a priest in 2009. She says, "I look through Jesus and I see Allah." How might this compare or contrast with Romans 4:9–17a?

No physical ceremony can produce the spiritual change that comes through grace.

Spiritual Autobiography: *The Journal of John Wesley*, by John Wesley. In this journal Wesley (1703–91), who was influenced by Martin Luther, gives an account of his coming to understand that only grace would change his behavior. This is in spite of the fact that he performed increasingly greater works of self-denial and charity (entering holy orders, shaking off "trifling acquaintances," studying harder, visiting the poor and infirm, getting rid of "all superfluities," and losing "no occasion of doing good" only to be counseled that "outward works are nothing"). What he realized was that he had been intent on his own righteousness, "zealously inculcated by the Mystic writers," "beating the air" as it were.[9]

Biography/Film: In the accounts of Martin Luther's life, he is seen as doing heavy penance, undergoing self-scourging, and lying on stone floors to achieve holiness. None of these acts bring him peace, which he finds only in being justified through faith. In the 1953 film biography *Martin Luther* (see the "Illustrating the Text" section for Rom. 1:16–17), starring Niall McGinnis, there is a scene that depicts Luther's misery and self-castigation.

In Judaism today, most practice Brit Milah (Covenant of Circumcision) when a boy is born. As in biblical times, it identifies the individual with the covenant that God originally made with Abraham. It is performed with much ceremony during the day on the boy's eighth day of life by a mohel (ritual circumciser). A sandek (similar to a godfather) holds the baby during the circumcision, blessings are recited, and the baby is given his Hebrew name. In the past, elegant tools were created for this special occasion. The photo shows a collection of them: sharp knives, shields, and cups for the blessing of the wine.

Romans 4:9–17a

Faith, Abraham, and the Christian

Big Idea *Abraham and the Christian experience justification before God in the same way: faith in God's promise, apart from works. For Abraham, it was faith in God and the promise that he would be the father of many nations. For the Christian, it is faith in God and in the promise that Jesus' death and resurrection atone for our sins, reckoning us righteous before God.*

Understanding the Text

The Text in Context

In Romans 4, Paul puts forth five arguments that Abraham was justified by faith. He has developed the theological (4:1–5), hermeneutical (4:6–8), historical (4:9–12), and logical (4:13–17a) arguments and now moves on to the experiential argument (4:17b–22). The apostle makes the point that both Abraham (4:17b–22) and the Christian (4:23–25) experience justification before God in the same way: by faith, apart from works.

1. Abraham's faith in God's promise that he would be the father of many nations (4:17b–22)
   a. The object of Abraham's faith: The God of the impossible (4:17b–19)
      i. Resurrection: Life out of death (4:17b)
      ii. Creation: Something out of nothing (4:17b)
      iii. Procreation: A child from an aged couple (4:18–19)
   b. The source of Abraham's faith: The promise of God (4:20–21)
   c. The result of Abraham's faith: Justification apart from human works to the glory of God (4:22)
2. The Christian's faith in God's promise that justification is based on Jesus' atoning death and resurrection (4:23–25)
   a. The object of the Christian's faith: The God of the impossible, who raised Jesus from the dead (4:24b)
   b. The source of the Christian's faith: The promise of God that Jesus' death and resurrection atone for our sins (4:25)
   c. The result of the Christian's faith: Justification apart from human works to the glory of God (4:23–24a, 25b)

Historical and Cultural Background

1. God's power to raise the dead to life (see Rom. 4:17b) was a cherished belief of most ancient Jews (see Deut. 32:39; 1 Sam. 2:6; Tob. 13:2; Wis. 16:13; cf. Rom. 8:11; 1 Cor. 15:22, 36, 45).

2. *Creatio ex nihilo* (creation out of nothing), a doctrine held in ancient Judaism (see Philo, *Spec. Laws* 4.187; 2 Macc. 7:28; *2 Bar.* 21.4; 48.8; *Mek.* Exod. 18.3; 21.37; 22.22; cf. Heb. 11:3), is probably alluded to in Romans 4:17b. Those who do not see an allusion here argue that the words "as though they were" (*hōs onta*) express the hypothetical (God's summoning of that which does not yet exist—the fulfillment of the promise to Abraham was still future for him), not the actual (the world that God has already brought into existence). But the words *hōs onta* can be used of an actual quality or reality (see BDAG, III.1).

Interpretive Insights

4:17b–19[1] *the God who gives life to the dead and calls into being things that were not.* Romans 4:17b–22 begins Paul's experiential argument in 4:17b–25 to the effect that Abraham (vv. 17b–22) and Christians (vv. 23–25) experience acceptance before God in the same way: by faith, apart from works. The same outline also pertains to Abraham and the Christian in this passage: both have the same object of faith, source

In Genesis 18, Abraham provides hospitality to three visitors. This scene is illustrated on this twelfth-century AD capital from a Catalan cloister. As they eat together, one of the visitors says, "I will surely return to you about this time next year, and Sarah your wife will have a son" (v. 10). Abraham believed that God had the power to keep his promise, which was fulfilled when Isaac was born to Sarah.

Key Themes of Romans 4:17b–25

The main theme is that both Abraham and the Christian are justified before God by faith. Three aspects of this faith are delineated:

- Its object is the God of the impossible.
- Its source is the promise of God. God's promise stirs up faith and obedience within the individual. The law, however, stirs up disobedience.
- Its result is that since God's promise causes faith to well up in a person, God is glorified because justification is not based in human effort but rather is rooted in God's grace.

of faith, and result of faith. The difference between the two is that God's promise to Abraham was that he would be the father of many nations, while God's promise to Christians is that they are reckoned righteous before him based on the atoning death

and resurrection of Jesus Christ. Romans 4:17b–19 presents the object of Abraham's faith: the God of the impossible. Abraham believed in the God associated with three miraculous feats: physical resurrection (v. 17b), which speaks life into death; the creation of the world out of nothing (*creatio ex nihilo*) (v. 17b; see "Historical and Cultural Background," above); and procreation on behalf of an aged couple in Abraham and Sarah (vv. 18–19).

The key to understanding 4:18–19 is to note that the opening paradoxical statement, "against all hope, Abraham in hope believed," governs verses 18–19. "Against all hope" refers to the mere human perspective, which told Abraham that the divine promise that he was about to have a child and would be the ancestor of many nations (note "So shall your offspring be" in Gen. 15:5 [cf. 17:5]) was ludicrous because he and Sarah were too old to have children (see Gen. 17:17). In terms of procreation, their bodies were as good as dead. But despite insuperable odds, Abraham "in hope believed" in the God of the impossible. This was the divine perspective that guided Abraham. Abraham's faith in God's promise never wavered.[2]

4:20–21 *he did not waver through unbelief regarding the promise of God.* In 4:20–21 Paul wants to make the point that God's promise to Abraham generated or created the faith of Abraham. Two matters indicate this. First, the words "promise" (*epangelia* [v. 20]) and "promised" (perfect tense of *epangellomai* [v. 21]) form an *inclusio* around verse 20b, "Abraham was strengthened in his faith." This structure appears to signal that Abraham's faith was generated by God's promise, with the outer two points shedding light on the middle point. Second, the verb *enedynamōthē* ("was strengthened" [v. 20]) is most likely a divine passive, meaning that the passive voice indicates God is the author of the action. If so, then the translation "was strengthened in his faith" implies that God's promise created and strengthened Abraham's faith.[3] This, together with the next consideration,

Here is a first-century AD tomb from lower Galilee with a rolling stone. The Gospel writers tell us that Jesus' body was placed in a tomb and a stone rolled across its entrance. On the third day Jesus arose. Paul writes in Romans 4:24, "God will credit righteousness—for us who believe in him who raised Jesus our Lord from the dead."

in 4:22, thereby rules out that Abraham's faith was in any way meritorious. Thus, the source of Abraham's faith was the divine promise and the power to deliver on that promise.

4:22 *This is why "it was credited to him as righteousness."* This verse spells out the result of Abraham's faith: he was reckoned as righteous before God (again cf. Gen. 15:6). This in turn glorified God's grace (compare 4:20 with 4:16). One can see in this the first half of Paul's experiential argument: Abraham's faith in the God of the impossible (4:17b–19) was born out of the divine promise (4:20–21), not out of Abraham's merit or work. Therefore, Abraham's experience of justification shows that God's grace alone should be glorified and not human works (4:22).

4:23–25 *for us who believe in him who raised Jesus our Lord from the dead.* The Christian experiences justification before God in the same way: by faith, apart from works. In that regard, the three-point outline in 4:17b–22 applying to Abraham (see "The Text in Context," above) pertains to the Christian in 4:23–25. Thus, according to 4:24b, the object of the Christian's faith is the God of the impossible—in this case, the God who raised Jesus the Lord from the dead (cf. 1:3–4). And according to 4:25, the source of the Christian's faith is the (implied) promise of God that whoever believes in Jesus' atoning death and resurrection will be justified by God.[4] The former, Jesus' atoning death and resurrection, generates or creates the latter, the believer's faith in God. Finally, 4:23–24a, 25b spell out the result of the Christian's faith: the Christian is reckoned as righteous before God based on the atoning death and resurrec-

The Suffering Messiah

Interpreters of Romans almost universally agree that in 4:25 Paul alludes to the Suffering Servant of Isaiah 53. That is, Paul sees Jesus as the Suffering Servant, who was delivered up for our sins. If we combine Romans 4:25 with 1:3–4 (Jesus the Davidic Messiah), we find that Paul, like other New Testament writers, identifies Jesus as the suffering Messiah.

This has sparked debate among biblical scholars. Did pre-Christian Judaism expect a suffering Messiah? The notion does not appear to surface in the Old Testament or any pre-Christian texts.[a] The truth more likely is that pre-Christian Judaism identified Israel, not the Messiah, with the Suffering Servant. It was the genius of Jesus to first combine the two figures of the Davidic Messiah and the Suffering Servant in himself to forge a new personage: the suffering Messiah.

[a] For more on this debate, see Kennard, *Messiah Jesus*, 325–26n24, and the extensive bibliography there.

tion of Jesus. In this lies the second half of Paul's experiential argument: as with Abraham, the Christian's belief in the God of the impossible (4:24b) was born out of God's promise (4:25) and therefore not out of human merit or works (4:23–24a, 25b). Thus, the Christian's salvation is based on the grace of God alone. In other words, God alone should be glorified for our justification because it is based on his grace (cf. 5:1–3, where the words "justification," "grace," and "glory" combine to express the same sentiment).[5]

Theological Insights

At least three theological insights emerge in Romans 4:17b–25. First, the Abrahamic covenant and the new covenant (even in the Old Testament) were based on faith, as opposed to the Mosaic covenant, which, if not initially, certainly in time became viewed legalistically by the Jews (against the New Perspective on Paul). The gospel of Jesus Christ too is rooted in faith. To put it another way, Paul's message in Romans 4 is that faith as the means of salvation is not new with his message of justification; it was already so with Abraham and with the prophets' longing for a new covenant. Second, related to the previous remark, faith is not a work; faith is the gift of God to humans so that they can respond to the gospel call (compare Rom. 4:17b–25 with Eph. 2:8–9). Third, and related to the previous two points, the word "call" (*kaleō*) in 4:17b is thought by Calvinists to involve the "effectual call" / "irresistible grace" of God whereby God's invitation to, even summoning of, a person to participate in salvation cannot be resisted. This in turn is connected to divine sovereignty and election, a topic that we will meet head-on in Romans 9.

Teaching the Text

For Romans 4:17b–25, "The God of the Impossible" is a sermon/lesson that could develop the four impossibilities that God performed: creation, procreation, resurrection, and justification. The first of these four miracles God did out of nothing. When it comes to the

The Shroud of Turin

origin of the universe, there really are only two possibilities: either matter is eternal or God is eternal. While in the past some scientists and philosophers argued for the former, these days the Big Bang theory is hospitable to the claim that the universe indeed had a beginning. And such an argument bodes well for those of us who believe that God created the cosmos. Simply put, God's calling the universe into being out of nothing is a miracle, a human impossibility, that the Judaic-Christian tradition cherishes, and for good reason.

The second miracle God did on behalf of Abraham and Sarah. To help people appreciate the faith of Abraham and Sarah in God's promise of procreation, one preacher put it this way: it would be like if today a hundred-year-old husband and his ninety-year-old wife were so confident that God was going to give them a natural-born son that they bought a home beside an elementary school to prepare for his arrival.

The third miracle, resurrection, God did for Jesus. His body was dead and buried, but God spoke the word and raised his Son to life. Recently, some scientists claimed to have solved the mystery of the Shroud of Turin, the supposed burial cloth of Jesus.

After months of reexamining the shroud, they concluded that it portrayed the resurrected face of Jesus, but as superimposed over the crucified face of the historical Jesus. Should these scientists prove to be correct, for the first time we humans would now see how the historical Jesus and the Christ of faith meet: at the intersection of the death and resurrection of Jesus Christ.

The fourth miracle is justification, whereby God calls righteousness out of nothing on behalf of the sinner whose faith is in Christ.

Illustrating the Text

God does the impossible: creation, procreation, resurrection, and justification.

Hymn Text: "All Creatures of Our God and King," by Francis of Assisi. Francis (1181/82–1226), a devout Italian monk, wrote the text for this great hymn. The music was added much later. The hymn echoes Francis's love for God's created world; it notes that all of creation get its life from God and should live in dependence, giving glory to God. "Let all things their Creator bless / and worship him in humbleness."

Poetry: "The Creation," by James Weldon Johnson. Johnson's short retelling of God's work in the Genesis creation story is full of energy and delight. It is intended to be poetical, not theological, but certainly it is usable. Audiences love it.

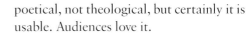

The relationship between faith and fact is complementary.

Bible: Compare the faith of Abraham and Sarah as described in Hebrews 11:8–19 with Paul's description in Romans 4:17b–25.

Spiritual Autobiography: See the conversion stories of well-known individuals who once were atheists or agnostics but who were converted to theism and even Christianity. There is a range of possibilities here. Here are some examples: Augustine, *Confessions*; C. S. Lewis (professor, apologist, writer), *Surprised by Joy*; Malcolm Muggeridge (journalist), *Jesus Rediscovered*; Josh McDowell (Christian apologist), *From Skepticism to Faith*; Anthony Flew (philosopher), *There Is a God: How the World's Most Notorious Atheist Changed His Mind*; Lee Strobbel (journalist), *The Case for Christ*.

Quote: John Calvin.

> Let us also remember, that the condition of us all is the same with that of Abraham. All things around us are in opposition to the promises of God: He promises immortality; we are surrounded with mortality and corruption: He declares that he counts us just; we are covered with sins: He testifies that he is propitious and kind to us; outward judgments threaten His wrath. What then is to be done? We must with closed eyes pass by ourselves, and all things connected with us, that nothing may hinder or prevent us from believing that God is true.[6]

The New-Covenant Blessings: Peace and Hope

Big Idea *Romans 5:1–11 presents three new-covenant blessings: peace, hope, and love (love will be covered in the next unit).*

Understanding the Text

The Text in Context

Romans 5 has been much debated in terms of its context: does it belong with 1:18–4:25, or does it begin a new unit?[1] Most scholars today believe that although chapter 5 does connect back to 1:18–4:25 (since the topic of justification so pervasive there occurs also in 5:1, 9, 16–19, 21), it most likely begins a new unit that concludes in 8:39. Several arguments indicate that this is the case. First, the opening words of 5:1, "Since we have been justified by faith," summarize the theme of 1:18–4:25 while preparing the way for a new topic. Second, the polemical tone of 1:18–4:25 is replaced in chapter 5 with one of camaraderie, signaled by Paul's use of the first-person plural. Third, the prevalence of key vocabulary from Romans 1:17—"the righteous will *live* by *faith*"—indicates that a shift in focus occurs between 1:18–4:25 and 5:1–8:39. Thus, the words "faith" and "believe" dominate 1:18–4:25, while "life" and "live" pervade 5:1–8:39.[2] The chart supplies the details:

	1:18–4:25	5:1–8:39
Faith/believe	33x	3x
Life/live	2x	24x

I agree with this assessment that chapter 5 begins a new unit. Moreover, it seems to me that the prevalence of "life/live" in 5:1–8:39 suggests that Paul is thinking in these chapters of the life of the new covenant—that is, the blessings of the new covenant. He describes this life as consisting of seven blessings corresponding to Old Testament covenant blessings (chapters 9–11 correlates with covenant curses). New-covenant blessings are based on the stipulation of faith in Christ apart from the law of Moses. In table 1, therefore, I summarize seven covenantal blessings paraded by Paul in this new unit.

With that context in mind, I suggest the following outline for Romans 5:1–4 (note that verses 2b–4 form a chiasm suggesting that hope is conditioned on suffering):

1. Peace with God (through justification) (5:1–2a)
2. Hope (through suffering) (5:2b–4)
   a. Hope of the glory of God (5:2b)

b. Suffering (5:3–4a)

a′. Hope (of the glory of God) (5:4b)

Historical and Cultural Background

1. Romans 5:1–8:39, as we saw above, taps into the covenant format, notably the blessings section of the covenant. This connects with the story of Israel—sin, exile, and especially restoration. Because of Israel's sin, God poured out on that nation the curses of the covenant in the form of exile. Yet God always held out the promise to Israel that if they repented, he would restore to them the blessings of the covenant. For Paul, those blessings are

- Peace with God is a new-covenant blessing through Jesus Christ.

- Hope is a new-covenant blessing, though, surprisingly, it is associated with suffering.

here now in Christ for those who believe in him.

2. The term *prosagōgē* (NIV: "access") in 5:2a probably has two backgrounds. The first may be cultic, in terms of the Jewish worshiper coming to God in the temple (the term does not occur in the LXX, but it has a parallel in the Dead Sea Scrolls [1QS 11.13–15]). Second, and more pronounced, in Paul's day the term would have evoked

Table 1: New-Covenant Blessings in Romans 5:1–8:39

	Blessing	Covenantal Connection
5:1–2a	1. Peace	Covenant peace promised to Israel (e.g., Num. 6:22–27; Ps. 55:18–19), especially in the new age of the new covenant (e.g., Isa. 9:6–7; 54:10; Ezek. 34:25–31; 37:26).
5:2b–4	2. Hope of glory	The future restoration of the lost glory of Adam to Israel (Rom. 1:21; 3:23), God's covenant people, but that now belongs to the Christian (Rom. 8:16–30) and is conditioned upon righteous suffering in this age.
5:5–11	3. Love	God's *hesed*, his faithful love to his covenant people, Israel, which now has devolved onto the church, as is demonstrated by the indwelling of the end-time Spirit (e.g., Isa. 32:15; 34:16; Ezek. 11:19; 36:26–27; Joel 2:28–32) and the death of Christ.
5:12–21	4. The new humanity in Christ as the new Adam	Israel (specifically unbelieving Israel, here and below) is still in the old Adam / old humankind, while Christ as the new Adam has made Christians the new humanity.
6:1–23	5. The new dominion through union with Christ	Israel is still enslaved to sin and has, like Adam, lost its dominion over the earth (see Gen. 1:26–28), but Christians have dominion over sin through their union with Christ.
7:1–25	5. The new dominion over sin is not by the law but by faith in Christ	Israel is still under the law, which empowers sin rather than breaks its dominion.
8:1–16	6. The Spirit of the new covenant is here in Christ	Israel remains under the law and the dominion of the flesh.
8:17–39	7. The Christian's destiny is the glorious resurrection body in the new creation	Adam's sin has enslaved all of creation, but the new covenant was expected to bring about the resurrection of Israel and the body (Ezek. 36–37).

access through the royal chamberlain into the king's presence (see Xenophon, *Cyr.* 7.5.45). Whether to translate *prosagōgē* as "introduction" or "access" is a matter of debate, but the first translation might imply that Christians have gained entrance before God only once, while the second rendering indicates continual appearance before God.

3. The theme of glory through suffering (see 5:2b–4) has two backgrounds: Adamic and eschatological. The first has to do with the cherished hope in Second Temple Judaism that righteous suffering would restore the lost glory of Adam (e.g., 1QS 4.22–23; CD 3.20; 1QHᵃ 4.15; *2 Baruch*; *4 Ezra*).[3] Second, Paul's term for "suffering" in 5:3, *thlipsis*, can simply indicate distress brought on by outward circumstances, but more likely it refers to the tribulation of the last days (compare, e.g., Dan. 12:1 LXX; Mark 13:19, 24; Rev. 6–19 with 2 Cor. 1:4, 8; 2:4; 1 Thess. 1:6; 2 Thess. 1:4), as I have argued elsewhere.[4] These two backgrounds—Adamic and eschatological— are related: the belief emerged in Second Temple Judaism that those who suffered the end-time tribulation for righteousness' sake would inherit the lost glory of Adam. Paul seems to be drawing on these backgrounds to say that Christians ensure the lost glory of Adam for themselves as they suffer for Christ in the tribulation of the last days. We also see in 5:2b–4 the "already but not yet" tension: Christians have the hope now (the "already") that they will share in the glory of Christ at his return (the "not yet").

Interpretive Insights

5:1–2a *we have peace with God . . . this grace in which we now stand.*[5] Verses 1–2a give the first blessing of the new covenant belonging to the Christian: peace with God based on justification by faith. We noted above that this peace is the peace associated with the new covenant. And such peace is based on the stipulation of faith in the Lord Jesus Christ (note that the full title is used here). The access, or acceptance, that believers have with God in Christ is their participation in the state of grace. The Dead Sea Scrolls are interesting in this regard, for they speak of entry into the "covenant of grace" (1QS 1.8; cf. 1QHᵃ 12.21–22; 15.30–31).[6] This seems to be what Paul has in mind in using the unusual description "this grace in which we now stand." Through faith in Christ believers have entered the new covenant of grace.

5:2b–4 *we boast in the hope of the glory of God . . . we also glory in our sufferings.* Here is the second new-covenant blessing: hope. We noted above that 5:2b–4 forms a chiasm, indicating that hope is conditioned on suffering. These verses also form a rhetorical *gra-*

The Roman emperors may have brought brief periods of peace to the Roman Empire, but Paul's focus in Romans is on peace with God through Jesus Christ. This is a bronze coin minted during the time of Nero (AD 54–68). It pictures the Temple of Janus with closed doors and the words PACE P(opuli) R(omani) TERRA MARIQ(ue) PARTA IANVM CLVSIT, which has been translated, "The peace of the Roman people having been established on land and sea, he closed (the temple of) Janus." In ancient Rome the Temple of Janus was located near the Roman Forum. From the time of Augustus it became the practice of emperors to open the doors during a time of war and close them during times of peace. Nero shut the doors in AD 66 after the defeat of the Parthians, and the coins were struck to commemorate that event.

ditio, whereby words are repeated creating a climactic effect: "suffering," "perseverance," "character," all of which crescendo in "hope" (cf. James 1:2–4; 2 Pet. 1:6–7). We also noted previously that this idea of suffering leading to the hope of the glory of God is both Adamic and eschatological. Suffering during the end-time tribulation for righteousness' sake will restore the lost glory of Adam to the believer. It is interesting that Paul juxtaposes suffering and the new covenant in 2 Corinthians: the former in 4:7–5:21, the latter in 3:1–4:6. Indeed, suffering for Jesus proved that Paul was a true apostle of the new covenant, even as it identifies the true Christian (see Rom. 8:16–17). All of this is to say that suffering for Jesus' sake is proof positive that a person is a member of the new covenant and awaits the full realization of the glory of the age to come.

Theological Insights

At least two theological insights can be gleaned from Romans 5:1–4. First, Paul's metaphor of reconciliation (v. 11) forms an *inclusio* with justification (v. 1) such that the two concepts are but different sides of the same coin. Reconciliation, with its personal touch, provides a nice balance to the legal language of justification that he has been using since 1:17. After all, God is the Father of Christians, and they are at peace with him. Second, suffering does not negate the fact that a person is a true Christian. Contrary to the "health and wealth gospel," which declares that well-being and

Paul encourages suffering believers to "glory in our sufferings, because we know that suffering produces perseverance; perseverance, character; and character, hope" (Rom. 5:3–4). The Circus Maximus was one place where Christians suffered horribly for their faith through Roman creativity and brutality, particularly under Emperor Nero. Located between the Palatine and Aventine hills, it was primarily used for chariot racing. The structure was continually enlarged and eventually held around two hundred thousand people, who could watch up to twelve chariots racing at once. This aerial view of a section of the modern city of Rome shows the remains of the Circus Maximus in the foreground.

prosperity are proof of genuine Christian faith, Paul maintains that it is suffering that marks true Christians, because in their afflictions they are identifying with the cross. Moreover, trials are intended by God to mature Christians and therefore should be welcomed. On the other hand, Paul is not promoting masochism. Christians need not bring about their own troubles, nor should they relish the pain that suffering inflicts. Indeed, the ultimate hope for Christians is the resurrection of the body and deliverance from all hurts (see Rom. 8:16–30).

Teaching the Text

In teaching or preaching Romans 5:1–4, it is useful to divide the two major points above into two messages. The first is "Romans 5:1–2a: Peace with God; Two Aspects." This would develop the two aspects of God's acceptance of the believer in Christ, justification (5:1) and reconciliation (5:11), since they are complementary ideas. As such, peace with God accords the believer a new legal standing before God as well as a restored relationship with him. Both aspects are needed. The former without the latter would provide a correct but cold relationship, while the latter without the former would fail to satisfy the holy character of God. Thankfully, we do not have to choose between the two, as they are different sides of the same coin. The second message is "Romans 5:2b–4: Hope in God—No Pain, No Gain." Two points emerge from these verses: suffering proves that one is truly a Christian, and suffering matures the Christian. Jesus said that we should rejoice if we suffer for his name's sake because it indicates that we are taking

up his cross and following him. Believers living in modern democracies know little about that aspect of the Christian life, but followers of Jesus living under totalitarian regimes or extremist theocracies experience such affliction daily for the sake of their Christian faith. One wonders what might await believers in the West as Christianity decreases in size and influence. The other positive aspect about suffering for Christ is that hardships make Christians stronger in their faith. The more God sees us through our afflictions, the more we learn to trust in him; and the more we trust him, the more we grow spiritually.

Illustrating the Text

Peace with God comes through justification and reconciliation, which he initiates.

Poetry: "The Hound of Heaven," by Francis Thompson. Thompson (1859–1907) was a poet and essayist who struggled throughout his life with an addiction to opium. His poem "The Hound of Heaven" is a powerful narrative of God's steady, majestic, but uncompromising pursuing and reconciling work in his life. Although the poet flees from him, God remains unhurried and unperturbed until finally the pursued understands that this is the true love of a determined God. It would be worth reading several of the memorable, often-quoted stanzas aloud.

Suffering allows the Christian to mature and to identify with the cross.

Film: *Molokai: The Story of Father Damien.* This moving film (1999) tells the true story of Father Damien (1840–89), a Catholic priest from Belgium who volunteered to go to the island of Molokai to minister to abandoned lepers, living in squalor and need. He was the first priest to go to Molokai. Although warned by his bishop not to touch lepers, he risked his health and life to reach them, and eventually he contracted leprosy himself. His influence was far-reaching; his pleas for help for these people were heard. His ministry is now often cited as an example of how society should care for persons with HIV/AIDS.

Personal Testimony: For over twenty-five years, my wife has suffered from a rare, chronic illness. Although through the years I (Marvin) tried to understand and comfort her, since I did not actually have the condition I could not really relate to her pain. So about thirteen years ago, I decided to ask the Lord to allow me to get the same disease so that I could meaningfully identify with her. And the Lord answered that prayer. About two years later I was diagnosed with my wife's rare condition. Now, I truly relate to her suffering and can better serve her. My suffering has allowed me to identify with her affliction.

A photo of Father Damien taken just before he died in 1889

Romans 5:1–4

The New-Covenant Blessings: Love

Big Idea *The preceding unit treated the covenantal blessings of peace and hope in 5:1–4. In this unit we look at the covenantal blessing of love in 5:5–11. Love is God's* hesed—*the covenant-keeping faithfulness of God to his people that is confirmed by the indwelling Holy Spirit and, above all, by the death of Christ.*

Understanding the Text

The Text in Context

We may outline Romans 5:5–11, the covenant blessing of love, thus:

1. The source of love is God (5:5a)
2. The medium of love is the indwelling Spirit (5:5b)
3. The proof of love is the death of Christ (5:6–11)
   a. Christ's death was eschatological (5:6)
   b. Christ's death was sacrificial (5:7–8)
   c. Christ's death provides eternal security (5:9–11)

Historical and Cultural Background

1. Christ's suffering and death as portrayed in Romans 5:6–11 recall two Jewish themes. The first is the Old Testament sacrificial system, which Paul alludes to in 5:6–8: Christ died "for" (*hyper* [4x]) us. The preposition *hyper* means "on behalf of" and is related to another term used for Christ's death in the New Testament, *anti*, meaning "in place of." Christ's dying for and in place of the sinner draws on the imagery of an animal being sacrificed on behalf of the worshiper for the remission of sins. Second, as James Dunn shows, Christ's sacrificial death is also portrayed against the backdrop of the Maccabean martyrs, whose deaths were viewed as atonement for the sins of ancient Israel (2 Macc. 7:9; 8:21; 4 Macc. 1:8, 10).[1]

2. The words "much more" in 5:9, 10, 15, 17 indicate that Paul is using another rabbinic hermeneutical technique, *qal wa-homer* (light and heavy) (see, in the unit on Rom. 4:1–8, the sidebar on Rabbi Hillel's rules of biblical interpretation). This is an argument from the major premise to the minor premise. Applied to 5:9–10, the argument goes like this:

Major premise: justified us in the past (5:9a)

Minor premise: will deliver us in the future (5:9b)

Major premise: reconciled us in the past (5:10a)

Minor premise: will deliver us in the future (5:10b)

The argument, then, says this: if God justified/reconciled us as sinners in the past (the really hard thing to do), then God surely will keep us eternally safe in the future (something that is relatively easy compared to saving us as sinners in the past). One can also see from the parallelism of 5:9–10 that justification and reconciliation are referring to the same reality—acceptance before God—but using different metaphors.

3. The term "reconciliation" (verb *katallassō*; noun *katallagē*) in 5:10–11 has a very interesting history that sheds wonderful light on these verses. "Reconciliation" is not used in ancient Greek literature for humans being restored to the deities they worshiped, since the mindset of the

- Paul expresses God's love in trinitarian terms: the source of divine love is God the Father; the medium of God's demonstration of love is the Holy Spirit; the proof of God's love is the death of Christ.

Greeks toward religion was that one could not have a personal relationship with the Greek pantheon of gods. The LXX is an obvious advancement over classical Greek thinking in that humans can be reconciled to God because they can have a personal relationship with him. But in the places where "reconciliation" is used of humans and God, it is uniformly the case that humans must initiate that restoration by once again obeying the Torah (2 Macc. 1:5; 7:33; 8:29). But here in Romans 5:5–11 (cf. 2 Cor. 5:18–21), Paul declares that God is the one who initiated our reconciliation with him by sending his Son to die for us, even when we were still sinners.

Interpretive Insights

5:5 *God's love has been poured out into our hearts through the Holy Spirit.* In 5:5–11 we meet with the third new-covenant blessing discussed in 5:1–11: love. The whole of the Trinity is involved in God's love for the believer: the source of love is God the Father (v. 5a); the medium of love is

The Greeks did not believe one could have a personal relationship with the gods of the Greek pantheon. This votive relief shows a gathering of Greek gods (400–350 BC). Zeus is at the top center with Persephone and then Hades, moving clockwise. Next to Zeus counterclockwise is Pan. The mask of the river god Achelous is on the table. The other gods cannot be identified.

the indwelling Holy Spirit (v. 5b); the proof of love is the death of Christ (vv. 6–11). Regarding the source of love, Paul's Greek phrase is *hē agapē tou theou* ("the love of God"). Based on the flow of Paul's thought in 5:5–11, it is undeniable that here the genitive ("of God") is subjective (= God's love for us) rather than objective (= our love for God). God the Father is the initiator of our salvation, even as he was for ancient Israel (Deut. 4:37; 10:15; see also Deut. 7:8; 23:5). It was the sheer love of God that called Israel into covenant with him, and it was God's *hesed*—faithful love—that maintained the covenant with Israel. Yahweh did not disqualify Israel; Israel disqualified itself from being the permanent people of God by breaking the stipulations of the covenant. Now God's covenant love rests upon the church, composed largely of Gentiles.

The medium of love is the indwelling Holy Spirit (5:5b). Many commentators rightly observe that the clause "God's love has been poured out into our hearts" should be equated with the indwelling Holy Spirit. Thus, the Holy Spirit is the subjective medium by which God com-municates his love for Christians. And not to be overlooked in this discussion is the well-known connection between 5:5 and the pouring out of the Spirit on the day of Pentecost, the inauguration of the new covenant (compare Acts 2:17–18 with Joel 2:28–29).

In Israel offerings for sin would be brought by individuals or by the priest on behalf of the community. The animals sacrificed for sin were usually bulls or goats, as prescribed by Mosaic law. This relief from Zincirli (eighth century BC) shows a man carrying a gazelle on his shoulders, perhaps bringing it as a sacrifice.

5:6–8 *at just the right time . . . While we were still sinners, Christ died for us.* In 5:6–11 Paul spells out the proof of God's love for us: the death of Christ. Paul here draws on three aspects of Christ's death: it is eschatological (v. 6), it is sacrificial (vv. 7–8), and it provides eternal security (vv. 9–11). The word *kairos* ("right time") in 5:6 indicates more than ordinary "time" (*chronos*). Here *kairos* taps into the early church's belief that the life, death, and resurrection of Jesus Christ inaugurated the age to come, the new covenant (see Rom. 13:11–14). Jesus' death spelled the defeat of this present age with its powerlessness before sin and has opened up the kingdom of God for sinners. Verses 7–8 indicate that Jesus' death was sacrificial; it was "on behalf of" (*hyper*) sinners. There has been much debate concerning these two verses, whether Paul here differentiates a righteous person from a good person relative to the death of Christ. They could be synonymous, or the first could be a morally correct person and the latter a benefactor. Either way, the point is the same: most people would not die for a well-respected, upstanding person, much less for a sinner. But that is precisely what Christ did. He died for us when we were still sinners.

5:9–11 *justified by his blood . . . saved from God's wrath*. Verses 9–11 highlight the eternal aspect of Christ's death as it relates to the believer's assurance on judgment day. As mentioned above, Paul uses the *qal wahomer* interpretive technique in 5:9–10 to the effect that if God has already accomplished the really difficult task of justifying/reconciling us as sinners to himself, then preserving the Christian spiritually on judgment day ("saved from God's wrath" / "saved through his life") is a relatively easy task by comparison. This message assures believers that they are eternally secure in Christ. In 5:11 the reader is returned to 5:1 in rejoicing that believers are reconciled with God, the flip side of justification. The first is relational, while the second is legal, but both convey the truth that Christians are accepted by God in Christ.

Theological Insights

Two important insights can be seen in Romans 5:5–11. First, God is the initiator of justification and reconciliation. It was his love for humanity that motivated him to send his Son to die for our sins. Second, the Christian's eternal destiny is secure in Christ. Since God saved us as sinners, he will keep us as his children for all eternity.[2]

The *Filioque* Debate

The *filioque* (Latin for "and [from] the son") debate centers on whether the Spirit proceeds only from the Father (so the Greek Orthodox Church) or from both the Father *and the Son* (so Augustine and the Western Church). The following illustrations depict the two positions:

Greek Orthodox Church

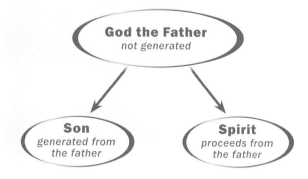

Augustine and the Western Church

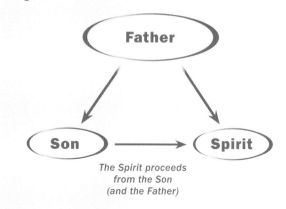

Augustine's argument better "completes" the Trinity than does the Greek Orthodox view.

Teaching the Text

A message on this unit is "Romans 5:5–11: The Love of the Trinity." This topic could simply use three subpoints from above: the source of love is God the Father; the medium of love is the Holy Spirit; the proof of love is the death of Christ. Augustine mused that love is at the basis of the Trinity's relationship in that the Spirit proceeds from both the Father and the Son (much to the vexation of the Greek Orthodox Church, which argues that the Spirit proceeds only from the Father [see the sidebar]). Here in Romans 5:5–11 Paul provides us with perhaps the most explicit mention of the delineation of the loving roles of the Father, the Son, and the Holy Spirit toward humankind. God the Father is the author of love. The love that he shares with the Son and the Spirit he also demonstrated by creating the world as the object of his love. In fact, God loved the world to the point that he was willing to give up his Son— that is, to withhold his love from his Son on the cross. The death of Christ on the cross for humankind obviously revealed his immense love for sinners. That love not only absorbed the sin of a hostile world but also was willing to suffer divine abandonment and hostility, even if only for a time. And the Holy Spirit is the one who transcends time in order to bring to the sinner's consciousness the depth of love displayed on the cross, making the death of Jesus an existential reality.

Illustrating the Text

The Trinity shows the source (Father), medium (Spirit), and proof (Son) of love.

Hymn Text: **"The Love of God," by Frederick M. Lehman.** Lehman (1868–1953) wrote this song in 1917 in Pasadena, California.

Detail of *The Trinity*, by Lucas Cranach the Elder (1472–1553)

The text is based on a Jewish poem called *Haddamut*, written in Aramaic in 1050 by Meir Ben Isaac Nehorai, a cantor in Worms, Germany. The cantor's poem has been translated into at least eighteen languages. The hymn is a beautiful testimony to the love of God, using metaphors to illustrate, and is summed up in the refrain: "O love of God, how rich and pure! / How measureless and strong! / It shall forevermore endure / The saints' and angels' song."

Art: *The Trinity*, by Lucas Cranach the Elder. A German Renaissance painter and printmaker, Cranach (1472–1553) is famous for his woodcut designs of the first edition of the German New Testament and for portraits of Martin Luther, who was a close friend. In *The Trinity*, a powerful painting in oil on wood, God the Father, crowned and robed as king, stands upright holding the limp, crucified Christ, on whose left knee is perched the Holy Spirit, in the form of a dove with unfurled wings. Around the edge of the painting are young angels looking on. It is an intriguing visual illustration (see photo).

Believers are eternally secure in Christ.

History: "A Confederate Soldier's Prayer," **author unknown.** This prayer is attributed to a battle-weary Confederate soldier whose body was found near the end of the Civil War. In his poem he expresses the irony that in response to everything he asked from God he was given the opposite, which created in him compassion and growth and blessing.

> I asked God for strength, that I
>   might achieve;
> I was made weak, that I might learn
>   humbly to obey.
> I asked for health, that I might do
>   greater things;
> I was given infirmity, that I might do
>   better things.
> I asked for riches, that I might be
>   happy;
> I was given poverty, that I might be
>   wise.
> I asked for power, that I might have
>   the praise of men;
> I was given weakness, that I might
>   feel the need of God.
> I asked for all things, that I might
>   enjoy life;

> I was given life, that I might enjoy
>   all things.
> I got nothing that I asked for, but
>   everything I hoped for.
> Almost despite myself, my unspoken prayers were answered.
> I am among all men most richly
>   blessed.

Love is the basis of the Trinity's relationship.

Book: *The Shack*, by William P. Young. This best-selling novel (2007) has captured Christians' imagination in its portrayal of the three persons of the Trinity as in a dynamic, loving relationship with one another. The book has been commended by some prominent biblical scholars such as Eugene Peterson, who calls it *The Pilgrim's Progress* for our time, and denounced by others, such as James DeYoung, who sees it as embedded with errors that strike at the heart of the gospel. Thus, the book's take on the Holy Spirit's relationship to the believer might be worth pursuing by way of discussion and education.

Moreover, the fellowship of the Trinity portrayed in *The Shack* taps into Augustine's view of the *filioque* debate mentioned above in that the Spirit proceeding from the Father and the Son "completes" the Trinity. Furthermore, Augustine said that the Holy Spirit is the love that connects Father and Son. Thus it is that *The Shack* dramatizes what the Spirit as love linking Father and Son might look like and how the Spirit might be experienced by the believer.

Adam, the Law, and the Curse of the Covenant

Big Idea *Paul presents another new-covenant blessing: Christians are part of the new human-ity created by Christ, the last Adam. Sin and death, instigated by the old-covenant law, began with the fall of the first Adam. This is the curse of the covenant. But Christ has undone the consequences of Adam's sin by obeying God and thereby creating the new humanity.*

Understanding the Text

The Text in Context

Romans 5:12–21 continues the theme begun in 5:1–11: the blessings of the new covenant have replaced the ineffective old covenant. The blessings specified in 5:1–11 are peace, hope, and love. Here in 5:12–21 the new-covenant blessing is the new hu-manity in Christ, the last Adam. Romans 5:12–21 divides into two units: verses 12–14 and verses 15–21. Verses 12–14 relate how it is that the world became the enemy of God: Adam's sin (and Eve's sin, though Paul does not mention her here; but see 2 Cor. 11:3; 1 Tim. 2:13–14) turned the world hostile to God. Verses 15–21 proclaim how it is that humanity is being reconciled to God: Christ's obedience to God is turning many to faith in him. Verses 12–14 unfold in two points:

1. Adam as the originator of sin and death (5:12)

2. The law of the old covenant as the instigator of Adam's sin (5:13–14)

Historical and Cultural Background

1. The first important piece of back-ground information is Jewish teaching about Adam and the fall. Although Second Temple Judaism could blame other culprits for perpetrating the fall of the human race (Satan [Wis. 2:23–24]; the Watchers, which were fallen angels [*1 En.* 6–36; cf. Gen. 6:1–7]; Eve [Sir. 25:24; *L.A.E.* 44; *Apoc. Mos.* 14; 32]), more often than not it placed the blame squarely on Adam's shoulders based on Genesis 2–3 (e.g., 1QS 4.22–23; CD 3.20; 1QHᵃ 4.15; *4 Ezra* 4.30; *2 Bar.* 23.4; 48.42). Paul agrees with the sentiment here in 5:12–14 (cf. 1 Cor. 15:21–22).

2. The ancient Hebrew phenomenon known as "corporate personality" may well be in play here. Corporate personality is the idea that one person's actions represent the many. Joshua 7:1–26 illustrates this in

the way it attributes Achan's sin to all of Israel (hence its defeat at the battle of Ai) and in the way that Achan's whole family was punished with him. Here Achan, like Adam, committed actions considered to be the actions of those whom he represented.[1] Hebrews 7:10 seems to tap into the same concept when it speaks of Levi being in the loins of Abraham when he gave a tithe to Melchizedek. That Paul has something similar in mind in Romans 5:12–21 is suggested by his usage of "the one" (12x) and "the many" (9x), common terms in ancient Judaism to designate the representative actions of an individual. The very structure of 5:12–21, which contrasts the two heads of the human race, Adam and Christ, also suggests this idea of corporate personality.

Interpretive Insights

5:12 *sin entered the world through one man.*[2] I suggest that 5:12–14 makes the case that the law of the old covenant occasioned the sin of Adam and the subsequent curse

Key Themes of Romans 5:12–14

- Death, both physical and spiritual, is the result of sin, and both sin and death began with Adam.
- Adam is the representative of the old humanity, while Christ, the last Adam, is the representative of the new humanity.
- Since Adam is the representative of the old humanity, his sin and death impact everyone.
- The law that Adam broke was the Torah before its inscription by Moses. More particularly, Adam transgressed the Torah for everyone.
- Indeed, the law of Moses as the stipulation of the old covenant provoked Adam to sin, which resulted in death. This is the curse of the covenant.

that it cast on all of humanity. In 5:12 Paul asserts that Adam is the originator of sin and death. That much is clear from verse 12a. But a storm of controversy has centered on the translation and meaning of two Greek words, *eph' hō,* that occur in verse 12b. There are four main views of the meaning of this phrase, described in table 1.

I think that Moo is correct. Pelagius's view has the correct translation but cannot explain how it is that every human being

Table 1: Four Views on the Meaning of *eph' hō* in Romans 5:12

Pelagius (fifth-century monk who opposed the concept of original sin)	Augustine (fifth-century bishop who opposed Pelagius)	John Calvin (sixteenth-century Reformer who introduced a "middle term" into the discussion: the sinful nature)	Douglas Moo (modern commentator who represents many who argue that 5:12 draws on the Jewish concept of corporate personality)
eph' hō = contraction of *epi toutō hoti* ("upon this that"), which should be translated as "because"	*eph' hō* = preposition and pronoun ("in him"), which should be translated as "in him [Adam]"	*eph' hō* = contraction of *epi toutō hoti* ("upon this that"), which should be translated as "because"	*eph' hō* = contraction of *epi toutō hoti* ("upon this that"), which should be translated as "because"
Pelagius took this to mean that Adam's sin affected only himself, and that every human being since Adam has chosen to sin. Thus, there is no original sin that has been passed onto the human race.	Augustine argued by this that all of humanity was biologically in Adam when he fell in the garden. Thus, each person sinned in Adam.	Calvin argued that Paul is basing the universal reign of death on the sinful nature that Adam's act created, not on individual acts of sin.	Moo argues that "because all sinned" means that humanity was in solidarity with Adam's sin due to his representative nature.

See Augustine, *Two Epistles of the Pelagians,* 4.4.7 (for both his and Pelagius's views); Calvin, *Institutes* 2.1.5–8; Moo, *Epistle to the Romans,* 327–28.

since Adam has, by personal volition, repeated his sin. To the contrary, there has to be some connection between Adam and humanity, such that the latter follows in his footsteps. Augustine's translation is no doubt incorrect. Calvin introduces an idea, the sinful nature, that may well be true but is no more than an implication in the text.

5:13–14 *sin was in the world before the law . . . death reigned from the time of Adam to the time of Moses.* Paul's second point is that the law of Moses, the stipulation of the old covenant, was the occasion for Adam's sin. The best way to develop this thesis is to state the seven steps upon which it is based.

1. Death reigned from Adam to Moses because of Adam's sin.

2. Sin assumes that a law has been broken. Notice that Paul's logic moves backward from Moses to Adam:

Moses	Humanity in Between	Adam
Law inscribed	Death ruled	Sin against law before its inscription

3. The law that Adam broke was the Torah before it was inscribed by Moses. Romans 7:7–12 will forcefully make that point, for it was a common assumption in Second Temple Judaism that the commandment that Adam and Eve broke was the command not to covet (to have the knowledge of good and evil and thus be like God), and that such a command summarized the entire Torah. James Dunn puts it this way: "Thus the commandment Adam received ('You shall not eat of it,' Gen. 2:17) could be seen not as an isolated rule but as an expression of the Torah, and in breaking it Adam could be said to have broken the statutes (plural) of God. . . . The oldest

The scenes of Adam and Eve's fall and Moses receiving the law are carved next to each other on this sarcophagus lid from fourth-century AD Rome. The law that Adam broke was the Torah in advance of its being inscribed by Moses.

form of this teaching may well be as early as Paul. Paul, in his repeated equation of 'the commandment' with '(the) law' in [Romans 7] vv. 8, 9, and 12, quite likely shows his familiarity with it."[3]

4. It was Adam's transgression against the Torah, the stipulation of the old covenant, that brought about the divine curse—that is, the curse of the covenant: death, not life.

5. If Paul indeed means in 5:13–14 that it was the Torah that Adam broke, then the meaning of the next clause—that humanity did not commit the same sin as Adam's transgression of the command not to covet—is resolved. While humanity between Adam and Moses might not have sinned against the Torah, Adam did, and he did so as the representative of all. Thus, in solidarity with Adam, humanity broke the Torah and now suffers the curse of the old covenant, which is death.

6. Ancient Israel saw itself as the new Adam and thought that its obedience to the law of Moses would result in a new humanity; that is, Israel was the last/eschatological Adam.[4] But in Romans 1:23 Paul hinted that Israel was still in the old Adam, as evidenced by their worship of the golden calf even as Moses was presenting God's law to them. Moreover, as I have argued elsewhere, Paul in 1 Corinthians 10:6–10 suggests that the law of the old covenant instigated Israel's idolatry in the wilderness.[5] Galatians 3:19; Romans 4:15; 5:20; 7:7–12 concur with Romans 5:13–14 that the law of Moses as the stipulation of the old covenant stirs one to disobedience, not obedience. All of this is to say that Paul believed that the law of Moses and the old covenant are still in Adam and participate in the old humanity.[6]

7. But the law of Moses is a part of the divine plan in that by increasing sin it prepares the way for the true, last Adam,[7] Jesus Christ. Christ, not Israel, is the founder of the new humanity, whose obedience to God has undone the first Adam's tragic legacy. This is why Paul can say that Adam is a type or pattern of the one to come,[8] because both men are universal representatives.

Theological Insights

Two key theological insights confront the reader in Romans 5:12–14. First, the biblical explanation of the origin of evil/sin is the fall of Adam and Eve. This view, of course, presumes that those two were real people. Second, sin is both individual and corporate in nature. Regarding the latter, no person is exempt from the network of sin that influences society. We inherit abuse, tragedy, disadvantage, and dysfunction, not to mention the consequence of poor choices by others. But the power of the gospel is able to free us from the shackles of past generations and indeed from our own mistakes and sins. As participants in the new humanity in Christ, we have the power to make wholesome decisions that honor God and help others.

Teaching the Text

A couple of sermons come to mind from Romans 5:12–14. The first is "What's Wrong with the World?" Here one could summarize theories regarding the origin of evil (Marxist, atheistic/evolutionary, and Eastern/dualistic) and discuss and defend the biblical view. Thus, Marxism argues that capitalism is the root of all evil because it divides humankind into haves and have-nots. And one day a classless society will emerge in which material goods are equally distributed to all. Atheistic evolution tries to allay our fears about evil by claiming that bad action on the part of humans is residual animal behavior that will extinguish itself in perhaps a few million years more. Eastern religion, with its principle of yin and yang, believes that good and bad are inherent to the universe and indeed are dualistically related. One cannot have the one without having the other. The Judeo-Christian tradition based on the Bible, however, argues that God created the first humans with a will, and with that will Adam and Eve chose to disobey God. This is the origin of evil, and that primeval choice has haunted humankind ever since.

Second, one might speak from this passage on the topic of "Adam, Me, and the 'Apple' in the Tree." This message could highlight the individual and corporate dimensions of sin mentioned above. But even assuming the accuracy of the discussion above regarding the influence of the intersection of individual and corporate decisions upon us, at the end of the day all of us will appear before God and will be evaluated on the basis of the decisions that we have made rather than on the basis of how others' choices have affected our lives.

Illustrating the Text

The origin of evil/sin is the fall of Adam and Eve.

Popular Theory: As noted in the "Teaching the Text" section, one could contrast the biblical position on the origin of evil with the Marxist, atheistic/evolutionary, and Eastern/dualistic theories. Quotes from primary sources could be shown or printed.

Literature: *Paradise Lost*, by John Milton. This epic poem by John Milton (1608–74) was first published in 1667 in ten books. Book 9 tells the story of the fall and the regret that follows. It is readable and emotionally engaging. It draws the reader into seeing and even feeling the "before and after" and the horror of sin.

Sin is both individual and corporate in nature.

News Story: One could prompt the audience to think about some of the CEOs of our day (e.g., Bernie Madoff, who defrauded many people of their retirement funds) whose individual decisions have spelled disaster for millions. Another example is the arsonist who sets a fire that burns thousands of acres, destroys hundreds of homes, and even takes lives.

History: Accounts from primary sources about the Holocaust (letters, eyewitness accounts, and memoirs) show the appalling nature of corporate evil. Two such resources are *The Diary of Anne Frank* (1947) and Viktor Frankl's *Man's Search for Meaning* (1946).

Film: *Judgment at Nuremberg*. This 1961 drama, directed by Stanley Kramer, revolves around a military tribunal in which four Nazi judges are accused of crimes against humanity for their activities during the Hitler regime. The chief justice, Dan Haywood (played by Spencer Tracy), makes an effort to comprehend how defendant Ernst Janning (played by Burt Lancaster) could have passed sentences resulting in genocide, and, how the German people could have ignored the Holocaust. The way in which individuals collude with state crimes is a focus of the film.

Literature: "The Lottery," by Shirley Jackson. This short story by Jackson (1916–65), published in *The New Yorker* in 1948, aroused great controversy following its publication. The story is set in a small village where the people are tightly knit together and tradition reigns supreme. An annual event is held in which one individual in the town is randomly selected to be brutally stoned to death by friends and family. This ritual, meant to ensure a good harvest, has been in existence for over seventy-seven years and is practiced by everyone in town. The tone of the story is almost light-hearted, at times festive, and it shows the power of corporate evil.

Preserved section of the barbed-wire fence and barracks at Auschwitz, the largest of the concentration camps erected by the Nazi regime. Here Nazi prisoners provided forced labor for Nazi enterprises. It was also a killing site with gas chamber and crematorium. It was here that Josef Mengele carried out his horrific medical experiments. Over a million people died in the three camps that made up the Auschwitz complex. The Holocaust still remains fresh in the minds of the Western world as an example of corporate evil.

The New Humanity as a Blessing of the New Covenant

Big Idea *Paul contrasts Christ, the last Adam, with the first Adam. This contrast reveals that Christ has inaugurated the new humanity, a blessing of the new covenant. In doing so, Christ has defeated the sin and death that characterized the old humanity and the old covenant. Christ has secured the life of the new covenant for those who believe in him.*

Understanding the Text

The Text in Context

Romans 5:15–21 qualifies Paul's concluding statement in 5:14 that Adam is a type[1] of Christ. Thus, on the one hand, Adam is a type of Christ in that his action, like Christ's, has had a universal impact (v. 14). On the other hand, Paul wants to show how diametrically opposed Christ is to Adam (vv. 15–21).

Verses 12–14 and verses 20–21 form an *inclusio* for verses 15–19, such that the contrasting paradigmatic pattern between Adam (vv. 12–14) and Christ (vv. 20–21) structures verses 15–21,[2] as shown in table 1.

So the cause-and-effect pattern that governs 5:15–19 is the result of the contrast between Adam (the law led to sin, which led to death [5:12–14]) and Christ (grace led to righteousness, which led to life [5:20–21]). The resulting cause-and-effect pattern is shown in table 2.

Table 1: The Contrast between Adam and Christ

5:12–14	5:15–19	5:20–21
Adam, old humanity, old covenant	Christ, new humanity, new covenant versus Adam, old humanity, old covenant	Christ, new humanity, new covenant
Pattern: Law led to transgression, which led to death	The reversal of the covenant blessings and curses	Pattern: Grace led to righteousness, which leads to life

In addition to the preceding macrostructure of the text, there are at least two individual features in Romans 5:15–21 that call for comment. First, 5:13–17 is an anacoluthon (interruption) that contains two asides made by Paul. (1) Verses 13–14, as we saw in the previous unit, specify the relationship between the sin and death Adam bequeathed to the world (v. 12). (2) Verses 15–17 qualify how it is that Adam is a type of Christ (so v. 14): both committed actions that continue to have universal consequences. Beyond that comparison, however, Adam and Christ have nothing in common. Second, Paul uses *qal wahomer* (see the sidebar in the unit on Rom. 4:1–8) in verse 15 and verse 17 (as he did earlier, in vv. 9–10), which is signaled to the reader by the words "how much more."

Historical and Cultural Background

The main background for Romans 5:15–21 is, I suggest, Deuteronomy 27–30. On Mount Ebal the Levites pronounced the curses of the covenant if Israel proved to be disobedient, while on Mount Gerizim the priests pronounced the blessings of the covenant if Israel was obedient to Yahweh's stipulations. The blessings and curses alternate like an antiphonal chorus, culminating in Deuteronomy 30:15–20, which presents the "two ways" tradition: the way of obedience and covenantal blessings, and the way of disobedience and covenantal curses. I suggest (and will defend in the next section) that the way Romans 5:15–21 contrasts the dire effect of Adam's sin with the blessing of Christ's righteousness is reminiscent of the alternating of the pronouncements of cov-

Key Themes of Romans 5:15–21

- Paul reverses the Deuteronomic blessings and curses: those who attempt to obey the law follow the first Adam, experiencing his transgression and death, while those who believe in Christ, the last Adam, apart from the law experience his righteousness and life. The latter is the dawning of the new humanity, a new-covenant blessing.
- Romans 5:12–14 and 5:20–21 contain a paradigmatic contrasting pattern:
  - Adam: The law of Moses led to sin, which led to death (vv. 12–14)
  - Christ: Grace led to righteousness, which leads to life (vv. 20–21)
- Romans 5:12–14 and 5:20–21 form an *inclusio* for 5:15–19, projecting the preceding pattern onto verses 15–19.

enant blessings and covenant curses upon ancient Israel in Deuteronomy 27–30. The difference is that Paul radically reverses the two: curses are on those who try to follow the Torah, but blessings rest upon those whose faith is in Christ. This is it say, the sins that Deuteronomy 27–30 warns Israel against cannot be avoided by keeping the Torah, for sinful nature will not submit to the divine law. It takes faith in Christ to produce genuine obedience to God and thereby ensure the covenantal blessings Deuteronomy promises.

Table 2: The Cause-and-Effect Pattern in Romans 5:15–19

5:15	Adam's transgression resulted in death.	God's grace expressed itself in the gift of Christ (his death), which results in life (implied in v. 15 but stated in vv. 17, 18, 21).
5:16	Adam's one sin snowballed into many sins and thus the judgment and condemnation of many.	The gift of God (God's grace through Christ's one act of obedience: his death on the cross) has overcome the snowball effect of sin on the human race by bringing justification to many.
5:17	Adam's transgression brought death and therefore showed life to be but temporary.	God's grace through the gift of Christ gives eternal life ("eternal" is implicit in v. 17 but is stated in v. 21).
5:18	Adam's transgression brought condemnation to the human race.	Christ's righteous obedience to God has brought justification to the new humanity.
5:19	Adam's one act of transgression made many sinners.	Christ's one act of obedience (at the cross) made many righteous.

Interpretive Insights

5:15 *But the gift is not like the trespass.* Verse 15 begins the series of contrasts between the two Adams. I presume the two tables above as we move through 5:15–21. Based on Deuteronomy 27–30 and the tradition that it generated (the Deuteronomistic tradition), Second Temple Judaism clung to the hope that after Israel was sent into exile for breaking the stipulation of the old covenant, the Jews' renewed commitment to the Torah would be the occasion for God to send the Messiah to establish the new covenant and the kingdom of God (see CD 3.12–21; 1QH[a] 9.32; *2 Bar.* 17.4–18.2; 51.3–7; *4 Ezra* 7.51, 89, 97; *Pirke Abot* 2.8; 6.7; cf. Jer. 31:31–34; Ezek. 36:24–31). Paul reverses that message in 5:15 (cf. v. 20): it was actually the law of the old covenant that provoked Adam to trespass against it in the first place, and that led to death for the old humanity. By contrast, God's grace through the gift of Christ's obedient death on the cross (which both fulfilled and terminated the law [see 10:4]) has clothed with righteousness those who believe in him. This has led to the blessing of the life of the new covenant that overflows to the new humanity in Christ. Robert Jewett has shown that Paul's terms for the beneficence of God mentioned in 5:15 ("grace," "gift," "overflowed") draw on the Jewish hope for the age to come because it would restore lost paradise (Isa. 25:6–8; 27:6; 65:17–25; Ezek. 47:9–12; Amos 9:13; *4 Ezra* 8.52). For Paul, the Messiah has indeed come and created a new humanity and a new paradise.[3] Moreover, all of this is based on grace, not the law.

5:16 *Nor can the gift of God be compared with the result of one man's sin.* The words "how much more" in 5:15 indicate that Paul is engaged in a *qal wahomer* argument, which is spelled out now in 5:16: Christ's one act of obedience did not merely overcome Adam's one act of disobedience, as if it were a tit-for-tat move; rather, Christ's obedience overcame the snowball effect of Adam's sin by which the whole world carried on his transgression. To paraphrase Paul in 5:15–16: if Adam's one act of sin was influential, how much more was Christ's one act of obedience influential in that it overcame both Adam's transgression and a whole world of trespasses that followed.[4]

5:17 *how much more will . . . the gift of righteousness reign in life.* Genesis 1:26–28 says that God granted Adam and Eve dominion over the earth. When the first couple fell, that blessing eventually went to Israel (compare Gen. 12:1–3 with 1:26–

The temptation and fall of Adam and Eve is depicted on this statue pedestal (AD 1210–20) at the cathedral of Notre Dame, Paris.

28).[5] But the incident of the golden calf demonstrated that, alas, Israel too was in Adam and suffered from his disobedience (see again Rom. 1:23). According to Paul, the law strangely is at the source of the problem, stirring up Adam and Israel to sin (cf. again v. 20). Instead of having dominion over the earth, those two are under the sway of death along with the old humanity. But Jesus Christ, the last Adam, by God's grace offers his righteousness and subsequent life to those who believe in him, apart from the law. Verse 17 also witnesses to Paul's use of a *qal wahomer* argument: if Adam's life only proved to be temporary, as is evidenced by the entrance of death into the world, how much more so is the life that Christ offers to his followers eternal, invulnerable to death (cf. v. 17 and Paul's remark in v. 21 that Christ's life is eternal). In concluding my comments on 5:17, I should mention that contrary to what some have claimed, Romans 5:12–21 does not teach universalism—the notion that God saves everyone because of Jesus' death. Such a sentiment is refuted by Paul's words in 5:17: Christ's blessings belong only to those who appropriate God's grace personally.

5:18 *one righteous act resulted in justification and life for all people.* Verse 18 resumes 5:12, completing the contrast that Paul started there:

- (The law) stirred up Adam's trespass, which brought condemnation (death) to the world (cf. 12–14).
- (Grace) sent righteousness (Christ's obedient death), which has brought justification and life to those who believe in him.

Many commentators correctly point out that "justification" is the present possession of the believer (the "already" aspect), while "life" is the eternal life that awaits the eschatological consummation (the "not yet" aspect).

5:19 *many will be made righteous.* Ancient Judaism harbored the illusion that obeying the Torah would make one righteous, and Paul counters that the mere attempt to obey the Torah makes one a sinner because that effort is itself an act of hubris in the light of the advent of the gospel. Rather, faith in Christ is the divinely prescribed means for becoming righteous.[6] The reference to Christ's obedience no doubt refers to his death on the cross (cf. Phil. 2:8) rather than to his obedient life as a whole. This is because Paul alludes to Isaiah 53:11 in 5:19. The Suffering Servant made "many" righteous by his death, just as Christ did by his death.

5:20–21 *where sin increased, grace increased all the more.* Verses 20–21 conclude the paragraph of contrasts between Christ and Adam. The law (of the old covenant) instigated Adam to sin, which resulted in death for what is now the old humanity. But God's grace through Christ produces righteousness in the new humanity, which is the eternal life of the new covenant. Three brief points about these verses are in order. First, the NIV's "was brought in" (*pareisēlthen*) is better rendered "entered." The same verb occurs in Galatians 2:4, where it describes the Judaizers' entrance into Antioch to push the Torah on Gentiles. No doubt the same negative connotation of the verb is intended here by Paul; the law entered for a negative purpose: to increase the trespass (used here as a generic term for transgressions). This leads to the second point: the law was designed by God to stir up sin, which gained momentum in human history, culminating in the crucifixion of Jesus. Third, the phrase "eternal life" is more typically Johannine than Pauline. For John, eternal life is here and now in Christ. For Paul, spiritual life in Christ both begins now (see, e.g., 5:17–18; 6:4) and will one day overcome physical death. This latter nuance informs the use of "eternal life" in 5:21.

Theological Insights

Two theological insights are central to Romans 5:15–21. First, the law and the old covenant lead to sin, which leads to death for the old humanity, while God's new covenant of grace in Christ leads to righteousness, which leads to eternal life for the new humanity. Second, Christ's obedient death on the cross has conquered Adam's sin and death, providing for the new humanity justification and spiritual life now and eternal life later.

Teaching the Text

One sermon on Romans 5:15–21 could be "Last Adam versus First Adam." Here the speaker can use table 1, supplied in "The Text in Context" section above, to cover the running contrasts between the two Adams. Thus, the first Adam's sin brought death, spiritually and physically, whereas Christ, the last Adam, has overcome that death by his own obedient death, so that his followers might live eternally (5:15). And the last Adam has, by his obedient life and death, more than matched the mounting effect of the first Adam's sin by bringing

justification to many (5:16). However, this action of Christ should not be misconstrued as universalism—the teaching that Christ's death and resurrection were so effective that everyone now is saved even apart from personal faith. In this view, all that the church needs to do is go into all the world (or not) and announce that all are justified because of the Christ event whether or not they believe for themselves. By contrast, the life that proceeded from the first Adam is only temporary because of the first couple's sin, but the life that the last Adam gives to those who believe in him is eternal (5:17). The two Adams are authors of two spiritual states: condemnation for those under the aegis of the first Adam, but justification for those in Christ, the founder of the new human race (5:18). The first Adam's sin has propagated a race of sinners, while the last Adam has created a race of righteous people.

Illustrating the Text

While Adam's offense brought death to all, Christ's obedience brought life.

Film: *To End All Wars.* This film (2001) is based on the true story of Ernest Gordon, former dean of the chapel at Princeton University who, as a Scottish soldier during World War II, spent three years in a Japanese POW camp. In the account, four Allied prisoners of war are treated brutally by their Japanese captors while being forced to build a highway through the Burmese jungle. What they demonstrate is great personal sacrifice in the face of impossible circumstances, showing the power of forgiveness over hatred and the reality of God's peace in the midst of tragedy. One prisoner in the movie, Dusty Miller, is a strong, Christlike figure whose persistent faith and serenity in the face of cruelty frustrate the Japanese guards and bolster his comrades.

Children's Book: *Hope for the Flowers*, **by Trina Paulus.** This simple book, published in 1972, still holds large appeal. It opens with a large group of caterpillars stepping all over each other in an effort to climb a caterpillar column, without any idea what is at the top. In contrast, another caterpillar, named Stripe, joins them, only to find out that he should follow Yellow, a butterfly who is not caught in the climb but who can fly. At the end, Stripe and Yellow soar above the earth while the other caterpillars continue arduously climbing. This could illustrate the difference between condemnation and justification.

Humankind can choose one of two spiritual destinies: death or life.

Film: *Dead Man Walking*. This 1995 film, which earned several Oscar nominations, is based on the book of the same name by Sister Helen Prejean. It tells the story of the relationship that she developed with Matthew Poncelet, a prisoner on death row for rape and murder. The nun works to effect a stay of execution (which is denied) for the prisoner, who claims to be innocent, though he is arrogant and racist. In a dramatic moment toward the end of the film, set in the final hours before his execution, Helen Prejean pleads with this hardened sinner to admit his guilt, to choose between death and life, to say the words. This is a powerful scene to illustrate the choice between spiritual life and death.

Poetry: "The Road Not Taken," by Robert Frost. This poem (1916) has been much misunderstood by readers, including Christian readers who have tried to liken it to the two paths offered in Scripture, one narrow, the other wide. Rather, Frost was making an existential statement about choice (note the word "sigh" in the poem). The author must choose one of two roads that lie before him, both of which appear pretty, and he realizes that there will be consequences for his choice. The sigh may be one of relief or sorrow. The poem is very usable for this scriptural point.

Christ's obedient death on the cross did not come easily. The Gospel writers, especially Luke (Luke 22:40–46), tell of his anguished time of prayer in the garden of Gethsemane the night of his arrest. This grove of ancient olive trees adjacent to the Church of All Nations is one of the traditional sites of the garden of Gethsemane.

New Dominion as a Blessing of the New Covenant: Dead to Sin

Big Idea *In chapter 6 Paul presents another blessing: new dominion. The first Adam forfeited his dominion over the earth. But Christ, the last Adam, inaugurated a new age and new covenant, restoring the lost dominion. Believers enter that new dominion by uniting with Christ's death and resurrection: they become dead to sin and alive to God.*

Understanding the Text

The Text in Context

While Romans 3:21–5:21 developed the theme of justification, Romans 6:1–8:16 is devoted to the topic of sanctification.[1] On the one hand, justification and sanctification are to be distinguished, as shown in table 1. On the other hand, justification and sanctification should not be completely separated, since the latter flows out of the former, as 6:1–14 demonstrates.

Table 1: The Distinction between Justification and Sanctification

Justification	Sanctification
Juridical: declared righteous	Moral: made righteous
Instantaneous decision	Lifelong growth
Imputed righteousness: the Christian's standing/ position before God	Imparted righteousness: the Christian's walk/ practice before God
Indicative mood: you are justified	Imperative mood: act like it
Union with Christ in his past death/resurrection	Communion with Christ in the present

Romans 5:20–21 and 6:14 form an *inclusio* for 6:1–13:

A Law/old covenant stirs up sin, which results in death (5:20–21)

B Grace/new covenant unites believers with Christ's death/ resurrection, which results in dominion over sin and newness of life (6:1–13)

A′ Law/old covenant enslaves one to sin (and death) (6:14)

Romans 6:1–14 can be outlined as follows:

1. The indicative of the Christian life: We have died and been raised with Christ (6:1–10)
   a. The issue: Shall we sin so that grace may increase? (6:1)[2]
   b. The answer: No, for one who has died to sin cannot continue to live in sin (6:2)
   c. The explanation (6:3–10)

i. Christians died to sin in union with Christ's death (6:3–5)

ii. Christians' dominion over sin is in union with Christ's life (6:6–10)[3]

2. The imperative of the Christian life: Now live like it (6:11–13)

3. Conclusion: We are under grace, not law (6:14)

Verses 1–7 are discussed below; verses 8–14 will be treated in the next unit.

Historical and Cultural Background

The major historical-cultural feature roughly contemporary with the New Testament that informs Romans 6:1–14 is the practice of baptism as an entry rite into a religious community. At least four religious groups required baptism of their new proselytes: rabbinic Judaism, the Dead Sea Scrolls community, the followers of John the Baptist, and the Greco-Roman mystery religions (see the "Additional Insights" section at the end of this unit).

Key Themes of Romans 6:1–7

- The logic of 6:1–14 can be expressed in a syllogism:
  Christ died to sin;
  Christians died with Christ; thus,
  Christians died to sin.[a]
- Sanctification flows from justification.
- Two ages overlap: the age to come has dawned (the indicative of justification) but is incomplete (the imperative of sanctification).
- Three tenses of salvation are intertwined: past (juridical/justification), present (moral/sanctification), future (eschatological).
- The old covenant is characterized by enslavement to sin and death, but the new covenant is characterized by dominion over sin and newness of life.

[a] For this logic, see Moo, *Epistle to the Romans*, 354.

Interpretive Insights

6:1 *Shall we go on sinning so that grace may increase?* Paul here states the issue: does the fact that God forgives us by his grace mean that we should go on sinning so that God's grace will be exalted in continuing to forgive us? This issue arises out of his comments in 5:20–21: sin increases trespass, but grace more than compensates for sin. No doubt the Jews or even Jewish Christians whom Paul encountered in the

The remains of a baptistery from a sixth-century AD church at Philippi

synagogues raised this issue regarding the apostle's understanding of grace and law.

6:2 *By no means! We are those who have died to sin.* Paul's reply is his impassioned *mē genoito* ("May it never be!"). Since Christians have died to sin, how could they possibly continue to live in sin? "Live in sin" is best understood through the lens of the overlapping of the two ages. (1) The age to come has dawned; therefore, Christians have been delivered from the habitual practice of sin—that is, the power and dominion of sin. (2) The age to come is not yet complete; therefore, Christians occasionally might sin in their struggle with the continued presence of sin in this age.

6:3–4 *all of us who were baptized into Christ Jesus were . . . buried with him through baptism.*[4] Verses 3–10 provide Paul's explanation regarding Christians having died and been raised with Christ. Verses 3–7 emphasize that Christians have died to sin in union with Christ's death, while verses 8–10 highlight that Christians have been raised to a new life in union with Christ's resurrection. Verses 3–4 offer a profound thought: Christians died with Christ on the cross and were buried with him by means of their present baptism experience.[5] Paul can say that believers died and were buried with Christ because God is eternal and timeless; therefore past, present, and future are before him at the same time. Thus, God sees Christians (in the future from the cross) as though they were on the cross with Christ (in the past). Moreover, death with Christ in the past is actualized for Christians in their present baptism.[6]

There is an Adamic underpinning to 6:3–5: the lost dominion of the first Adam—life and glory—is being restored to the believer in Christ. Israel fared no better than Adam. The last words in 6:4 indicate this: "so we too might walk in newness of life" (NRSV). As James Dunn notes, "walk" (*peripateō*) is

The rock of Calvary, the traditional place of Christ's crucifixion, is located under the Greek Chapel, shown here, in the Church of the Holy Sepulchre, Jerusalem.

an Old Testament metaphor for obeying the law and statutes of Moses, which was supposed to bring life; instead, such attempts brought death for Israel.[7] But, according to Paul, faith in Christ removes one from the disobedience and death of the old covenant and places one in the new covenant, where there is obedience and life.[8]

6:5 *united with him in a death like his . . . united with him in a resurrection like his.* Verse 5 calls for two comments. First, dying in the "likeness" (*homoiōma*) of Christ's death probably means that the Christian's participation in Christ's death is real but not an exact correspondence, because Christ did not die for his own sins (he had none). Instead, Christ, the perfect one, took our sins upon himself in order to give us his righteousness (see 2 Cor. 5:21). Second, being united with Christ in his resurrection attests to the overlapping of the two ages. Thus, Christ's resurrection inaugurated the age to come, and therefore Christians have resurrection life (a "spiritual resurrection") now; however, the believer's body will not be resurrected until the return of the Lord. Until then, the Christian also lives in this age, an indication that the age to come is not yet fully here.

6:6 *our old self was crucified with him so that the body ruled by sin might be done away with.* Verses 6–10 highlight the fact that Christians have been raised to newness of life in union with Christ's resurrection. The "old self" (literally, "old man") is the first Adam (cf. Col. 3:9; Eph. 4:22), whose primeval action placed this age under the dominion and rule of sin. Christ's death and resurrection defeated the tyranny of sin and initiated the age to come and righteousness. Because the believer is united to

"In Christ" Mysticism

Paul's "in Christ" mysticism is manifest in Romans 6:3–11 in two ways: in Paul's *syn-* ("with") words and in the actual phrase "in Christ Jesus" (v. 11). "In Christ" or some similar wording occurs about 164 times in Paul's letters, signifying the believer's spiritual union with Christ: Christ is in the believer, and the believer is in Christ. On the cross Christ absorbed the Christian's sin and gave his righteousness to the believer. The qualities and abilities of Christ flow to the Christian throughout his or her life. Adolf Deissmann first popularized this notion of "in Christ" mysticism in his book *Paul: A Study in Social and Religious History*, though I believe that Deissmann overstated his case.[a] Related to this are Paul's *syn-* words in 6:4–8, which no doubt are his coinage: "buried with" (*synetaphēmen* [v. 4]); "united with" (*symphytoi* [v. 5]); "died with" (*apethanomen syn*) Christ (v. 8); "crucified with" (*synestaurōthē* [v. 6]); "live with" (*syzēsomen* [v. 8]).

[a] Deissmann, *Paul*, 137–42; see Pate, *End of the Age*, 26–27.

Christ's death and resurrection, the body of sin can be done away with. "Body ruled by sin" does not refer to only the physical body, nor does it suggest that the human body is sin. Rather, the body is the instrument or vehicle by which humans live in the world and through which sin (or righteousness) operates (see 6:12–13). Paul declares that sin's influence over the human being as a body in this world is broken. "Done away with" (NIV mg.: "rendered powerless") represents the verb *katargeō*, which means "to make powerless, ineffective," as we have seen several times before. Thus, the law, the old covenant, and sin no longer have mastery over the believer.

6:7 *anyone who has died has been set free from sin.* Verse 7 might reflect a general rabbinic maxim: "When a man is dead, he is freed from fulfilling the law" (*b. Shabb.* 151b [see Str-B 3:232]). If so, Paul specifically applies it to Christians: in their union with Christ's death and resurrection, they have been delivered[9] from sin and the law.

Theological Insights

At least two key theological insights emerge from Romans 6:1–7. First, the indicative of justification precedes the imperative of sanctification. Otherwise, sanctification could degenerate into legalism. Second, it is no doubt the case that Paul and the early Christians would have been surprised to meet an unbaptized Christian. Not that there were not any; it is just that the normal expectation would have been for believers to identify themselves publicly as followers of Jesus by being baptized (cf. Rom. 10:9–10).

Teaching the Text

An appropriate sermon based on Romans 6:1–14 is "Become What You Are!" Here the speaker could make the first two points shown in the outline above: the indicative of the Christian life (6:1–10) and the imperative of the Christian life (6:11–14). Both of these principles require faith to put into action. The first, the indicative, demands that Christians believe something that they cannot see: they are dead with Christ on the cross, buried with him, and now alive in his resurrection power and life. Yet, even though this cannot be seen with the human eye, the Christian's union with Jesus' death, burial, and resurrection is theologically true because it is the way God perceives the situation, which is ultimate reality.

The second principle, the imperative, likewise requires faith on the Christian's part because living out the death, burial, and resurrection of Christ depends on volition, not feelings. Thus, when believers are tempted, they must will their way through

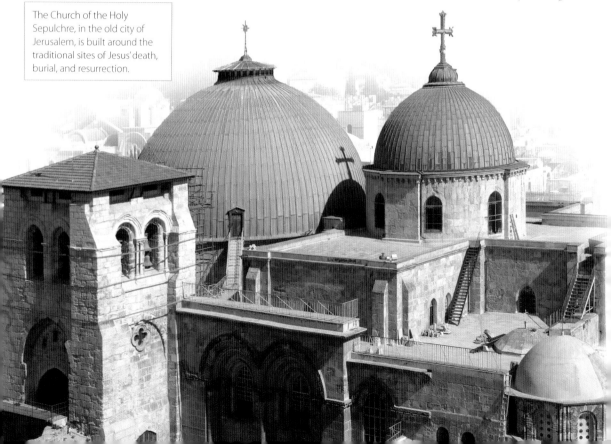

The Church of the Holy Sepulchre, in the old city of Jerusalem, is built around the traditional sites of Jesus' death, burial, and resurrection.

the solicitation relying upon the Holy Spirit to guide them. Or when Christians have God-given tasks, they must perform them whether or not they are excited about them, all the while depending on God's strength to empower them. Or when believers face daunting trials, by faith they must endure those afflictions knowing that God will see them through. And so it is that Christians need to become what they are in Christ. God presents us with tasks and trials and allows us to face temptations in order to develop our faith, which translates the indicative into the imperative.

Illustrating the Text

Sanctification must build on the foundation of justification.

Quotes: Two well-known statements from two famous literary figures could be contrasted with the teaching of a Christian catechism. The Enlightenment skeptic Voltaire (1694–1778) once said sardonically, "God will forgive; that is his business." In poet W. H. Auden's (1907–73) insightful Christmas oratorio *For the Time Being*, Herod contemplates the implications of God coming to earth as a child. Justice, he thinks, will be replaced with "Pity," upsetting what he sees as the natural order: "I like committing crimes. God likes forgiving them. Really, the world is admirably arranged." In sharp contrast, the Westminster Larger Catechism asks, "Wherein do justification and sanctification differ?" It answers, "Although sanctification be inseparably joined with justification, yet they differ, in that God in justification imputes the righteousness of Christ; in sanctification his Spirit infuses grace, and enables to the exercise thereof; in the former, sin is pardoned; in the other, it is subdued" (Question 77).

The Christian must make spiritual progress.

Literature: *The Pilgrim's Progress*, by John Bunyan. In *The Pilgrim's Progress* (1678), after Christian has been to the cross, lost his burden, and fallen asleep on the Hill of Difficulty as a failure, he comes for a time of rest to the House Beautiful. Here, he is fed well, mentored, and encouraged spiritually by four women: Discretion, Piety, Charity, and Prudence. The women also ask him pointed questions about where he came from, how he thinks about his past, and so on in order to ascertain where he stands in his Christian life and to mark his progress in preparation for what is to come.

Television: *The Good Wife*. In the first season of this show, the episode "Heart" has some dialogue not typically heard in popular television shows. Peter Florrick, a politically connected man and the husband of Alicia Florrick, has fallen sexually multiple times and has been in jail for misusing public money. He is now under house arrest, and he is trying to court a black pastor, Isaiah Easton, to make points with the black community. Isaiah instead approaches Peter about his spiritual condition, eventually backing him into a corner and telling him he must want to change; this will come through knowing Jesus and allowing Jesus to effect a complete internal transformation. Otherwise, the pastor assures Peter, his marriage will not heal, nor will life work.

The Backgrounds of Christian Baptism

Several background issues provide additional insight into the Christian practice of baptism.

First, rabbinic Judaism required that Gentiles who wanted to become Jewish be circumcised, embrace the whole Torah, and be baptized (*b. Ker.* 9a). This was in contrast to the less stringent requirements upon God-fearers, those Gentiles who worshiped Israel's God and had to submit to only the Noahic laws or a summary of the Torah.

Second, the Dead Sea Scrolls are fascinating in terms of comparing the Essenes'[1] practice of baptism with that of the New Testament church, especially since both communities claimed to be already participating in the new covenant (see CD 6.19; 19.33–34; Luke 22:20; 1 Cor. 11:25; 2 Cor. 3:1–4:6; Heb. 8–9). Essene proselytes were initiated into the fellowship by submitting to baptism, as were early Christians. Two foundational documents of the Essenes—the *Rule of the Community* (1QS) and the *Damascus Document* (CD) (both ca. 150 BC)—indicate that Essenes celebrated the initiate's baptism as a new-covenant ritual (e.g., 1QS 3.4–9; 4.20–22; 5.13–14). Indeed, the entire community annually renewed its commitment to God by renewing the new covenant. Note, as shown in table 1, how all the covenant components of Deuteronomy inform these two documents, which is reminiscent of my outline of Romans (see "The Genre/Outline of Romans" in the introduction).

Third, there is a strong possibility that John the Baptist, who provided a direct precedent for the inclusion of baptism in the Christian message (Matt. 3; Mark 1:1–11; Luke 3:1–22; John 1:29–34 implicitly), once belonged to the Essene community.[2] If so, his message of a baptism of repentance to Jews may have originated with the Essenes, who also required Jewish initiates to be baptized, a practice normally reserved for Gentiles.

Fourth, it used to be fashionable among scholars to root Paul's message of baptism in the mystery religions. Richard Reitzenstein and Wilhelm Bousset claimed that such wide-ranging religions as the Eleusinian mysteries and the cults of Isis and Osiris, Attis, and Mithras shared two commonalities with Paul's message of baptism (and the Lord's Supper): both focused on the dying and rising of their respective gods/goddesses, and both taught that the initiate enters into mystical union with these gods/goddesses by participating in the sacraments of baptism and the sacred meal.[3] Paul therefore borrowed his concept of baptism from the mystery religions. But more recent scholarship has rightly jettisoned this view, on at least five grounds. (1) The mystery deities' deaths were not vicarious, whereas for Paul, Christ's death was atoning. (2) The mystery deities did not die voluntarily, but Christ did. (3) The deities were mythological figures, but Jesus Christ was a historical person. (4) There

Table 1: The Covenant Structure in the *Rule of the Community* and the *Damascus Document*

Covenant Form	*Rule of the Community* (**1QS**)	*Damascus Document* (**CD**)
1. Preamble	1.2, 16: Yahweh the covenant-keeping God	1.1: Yahweh the covenant-keeping God
2. Historical Prologue	1.16–22: God's mighty deeds of salvation on behalf of the Qumran community	1.1–12: A summary of God's saving acts on behalf of the Qumran community, notably connecting it to the true interpretation of the law by the Teacher of Righteousness
3. Stipulations	Columns 1–4: The general requirements of the law of Moses; columns 5–11: the specific expression of that in terms of loving the Qumran community	3.14–16: The general stipulations of the law of Moses as reinterpreted by the community leaders; 3.17–13.22: the specific application to the Qumran community, including loving the members of the community
4. Blessings and Curses	1.21–4.26: The two spirits: the spirit of disobedience, which leads to the covenantal curses, and the spirit of obedience, which leads to the covenantal blessings	1.10–18: Blessings are pronounced upon the Teacher of Righteousness and his community, while curses are uttered upon those Jews outside the Qumran covenant community.
5. Document Clause	1.1: The book of the Community Rule is the public document stating the terms of the new covenant.	The Damascus Covenant, like the Community Rule, is a public document containing the terms of the new covenant.
6. Appeal to Witnesses	8.1–15: The Qumran community is the testimony of truth to God's faithfulness.	14.1–22 (especially lines 17–22): The Qumran community is the true testimony of God's law.[a]

[a] These outlines are my own suggestions.

was no apocalyptic framework for the mystery religions, but eschatology plays a pivotal role in how Paul interprets Jesus' death and resurrection. (5) The mystery religions never actually taught that their deities were resurrected; rather, they were resuscitated. Not so for Paul and the early church: the bodily resurrection of Jesus Christ was the bedrock of the Christian faith.[4]

In the foreground are steps leading down into a ritual bath known as a *miqvah* (mikveh) located at the archaeological excavations of the Qumran community near the Dead Sea in Israel. Ritual purity could be restored by immersing oneself completely in "living water" such as rivers, springs, the ocean, or baths, like this one, that collected acceptable water. The Dead Sea Scrolls, which document the baptism practices of the Essenes, were found in caves near this archaeological site.

New Dominion as a Blessing of the New Covenant: Alive to God

Big Idea *In the preceding unit we saw that in chapter 6 Paul presents another blessing: the new dominion inaugurated by Christ. Believers enter that new dominion by uniting with Christ's death and resurrection: they become dead to sin, alive to God. Now Paul urges believers to live lives befitting their status as those who have been brought from death to life.*

Understanding the Text

The Text in Context

See Romans 6:1–7 for an outline of Romans 6:1–14.

Historical and Cultural Background

The reader should consult the "Historical and Cultural Background" section presented for Romans 6:1–7 and the "Additional Insights" following that unit.

Interpretive Insights

6:8 *if we died with Christ . . . we will also live with him.* Verse 8 focuses on believers. This verse, like 6:5, taps into the overlapping of the two ages: the age to come came with Christ's death and resurrection, and therefore Christians share in his resurrection life now. But the age to come will not be complete until the parousia (the return of Christ); only then will believers receive

their resurrection body. Both occur by virtue of the believer's union with Christ.

6:9–10 *The death he died, he died to sin once for all.* Verses 9–10 focus on Christ and root the Christian's new dominion over sin in Christ's death and resurrection. "He died to sin" does not suggest that Christ was sinful and died because of it. Instead, it reflects the same sentiment that we saw in 6:5 and the "likeness" (*homoiōma*) of his death: Christ died for our sins; he had no sins of his own. "Once for all" refers to the fact that Christ's death once and for all atoned for sin. This is often referred to by theologians as "the finished work of Christ on the cross."

6:11–13 *count yourselves dead to sin but alive to God in Christ Jesus.* Verses 11–13 record both the indicative and the imperative of the Christian life: since believers are counted as dead, buried, and resurrected with Christ, they should walk in newness of life. In other words, they *should* become (imperative) what they *are* (indicative). Or, more accurately, they should become what they are becoming. Paul uses four imperatives in verses 11–13: "count" yourself dead to sin but alive to God (v. 11); "do not let sin reign" in your present life (v. 12); "do not offer" any part of yourself to sin (v. 13); "offer" your whole self to God (v. 13). "Count" is the same word, *logizomai*, used in 4:1–8 of God counting as righteous those who believe his promise. The same idea is present here in 6:11: Christians should believe it to be true that they have died and been raised with Christ to a new life. Here we see that not only is justification by faith, but also sanctification likewise is by faith. Faith is required to live a holy life because the Christian still lives in this age of struggle.

6:14 *you are not under the law, but under grace.* Verse 14 with 5:20–21 forms an *in-*

Key Themes of Romans 6:8–14

- In baptism believers share in Christ's death, dying to sin, but also they will share in his resurrection, living to God.
- Although believers do not yet have a resurrection body, they share in Christ's resurrection life now by virtue of their union with him.
- Because believers share in Christ's resurrection life now (the indicative), and because they are under grace, not law, they must live as instruments of righteousness, not sin (the imperative).

clusio for 6:1–13 by way of contrast. The pattern is the same pattern that we saw relative to 5:12–21: law leads to sin, which leads to death.[1] By way of contrast, grace leads to righteousness, which leads to life.

The Church of the Holy Sepulchre, or the Church of the Resurrection, in the Old City of Jerusalem is the traditional site of Jesus' death, burial, and resurrection. It has been damaged, destroyed, and rebuilt since its initial construction by Constantine in the fourth century AD. Today, in the rotunda under the dome is the edicule, a small building that covers the site of Christ's tomb. Inside the edicule a marble slab, pictured here in the foreground, covers the traditional spot where Jesus' body lay until he rose from the dead.

Theological Insights

Two theological insights nicely cover Romans 6:8–14. First, the Christian is in union with Christ through the Spirit. Such a connection amounts to the believer having a spiritual parallel life: we are simultaneously on this earth while spiritually in Christ in heaven (compare 6:8–13 with Eph. 2:4–7; Col. 3:1–4). This is not psychological disassociation or medical schizophrenia but a metaphysical reality for the believer. Becoming cognizant of our union with Christ actually makes us better people here in this world. But what exactly does it mean to say that the Christian is in union with Christ? On the one hand, the Christian's union with Christ is not to be interpreted liter-

ally, such as when some theologians in the past claimed that the believer is absorbed into Christ, which produces a light, ethereal form of existence. But, on the other hand, neither should the Christian's intimate association with Christ by the Spirit be reduced to mere figurative language, as even more New Testament scholars are prone to do today. To better understand Paul's mysticism as reflected in his phrase "in Christ," we should turn to Ephesians 1:1–2:7. There we read that the believer has a past, present, and future in the mind of God. Thus, God chose the Christian and the church in eternity past. And God raised the believer to heaven with Christ at his resurrection. Furthermore, in the age to come in heaven,

This relief on the Trajan column, completed in AD 113, shows Roman soldiers using the tortoise formation as a battle tactic. Strict discipline in a soldier's training, individually and as part of a unit, produced the successful fighting force that characterized the Roman legions. It took practice and teamwork to learn to produce this formation, which shielded a unit of soldiers on all sides.

God will showcase the Christian as a trophy of divine grace. While these three tenses are sequential to the human perspective, with God they are simultaneously before him. And it seems that this is the key to understanding our union with Christ. It is in the *mind of God* that the believer has already been raised to the heavens with Christ and seated on the divine throne with him. Thus, we are permitted to say that Christ is in the Christian on earth by the Holy Spirit while the believer is in heaven in the mind of God, where past, present, and future coincide.

Second, discipline is the key to successfully living the Christian life. The militaristic background of Romans 6:12–14 attests to this principle. Rising before the crack of dawn, rigorous regimens of exercise, endless practice drills, unencumbered by civilian life, and committed to one's country to the point of death—these are the ways of disciplined soldiers. And such should be the case for the follower of the cross of Christ. I teach young people at a Christian university, and one of the first things I share with them at the beginning of a course is this spiritual axiom: discipline is the key to living for the Lord (and to passing my course!). I challenge them to dare to believe that discipline leads to delight, that faithfulness brings fulfillment, and that obedience results in joy.

These two theological insights are very much related: drawing on our union with Christ and his Spirit is the way to become disciplined in the Christian life. Discipline without union with Jesus degenerates into the energy of the flesh, but through the power of the indwelling Spirit of Christ, believers discover the resources that they need to say no to sin and yes to God.

Spiritual Warfare

In Romans 6:12–14 Paul employs three ideas with militaristic overtones. (1) The verbs "to be lord over" (*kyrieuō* [v. 14]) and "to reign" (*basileuō* [v. 12]) denote a monarch ruling over a kingdom. (2) The term "instruments" (*melos* [v. 13]) probably indicates weapons of warfare, referring to the believer's body as an instrument of righteousness in the service of the kingdom of God. (3) The emphasis on obedience also suggests a military setting. Thus, 6:12–14 (cf. vv. 4b, 6b, 11) probably draws on a theme familiar to early Jewish and Christian apocalyptic writers: at the end of the age the saints of God will wage war against the sons of evil (see Dan. 7:12; 1QM 15; Rev. 19). For Paul, however, the believer's quarrel is not with flesh and blood, but rather against the spiritual enemies of God (see Eph. 6:10–16). What Romans 6:12–13 thus presents is an internal, spiritual holy war between the dominion of sin and the kingdom of God (hence the injunction to Christians to align themselves with the forces of righteousness). The battle is already won by virtue of the believer's union with Christ's resurrection.

Teaching the Text

In teaching the theological insight of union with Christ, the speaker may want to discuss Romans 6:8–14 in conjunction with Ephesians 1:1–2:7 and Colossians 3:1–4, both of which deal with the Christian's parallel spiritual life in heaven. The teacher could use my suggestion that the past election of believers, their present reign in Christ in heaven, and their future praise to the glory of God the heavenly Father are in the mind of God, before whom all tenses are present at once. This might allay any fear that Paul or Christians are mentally unbalanced in trying to describe their intimate association with Christ by his Spirit! Once again, the key to all of this is for the Christian to believe in that spiritual reality even if they do not feel it. I would use the touching poem "Footprints in the Sand" to drive home the last comment. Even as the author of that piece expressed concern to God that there was only one set of footprints in the sand during the worst times of life, it was in actuality because God was carrying the author. In a similar way, as believers step out in faith to accomplish their tasks, resist their temptations, and endure their trials, it is often only after those actions are completed that Christians come to realize that God was with them all along, empowering their every step.

In driving home the lesson that discipline is the key to the Christian life, the teacher could read in staccato-like style the imperatives in verses 11–13: "Count yourselves dead to sin but alive to God!" "Do not let sin reign" in your present life! "Do not offer" your body to sin! "But rather offer yourselves to God!" Uttering these commands in that way gives the impression that the audience is in boot camp. This can be reinforced by listing the militaristic images in verses 12–14: "be lord over," "reign," "instruments of righteousness," "obedience." The effect of pronouncing these commands and military images with the tone of a drill sergeant can make the passage come alive. Reciting a hymn like "Onward Christian Soldiers" could further rouse the congregation to a newfound discipline to be soldiers of the cross. Furthermore, the teacher of this passage can encourage listeners that after a while discipline becomes a way of life, a matter of habit. Difficult but good habits that we develop over time become second nature to us, and we feel incomplete when we neglect them, however briefly that may be.

Illustrating the Text

Christians are called to union with Christ.

Film: *Avatar.* James Cameron's Oscar-winning movie (2009) provides a nice il-lustration for grasping the spiritual parallel life of the Christian in union with Christ. The lead character in the movie undergoes moral struggle in deciding between being faithful to his military commander's orders to forcibly relocate the "Na'vi" people and defending these creatures he has now come to love. That struggle is intensified by the fact that the hero of the story can change from his earthly body into the incredible body of the Avatar. But the more he lives in his newly found parallel universe, the more he wants to leave his frail earthly body. This is similar to Christians who live life on earth with all of its struggles while longing to assume their heavenly existence. They are caught between two worlds, two ages. But the more believers concentrate on their spiritual existence in heaven in the mind of God, the more effectively they can serve Christ and his church on earth.

Discipline is key to the Christian life.

Personal Testimony: A profound experience early in my life has taught me (Marvin) the importance of discipline in the Christian life. When at age sixteen I sensed that the Lord was calling me into the ministry, I reasoned that if I was going to preach the Bible then I needed to start studying the Bible for myself and not depend solely on the preacher's sermons or on devotional booklets. So I began getting up an hour earlier each day in order to read and meditate on the Bible and then pray. I did this for about a year, but without getting anything out of my study times. I wanted to quit my devotional time with the Lord on a number of mornings because it seemed so dry. Yet I did stick with my daily devotional plan for a whole year without any noticeable change.

After that first year of Bible study, however, something amazing happened—the Bible and prayer came alive to me! In fact, my Bible study became so exciting that I began to take notes on each verse I contemplated, eventually filling whole notebooks on one biblical book after the next. I sometimes think that the Lord was testing me during that first year to see if I really meant business. By the power of the Spirit I remained disciplined during the dull times of my early devotional studies, which eventually gave way to what has for forty-two years become the most meaningful part of my day. And that morning talk with God has in turn increased spiritual discipline in my life. I believe it will do the same for others.

Hymn Text: "Onward Christian Soldiers," by Sabine Baring-Gould.

> Onward, Christian soldiers,
> marching as to war,
> with the cross of Jesus
> going on before.
> Christ, the royal Master,
> leads against the foe;
> forward into battle
> see his banners go!
>
> Onward, Christian soldiers,
> marching as to war,
> with the cross of Jesus
> going on before.
>
> At the sign of triumph
> Satan's host doth flee;
> on then, Christian soldiers,
> on to victory!
> Hell's foundations quiver
> at the shout of praise;
> brothers, lift your voices,
> loud your anthems raise.
>
> Onward, Christian soldiers,
> marching as to war,
> with the cross of Jesus
> going on before.

The Christian's New Dominion:

Dedicated to Righteousness

Big Idea *The familiar contrast that runs from 5:12 through 6:14 continues in 6:15-23: the law of Moses cannot rescue from sin, which leads to death, but the grace of God in Christ engenders righteousness, which leads to eternal life. The new component of this contrast in 6:15-23 is Paul's usage of the metaphor of slavery.*

Understanding the Text

The Text in Context

Romans 6:15-23 continues Paul's enumeration, begun in 6:1-14, of the blessings of the new dominion as a part of the new covenant. Romans 6:1-14 was devoted to the believer's deliverance from the law, sin, and death by virtue of union with Christ's death and resurrection. Now 6:15-23 discusses how dedication to righteousness is incumbent upon believers as participants in the new dominion. The general outline of 6:15-23 is quite similar to 6:1-14:

1. The question: Since Christians are not under the law, can they live in sin? (6:15a)
2. The answer: Absolutely not! (6:15b)
3. The explanation: Everyone has a master, either sin or righteousness (6:16)
4. The application: Choose to be a slave to righteousness (6:17-23)

More specifically, I suggest that verse 15 and verse 23 form an *inclusio* for verses 15-23:

Not under the law, but under grace (6:15)

Not under the wages of sin (brought about by the law), but under the gift of eternal life (brought about by God's grace in Christ) (6:23)

The net result of this *inclusio* is that it imprints the intervening verses 16-22 with a now familiar contrast: law brings sin, which leads to death, but grace brings obedience/righteousness, which leads to eternal life. This basic contrast undergirds the antitheses that occur in verses 15-23, as laid out in table 1.

Historical and Cultural Background

The main historical and cultural background for Romans 6:15-23 is the ancient institution of slavery. Slavery was a basic reality in Greco-Roman society, reaching its highest proportion in the first centuries BC and AD. According to varying estimates, from one-fifth to one-third of the population was enslaved. The slave revolts in Italy and Sicily in the late republic confirm widespread social discontent at the time. Cato's account of slave labor in agriculture reveals a taskmaster mentality reminiscent of slavery prior to the Civil War in the United States. Seneca relates that a proposal in the Roman senate that slaves be required to follow a distinctive dress code was defeated lest the slaves discover how numerous they were. Slavery was a despicable institution, devaluing the dignity of the human being. The legal status of a slave was that of a "thing." Aristotle defined a slave as "living property" (*Pol.* 1.2.4–5) and said "a slave is a living tool and the tool a lifeless slave" (*Eth. nic.* 8.2). In short, the slave was subject to the absolute power of the master. Although early Christianity did not officially challenge slavery (to do so would be to invoke the wrath of mighty Rome against Christians), the gospel did sow the seeds that have contributed toward the overthrow of that hideous institution. Indeed, Paul's

Key Themes of Romans 6:15–23

- There is no middle ground when it comes to spiritual slavery: either one is enslaved to the master of sin or one is captivated by the master of righteousness.
- Being under the law of Moses means being in bondage to sin, which results in eternal death, but being under the grace of God in Christ brings righteousness, which results in eternal life.
- The indicative of deliverance from sin leads to the imperative of dedication to righteousness.

claim in Galatians 3:28 that in Christ there is "neither slave nor free," his holding masters accountable in Ephesians 6:5–9, and his strong encouragement to Philemon to let his slave Onesimus go free hopefully will contribute to the downfall of slavery.[1]

Interpretive Insights

6:15 *Shall we sin because we are not under law but under grace?* The question here is very similar to 6:1: both verses expose a misguided inference from Paul's message of justification by faith apart from the works of the law that it does not matter how Christians live, since they are under grace. The difference between the two verses is that the assumption in 6:1 errs by

Table 1: The Antitheses in Romans 6:15–23

6:15 (*inclusio* A)	Slaves to (under) the law of Moses	Slaves to (under) grace	
6:16	Slaves to sin and death	Slaves to obedience and righteousness	
6:17	Past: slaves to sin	Present: obedient from the heart	Indicative
6:18	Past: slaves to sin	Present: set free to be slaves to righteousness	Indicative
6:19	Past: you offered your bodies to sin	Present: offer your bodies to sanctification/holiness	Imperative
6:20–22	Past: slaves to sin, fruit of impurity, shameful	Present: slaves to God, set free to sanctification/holiness	Indicative
6:23 (*inclusio* A′)	Wages of sin (brought about by the law) bring death	Gift of God (grace in Christ) brings eternal life	

suggesting that the more we sin, the more God's grace increases, while the perspective in 6:15 goes astray in assuming that since believers are no longer under the law, they are under no obligation to live a holy life (cf. 3:5–8). Robert Jewett notes that the phrase "under the law" probably originated as a slogan coined by Judaizers in the Galatian crisis who followed early rabbinic interpretation of Exodus 19:17 and Deuteronomy 4:11 to the effect that the law was hanging in a threatening manner over their heads.[2] As we have seen before and will see again in 6:23, the pattern that Paul presumes in 6:15 is this: law leads to sin, which brings death; on the other hand, God's grace in Christ brings obedience and righteousness, which lead to life. But grace should not be turned into licentiousness; hence Paul's vitriolic answer to the question of whether a believer has no obligation to live a holy life: *mē genoito* ("May it never be!"). That is, on the contrary, Christians are obligated to live holy lives.

6:16 *you are slaves of the one you obey.* Here Paul explains his answer in 6:15: there is no middle ground when it comes to sin or righteousness, for one is either a slave to sin or a slave to holiness. Many commentators note that the phrase *eis hypakoēn* ("unto obedience") occurs here and in Romans 1:5; 15:18; 16:26, in each case as shorthand for the "obedience of the faith" of the Gentiles. Thomas Schreiner catches the significance of this: "The liberation of the Roman Christians from the power of sin fulfills God's promises of liberation made to Israel in the OT. Israel would no longer be in exile when their sins were forgiven and they were free from bondage to other nations (cf. Dan. 9). Believers in Christ have now experienced the freedom and joy promised in the OT."[3] In other words, Gentiles are now experiencing the end-time conversion promised in the Old Testament, and this *before* the restoration of Israel. Indeed, Gentile Christians are participating in the true restoration of Israel.

6:17 *though you used to be slaves to sin.* Paul points to his audience's conversion story to support the principle in 6:16: in the past the Roman Christians were enslaved to sin, but now in Christ they are slaves to obedience. As R. A. J. Gagnon notes, two contrasts between the old covenant and the new covenant are alluded to in the phrases "wholeheartedly obeyed" and "the form

This stone carving depicting a sculptor at work is from a larger relief on a sarcophagus that shows a sculptor's workshop (Ephesus, second century AD). In Rome many of the skilled artisans were slaves that were formerly prisoners of war who had practiced these trades in their home countries. Paul uses the metaphor of slavery to help his readers think about what has mastery over them—sin or righteousness—and challenges them to be slaves to righteousness.

of teaching." The former contrasts the old covenant and its law written on tablets of stone with the new covenant and the obedience to God from the heart because of the indwelling of the Holy Spirit.[4] The latter is the *typos didachēs*, the type or imprint of teaching to which the believers are delivered (a divine passive for God): obedience to God by faith apart from the works of the law fulfills the promise of the new covenant, and this by Gentiles![5]

6:18 *You have been set free from sin.* As in 6:17, Paul expresses the Roman Christians' conversion in the indicative mood: their break with enslavement to sin is manifest in their present enslavement to righteousness.

6:19 *offer yourselves as slaves to righteousness.* Now Paul employs the imperative mood to challenge his audience to continue to be slaves to holiness. Two comments can be made about this verse. First, Paul speaks in the general sense in 6:19a: because human nature is weak in understanding spiritual matters (in this case the obligation incumbent on Christians to live holy lives), imperfect analogies can be of help in illuminating theological truth (in this case the metaphor of slavery).[6] Second, now that Paul has made clear in Romans 1–5 that righteousness is imputed to believers apart from their own merits, the apostle has no qualms about saying in 6:19b that righteousness produces ethical results: sanctification or holiness (*hagiasmos*).

6:21 *What benefit [fruit] did you reap at that time from the things you are now ashamed of?*[7] In 6:20–22 Paul returns to the indicative mood in contrasting the Roman Christians' former lifestyle of impurity and shame with their present dedication to holiness/sanctification. I suggest that the "fruit"

(*karpos*) of impurity that Paul has in mind in 6:21 was stimulated by the law of Moses, since he uses the same word for the law's work in 7:5: "For when we were in the realm of the flesh, the sinful passions aroused by the law were at work in us, so that we bore fruit for death."

6:23 *For the wages of sin is death, but the gift of God is eternal life.* Jewett makes an important comment about the contrast here between the wages or earnings (*opsōnion*) of sin as being death and God's gift as being eternal life: "In Paul's view, these gifts [salvation and mercy] were granted without regard to whether or not one has fulfilled the requirements of the law. In Romans 4:4, this was connected to the matter of wages [*misthos*] in a manner that provides the premise of 6:23: to one who works, his wages are not reckoned as a gift but as his due."[8] I agree, and I suggest that "wages of sin" in Paul's mind is related to the "works of the law," by which no one will be justified, because the law reveals, even stirs up, sin (3:19–20). If I am correct on this point, then 6:23 does indeed form an *inclusio* with 6:15: law leads to sin, which brings death, but grace leads to righteousness, which brings eternal life in Christ Jesus our Lord.[9]

Theological Insights

Three theological insights impress me when reading Romans 6:15–23. First, as Jesus said, "No one can serve two masters" (Matt. 6:24). Paul agrees, for all humans serve one of two lords: sin or righteousness. Anticipation of the outcome of those two dominions—sin brings death, and righteousness brings life—should be ample motivation to choose the latter rule. Second, being delivered from sin by grace should motivate one to be dedicated to holiness. Third, neither legalism nor licentiousness should characterize Christians; rather, what should characterize them is faith leading to sanctification.

Teaching the Text

Two sermon themes come to mind based on Romans 6:15–23. The first one is "Whose Slave Are You?" This provocative title could lead into discussion of the familiar pattern that we have noted a number of times now: law leads to sin, which leads to death, but grace brings righteousness, which brings life. Martin Luther's trenchant treatise against Erasmus, *On the Bondage of the Will* (1525), rejected Erasmus's attempt to steer a middle way between Augustine's emphasis on total depravity and Pelagius's on free will—that is, that humans have the ability to turn toward or away from salvation. Luther wrote, "We neither accept nor approve that middle way. . . . We must therefore go all out and completely deny free choice, referring everything to God."[10] It does seem that Paul's sentiments lie with Luther, since

according to the apostle, the human will has only the capacity to disobey the law (especially if the law stirs up the will to rebellion in the first place). Second, "What Happened at the Cross Stays at the Cross!" is a sermon that conveys a double meaning: our sins were buried with Christ at the cross so that no one can bring them back up to shame us, and our sinful lifestyle should remain a thing of the past, buried at the cross. Here again is tension between the indicative and the imperative. The former taps into the fact that Jesus' death was for our sins, his burial removed those sins

The Greek god Dionysus, incorporated into the Roman pantheon and renamed Bacchus, is depicted by this terracotta bust from Rome (AD 50–100). He was the god of wine and of all the carousing that occurs with overindulgence. Festivals to honor him often deteriorated into orgies, and the Roman Senate outlawed these celebrations in the second century BC. Perhaps some of the Roman believers had been slaves to impurity by participating in Bacchian worship prior to their conversions.

from human purview, and his resurrection is proof positive that God accepted his Son's sacrifice for our sins. The last becomes a spiritual reality when believers moment by moment draw upon the resurrection power of the risen Christ by his Spirit to replace disobedience with obedience to God.

Illustrating the Text

Everyone serves one lord: sin or righteousness; there is no middle ground.

Film: *The Two Towers.* This movie (2002) is the second installment of the film adaptation of J. R. R. Tolkien's novel *The Lord of the Rings.* The scene showing the struggle between good and evil in the character of Gollum is powerful. Gollum was originally named Smeagol, a hobbit of the River-folk, but later is called Gollum because he has a habit of making a "horrible swallowing noise in his throat." Gollum has lived longer than expected because he possessed the One Ring. It becomes his obsession, and he pursues it for decades after losing it to Bilbo Baggins. This obsession has caused a split in his personality. While his one side, Smeagol, has vague recollections of beauty, love, and friendship, Gollum, his other side, is deceitful and violent. Then Smeagol's dual personalities begin to converse, even battling each other. The battle is poignant and vividly illustrates the principle that good and evil cannot comfortably coexist, that there is no middle ground. Gollum loses the battle to evil.

Deliverance from sin motivates the believer to make a commitment to holiness.

Literature: *A Tale of Two Cities,* by Charles Dickens. The well-known novel (1859), set in London and Paris before and during the French Revolution, follows the lives of its main characters through a series of events, many of them catastrophic. Sydney Carton, a shrewd British lawyer, endeavors to redeem his poorly lived life out of love for the wife of a virtuous French aristocrat who has fallen victim to the excesses of the French Revolution. In an act of sacrificial love, Carton ultimately gives his life for the husband so that the couple might escape together. Although Dickens seldom mentions God, and never as a personal saving force, his books often tell stories of redemption.

Freedom from the Law through Christ, Enslavement to the Law through Adam

Big Idea *Paul focuses on the Mosaic law's relationship to new dominion in Christ. A stark contrast emerges: freedom from the law because of union with Christ versus enslavement to the law because of union with Adam. This relationship is paradoxical: union with Christ and with Adam both pertain to the Christian (7:13–25 will expound on this).*

Understanding the Text

The Text in Context

Romans 6:23 pronounces that the Christian is in union with Christ and therefore free from the law. This is illustrated in 7:1–6. But things are not so simple. Because this age is dominated by Adam's sin, the law and death remain a present reality (7:7–12).

We may outline 7:1–6 as follows:

Romans 7:1–6	Law	Grace
7:1–4a	Bound to the old husband	United with the new husband
7:4b–5	Fruit of death	Fruit of life
7:6	Letter / old covenant	Spirit / new covenant

To outline 7:7–11 (v. 12 is a concluding statement qualifying vv. 1–11) I have chosen to use comparisons with the Adam narrative, especially Genesis 2–3. These comparisons are shown in table 1.

Table 1: Romans 7:7–11 and the Adam Narrative in Genesis 2–3

Romans 7:7–11	Genesis 2–3
7:7: "You shall not covet."	3:1–6: Adam and Eve desired to be like God and broke God's commandment not to eat of the tree of knowledge of good and evil.
7:8: Sin is personified.	3:1–6: The serpent personifies sin.
7:9a: "I was alive apart from the law."	1:26–2:14: Only Adam and Eve were alive before the advent of the law, God's commandment not to eat from the forbidden tree (2:17).
7:9b–10: "I died."	2:17: God warns that if the couple eats from the tree of knowledge of good and evil, they will die (which did happen).
7:11: "Sin . . . deceived [*exapataō*] me" (cf. 2 Cor. 11:3; 1 Tim. 2:14). (The verb *exapataō* is an intensive form of *apataō*.)	3:13 LXX: "The serpent deceived [*apataō*] me [Eve]."

Historical and Cultural Background

The Jewish view of marriage differed from the Greco-Roman understanding of that institution. According to Jewish law, only the husband could divorce his wife (see Deut. 24:1), and therefore the woman was bound to her husband as long as he lived; in Roman law, either mate could initiate divorce.[1] It is clear that in the illustration used in Romans 7:1–6, the man holds all the cards in the marital relationship, as the woman is not free to remarry until her husband dies.

Interpretive Insights

7:1–4a *the law has authority over someone only as long as that person lives.* The rabbis said that a person who has died is free from obligation to the Mosaic law (*b. Shabb.* 30a). Jews, of course, knew this, but former Gentile God-fearers, such as those who constituted the majority of the Roman house churches, likewise would have been aware of such teaching because prior to their conversion to Christ they worshiped in the synagogues. The "law," then,

Key Themes of Romans 7:1–12

- Paul uses the analogy of the death of a spouse in marriage to illustrate the believer's death to the law by virtue of being united with Christ (7:1–6).
- Paul draws on the story of Adam's disobedience to the law to communicate humanity's continued union with Adam (7:7–12).

to which Paul refers in 7:1 is the Torah. The specifics of Paul's analogy of marriage are not quite clear. In 7:1–4a Paul talks about the husband dying, and then in 7:4b he talks about Christians dying. Most likely Paul has in mind the following identifications: law = first husband; wife = Christians; new husband = Christ. In any case, Paul's point is clear: Christians died to the law when they died with Christ.

When Paul uses marriage to illustrate the authority of the law, he is thinking of the regulations of marriage under the Mosaic law, where a woman was bound to her husband as long as he lived. Under Roman law, only Roman citizens could have a legal marriage, and the wife remained under her father's authority rather than her husband's. This made divorce much easier, since the wife did not become a member of the husband's family and could get her dowry back if the marriage ended. Pictured is a funerary monument showing a married couple with their young son (AD 25–50, Rome).

7:4b–5 *fruit for God . . . fruit for death.* Paul speaks about two different kinds of fruit, one that comes from being freed from the law, and one that comes from trying to obey the law. He says clearly that the law stirs up sin, which brings the fruit of death (cf. 3:20–21; 4:15; 5:12–14, 20). But union with Christ's resurrection brings the fruit of righteousness and life to the believer (recall 6:15, 20–23).

7:6 *we serve in the new way of the Spirit, and not in the old way of the written code.* As many commentators note, this verse contrasts the ineffective law of the old covenant with the obedience that the Spirit engenders for those in the new covenant (cf. 2:29). Interestingly, back in verse 5 Paul uses the same word that he has used before relative to the negative side of the law: *katargeō* ("work" [compare 7:5 with 3:31; 4:14; 6:6]). Moreover, the unusual term Paul uses for the new covenant in 6:4, *kainotēs* (NIV: "new life"), also occurs here in 7:6 (NIV: "new way").

7:7a *Is the law sinful? Certainly not!* In this verse and in 7:12 Paul offers a much-needed positive assessment of the law of Moses. Here he praises the law by making the point negatively. "Is the law sinful?" he asks. From everything that he has said about the law up until this point, one might expect him to answer yes. But Paul thunders forth with his emphatic *mē genoito*—absolutely not! Rather than being sin, the holy law of God exposes sin.

7:7b *if the law had not said, "You shall not covet."* Following Paul's positive assessment of the law in 7:7a is an autobiography of his experience with the law, expressed in the first-person singular, in 7:7b–12. The identification of the "I" in these verses is debated (see sidebar), but we can say that in 7:7b Paul alludes to Adam's and Eve's disobedience of the Torah in its summarized form: "You shall not covet." Thus, the big picture of 7:7–12 is that the believer is still influenced by Adam's realm and therefore struggles with enslavement to the law.

7:8 *But sin . . . produced in me every kind of coveting.* Verse 8 depicts sin acting like a person and thereby distinctly brings to mind the personification of sin in the form of the serpent in Genesis 3:1–6. Just as the serpent pounced on God's commandment to Adam and Eve not to eat of the forbidden tree, thus creating in them the opposite effect, so sin jumps at the opportunity to use God's holy law to stir up in humans the opposite of holiness—every kind of evil desire.

7:9a *Once I was alive apart from the law.* The only persons in

In Romans 7:8, sin is personified, perhaps reminding the reader of the serpent in Genesis 3:1–6. The serpent seized the opportunity afforded by God's command to Adam and Eve, producing in them the desire to taste what was forbidden. This late twelfth-century AD stone capital from a cloister in Catalunya shows the serpent with Adam and Eve.

history who were alive before God's law was introduced into the world were Adam and Eve, however short that period might have been. The first couple was created and placed in the garden to care for it (Gen. 1:26–2: 15). Only after that did God issue his commandment regarding the forbidden tree (Gen. 2:16–17). The Adamic background of 7:9a works better than the other major theory regarding the sentence "I was once alive apart from the law," which is that it reflects the bar mitzvah of the Jewish male who, at the age of thirteen, was pronounced a "son of the Torah." However, Jewish boys were instructed in the law from their earliest years (cf. 2 Tim. 3:15; Josephus, *Ag. Ap.* 2.178; Philo, *Embassy* 115, 210), not just beginning at the age of thirteen.

7:9b–10 *sin sprang to life and I died.* The narrative of Genesis 2–3 continues to govern Paul's thought in 7:9b–10. His words "I died" draw upon Genesis 2:17 and God's warning to the first couple that if they ate from the tree of the knowledge of good and evil, they would die. That indeed happened: Adam and Eve ate from the restricted tree, and they died spiritually on the spot (see Gen. 3:7–19). Later they died physically, setting mortality in motion for the human race. The paradox is striking: the divine commandment given to preserve their lives spiritually and physically became, in the hands of the serpent, the occasion for death. Moreover, Paul taps into Israel's history: the law of Moses, which was supposed to bring life, actually resulted, when in the hands of sin, in death for that nation.

7:11 *sin . . . deceived me.* Paul uses an intensive form of the word "deceived" (*exapataō*), applying to himself a word used in Genesis 3:13 LXX (*apataō*) of Eve in the

The "I" of Romans 7:7–12

The identification of the "I" in 7:7–12 is debated, but many Pauline scholars take it to signify three experiences. The first referent is Paul himself. Thus, here Paul speaks of his experience with the law. Before he met the risen Christ, his assessment of the law was positive (see Gal. 1:13–14; Phil. 3:3b–6), but after that encounter his perspective changed. Now he saw the law as preparation for the gospel, with the negative purpose of exposing human sin in order to drive people to Christ.

Second, the "I" probably also alludes to Israel's constant disobedience to the law in the Old Testament. This was so from the beginning at Mount Sinai when, just as Moses was delivering God's law, Israel was worshiping the golden calf.

Third, and most pronounced, are echoes of Genesis 2–3 throughout 7:7–12. In 7:7 Paul harks back to God's commandment in the garden of Eden that the first couple not eat from the tree of knowledge of good and evil (Gen. 2:17). Adam and Eve disobeyed, coveting to be like God. Paul's words here may be the first record of what became a fairly pervasive belief in rabbinic literature: the Torah was present with Adam in the garden. Indeed, many thought that the Torah existed before creation (e.g., *Tg. Yer.* Gen. 3.24; *y. Hag.* 2.77c; *Gen. Rab.* 8.2). Moreover, many Jews believed that God's commandment to Adam was representative of the whole Torah (e.g., *4 Ezra* 7.11; *Tg. Neof.* Gen. 2.15; *Gen. Rab.* 16.5–6; 24.5; *Deut. Rab.* 2.25; *b. Sanh.* 56b). Also, Second Temple Judaism considered coveting, forbidden in the tenth commandment, to be the root of all evil (e.g., Philo, *Creation* 152; *Decalogue* 142, 150, 153, 173; *Apoc. Mos.* 19.3; *Apoc. Ab.* 24.10; cf. James 1:15).

garden (cf. 2 Cor. 11:3; 1 Tim. 2:14), making it all the more likely that Genesis 2–3 continues to weigh heavily in Paul's argument in 7:7–12. As he mentioned in 7:8, so the apostle repeats in 7:11 more intensely that the serpent/sin in the garden and sin in humanity perverted the holy law of God into disobedience. It is difficult to say precisely what Paul means by "sin . . . deceived me" by perverting the law into death and not life. For Adam and Eve, it meant that the serpent duped Eve into breaking the divine commandment in the hope that she and Adam could be like God. But that action in reality brought about their death.

And Paul once thought (and Israel tragically still did) that one could obey God's law and live. This for Paul was an attempt to be justified before God based on righteousness by works (cf. Rom. 9:3–10:4). But this is the deception of sin, since no one can be accepted before God on that basis.

7:12 *the law is holy*. Verse 12 is a concluding statement qualifying verses 1–11 and is reminiscent of verse 7. Here in verse 12, Paul reiterates that the law is not the culprit in bringing about disobedience to God; sin is the perpetrator of disobedience. Rather, the law (the entire law of God to Moses) or commandment (a summary command of that law) is holy, righteous, and good. The law originated from God's holy character and prescribes just conduct, and it is good because it is applicable to all humanity, proceeding as it does from the ultimate good—God himself.

Theological Insights

Three theological insights surface in Romans 7:1–12. First, the Christian's union with Christ produces a holy lifestyle, something that the law cannot do. Second, this age and the old covenant still tug at the believer's heart. Therefore, the believer's obedience to God will not be perfect in this life. Third,

the law is holy because it is an expression of the character of God. The problem with the law is that sinful human nature perverts it into the instrument of death.

Teaching the Text

Two sermons emerge from Romans 7:1–12. The first one, based on 7:1–6, could be entitled "Freedom from the Law because of Union with Christ." The three-point outline in the chart above (old husband versus new husband; fruit of death versus fruit of life; the letter of the old covenant versus the Spirit of the new covenant) would nicely guide that message. We might imagine the before-the-law and after-the-law relationships concerning the Christian as being like an abusive marriage. It is a well-known and tragic fact that women who are involved in abusive marriages often have great difficulty leaving the relationship. We might compare that to the believer who wants to go back to the suppressive relationship of living under the law. Only the fruit of death awaits that decision. But the Christian needs to see the potential for life in the new covenant in Christ in the way a downtrodden wife needs to see the hope for a better life apart from her abusive husband.

Second, a message entitled "Romans 7:7–12 and the Hijacking of the Law by Sin" could be preached by rehearsing Paul's

The grave of John Newton is located in the churchyard of the Parish Church of St. Peter and St. Paul, Olney, England, where he served as curate between 1764 and 1780. The epitaph, which he composed himself, speaks of his transformation from sinner to servant by God's mercy. It reads, "John Newton, Clerk, once an infidel and libertine, a servant of slaves in Africa, was, by the rich mercy of our Lord and Saviour Jesus Christ, preserved, restored, pardoned, and appointed to preach the faith he had long laboured to destroy."

argument regarding those verses. The main point to make is that the serpent/sin turned the holy law of God into the occasion for Adam and Eve's sin. And so it is today: the sin principle in all humans distorts the good laws of God into disobedience, even the idolatry of trusting in our own good efforts to commend us to God. Thus it is sin that is the culprit, not the law.

Illustrating the Text

We are free from the law because we have been joined with Christ.

Spiritual Biography: The story of the life of British cleric and poet John Newton (1725–1807) powerfully illustrates the liberty found in Christ, as do the words of his ever-popular hymn "Amazing Grace."

The early life of George Müller (1805–98) is probably less well known than his later life, when he established orphanages in England. He is often thought of as the "man who got things from God," as he experienced many answers to prayer while opening and maintaining those orphanages. However, his story is far more complex than those dramatic accounts. Müller spent many of his early years living a sinful lifestyle, undeterred even by his mother's death. Invited one evening to a Christian meeting at a friend's house, he experienced something that he said he had been seeking his whole life. That was the beginning of Müller's freedom from the bondage of sin.

Sin (this age and the old covenant) tugs at the heart.

Church Fathers: Augustine's *Confessions* provides a classic illustration of prohibitions awakening in humans the desire to transgress those very laws. Augustine tells about a time as a boy when he joined his friends in stealing pears, not because they wanted them to feed the pigs, but because they wanted the pleasure of disobeying the law.

Literature: "The Man That Corrupted Hadleyburg," by Mark Twain. This parabolic tale (1899) tells the story of a town whose motto has been "Lead us not into temptation." The people in Hadleyburg live smugly, sure of their virtue and their spiritual standing. One night a stranger, seeking revenge for an offense by the town, drops off a sack at the home of Mr. and Mrs. Richards, claiming that it is filled with gold. He directs that the sack be given to the man who purportedly gave him some good advice and twenty dollars in a time of need. Anyone claiming to know what that advice was should write it down, he tells the couple, and hand it to Reverend Burgess, who will open the sack at a public meeting and find the actual words of advice inside along with the gold. The gold will be given to the person who knows the right answer. The temptation that comes upon this town proves irresistible, and what ensues is proof, in the author's thinking, that everyone can be bought. A short version of a PBS film based on the story was released on DVD in 2004.

Hymn Text: "Come Thou Fount of Every Blessing," by Robert Robinson. Robinson (1735–90) writes, with what could be read as muted desperation, "Prone to wander, Lord I feel it; Prone to leave the God I love." In light of that reality, he cries, "Here's my heart, O take and seal it; Seal it for the courts above."

"Wretched Man That I Am": Battle of the Two Ages within the Christian

Big Idea *Paul shares how the battle of the two ages rages within him. The good law of God exposes sin, only for that sin to drive him to disobey the law, which results in death. He documents his struggle between wanting to obey the law and being unable to do so because his sinful nature drives him to disobedience.*

Understanding the Text

The Text in Context

Before outlining Romans 7:13–25, I must summarize the hermeneutical debate regarding these verses. This enigmatic passage has generated at least three major interpretations: (1) it speaks of Paul's, and all Christians', present engagement with sin;[1] (2) it refers to Paul's past life as a rabbi, one checkered by frustration with the law;[2] or, it points back to Paul's preconversion days of discontent with the law, as seen through his Christian eyes;[3] (3) it draws on life under the law as experienced by the unregenerate.[4] I will briefly address these in reverse order.

The third view has against it the undeniable fact that the present tense is consistently used throughout 7:14–25 (in contrast to the past tenses in 7:7–13), thus pointing to Paul's present Christian experience, not to his bygone preconversion days. Moreover, this interpretation stumbles on 7:25b, "So then, I myself in my mind am a slave to God's law, but in my sinful nature a slave to the law of sin," a poignant description of Paul's contemporary experience.

The second interpretation is also contradicted by the sustained usage of the present tense in 7:14–25, not to mention Paul's positive assessment elsewhere of his preconversion ability to keep the law (Gal. 1:14; Phil. 3:6b).

That leaves us with the first view. The only substantial disagreement that can be voiced against this understanding of the passage is that it seems to paint too negative a picture of the Christian life, especially when it is compared with the victorious presence of the Spirit in the Christian as recorded in Romans 8:1–16. However, this criticism is more apparent than real. Actually, 7:14–25 portrays a bad side and a good side to a Christian, and their admixture is the result of the overlapping of the two ages. This produces within Christians a deep-seated struggle between obedience and disobedience to God. Stated another way, the eschatological tension resident within Christians is evidence that they are genuinely saved. This also explains the divided "I" that is pervasive in 7:14–25: it is not anthropological dualism (the sinful body versus the mind) but rather eschatological dualism that informs Paul's and every Christian's struggle. The believer is caught between the two ages, between wanting to obey God (the age to come) and not in fact doing so (this age).

Now I supply an outline of Romans 7:13–25:

1. The thesis statement: The good law of God brings sin to light only to have that sin drive Paul / the Christian to disobey the law of Moses (7:13)
2. The development of the thesis (7:14–24)
   a. The "divided I" (7:14–20)
   b. The two laws, a summary of vv. 14–20 (7:21–24)
3. The transition statement (7:25)
   a. Anticipation of Romans 8 and the victory over sin (7:25a)
   b. Summary of Romans 7 and the struggle with sin (7:25b)

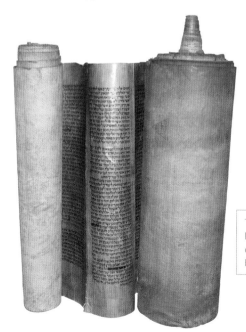

Key Themes of Romans 7:13–25

- The main theme that undergirds this passage is that the struggle within Paul and the Christian is the result of the overlapping of the two ages: the already (the age to come that has dawned in Christ) and the not yet (this age is still a present reality).
- Since Christians are participants in the age to come, they desire to obey God. Yet since they still are participants in this age, they have a sinful nature, which wars against their desire to obey God.

Romans 7:14–20 compares the already and the not yet as laid out in table 1.

The reader may also notice that 7:14–17 parallels 7:18–20:

> The good law versus sinful Paul (7:14 // 7:18)
>
> Paul wants to do the good but does not do it (7:15–16 // 7:19)
>
> Sin drives Paul to do the bad (7:17 // 7:20)

The following parallels between the two laws can be seen in 7:21–25:

The age to come has dawned—the good law of God (7:21a)	This age is still in effect—the principle (power) of sin (7:23a)
I want to do the good (7:21b)	Another law is at work (7:23a)
My inner being delights in God's law (7:22)	Sin within me wages war against the good and drives me to sin (7:23b)
The law of my mind (7:23b)	The body of death (7:25b)

Historical and Cultural Background

The main information in Romans 7:13–25 that finds parallels approximate to Paul's

This handwritten Torah scroll from the 1740s is on display at the Ramhal Synagogue, Acre, Israel. In the previous passage Paul described the law as holy because it expresses the character of God. Here he continues to characterize the law as spiritual and good.

Table 1: The Already and the Not Yet in Romans 7:14–20

Romans 7:14–20	The Already: The Age to Come Has Dawned	The Not Yet: This Age Is Still in Effect
7:14	The law is spiritual.	But I am unspiritual (of the flesh).
7:15–16	I want to do the good law of God.	But I do not do the good.
7:17	(Implied) I want to do the good.	But sin living in me does not let me do the good.
7:18	I desire to do the good.	But I am sinful.
7:19	I want to do the good.	But I do evil.
7:20	I want to do the good.	But sin living in me does not let me do the good.

day is the internal struggle to do good, only to capitulate to evil. Judaism had its duel of the two impulses (see, e.g., *4 Ezra*). So did the Greco-Roman writers. Thus Ovid wrote, "I see and approve the better course, but I follow the worse" (*Metam.* 7.21). And Epictetus wrote, "Every sin involves a contradiction. For since he who sins does not wish to sin, but to be right, it is clear that he is not doing what he wishes" (*Disc.* 2.26.1–2; cf. 2.26.4–5). Much further removed from Paul's understanding is the Platonic notion of *soma-sema*: the body is the prison of the soul because the two are at war with each other.

The theme of the internal struggle between good intentions and wrong actions reflected in Romans 7 can be found in the writings of earlier Greek and Roman authors. For example, in Ovid's *Metamorphoses*, Medea, while pondering her attraction to Jason, muses, "I see and approve the better course, but I follow the worse" (*Metam.* 7.21). Shown here is a statue of Ovid in Ovid's Square, Constanța, Romania, designed by Ettore Ferrari in 1887. The Roman poet was exiled to the ancient Greek colony of Tomis, now Constanța, in AD 8 by Emperor Augustus.

Interpretive Insights

7:13 *Did that which is good, then, become death to me? By no means!* Verse 13 states the thesis of 7:13–25: the law of Moses is not culpable for bringing death to the human race. Rather, the law exposed sin, only for sin to use the law to bring about transgression and death. Sin's perversion of the good law of God is thereby shown to be the real culprit behind death.

7:14–20 *the law is spiritual; but I am unspiritual . . . I have the desire to do what is good, but I cannot carry it out.* The thesis of 7:13 is developed in 7:14–23, which divides into two parts: the divided "I" (vv. 14–20) and the two laws (vv. 21–23). Because verses 14–20 contain parallels (see the outline above), we may conveniently treat the paired verses together (vv. 14, 18; vv. 15–16, 19; vv. 17, 20).

Verse 14 states that the law is spiritual, meaning that its origin is the Holy Spirit (cf. Ps. 19:7–11; *t. Yad.* 2.14; see Str-B 3:238). But Paul is "fleshly" (*sarkinos* [NIV: "unspiritual"]), which means that Paul/everyone is sinful (for the same use of *sarkinos*, see 1 Cor. 3:1). Verse 18 essentially repeats the sentiments of 7:14, where Paul contrasts the good (law) with his sinful nature.

Verses 15–16, 19 focus on Paul as the divided "I," wanting to do right (obey the law) but doing wrong. I understand these verses to reflect the Christian struggle between good and evil as born out of the overlapping of the two ages within the believer. Christians want to obey God because they are citizens of the age to come, the kingdom of God. But because Christians still live in this present age of sin, they oftentimes do wrong.

Verses 17, 20 focus on the culpability of sin in the Christian's inner battle: it is sin that drives Paul and all Christians to do wrong. In saying this, Paul is not avoiding the personal responsibility that all believers have to resist sin and do right; he is simply saying that in and of themselves, humans are no match for sin (but the Spirit is, as Rom. 8 will explain).

7:21–23 *I delight in God's law; but I see another law at work in me.* Verses 21–23 summarize 7:13–20 by rooting the divided "I" in the two laws that govern the spiritual realm: the law of Moses (God) and the law or power/principle of sin. Before spelling out the distinctive actions associated with those two laws, I first must mention that biblical interpreters are divided over whether the second law (that of sin) is the Mosaic law or in this case *nomos* should be translated as "principle" or "power." James Dunn, for example, says that *nomos* is the Mosaic law throughout 7:13–25.[5] He takes the law of God (Moses) to be now freed from this age, and Israel's misuse of it to create social barriers. This New Perspective on Paul looks like this:

This Age	Age to Come
The law of Moses misused to produce sin	The law of Moses freed from sin's misuse

In my view, since Romans 3:27–31 records three different renderings of *nomos* (law of Moses, principle/power, and covenant), I see no reason why *nomos* could not be rendered in different ways in 7:21–23: the law of Moses and the principle/power of sin. Thus, 7:21–23 documents the contrasting two laws: the law of God, which Paul desires to serve in his inner being/mind, versus the law/principle of sin, which Paul actually serves in his body of sin/death (7:24). Paul's dichotomy between inner being/mind and body of sin/death sounds Platonic, but as we noted above, it is more eschatological in orientation:

This Age	Age to Come
Body of sin/death (the physical body is not evil, but is the instrument of sin and death)	New nature ("inner being")/mind (on the new nature, cf. 2 Cor. 4:16; Eph. 3:16; on the renewed mind, cf. Rom. 12:1–2)

So the Christian's struggle proceeds from the reality of living simultaneously in both worlds.

7:24 *What a wretched man I am!* The wretched status of Paul and the Christian is the state of being torn between the age to come and this age, between the new nature and the old nature.

7:25 *Thanks be to God, who delivers me through Jesus Christ our Lord!* Verse 25 is a transitional statement: verse 25b summarizes the plight of the believer as spelled out in 7:13–24, while verse 25a anticipates the victory of the new nature in Christ by the power of the Spirit, as is beautifully explained in Romans 8.

Theological Insights

We meet with two theological truths in Romans 7:13–25. First, the law of Moses is not to blame for death. But, since in the order of salvation history the law still belongs to this age, it suffers from misuse by sin, resulting in death. Second, the struggle in the Christian life is normal. It means that the entrance of the new nature into the believer at conversion no longer allows sin to go unhindered.

the kingdom of God is not yet complete. Moreover, in Romans 8 Paul asserts that the indwelling Spirit's power can make the difference in the believer's life for godliness. The Holy Spirit can succeed in leading Christians into a life of holiness in a way the Old Testament law could not. This too is a sign that the age to come has dawned in Jesus the Messiah.

Teaching the Text

A good sermon idea based on Romans 7:13–25 is to develop Martin Luther's famous description of the Christian as *simul justus et peccator*—saint and sinner at the same time. The message could discuss the divided "I" in 7:14–20 and the two laws in 7:21–24. Regarding the former, three statements summarize Paul's comments there. First, the law is good, but Paul (and all of humankind) is evil. Second, Paul nevertheless deeply desires to do the good. Third, he does the bad anyway because sin drives him to do so. The discussion of two laws in 7:21–24 registers a similar plight. Thus, because the age to come has dawned, Paul and all Christians are in Christ and possess the Spirit and therefore have a desire and a capacity to serve God. But because the age to come is not complete, the law of the sinful flesh still resides in the believer's heart, hampering the attempt to obey God. But rather than bring the Christian to despair, such a struggle signals the good news that the believer is, after all, a citizen of the age to come, even though

When Paul talks about being "sold as a slave to sin" in Romans 7:14, he creates an image that his readers would understand. This is a bill of sale for a six-month-old slave girl from third-century AD Greece. The purchase price was fifteen silver pieces.

Illustrating the Text

Christians have an appetite for holiness but a proneness to sin.

Poetry: "Holy Sonnet XIV," by John Donne. One of the most articulate expressions of the Christian's dilemma is this sonnet by the metaphysical poet Donne (1572–1631), who also became the dean of St. Paul's Cathedral in 1621. Donne led a conflicted early life, after which he was converted. The sonnet describes the believer's struggle between the old and new natures:

> Batter my heart, three-person'd
>   God; for you
> As yet but knock, breathe, shine,
>   and seek to mend;
> That I may rise, and stand,
>   o'erthrow me, and bend
> Your force, to break, blow, burn,
>   and make me new.
> I, like an usurp'd town, to another
>   due,
> Labour to admit you, but O, to no
>   end.
> Reason, your viceroy in me, me
>   should defend,
> But is captived, and proves weak or
>   untrue.
> Yet dearly I love you, and would be
>   loved fain,
> But am betroth'd unto your enemy;
> Divorce me, untie, or break that
>   knot again,
> Take me to you, imprison me, for I,
> Except you enthrall me, never shall
>   be free,
> Nor ever chaste, except you ravish
>   me.[6]

Film: *The Passion of the Christ*. This film (2004) is a powerful and graphic portrayal of the suffering and death of Jesus. In one scene, Jesus is praying in the garden of Gethsemane, clearly in great distress over his approaching death. At this moment, Satan appears in the form of a woman with a man's voice and asks Jesus if he believes that one man can sustain the burden of the sin of all humankind. The question is not sincere, as Satan's questions never are, and he proceeds to answer it himself by saying that no one can do it, for "the burden is too heavy." Jesus is face down on the ground when a serpent slides out from under Satan's robe and makes its way toward Jesus, touching his hand. Satan smiles, as if sure that Jesus has been defeated. But Jesus then rises from the ground and crushes the head of the serpent. He gains new resolve to do what he must: sacrifice himself for the sins of the world in obedience to his Father.

Film: *The Apostle*. In this film (1997), Euliss "Sonny" Dewey (played by Robert Duvall) is a married, charismatic preacher in Texas with a wandering eye and a number of other serious faults. Nevertheless, he keeps witnessing to the power of God, eventually moving to Louisiana, where he starts a church with a racially integrated congregation. He even succeeds in leading a violent racist to the Lord. Although Sonny is maddeningly flawed, there seems to be little question that in this film Duvall, who wrote and directed the film, is exploring the mixed nature of God's children.

The Holy Spirit and the Blessings of the New Covenant

Big Idea *Second Temple Judaism longed for the return of God's Spirit, as evidenced in Joel 2:28–29. Paul's use of the term "Spirit" in chapter 8 signifies that Joel's prophecy has come true. The chapter is chock-full of covenantal blessings of the Spirit—given to Gentiles, no less, because they have accepted Jesus as the Christ.*

Understanding the Text

The Text in Context

Romans 8:1–17 discusses six new-covenant blessings to the believer that proceed from the Spirit: justification (v. 1), obedience (vv. 2–8, 12–13), indwelling (vv. 9–10), resurrection (v. 11), adoption (vv. 14–16), and inheritance (v. 17). Romans 8:18–30 adds one more new-covenant blessing of the Spirit, glory (through suffering), which I will discuss in the next unit.

Historical and Cultural Background

The background of the term "adoption" (*huiothesia*), first appearing in Romans 8:15, is twofold. According to Roman custom, a father could legally adopt a boy outside the father's family as a son. When the boy reached the age of thirteen or fourteen, the father bequeathed to his adopted son the father's inheritance.[1] Moreover, although adoption as a legal act was not a Jewish institution, Jews did sometimes raise the children of others, treating them as their own (Gen. 15:2–4; Esther 2:7; cf. Exod. 2:10). But even more important is the fact that Israel was adopted as God's son in the Old Testament (e.g., Exod. 4:22; Jer. 3:19; 31:9; Hos. 11:1). This background may be the nearest influence on Romans 8:15.

Interpretive Insights

8:1 *there is now no condemnation for those who are in Christ Jesus.* The adverb "now" signifies that the age to come dawned with the coming of Christ and the Spirit. For those in Christ, the condemnation that the law brought no longer applies to them. Instead, Christians now have end-time justification. As we saw in 1:17, justification is the saving act of God associated with the restoration of Israel and the new covenant. Paul declares in 8:1 that that reality now belongs to Gentile Christians.

8:2–4 *the law of the Spirit who gives life has set you[2] free from the law of sin and death.* The identity of the two laws mentioned in 8:2 is much debated. Some think that both occurrences of *nomos* refer to the Torah. Thus, Paul would be contrasting the Torah as the instrument of sin and death in this age with the Torah of the age to come, which can now be fulfilled by the power of the Holy Spirit.[3] But the majority of commentators, rightly I believe, take the "law" of the Spirit to be the principle/power of the Spirit (not the Torah), while the second law is the inept Torah. We saw Paul use *nomos* in differing ways in 3:27–31; 7:21–23, and apparently he does the same here in 8:2–4. Thus, 8:2 asserts that the Spirit has brought the life of the new covenant, whereas the Torah of the old covenant brings only sin and death.

Verse 3 points to the ultimate reason for the failure of the Torah: it is incapable of engendering obedience because of the sinful nature of humans. But God solved the dilemma of how to empower humans to obey him by sending his Son as a human to defeat sin. Christ's sacrificial death defeated sin and replaced it with obedience in the Christian. The new-covenant prophecies of the Old Testament (e.g., Jer. 31:31–34; Ezek. 26:26–28) associated the new covenant with obedience from the heart accomplished by the Spirit.

Verse 4 declares hope to be a present reality: Christians by the indwelling

Key Theme of Romans 8:1–17

- The Holy Spirit grants to Christians numerous blessings of the new covenant: justification, obedience, indwelling, resurrection, adoption, and inheritance.

Spirit obey the just requirement (*dikaiōma*) of the law. A comparison of this statement with Romans 13:8–10 and Galatians 5:14 suggests that Paul believed that love for others (and God) is the ultimate fulfillment of the essence of the law (cf. Mark 12:28–31).

8:5–8 *The mind governed by the flesh is death, but the mind governed by the Spirit is life and peace.* A chart best captures Paul's sentiments in 8:5–8, after which I offer three brief comments. There is a running contrast in these verses between the two dominions of flesh and Spirit.

	Flesh/Law	Spirit
8:5	Sinful nature: mindset of flesh	Spiritual nature: mindset of Spirit
8:6	Result: death	Result: life
8:7–8	Hostile, unpleasing to God	(Implied) Obedient, pleasing to God (cf. 8:1–4)

First, in these verses Paul speaks in the indicative mood, not the imperative. Thus, he is describing the spiritual reality: those

Prior to the temple, the Israelites offered their sacrifices at the tabernacle according to the requirements of the Mosaic law. This model of the tabernacle at Timnah, Israel, shows the altar outside the tent of meeting. Because following the law could not overcome sin, God sent his Son as a sin offering.

following the flesh displease God and die, but those following the Spirit obey God and live. Second, a comparison of 8:5–8 with chapter 7 (and even 8:3–4) makes it clear that it is the Torah that stirs up the flesh to sin (though sin is to blame, not the law). Third, 8:5–8 therefore reverses the old-covenant blessings and curses:

Old Covenant	New Covenant
Law leads to death	Spirit leads to life

8:9–10 *if indeed the Spirit of God lives in you . . . if Christ is in you.* A third blessing of the new covenant is spelled out in 8:9–10: the indwelling of the Holy Spirit. The Spirit's residence in the Christian should be understood against the backdrop of the covenant formula: "I will dwell among the Israelites, and I will be their God" (Exod. 29:45; cf. Exod. 25:8; Lev. 26:12; Jer. 32:38; Ezek. 37:27; 2 Cor. 6:16; Rev. 21:3).

For Paul, there is no in-between: either one has the Spirit and is therefore a Christian or one does not have the Spirit and is therefore not a Christian (8:9). Verse 10 should be translated as a concessive: "But if Christ is in you, then even though your body is subject to death because of sin, yet your spirit is alive because of righteousness" (NIV mg.). The body here is the vehicle of sin that will culminate in death. Nevertheless, Christians will live eternally in a resurrection body (see 8:11) because they possess the Holy Spirit, who places believers in union with Christ's righteousness and life.[4]

8:11 *he who raised Christ from the dead will also give life to your mortal bodies.* Here is the fourth blessing of the Spirit of the new covenant: the future resurrection of the believer. According to Ezekiel 36–37,

one of the attendant circumstances of the new covenant will be the resurrection of Israel as a nation—that is, the restoration of Israel. Alongside the future hope of Israel's national resurrection, Daniel 12:1–3 places the individual resurrection body of the believer. Paul's Jewish heritage combined those two aspects, and so does the apostle in Romans 8:11. The Spirit who raised Jesus from the dead will also raise Christians from the dead. For Paul, Jesus' resurrection began the true restoration of Israel, one that includes Gentiles and the future hope of the resurrection body.

8:12–13 *if by the Spirit you put to death the misdeeds of the body, you will live.* Verses 12–13 switch to the imperative side of the Christian life: by the power of the indwelling Spirit Christians are to mortify, or kill, the acts of the sinful nature. The pattern is the same here as in 8:5–8: the sinful nature leads to death, but the Spirit empowers believers to overcome their sinful desires and thereby live. No doubt the Torah is still in Paul's mind in 8:12–13, in that the law stirs up the sinful nature, but the Spirit defeats it.

8:14–16 *For those who are led by the Spirit of God are the children of God.* Verses 14–16 register a fifth blessing from the Spirit of the new covenant: adoption (*huiothesia*) as the children of God (8:15). We saw earlier that the background of adoption most familiar to Paul was God's adoption of Israel as his sons (Exod. 4:22; Jer. 3:19; Hos. 11:1; Rom 9:4). Furthermore, James Scott has demonstrated that the restoration of Israel would include the restoration of Israel to the status of children of God.[5] For Paul, therefore, to apply the label "children of God" to Gentiles would have been dramatic: Gentile Christians are included in the restoration of Israel! The Holy Spirit bears witness with the spirit of Christians (the only instance where "spirit" in Rom. 8 is the human spirit) that they are the children of God (8:16). So incredibly intimate is the believer's relationship with the heavenly Father that by the Spirit the child of God calls him "Abba," an Aramaic term of endearment for a father roughly equivalent to "daddy" (in Mark 14:36 Jesus calls God "Abba"; in Gal. 4:6 Christians call God "Abba").[6]

8:17 *heirs of God and co-heirs with Christ, if indeed we share in his sufferings.* Here Paul mentions a sixth blessing from the Spirit of the new covenant: inheritance ("heirs" [*klēronomos*] and "co-heirs" [*synklēronomos*]). In the Old Testament the inheritance of Israel was the land of Canaan, but in Second Temple Judaism inheritance was also

At age 46, Tiberius was adopted by Augustus as his son and therefore legitimate heir. This bronze bust of Tiberius was created to commemorate that event, which took place in AD 4. Tiberius became emperor after the death of Augustus and ruled during the time of Christ (AD 14–37). Paul tells Roman believers that the Holy Spirit brought about their "adoption to sonship" (Rom. 8:15), that they are children of God, and if they are children, then they are heirs.

understood to involve the spiritual realm (4 Macc. 18:3; *Pss. Sol.* 14.5–10; *1 En.* 40.9; *2 En.* 9.1). For Paul, the heavenly inheritance is now the possession of the Christian (Eph. 1:1–3) and is the culmination of the Abrahamic covenant (Gal. 3:14, 29), which includes being heir of the world. But such a glorious inheritance comes with a cost: sharing in Christ's suffering; this will be the theme of 8:18–30. Thus, 8:17 serves as a transition between 8:1–16 and 8:18–30.

Theological Insights

A couple of spiritual truths stand out in Romans 8:1–17. First, the Holy Spirit is the key to the Christian life, blessing the believer with justification, obedience, indwelling, and the hope of the resurrection, confirming inclusion in God's family, and making Christians participants in the heavenly inheritance. These blessings of the new covenant far outdo the failures of the old covenant. Second, Jesus Christ's death and resurrection and the Holy Spirit's residence in believers grant them unparalleled spiritual intimacy with God as their Father, even as Abba.

Teaching the Text

Perhaps the best sermon to preach on Romans 8:1–17 is one that covers the six blessings from the Spirit of the new covenant. The point of emphasis of such a message is to highlight the reality that these six end-time blessings of the new covenant belong now to the believer. First, the Spirit is the one who places the sinner into Christ at the moment of faith, at which time God declares that person justified in anticipation of judgment day (8:1). Second, the Spirit is the one who fulfills the prophecies of the new covenant: through Christ he resides within the people of God, giving them the power to obey all the law of Moses envisioned but without being under the law (8:2–8, 12–13). This is important to note, because Paul is not antinomian; that is, he

does not advocate that the believer has no responsibility to live a holy life. Rather, he knows well that the flesh is incapable of obeying the law. Only through the enabling Holy Spirit does one find the capacity to please God. Third, the presence of the Spirit of God, as mentioned above, fulfills the long-awaited Old Testament promise that God's Spirit would be poured out beyond Israel onto all flesh (compare 8:9–10 with Joel 2:28–29)—that is, those who believe in Jesus Christ. Fourth, the presence of the Spirit within the Christian is the down payment of the future resurrection body to be given to the believer at the return of Christ (compare 8:11 with 2 Cor. 5:5; Eph. 1:13–14). Fifth, the indwelling Spirit gives believers the inward sense that God is their heavenly Father (8:14–16). Sixth, the Spirit

This painting by Duccio di Buoninsegna of Siena (fourteenth century AD) shows the Holy Spirit being poured out on the day of Pentecost.

is also proof that believers are destined for heavenly glory, all the while empowering them to suffer with Christ (8:17).

Illustrating the Text

While Christians battle the old nature, the Holy Spirit gives them strength.

Literature: *The Pilgrim's Progress*, by John Bunyan. This book (1678) is excellent for illustrating theological tenets in Romans, particularly those scenes in the Interpreter's House before Christian loses his burden at the cross. There are seven such teaching scenes in this section. In one of these, Christian sees the Interpreter lead a man to the door of the Palace, where many men are gathered, apparently wanting admission. Also at the door are men in armor appearing to prevent their entrance, acting threateningly and potentially harmfully. This intimidates those standing there except for one man who, with a great look of purpose on his face, asks that his name be written down. Taking his sword in his hand, he puts on a helmet and rushes at those who would keep him out. The battle is fierce, and the man is wounded, but he fights until he wins entrance and finds eternal glory inside. The lesson seems clear; a fierce war may be waged between the old and the new natures, but pressing on will ensure victory.

Christ's sacrifice and the Spirit's indwelling give us intimacy with Father God.

History: When Oliver Cromwell served as Lord Protector of England, a young soldier was sentenced to die when the curfew bell rang. His fiancée begged Cromwell to save his life by giving him a pardon, but he refused. As the church sexton over and over pulled the rope at curfew, the bell remained silent. The young man's fiancée had climbed into the bell tower and wrapped herself around the clapper to keeping it from striking the bell. She refused to let go in spite of the injuries she was incurring. When she finally climbed down to the place of execution, Cromwell, deeply impressed by such heroic and sacrificial love, commuted the sentence. The story is immortalized in a poem called "Curfew Will Not Ring Tonight," by Rose Hartwick Thorpe, which illustrates vividly Christ's sacrifice on the cross, which likewise keeps us from judgment.[7]

The Spirit and the Glory of the Age to Come and the New Covenant

Big Idea *Paul showcases another blessing from the Spirit of the new covenant: glory. More particularly, the Spirit is a sign of the glory of the age to come and the new covenant. And yet, that glory occurs in the midst of this age and suffering.*

Understanding the Text

The Text in Context

1. Suffering/glory (8:18)
2. Three groanings (8:19–27)
   a. Creation groans (hope for the revelation of the children of God) (8:19–22)
   b. Believers groan (firstfruits of the Spirit / by hope we were saved) (8:23–25)
   c. The Spirit groans (the Spirit helps us in our weaknesses) (8:26–27)
3. Suffering/glory (8:28–30)[1]

Each of these points—suffering/glory, the groaning of creation, the groaning of Christians, and the groaning of the Spirit—includes blessings of the age to come and the new covenant that have already dawned for Christians but are not yet complete.

Historical and Cultural Background

1. Verses 17–18 and verses 28–30, preoccupied with the themes of suffering and glory as they are, form an *inclusio* around Romans 8:19–27. These two themes combined to form a prominent notion in Jewish apocalyptic writers, who believed that the suffering of the people of God in the present age would bring them glory in the age to come (e.g., *1 En.* 1.2–8; 96.3; *2 Bar.* 48.49–50; 51.3–11; *4 Ezra* 7.15–16, 95–98). Yet for Paul, as for the early Christians, the relationship between suffering and glory no longer was consecutive (the one would lead to the other) but rather was dialectical (the one is intermingled with the other). Because of the death and resurrection of Christ, the glory of the age to come has broken into this age of suffering. Thus, the two are intertwined in the Christian's life, as

Romans 8:17–18 makes clear. God's glory is already the possession of the believer, even in this age of suffering. But the divine glory is presently invisible, residing in the Christian's heart. Only at the parousia (the return of Christ) will it be revealed publicly in the believer's resurrection body (see 2 Cor. 4:16–5:10; Phil. 3:20–21; Col. 3:1–4).

Romans 8:28–30 presents the same pattern: divine glory is the present possession of the believer, but it coexists with suffering. The former aspect is delineated in 8:29–30, which showcases a dazzling display of theological terms to describe the present aspect of the Christian's salvation ("foreknew," "predestined," "called," "justified," "glorified"). It is not accidental that "glory" (8:30) is the term used to conclude that list, for it returns the reader to the thought that initiated the paragraph (8:17). The latter aspect, suffering, is the conceptual antecedent of the words "in all things God works for the good of those who . . . have been called according to his purpose" (8:28). In context, the "all things" are the afflictions that God uses (8:17–25) to conform believers to the image and glory of Christ (8:29).[2]

2. Romans 8:22, at first glance, is enigmatic: "We know that the whole creation has been groaning as in the pains of childbirth right up to the present time." Moreover, Paul attributes humanlike qualities to creation when he asserts, "The creation waits in eager expectation for the sons of God to be revealed" (8:19 [cf. the similar description in 8:21]). The longing of the

Early Western Christian artists often depicted Christ on his throne ruling the world, as shown in this reproduction of a painting on parchment by Haregarius (AD 844–51). This artistic representation became known as *Christ in Majesty* or *Christ in Glory*. One day believers will share in Christ's glory.

Key Themes of Romans 8:18–30

- Suffering with Christ in this age assures the Christian of the glory of the age to come and the new covenant.
- Creation groans for the new creation.
- Christians groan for the resurrection body.
- The Spirit groans in prayer on behalf of the believer.

cosmos for the final glorification of the people of God and the simultaneous restoration of the earth is a dominant refrain in Jewish apocalypticism and is succinctly summarized in the modern expression *Urzeit-Endzeit* ("original time–end time"). This means that the end of time, or the age to come, will recapitulate the paradisiacal setting of the beginning of time (see Isa. 11:6–8; 65:17–25; Ezek. 34:25–27; *Jub.* 1.29;

Romans 8:18–30

1 En. 45.4–5; 2 Bar. 32.6; 49; 73.5–7; 4 Ezra 6.16; 7.25, 119–26; cf. Rev. 21–22).

Interpretive Insights

8:18 *present sufferings are not worth comparing with the glory that will be revealed in us.* Verse 18 continues the theme of suffering leading to glory from 8:17. Three comments can be made about this theme. First, as noted earlier, suffering for righteousness' sake in this age leading to the glory of the age to come is apocalyptic in orientation. Second, it is also rooted in the new covenant. Paul makes this clear in 2 Corinthians 3:1–5:21, where he talks about the glory of the new covenant over the old covenant (3:1–4:6) but says that such a new covenant is rooted in suffering (4:7–5:21). Third, in participating in the suffering/glory paradigm, the Christian participates in Christ's suffering and glory (compare Rom. 8:17–18 with 2 Cor. 3:1–5:21; Phil. 3:10, 21; Col. 3:4; 2 Thess. 2:14; Heb. 2:7–10).

8:19–22 *creation waits in eager expectation . . . the whole creation has been groaning.* The suffering/glory theme now gets expressed in terms of the groanings of creation (8:19–22), of the Christian (8:23–25), and of the Spirit (8:26–27). Regarding the groaning of creation, the future glory of the nonhuman world is linked to the return of Christ and the glorious resurrection body that awaits the believer (8:19, 21b). The assumption here is that the new creation that Christ brings will restore lost paradise—the *Urzeit-Endzeit* pattern (compare Gen. 1–3 with Rev. 21–22). All of creation has been groaning for that day since Adam's sin brought the divine curse on the earth (compare Rom. 8:20–22 with Gen. 3:17).[3] Perhaps, as in Romans 5:12–14, we are to see

in Romans 8:19–22 the dynamic of the law of the old covenant stimulating Adam's sin and the resulting curses on humanity as well as on the nonhuman world. But already in the garden of Eden God held out the hope that the Messiah would come and restore all things (compare Rom. 8:20 with Gen. 3:15, the *protoevangelion*).[4]

8:23–25 *we ourselves, who have the firstfruits of the Spirit, groan inwardly as we wait.* The groaning of the Christian also evokes the suffering/glory paradigm. Thus, believers groan because they, like creation, are subject to Adam's curse in this present evil age. But Christians also groan because they know that the indwelling Spirit is proof that the glorious resurrection body certainly awaits them. And such a hope sustains the believer in the meantime (8:24–25). So the groaning is both negative (suffering in this age) and positive (glory in the age to come).[5]

Two more comments can be made about the believer's glorious body, both connected to the new covenant. First, the future glorious resurrection was associated by the prophets with the restoration of Israel and the arrival of the new covenant (e.g., Ezek. 36–37; Dan. 12:1–3). Second, Revelation 21–22, the quintessential description of the future resurrection and the new creation, intimately associates such realities with the new covenant: "God's dwelling place is now among the people, and he will dwell with them. They will be his people, and God himself will be with them and be their God" (21:3). Such a classic formulation of the covenant is not far removed from the doctrine of the indwelling of the Spirit, who provides certain hope for the glorious resurrection and new creation.

8:26–27 *the Spirit himself intercedes for us through wordless groans . . . in accordance* *with the will of God.* These mysterious and wonderful verses point out that the indwelling Holy Spirit groans on behalf of the believer. Such groaning, like that of creation and the Christian, is evidence of the overlapping of the two ages. The Spirit groans on behalf of the believer who suffers in this age. But the Spirit's groaning is also a sign that the age to come has dawned. Thus, the Spirit intercedes with the Father when the believer is not sure what the will of God is. This understanding, rather than ecstatic speech, is most likely what Paul has in mind in 8:26–27. Access to the throne of God via the guidance of the Spirit assures the Christian that God hears now and will grant the glory of his Son (cf. 8:30).

8:28 *in all things God works for the good of those who love him.* We earlier noted that the suffering/glory paradigm imprints 8:28–30. The "all things" consists of the sufferings of this age (8:19–27), which God uses to conform the believer to the image of his Son, in whose glory the believer shares (8:30).[6]

8:29–30 *those God foreknew he also predestined . . . those he predestined, he also called; those he called, he also justified; those he justified, he also glorified.* The cluster of theological terms in these verses— "foreknew," "predestined," "called," "justified," "glorified"—assures believers that God's gracious election will see them through the purging process so that they become like Christ, with all the glory that entails. We should also note that several words here convey a covenantal nuance. First, "foreknow" (8:29) is rooted in God's covenantal love for Israel (e.g., Gen. 18:19; Exod. 33:13; Ps. 18:43; Prov. 9:10; Jer. 1:5; Hos. 13:4). Second, to "love" God (8:28)

Divine Foreknowledge

Debate rages over the word "foreknew" (Rom. 8:29). Does it mean that God *knew* beforehand or *chose* beforehand those who would be saved? It appears that *proginōskō* refers to God's choice beforehand (cf. Acts 2:23; Rom. 11:2; 1 Pet. 1:2, 20). Another possibility is that Paul is referring to God's corporate election—the choice of Israel or the church. However, in light of Romans 9:6–29 and God's choice there of individuals, the corporate view of election probably is ruled out. (These three views of foreknowledge—Calvinist, Arminian, and corporate—will be discussed further in the commentary on Romans 9:6–29.)

is the stipulation of the old covenant (e.g., Exod. 20:6; Deut. 5:10; 6:5; 7:9; Josh. 22:5; 1 Kings 3:3; Neh. 1:5). Third, Jesus the "firstborn" Son (8:29) alludes to Israel as God's firstborn son (e.g., Exod. 4:22; *Pss. Sol.* 18.4). But Paul applies these terms to Christ and his followers as participants of the new covenant.

Theological Insights

Several theological truths encourage the reader of Romans 8:18–30. First, suffering does not negate the fact that a person is a Christian; rather, it proves that the Christian's profession of faith is genuine. Second, Christians should have respect not only for the human body but also for the nonhuman creation, for both will participate in the new creation. Third, the Holy Spirit intercedes for believers even when they do not know what God's will is. Fourth, God's saving action on behalf of his people will keep them secure for all eternity.

Teaching the Text

A good way to preach or teach Romans 8:18–30 is to use the outline that I suggested (see "The Text in Context" section above). The suffering/glory motif is the key to interpreting the three groanings in these verses because it forms an *inclusio* for the paragraph: suffering now in this age ensures the glory of the age to come. But since the overlapping of the two ages governs Paul's thought here, we could just as well say that the glory of the age to come has broken into this present age. Thus, because of the first coming of Christ there is a sense in which inanimate creation inherently grasps that its own destiny is tied into the future resurrection of the children of God at the parousia. That is, when Christ returns and his followers are resurrected, so too the old creation will be transformed into paradise regained.

Thus, the groaning of the cosmos is both positive and negative: negative because creation suffers under the curse of Adam's sin, but positive because it longs for the new creation. And Christians understand that the dawning of the age to come at the first coming of Christ ensures for them a future body like Jesus' glorified body. So believers' groaning is negative in that they are subject to Adam's sin, but positive in that they know their destiny is celestial. Furthermore, the Spirit's groaning is testimony to the overlapping of the two ages. The Spirit groans within believers because they struggle over what to pray for in this present evil age. This is the negative aspect of the Spirit's groaning. But such intercession of the Spirit on behalf of believers is also positive in that the heavenly Father knows the mind of the Spirit as to what is best for each struggling Christian and answers accordingly.

Illustrating the Text

Both creation and Christians groan for release from suffering and frustration.

Film: *Cocoon*. In this science-fiction movie (1985), aliens are portrayed as having human bodies clothed in an invisible, but clearly glorious form, illustrating the "now but not yet."

Creation and mankind groan because of Adam's sin. In Genesis 3:17 God says, "Cursed is the ground because of you; through painful toil you will eat food from it all the days of your life." This section of a sarcophagus shows God handing over the symbols of work to Adam and Eve (AD 330–40).

Poetry: "Who Am I?," by Dietrich Bonhoeffer. This poem is found in Bonhoeffer's *Letters and Papers from Prison*. Bonhoeffer (1906–45) was a great German pastor, theologian, and writer who was martyred for his resistance to Adolf Hitler and the Nazis. He is known for his unflinching courage while in a concentration camp where he died, but this poem candidly and poignantly expresses his anguish and self-doubt in the midst of suffering.

Poetry: "Sympathy," by Paul Dunbar. Dunbar (1872–1906) was the first African American to gain national recognition as a poet. Maya Angelou (b. 1928), a contemporary African American writer, titled her autobiography with a line from this poem, "I know why the caged bird sings." The whole poem could be used as an illustration, but the last stanza is particularly apt in describing suffering in the Christian life.

> I know why the caged bird sings,
>   ah me,
>   When his wing is bruised and his
>   bosom sore,—
> When he beats his bars and would
>   be free;
> It is not a carol of joy or glee,
>   But a prayer that he sends from
>   his heart's deep core,
> But a plea, that upward to Heaven
>   he flings—
> I know why the caged bird sings!

A Christian's hope is in the Spirit, who helps us pray and intercedes for us.

Film: *The Legend of Bagger Vance*. This film (2000) tells the story of a golfer, Rannulph Junuh (played by Matt Damon), who is the best that Savannah, Georgia, has ever seen. He returns from World War I traumatized and lives on the edges of life as a drunk. Through a series of events, he is chosen to be a local participant in a golf tournament. One night as Junuh is trying to hit golf balls, a stranger carrying a suitcase appears, gives his name as Bagger Vance (played by Will Smith), and says he will be Junuh's caddy. He begins to help Junuh deal with what is haunting him and with his golf game. When Junuh follows his wise advice, it works, and Junuh begins to win and come into his own, personally and professionally. Bagger decides that Junuh does not need him anymore and disappears as mysteriously as he arrived. Some critics have noted that this movie is a good portrayal of how the Holy Spirit comes into our lives in the midst of our "groaning" and brings us the gift of guidance and peace.

Hymn Text: "Spirit of God, Descend upon My Heart," by George Croly. In this beautiful hymn, Croly (1780–1860) very personally addresses the Holy Spirit, asking him to "make me love Thee as I ought to love," to "take the dimness of my soul away," and to give "the patience of unanswered prayer."

Romans 8:18–30

Justification before God because of the Love of Christ

Big Idea *Romans 8:31–39 forms an* inclusio *with Romans 5:1–11, thereby summarizing the blessings of the new covenant delineated in chapters 5–8. Thus, 8:31–39, like 5:1–11, relates two summary blessings of the new covenant: justification before God (8:31–34), because of the love of Christ (8:35–39).*

Understanding the Text

The Text in Context

Romans 8:31–39, like 5:1–11, declares that the Christian is justified before God because of the atoning sacrifice of Christ, which is rooted in the love of Christ. More specifically, 8:31–39 divides into two sections:

1. Justification before God because of the atoning sacrifice of Christ (8:31–34)
2. Justification is rooted in the love of Christ and love of God (8:35–39)

Historical and Cultural Background

The main background material in this unit is the juridical language in 8:31–34, which I will discuss in the "Interpretive Insights" section.

Interpretive Insights

8:31 *What, then, shall we say . . . If God is for us, who can be against us?* Paul be-

gins this section with two questions. First, "What, then, shall we say in response to these things?" Here, "these things" (*tauta*) refers to all that Paul has been saying since chapter 5 with regard to the blessings of the new covenant. Second, "If God is for us, who can be against us?" "For us" translates *hyper hēmōn* ("on our behalf"), which Paul regularly uses to depict the vicarious atonement of Christ (see especially 5:6–8). Here *hyper* applies to God's work on behalf of Christians. No matter who the enemies of Christians are, God is on his children's side and will protect them.

8:32 *He who did not spare his own Son . . . how will he not also, along with him, graciously give us all things?* The words "He who did not spare his own Son, but gave him up for us all" echo the offering of Isaac (Gen. 22:1–18). Later Jewish tradition interpreted Abraham's offering of his son (known as the Aqedah) as an atonement for sin. Besides *hyper hēmōn* in 8:31, we meet with another juridical action of God in the phrase "gave him up." The verb here is *paradidōmi*, which the Gospel passion predictions pick up from Isaiah 53 and apply to Jesus. The next clause in 8:32, "how will he not also, along with him, graciously give us all things?" is a "major to minor" argument (recall our treatment of *qal waḥomer* in the discussion of Rom. 4:1–8): if God gave his Son for us (major argument), how will he not also give us all things (minor argument)? In other words, if God did not spare his Son for us, then neither will he deny us anything pertaining to salvation.

8:33–34 *Who will bring any charge against those whom God has chosen?* The correct way to punctuate 8:33–34 is debated, but the NIV seems to offer the best solution: first question, then answer; this pattern occurs in both verses.[1] Four juridical terms occur in these verses. "Bring a charge" (*enkaleō*) is used of Paul's court trials (Acts 19:38, 40; 23:28–29; 26:2, 7).[2] "Justify" (*dikaioō*) is a forensic term, as is "condemn" (*katakrinō*). "Intercede" (*entynchanō*) is used in Hebrews 7:25 of Christ's high priestly intercession for his followers. This term is also used of angels interceding for the righteous (*1 En.* 13.4) and, closer to home, of the Spirit's intercession for believers (Rom. 8:27). In the New Testament Jesus' intercession for his followers at the right hand of God is referenced with allusion to Psalm 110:1, often applied to his ascension (Matt. 22:44; 26:64; Acts 2:33–34; 5:31; 7:55–56; Eph. 1:20; Col. 3:1; Heb. 1:3, 13; 8:1; 10:12; 12:2; 1 Pet. 3:22).

Key Themes of Romans 8:31–39

- Paul declares that Christians are justified before God through the atoning sacrifice of Christ. Paul uses various juridical terms to make that point: "on behalf of," "hand over," "bring charge," "justify," "condemn," and "intercede."
- Paul roots the justification of the believer in the love of Christ and love of God. "Love" occurs three times in these verses: "love of Christ," "him that loved us," and "love of God . . . in Christ Jesus."

Paul's argument in 8:33–34 is that if God justifies the Christian, and Christ died, was raised, and intercedes for the Christian, then who could possibly hold anything against believers?

8:35 *Who shall separate us from the love of Christ?* Earlier I called attention to the love of Christ/God as being the theme of

The sacrifice of Isaac from a cast made of the sarcophagus of Junius Bassus. The original sarcophagus (AD 359) is in the Museum of St. Peter's Treasury in Rome. In Genesis (22:12, 16) God recognizes that Abraham did not "withhold" Isaac even when asked to sacrifice him. In the Septuagint, the verb used for "withhold" in Genesis 22 is the same one used by Paul in Romans 8:32 (NIV: "spare").

8:35–39 (note vv. 35, 37, 39). Verse 35 consists of one of Paul's *peristasis* catalogues (a list of afflictions) (cf. 2 Cor. 4:7–16; 6:3–10; 11:21–29; 12:10). All of the items except the last one are found in Paul's apostolic hardship lists in 2 Corinthians 11:26–27; 12:10. These afflictions may be general trials, but more probably they refer to the messianic woes of the end time (see the sidebar).[3]

8:36 *"For your sake we face death all day long; we are considered as sheep to be slaughtered."* Paul cites Psalm 44:22 (43:23 LXX), from a passage that laments the suffering of the righteous. In similar fashion, the apostle wants his readers to know that suffering for Christ is to be expected (cf. Rom. 12:14–21).

8:37 *in all these things we are more than conquerors through him who loved us.* Paul assures the believer of future victory with his choice of words "more than conquerors" (*hypernikaō*). *Nikaō* is a favorite word

of Revelation for the victorious destiny of believers who are faithful to Christ despite being persecuted for their faith (e.g., 2:7, 17, 26; 3:5).

8:38–39 *neither death nor life . . . nor anything else in all creation, will be able to separate us from the love of God.* Verses 38–39 eliminate any possibility of Christians being separated from the love of God in Christ: neither death nor life, angels nor rulers (demons?), present nor future, height nor depth (astronomical, not astrological terms), nor any power, nor anything in creation that Paul fails to mention. The believer could not be more secure. Note also that Paul equates the love of Christ (8:35, 37) with the love of God (8:39), an indication that the two—Christ and God—are equally divine. This is the apex of Christology.

Paul tells believers that death cannot separate them from God's love. The Jewish population of Rome buried their dead in underground rock niches to create tombs similar to those that were used in Palestine. As Christianity flourished, believers created Christian areas underground in which to bury the dead, later known as catacombs. You can see the passageways and horizontal tiers of graves in this photo from the Priscilla catacomb (second to third century AD). Archways above and between the tombs were often decorated with Christian symbols, and frescos or drawings of biblical stories were painted especially in areas where the wealthy or martyrs were placed.

Theological Insights

Here is a good place to summarize the blessings of the new covenant that belong to the church as spelled out in Romans 8. We can do no better than to quote Thomas Schreiner on this point:

One of the striking themes in chapter 8 is that the blessings originally promised to Israel have become the province of the church. Israel was promised the Holy Spirit (Ezek. 36:26–27) so that they could keep the ordinances of the law, but this promise has come to fruition in the church through the gift of the Holy Spirit (Rom. 8:4). Israel had the pledge of a future resurrection (Ezek. 37), and yet Paul speaks of the resurrection of believers (Rom. 8:10–11). Israel was God's son (Exod. 4:22), but now believers in Christ are sons and daughters of God and adopted as his own (Rom. 8:14–17). The future inheritance was promised to Israel (Isa. 60), but now it is pledged to the church (Rom. 8:17). Israel was God's chosen people and the only one foreknown among the nations (Amos 3:2), and yet now the church is said to be foreknown and chosen by God (Rom. 8:29–30). Yahweh had promised never to forsake Israel (Deut. 31:6), yet now this promise is extended to the church (Rom. 8:38–39; cf. also Heb. 13:5).[4]

Teaching the Text

Romans 8:31–39 can be preached or taught according to its twofold division: there is no condemnation because of Christ's atonement (vv. 31–34); there is no separation because of Christ's love (vv. 35–39). The title "More Than Conquerors" is a fitting one for this magnificent passage. The first paragraph might best be presented as if the

Paul's *Peristasis* (Afflictions) Lists

There are at least three major comparisons between Paul's *peristasis* lists and Jewish apocalypticism, each of which has been transformed by the Christ event.

First, the paradoxical structure of Paul's *peristasis* texts (suffering/glory, death/life, afflictions/deliverance, etc.) is the result of the modification of the two-age structure of Jewish apocalypticism (e.g., *4 Ezra* 4.27; 7.12, 89; *2 Bar* 15.8; 48.50) by the death and resurrection of Christ. That is, the age to come has broken into this present age.

Second, the suffering that Paul, and all Christians, experience is none other than the messianic woes that Jewish apocalypticism expected would immediately precede the appearance of the Messiah (*4 Ezra* 7.1–9.14; 1QS 3.23; etc.), though Paul believes that Jesus' resurrection has brought eschatological comfort and joy into the midst of such affliction. Thus the "already" (hope and joy) / "not yet" (messianic woes) eschatological tension initiated by the Christ event becomes the very foundation of Paul's concept of suffering.

Third, like Jewish apocalyptists, Paul too views suffering as pedagogical; it is designed by God to better, if not purify, his people (see Sir. 2:1; *Pss. Sol.* 13.9; 16.11; etc.). Yet, for Paul, this too is transformed by Christ in that his victory over death becomes the divine pattern for the Christian, whose affliction, therefore, produces life. In other words, suffering works for, not against, the believer.

It becomes apparent from this discussion that one need not look to Stoicism as a formative element in Paul's concept of affliction, as some scholars do. In fact, there are significant differences between the two. First, Paul is deeply affected by his hardships, whereas the Stoic sage is not. Second, Paul's trust in times of trouble is solely in God, whereas the Stoic's confidence is in his own reason and ability. Third, Paul's contrasts between the inner and outer man, spiritual and physical existence, and so forth are rooted in Jewish eschatological, not Stoic anthropological, dualism. That is to say, such language attests to the impact of the overlap of the two ages upon the totality of the Christian's being. Fourth, unlike with the Stoic sage, Paul's suffering benefits others (though it is not vicarious).

audience were witnessing the drama of a heavenly courtroom scene. The accused (the sinner) is on the witness stand and is being grilled with questions by the prosecuting attorney, Satan (the accuser), who throws the book at the accused. The prosecutor brings up every sin that the accused has ever committed—in thought, word, and deed. The accused deserves justice not mercy, hell not heaven. When the prosecution has finished its testimony, the defendant apparently has no chance. But then the defense lawyer, Jesus Christ, provides his evidence as to why the defendant should be acquitted. He shows his nail-pierced hands and feet, his thorn-cut brow, and his spear-punctured side. The hymnist Eliza Hewitt (1851–1920) put the defense well:

> My faith has found a resting place,
>   not in device or creed.
> I trust the ever-living One,
>   his wounds for me shall plead.
> I need no other argument,
>   I need no other plea;
> It is enough that Jesus died,
>   and that he died for me.

God, the judge, then pronounces, "Case dismissed!"

Regarding 8:35–39, one could name the obstacles and challenges that Paul mentions—trouble, hardship, persecution, famine, nakedness, danger, sword, death/life, angels/demons, present/future, height/depth—and then ask the audience if Paul left out anything. If the audience mentions an obstacle, the speaker could place it in one of the categories mentioned in 8:35–39. The point, of course, is that absolutely nothing can come between the love of God in Christ and his children.

Illustrating the Text

Because of Christ's atonement, we are no longer under condemnation.

Film: *Camelot.* This film (1967), an adaptation of the musical by the same name (1960),
is based on the legends of King Arthur, who defended Britain against Saxon invaders in the early sixth century, according to medieval histories and romances. King Arthur gathered around him the Knights of the Round Table, who were devoted to a stringent code of honor. His most trusted knight, Lancelot, betrayed code and king by having an affair with Arthur's wife, Guinevere. Caught in adultery by the hostile Mordred, Arthur's illegitimate son, Lancelot escapes. Guinevere, however, is sentenced to be burned at the stake. Everyone wonders if the king will let her die. Mordred sings, "Arthur! What a magnificent dilemma. . . . Which will it be, Arthur? Do you kill the Queen or kill the law?" Arthur resolves to uphold the law, but looking on as his beloved comes to the place of execution, he cries, "I can't! I can't! I can't let her die!" even hoping that Lancelot will save her. Mordred taunts, "Well, you're human after all, aren't you, Arthur? Human and helpless." King Arthur's struggle out of human love might be compared to that of God, who also watched as his beloved Son was led to execution. Yet God, in contrast, out of divine love bore the pain, allowing his Son to die that we might be set free.

Though we may suffer, we will never be separated from the love of God.

Spiritual Autobiography: *The Hiding Place,* **by Corrie ten Boom, with John and Elizabeth Sherrill.** This autobiography (1971), later made into a film (1975), is the account of Corrie ten Boom, filled with stories of her growing understanding of God's love in the midst of tragedy. Four members of the ten Boom family gave their lives because of their work in the Dutch underground during World War II, hiding Jews from Nazi persecution. Corrie and her sister were imprisoned in three different camps, including the notorious Ravensbrück near Berlin, the camp where Betsie ten Boom died and from which Corrie was released. Corrie is famous for the words she learned from her sister: "There is no pit so deep that God's love is not deeper still," and "God will give us the love to be able to forgive our enemies."

Hymn Text: "O Love That Wilt Not Let Me Go," by George Matheson. The story of Matheson (1842–1906), known as "the blind preacher," is an illustration of this passage. The oldest of eighteen children, he graduated from the University of Edinburgh with degrees in the classics, logic, and philosophy. Engaged to be married, he discovered that he was going blind. Subsequently, his fiancée broke the engagement. Completely blind by the time he was twenty, Matheson became a pastor. He said that the text of this great hymn was the fruit of "the most severe mental suffering." Particularly poignant is the following stanza:

> O Joy that seekest me through pain,
> I cannot close my heart to thee;
> I trace the rainbow through the rain,
> And feel the promise is not vain,
> That morn shall tearless be.

Paul was brought before the proconsul Gallio at this *bēma* (or judgment seat) in Corinth. It was likely from Corinth that Paul wrote Romans. Even though it was a few years after he stood before the proconsul, this image of worldy judgment would have been fresh in his mind. But he declares that it is ultimately God who will judge.

Israel and the Present Curses and the Past Blessings of the Covenant

Big Idea *Chapters 9–11, which correspond to the curses component of the covenant (chaps. 5–8 enunciate the blessings), answer the question "Have God's promises to Israel failed?" Paul answers, "No!" In 9:1–5 he broaches the problem of Israel's unbelief. Israel previously enjoyed the blessings of the covenant but is now under its curses for rejecting the Messiah.*

Understanding the Text

The Text in Context

In order to situate Romans 9:1–5 in its literary setting I must briefly make four points. First, what is the relationship between Romans 9–11 and Romans 1–8? The scholarly consensus is that Romans 9–11 forms an integral part of Paul's argument in Romans in two ways. Had Paul left his argument with Romans 8, he would have given the distinct impression that God was finished with Israel, as indeed he was finished with the old covenant. But if God were finished with Israel, what then of the Old Testament promises to restore Israel in the end time? Furthermore, if God abandoned his Old Testament people, could he not also abandon the church, the new-covenant people? Therefore, Paul must demonstrate that God has kept his promises to Israel, as indeed he will keep his promises to the church.

Second, Romans 9–11 develops in the following way:

1. Introduction (9:1–5)
2. God's promises to Israel have not failed (9:6–29)
3. Gentiles are included in the promises of God (9:30–11:10)
4. Israel's future spiritual restoration (11:11–32)
5. Doxology to God (11:33–36)

Third, a contrast runs right through Romans 9–11, as James Dunn has noted, to which I correlate the covenantal curses and blessings, as shown in table 1.[1]

Fourth, Romans 9:1–5 divides into two parts:

1. Israel's present curses under the covenant (9:1–3)
2. Israel's past blessings under the covenant (9:4–5)

Table 1: The Covenantal Blessings and Curses in Romans 9–11

Romans 9:1–11:32	Covenantal Blessings	Covenantal Curses
9:1–5	Israel's past	Israel's present
9:6–29	Election of mercy	Purpose of wrath
9:30–10:4	Gentiles: righteous by faith	Israel: not righteous because of the law
10:5–21	Gentiles and the remnant	The majority of Israel
11:1–10	A remnant according to grace	The rest hardened
11:11–27	Israel's future restoration	Warning to the Gentiles that they can be cut off
11:28–32	Israel's future / Gentiles' present	Israel's present

Historical and Cultural Background

1. The term that Paul uses in 9:3, "cursed," is the Greek word *anathema*, which in the LXX translates the Hebrew word *herem*. The *herem* was something devoted to God to be destroyed: idols (Lev. 27:28; Deut. 13:17 [13:18 LXX]; Zech. 14:11), Achan (Josh. 6:17–18; 7:1, 11–13; 22:20; 1 Chron. 2:7), Jerusalem because of its idolatry (Isa. 43:28; Mal. 4:6).[2] It is interesting that each of these settings is that of the covenant. Thus, idols break covenant with God. Achan's sin broke the covenant with God, necessitating his death and a renewal ceremony of the covenant with God. Jerusalem's perpetual idolatry caused God to hand the city over to Babylonia, the unwitting enforcer of the covenant curses. I will say more on this in comments on 9:3.

2. In 9:4 Paul calls his kinsfolk "Israelites." Two observations enlighten Paul's choice of this word. (a) "Israel" was first

Key Themes of Romans 9:1–5

- Paul could wish to exchange places with Israel such that he would gladly take the covenant curses for himself instead of his kinsfolk according to the flesh.

- Israel in the past enjoyed the blessings of the covenant before they gave way to the covenantal curses.

used of Jacob and then of the twelve tribes (Gen. 32:28; 35:10–12). As such, it was the covenant name for the Hebrews. Indeed "Israelite" and "children of Israel" were the preferred names of the Hebrews before the exile (e.g., Pss. 25:22; 53:6; 130:7–8; Isa. 49:3). After the exile, the Hebrews were called "Jews" (see Philo, *Against Flaccus* and *Embassy to Gaius*). (b) Paul uses the name "Jew" in Romans 1–3 nine times and in Romans 9–11 only twice (9:24; 10:12). But he predominantly uses the name "Israel/Israelite" in Romans 9–11 (9:6, 27, 31; 10:19, 21; 11:1, 2, 7, 25, 26). This is because in Romans 9–11 Paul is speaking as an insider, and the name "Israel" evokes his people's sense of being God's elect, the covenant people of the one God.[3]

Interpretive Insights

9:1–3 *I speak the truth in Christ . . . I could wish that I myself were cursed.* Verses 1–3 express Paul's deep concern for his Jewish kinsfolk. No doubt Paul is answering those critics who accused him of being anti-Jewish in light of his commitment to evangelize Gentiles. Here Paul solemnly expresses his concern for Israel by beginning with an oath, stated both positively ("I speak the truth in Christ") and negatively ("I am not lying"). To reinforce the truthfulness of his oath, Paul says that his conscience is confirmed by the Holy Spirit. Then comes his concern: "I have great sorrow and unceasing anguish in my heart." It is implied that his anguish is because Israel has not accepted Jesus the Messiah. Then Paul expresses the depth of his anguish: he is willing to be cursed, separated from salvation in Christ, if that would somehow bring his compatriots to Christ. But the potential indicative *euchomēn* ("I could wish") indicates that such a wish is not possible. Only Christ's death can atone for others, and those others must make the choice for themselves whether or not to accept Christ. Paul's request brings to mind Moses' similar request to be cut off from the covenant rather than the children of Israel (Exod. 32:32).

I suggest that Paul's use of the word "curse" (*anathema*) evokes the curses of the covenant, for five reasons. First, as we just noted, Paul's request resembles the one made by Moses, who hoped to prevent God from cutting his people off from the covenant after their worship of the golden calf. Second, Paul's lament in 9:1–3 recalls the Old Testament laments over Israel's sin, the destruction of Jerusalem, and the exile to Babylonia (Jer. 4:19; 14:17; Lamentations; Dan. 9:3; cf. *T. Jud.* 23.1; *4 Ezra* 8.16; 10.24, 39; *2 Bar.* 10.5; 35.1–3; 81.2;

4 Bar. 4.10; 6.17). Third, Paul's combination of *lypē* (sorrow) and *odynē* (anguish) occurs in the LXX in Isaiah 35:10; 51:11, which predict that Israel will be restored to the land, leaving behind the sorrow (both times *lypē* and *odynē* are used to render the Hebrew word meaning "sorrow") of the covenant curses of the exile. Fourth, the Greek word *anathema* ("curse") translates in the LXX the Hebrew word *herem*. This *herem*, or God's ban, as we observed above, clusters around three themes: idols, Achan, and the destruction of Jerusalem for its idolatry. Each of these themes is connected to the breaking of God's covenant relationship with Israel. It seems, then, that Paul's "curse" ties into that theme: he is willing to exchange places with Israel—he will take upon himself the covenantal curse that rests upon his kinsfolk—so that they can receive the blessings of the new covenant in Christ. Fifth, indeed, in 9:4–5 he will go on to list the past blessings of the covenant that Israel once enjoyed but now have been replaced with the covenant curses.

9:4–5 *Theirs is the adoption to sonship . . . the temple worship and the promises.* Verses 4–5 rehearse the various blessings associated with Israel and the Old Testament covenant. Paul introduces

In Romans 9:5, Paul includes the patriarchs, through whom the Messiah will come, as one of the blessings of Israel. Abraham, forefather of the Jewish people, purchased the cave at Machpelah as a burial site for his wife, Sarah. Eventually Abraham himself, Isaac, Rebekah, Joseph, and Leah would be buried there, and it would become a sacred site. Herod the Great recognized it as such and commissioned a large enclosure wall to be erected and cenotaphs to be constructed to honor the patriarchs. This building, known as the Tomb of the Patriarchs, is shown here. Underground tombs exist beneath the building, but they have not been extensively excavated.

the list with "Israelites," which, as we saw above, evokes the idea that Israel was God's elect covenant people. The "adoption to sonship" (*huiothesia*) refers to Israel's sense of being God's son(s) (Deut. 14:1; Isa. 43:6; Jer. 31:9; Hos. 1:10; cf. Wis. 9:7; *Jub.* 1.24–25). The "divine glory" (*doxa*) recalls the glorious presence of God with Israel in the tabernacle and in the temple (Exod. 16:10; 24:25–27; 40:34–35; Lev. 9:23; Num. 14:10). Paul may also have thought of the promise that Israel would be the glory among the nations in the end time (Isa. 35:2; 40:5; 59:19; 60:1–3; 66:18–19).[4] "The covenants" (*diathēkai*) refers especially to God's covenant with Israel (Exod. 19:5–6), reaffirmed in Deuteronomy 29–31 and Joshua 8:30–35, but also to the covenant with Abraham (Gen. 15; 17), the covenant with David (2 Sam. 7; 23:5), and the new covenant (Jer. 31:31–34; Ezek. 36:24–27). The "gift of the law" (*nomothesia*) was Israel's charter of the covenant, and the "service" (*latreia*) constituted the worship of the temple cult (Josh. 22:27; 1 Chron. 28:13; cf. 1 Macc. 2:22). The divine promises (*epangeliai*) are those to the patriarchs (*pateres*)—Abraham, Isaac, and Jacob—of a land and people (Gen. 12:1–3; 15; 18:18; 22:18; 26:4; 28:14; cf. Sir. 44:21; Acts 3:25). Most important is "the Messiah" (*ho Christos* [note the titular usage]), who obviously was Jewish. It may be that Paul infers that the promise of the Messiah is also one of the divine promises to Israel (e.g., Gen. 3:15; 49:10). There is a delightful stylistic pairing of these blessings: three sets of words, each set ending in the same letters: *huiothesia*/*nomothesia*; *doxa*/*latreia*; *diathēkai*/*epangeliai*.

Does Paul Call Christ "God" in Romans 9:5?

Paul's concluding statement in 9:5 has occasioned a huge debate. Does Paul call Christ "God" there? The question involves how the Greek text should be punctuated (recall that the original manuscripts had no punctuation). There are two major options:[a]

1. "the Christ, who is God over all, forever blessed!" (cf. NIV). This rendering equates Christ with God, the highest possible Christology.
2. "the Christ. God who is over all be forever blessed!" (cf. NIV mg.). This rendering does not elevate Christ to the status of God.

Most commentators prefer the first option, and there are several reasons for doing so: (a) Christ according to the flesh (v. 5a) would be balanced by Christ as God (v. 5b), as we saw was the case in Romans 1:3–4; (b) Paul elsewhere equates Christ with God (Phil. 2:6–11) or calls him "God" (Titus 2:13); (c) the participial phrase *ho ōn* ("the one who is") best refers to "Christ" as the antecedent; (d) it would be awkward for "blessed" to refer to "God" since it follows, whereas "blessed" typically appears before "God" in other blessing formulas (e.g., Gen. 9:26; 14:20; Exod. 18:10; Ps. 28:6; Luke 1:68; 2 Cor. 1:3).[b]

[a] See Dunn, *Romans 9–16*, 528–29.
[b] For an excellent handling of the evidence, see Jewett, *Romans*, 567–68.

Theological Insights

A number of truths emerge from Romans 9:1–5. First, we learn from Paul's love for Israel that there should be no anti-Jewish attitude among Christians. The children of Israel were God's chosen people, and the Savior was Jewish. Second, nevertheless the curses of the covenant remain on Israel until such time as they receive Jesus as the Messiah. Third, the blessings of the new covenant now rest on the church. Christians are the children of God; they possess the glory of God within; they are participants of the Abrahamic, Davidic, and new covenants; they have the indwelling Spirit for obedience's sake; they worship God in truth and Spirit; and they have the ultimate promise of the patriarchs—Jesus Christ.

Teaching the Text

An entire sermon or lesson could be devoted to Romans 9:1–5 entitled "Present Curses and Past Blessings: Israel and the Covenant." I would divide the message into its two constituent parts: present curses (9:1–3) and past blessings (9:4–5). I would conclude the message by applying the blessings of the new covenant to Christians, as I did in the "Theological Insights" section. Thus, the present curses currently rest on non-Christian Jews because they make obedience to the

Modern Jewish men praying at the Western Wall in Jerusalem. Like these, the Jews in Paul's day were striving to fully keep the law of Moses.

Torah the stipulation of the covenant rather than faith in Christ (9:1–3). This is a tragic turn of events, especially when one remembers all of ancient Israel's past blessings: children of God; possessors of divine glory, the covenants, and the law; observers of the temple cult; and recipients of the promises of the patriarchs, especially the Messiah. Paul may offer an important key as to why Israel once enjoyed these blessings but now stands under the divine curses of the covenant. Note that in the list of blessings, the covenants precede the giving of the law. That is to say, Paul may be hinting that Israel was to enter the covenants with God by faith and in the same manner keep the law: by faith. Instead, Jews reversed the order: obey the law in order to enter and keep the divine covenants. Somehow Israel lost sight of faith as the stipulation for entering and maintaining the covenant and turned it into legalism. Ironically, now Gentiles enjoy the blessings of the new covenant because they understand that the stipulation for doing so is faith in Christ, not works.

Illustrating the Text

Christians should respect the Jews as God's chosen people; the Savior was Jewish.

Biography: Concern for the Jews was the burden of Dietrich Bonhoeffer's (1906–45) calling in Nazi Germany. A Lutheran pastor and theologian, he participated in the German resistance movement and was part of several plots to assassinate Adolf Hitler, for which he was arrested and later hanged. His demeanor while in prison was courageous and heroic. Opposed to the Nazi regime from its incipience, he was disheartened by the complacency of the German Lutheran church and spoke out against it with force, even disagreeing with prominent theologians such as Karl Barth. It would be very useful to look at biographical material about Bonhoeffer as an example of a Christian ("he could wish himself accursed") who stood up for the Jews, putting his life on the line. His own *Prisoner for God: Letters and Papers from Prison* (1953) would also be helpful. In 2006 a feature-length documentary of his life was aired on PBS.

Personal Stories: Maximilian Kolbe was a Polish priest who died in 1941 as prisoner 16670 in Auschwitz, one of the Nazi extermination camps. When a prisoner escaped from the camp, the commandant chose ten others to be killed by starvation in the "hunger bunker" as punishment for that escape. One of the ten, Franciszek Gajowniczek, pleaded to be spared because he had a wife and children. At this, Father Kolbe stepped forward and asked to die in his place. He told the commandant, "He has a wife and family. I am alone. I am a Catholic priest." His request was granted. As the ten men were led to their death, Father Kolbe supported a fellow prisoner who could hardly walk. No one emerged from the "hunger bunker" alive, and Father Kolbe was the last to die.

The covenant curses remain on Israel until they receive Jesus as Messiah; the new-covenant blessings now rest on the church.

Literature: An examination of curses and spells put on various individuals throughout literature provides an interesting comparison to the sections on curses and blessings written to Israel in Scripture (Lev. 26–27; Deut. 28–29). The Harry Potter series, for instance, uses a number of spells and curses. The spells consist of a gesture made with the character's wand, combined with a spoken or mental incantation. For example, *Avada Kedavra* (the killing curse) causes instant, painless death to whomever the curse hits. The only two people in the series to survive this curse are Harry Potter and Voldemort. Questions to ask about curses and spells in literature might include the following: "What was the original reason and intention of the curse?" "How was the curse overcome?" and "What is the difference between biblical hope and fairy-tale hope to overcome a curse?"

Hymn Text: "Come, Thou Fount of Every Blessing," by Robert Robinson. This hymn is rooted in the life experience of Robinson (1735–90). It reflects the story of a man who is given a reprieve, then fights against the covenant grace of God for three years before finding a measure of peace.

Comics: *A Contract with God*, by Will Eisner. Eisner (1917–2005) wrote what many believe to be the first "graphic novel." *A Contract with God* (1978) is a trilogy of stories ("A Contract with God," "A Life Force," and "Dropsie Avenue") about growing up in the Great Depression. It begins with the tale "A Contract with God." Here Eisner interacts with the issue of a vengeful God. The preacher or teacher could use this story to explore the difference between "covenant" and "contract."

Covenantal Curses on Israel, Covenantal Blessings on Gentiles

Big Idea *Responding to anticipated objections about his presentation of salvation history, Paul shows that God's promises were only to spiritual Israel, and that God sovereignly has mercy on whomever he chooses. In the past, God poured out mercy on Israel but wrath on Gentiles. In the present, God pours out wrath on Israel but mercy on Gentiles and the Jewish remnant.*

Understanding the Text

The Text in Context

Romans 9:6–29 proceeds from Paul's remarks in 9:1–5: in the past Israel enjoyed the covenant blessings (vv. 4–5), but in the present Israel is under the covenant curses (vv. 1–3). This sounded to Jewish ears like a failure of God's covenant promises to Israel. Paul answers that criticism in 9:6–13, and then he responds to a second criticism in 9:14–29 that God's ways are unfair. Therefore, 9:6–29 should be outlined thus:

1. Objection #1: God's covenant promises to Israel have failed (9:6a).
   Paul's answer: God's promises were given not to national Israel but to spiritual Israel (9:6b–13).
2. Objection #2: God's ways are unfair; he arbitrarily chooses some but not others (9:14).

Paul's answer: God sovereignly chooses to show mercy to whomever he wishes, but it all balances out (9:15–29).
   a. Past: Mercy on Israel, but wrath on Gentiles (9:15–18)
   b. Present: Mercy (covenant blessings) on Gentiles, but wrath (covenant curses) on Israel (9:19–29)

Paul concludes his argument begun in Romans 9:6–29 in 9:30–10:21. The former (9:6–29) emphasizes God's sovereignty, while the latter (9:30–10:21) emphasizes human responsibility.

Historical and Cultural Background

In Romans 9:6–29 Paul draws on the concept of the remnant, which runs throughout Scripture in a wide variety of texts and contexts. The central idea of the remnant concept/theology is that in the midst of seemingly total apostasy and the consequental terrible judgment and/or destruction, God has always had a small, faithful group that he delivered and worked through to bring blessing.

Interpretive Insights

9:6–9 *It is not as though God's word had failed.* Verse 6a raises the first criticism of Paul's view of salvation history. Verses 6b–13 provide Paul's rebuttal. The criticism, no doubt from a Jewish perspective, takes umbrage at Paul's claim that the covenant curses rest on Israel (cf. 9:1–5). This is tantamount to saying that God's Old Testament promises to Israel of the covenant blessings have been revoked. Verse 6b bluntly states Paul's answer: God never promised these blessings to Israel based solely on their national identity; rather, God's promise belongs to spiritual Israel. Verses 7–9 illustrate the principle of divine selectivity: God chose spiritual Israel (the true children of Abraham) out of national Israel (illustrated by Ishmael). Table 1 shows the differences.

Table 1: The Not Chosen and the Chosen

Romans	Not Chosen (Mere National Israel)	Chosen (Spiritual Israel)
9:7–9	Abraham's physical descendants, natural children; Ishmael	true children of Abraham, children of the promise of the covenant; Isaac
9:10–13	Esau	Jacob
9:14–18	Pharaoh/ Egyptians	Moses/Israel
9:19–23	vessels of wrath	vessels of mercy
9:24–26	Jews	Gentiles (and believing Jews)
9:27–29	national Israel	remnant

Key Themes of Romans 9:6–29

- God's covenant promises in the Old Testament were made to spiritual Israel, not necessarily national Israel.
- God in his sovereignty shows mercy to those who do not deserve it: Israel in the past, Gentiles in the present.
- God in his sovereignty pours out wrath on those who deserve it: Gentiles in the past, Israel in the present.

9:10–13 *Rebekah's children were conceived at the same time . . . "Jacob I loved, but Esau I hated."* Verses 10–13 provide a second illustration of God's principle of election in the Old Testament: he chose Jacob to be the recipient of the covenant over against Esau. Three points sharpen God's principle of election here. First, Jacob and Esau came from the same parents, Rebekah and Isaac (9:10).[1] Second, God chose the one (Jacob) even before the twins were born. Thus, God's choice had nothing to do with the boys' actions, whether good or bad (9:11–12b). God's purpose was to elect Jacob as heir of the Abrahamic covenant. Third, God reversed the law of primogeniture (the oldest son receives the most honor and inheritance) by determining that Esau, the older, should serve Jacob, the younger. The rationale for God's decision was that he loved Jacob but hated Esau (compare 9:12c with Mal. 1:2–3). The visceral terms "love" and "hate" are not emotional in disposition but rather are logical: God accepted Jacob but rejected Esau.[2]

9:14–18 *Is God unjust? Not at all! . . . God has mercy on whom he wants to have mercy.* Verse 14 raises a second criticism of Paul's position: if God chooses whomever he wills for his purposes, does that not make him unfair and unrighteous? Paul's immediate response to that accusation is his impassioned *mē genoito* ("May it never be!").

Then Paul provides a lengthy logical answer in 9:15–29 to the criticism that God is unfair, revealing to the contrary that God is just. In 9:15–18 he explains that in the past God poured out mercy on Israel at the exodus while pouring out wrath on the Gentiles (Pharaoh and the Egyptians). In 9:19–29 Paul further explains that in the present God has poured out wrath (the covenant curses) upon Israel while pouring out mercy (the covenant blessings) upon the Gentiles and the remnant. It becomes clear from this that God is no respecter of person: he pours out both wrath and mercy on Gentile and Jew alike.

Verses 15–18 highlight how God raised up Pharaoh precisely to pour out divine wrath on him and the so-called gods of Egypt (compare 9:17 with Exod. 9:16; 12:12; 14:4). The way God "set up" Pharaoh for judgment was by hardening his heart toward God and the Israelites (compare 9:18 with the some fourteen occurrences of "harden" in Exod. 4–14). Some might downplay the fact that God hardened Pharaoh's heart by countering that Pharaoh hardened his own heart. But the first references to God hardening Pharaoh's heart (e.g., Exod. 4:21; 7:3) occur before the first occurrences of Pharaoh hardening his own heart (Exod. 8:11, 28). This indicates that Pharaoh

became unrepentant because God predisposed him to be so. But God's purpose for hardening Pharaoh's heart and destroying his army was to display might and mercy on behalf of the Israelites (9:15 [cf. Exod. 33:19], 16, 18).

9:19–23 *"Then why does God still blame us? For who is able to resist his will?"* Romans 9:19–29 reveals that God's flow of wrath and mercy can be reversed relative to people groups. Thus, in the present God has poured out his wrath (covenant curses) on Israel while pouring out his mercy (covenant blessings) on Gentiles and only a minority of Jews (the remnant). If 9:15–18 had to do with the exodus, then 9:19–29 has to do with acceptance or rejection of Christ.

Romans 9:19–23 has to do with God's judgment on Israel for (by implication) rejecting Jesus the Christ. Verse 19 begins the discussion by again criticizing Paul's position: why should God punish anyone, since he sovereignly dictates the destiny of humans? Paul replies in 9:20–23 by using the Old Testament metaphor of God the creator/potter and humans the creation/clay. Verses 20–21 make the point that the

Just before God sends the plague of hail on the Egyptians, he gives Moses words to speak to Pharaoh, a portion of which Paul quotes in Romans 9:17. This scene of the seventh plague is an illustration in the Sarajevo Hagada, a fourteenth-century AD Hebrew manuscript from Spain. God in his sovereignty pours out wrath and mercy.

creation/clay has no right to question the purposes of God the creator/potter. In using this metaphor, Paul draws on several Old Testament texts, each of which occurs in the context of the coming judgment and exile upon Israel for their sin (Isa. 29:16 [cf. 10:15]; 45:9; 64:8; Jer. 18:6).

Verse 22 continues that theme. Even though God waited patiently for Israel to repent, they never did. Consequently, God delivered Israel over to destruction and exile. Such divine wrath was the fulfillment of the covenant curses (cf. 1 Thess. 2:15–16). This indictment harks back to 9:1–5 as well as anticipates 9:30–10:4.[3] Verse 23, then, alludes to Christians as being the objects, or vessels, of God's mercy (covenantal blessings). That interpretation is confirmed in 9:24–26.

9:24–26 *even us, whom he also called, not only from the Jews but also from the Gentiles.* Here Paul quotes Hosea 2:23 (Rom. 9:25) and Hosea 1:10 (Rom. 9:26). Hosea applies his prophecy to the future restoration of Israel: even though the exile has turned Israel into not being God's people/children, the restoration will restore their original status. But Paul applies Hosea's prophecy to Gentiles: even though Gentiles in Old Testament times were not the people of God and the children of the covenant, now faith in Christ (see 9:30–33) has constituted them as such.

9:27–29 *"only the remnant will be saved."* Paul finishes his catena of Old Testament quotations in 9:25–29 by quoting Isaiah 10:22–23 (cf. Hos. 1:10) and Isaiah 1:9. The intent of these verses is to say that when God has finished judging Israel, only a few—a remnant—will survive to return to their homeland. Paul interprets this rem-

nant to be those few Jews who accepted Christ in the first century.

Theological Insights

Here I briefly raise the thorny issue of how one is to interpret Paul's concept of election in Romans 9:6–29 (for further discussion, see the "Teaching the Text" section). There are three main views on election: the Calvinist view, which emphasizes God's sovereignty; the Arminian view, which focuses on human choice; and the corporate view, which proposes its own solution to the tension between divine sovereignty and human responsibility. The first view argues that God chose from eternity past which individuals are to be saved or lost. The second view claims that God only knew beforehand who would choose to accept or reject him. The corporate perspective suggests that God chose entities—Israel in the Old Testament to be his people, and Christ in the New Testament to be the means of salvation—and it is up to each person to choose the entity that God has chosen.

Teaching the Text

Romans 9:6–29 is a most difficult text to preach and teach. I would divide a message on this passage into two parts: interpretation and application. The interpretation section summarizes my outline of 9:6–29: (1) God's word has not failed, because his promises were to spiritual Israel (vv. 6–13); (2) God's ways are not unfair, because in the past he judged Gentiles but saved Jews, while in the present he judges Israel but saves Gentiles (vv. 14–29). The application section covers the three views of Romans 9:6–29: Calvinist,

Arminian, corporate. We now delve a little more deeply into these views. First, there is the Calvinist view of election, which can be summarized by the acrostic TULIP:

T — total depravity of humanity

U — unconditional predestination of the elect by God

L — limited atonement (Christ died for only the elect)

I — irresistible grace (sinners cannot resist God's effective call to salvation)

P — perseverance of the saints

Thus, the Calvinist focuses on God's sovereign election of the saved (vessels of mercy) and the lost (vessels of wrath) in Romans 9:6–29. Before anyone was even born, God chose in eternity past those who would be the elect and the nonelect. This viewpoint is called "double predestination." Obviously, it leaves little if any room for human choice in the matter.

Second, the Arminian school of thought begs to differ with the Calvinist on the matter of election. The Five Articles of Remonstrance is its point-by-point disagreement with TULIP (see table 2). So, the Arminian argues that God knows who will have faith in him before they are born, not that God chooses who will have faith in him. This view takes seriously human responsibility but tends to downplay divine sovereignty.

The third view, the corporate view, was popularized by Karl Barth (*Church Dogmatics* II/2). It claims that Romans 9:6–29 teaches that God chooses entities, not individuals. Thus, in the Old Testament God chose Isaac/Jews not Ishmael/Arabs, and Jacob/Israel not Esau/Edom, and Moses/

Table 2: The Five Articles of Remonstrance

Remonstrance	TULIP
God's decree—appointed Christ as means of salvation.	U
God decreed that all could repent and be saved.	L
Prevenient grace compensates for total depravity.	T
Therefore, humans choose to be saved or not on their own.	I
God predestines those who he foreknows will believe (thus it is eternal salvation not eternal security).	P

Israel not Pharaoh/Egypt. And it was up to each individual to decide whether or not to align with God's corporate people. In the New Testament, God chose Christ to be the savior, and double predestination was fulfilled in him: God's wrath for sinners was poured out on Christ on the cross, so that God's mercy could be poured out on those same sinners. One can see from this that those who hold the corporate understanding of election claim to have resolved the tension between divine sovereignty and human responsibility.

I would like to side with the corporate view, but the objections raised by Paul's critic(s) (Rom. 9:6, 14, 19) are precisely what one would expect if God were choosing some individuals for eternal salvation and others for eternal damnation. One would not expect the corporate view of election to elicit those protests.

Furthermore, I do think that Romans 9:6–29 focuses on God's sovereignty in electing individuals for his purposes, but that Romans 9:30–10:21 focuses on human responsibility. Therefore, there is a middle view between Calvinists and Arminians: Calminians! According to this rather playful label, God sovereignly chooses individuals' destinies, but paradoxically humans have the power and responsibility to choose Christ for themselves. These two opposing truths do not sit well with Western rationalism, but the ancient Hebrews seemed content to accept such antinomies.

Illustrating the Text

God's promises will be fulfilled through the true remnant of Israel.

Medicine: During reconstructive surgery, "preserving the remnant" of the original organ, tissue, or ligature is important to bringing a patient back to full health. Often part of the process includes grafting other tissue to the original tissue. Doctors believe that by so doing, they will enable patients' bodies to accept the procedure.

Personal Stories: Harry Ironside tells about a man who was wonderfully saved and arose in a class meeting to testify to his newly found joy. When he had finished, the legalistic class leader said, "Our . . . brother has told about God's part, but he forgot to tell his part before he was converted. Brother, haven't you something more to tell us about it?" Without hesitation, the man exclaimed, "I shore did my part. I was doin' my part running away from God as fast as I could for thirty years, and God took after me till He run me down. That was His part."[4] This is an example of how God pursues his people.

God's ways are not unfair.

Human Experience: Many teachers have experienced a student's insisting on a higher grade. The student says to the teacher, "Look, I missed the A by only one-tenth of a point." The teacher may, on occasion, give that student the A. The teacher may reply to another student, however, "No, sorry, this is the grade." Is the teacher wrong to withhold the higher grade when asked? No. The teacher may simply elect to give a higher grade or not, based on the particulars of each individual situation. The teacher is not wrong in either case.

Personal Stories: R. C. Sproul tells about students questioning his fairness as a professor. When he gave some of his students an extension for a late term paper, they began to take his mercy for granted. They, and some other students too, were late with the next term paper. Again he gave them a break. When they and even more students were late with the third term paper, he finally gave them what they had earned, an F. They were angry, and one student protested that he was not being fair. Sproul replied, "It's justice you want? I seem to recall that you were late with your paper the last time. If you insist on justice, you will certainly get it. I'll not only give you an F for this assignment, but I'll change your last grade to the F you so richly deserved." The student apologized and was happy to settle for one F instead of two. Sproul concludes, "The normal activity of God involves far more mercy than I showed those students with their term papers."[5]

The Reversal of the Deuteronomic Curses and Blessings: Replacing Law with Faith

Big Idea *The key issue in this controversial text is the role of the law in light of the work of Christ. Paul reverses the Deuteronomic curses and blessings: non-Christian Jews experience the Deuteronomic curses because they attempt to be justified by the law, while believing Gentiles are justified because their faith is in Christ, so to them belong the Deuteronomic blessings.*

Understanding the Text

The Text in Context

Romans 9:30–10:21 forms the second unit in Romans 9–11 (9:1–29 is the first, and 11:1–32 is the third). The theme of Romans 9:30–10:21 is the reversal of the Deuteronomic curses and blessings. The former pertain to non-Christian Jews (and unbelieving Gentiles), while the latter apply to Christian Gentiles (and Christian Jews as well). These two themes form a simple chiastic structure for Romans 9:30–10:21.

  A Deuteronomic blessings on Gentiles because of faith righteousness (9:30)

    B Deuteronomic curses on Israel because of law righteousness (9:31–10:18)

  A′ Deuteronomic blessings on Gentiles because of faith righteousness (10:19–21)

We may conveniently divide 9:30–10:21 into five sections: 9:30–10:4; 10:5; 10:6–8; 10:9–13; 10:14–21. I will cover the first two of these sections in this unit, leaving 10:6–21 for the next unit.

Historical and Cultural Background

Two key pieces of background information illuminate Romans 9:30–10:5. I simply list them here (for fuller discussion, see the "Additional Insights" section): (1) the Deuteronomic tradition; (2) Paul's mention of the word "zeal" in Romans 10:2 regarding Israel's commitment to the Torah taps into a storied tradition in the Old Testament and in Second Temple Judaism.

Interpretive Insights

9:30–10:4 *the Gentiles, who did not pursue righteousness, have obtained it, . . . but the people of Israel, who pursued the law as the way of righteousness, have not attained their goal.* Here are three indications that combine to show that 9:30–10:4 reverses the Deuteronomic curses and blessings. First, as we develop below, the Deuteronomic tradition is embedded in the overall argument of chapters 9–11. Second, more specifically, we earlier noted that 8:1–16 (cf. chap. 7) is well understood as Paul's reversal of the Deuteronomic curses and blessings. Third, Paul continues to think along such lines in 9:25–29, where, in quoting Hosea 2:23 (v. 25), Hosea 1:10 (v. 26), Isaiah 10:22–23 (v. 27), and Isaiah 1:19 (v. 27), he draws on the motifs of the exile (Deuteronomic curses on the unfaithful) and the remnant (Deuteronomic blessings on the faithful). In light of these considerations, it can be understood that 9:30–10:4 transposes commonly held Jewish expectations: according to Paul, those who do not attempt to be justified by the works of the law but rather place their faith in Christ alone (Gentile believers) are currently experiencing the Deuteronomic blessings, while those who attempt to be saved through adherence to

Key Themes of Romans 9:30–10:5

- The Deuteronomic (covenant) curses are upon the people of Israel because they tried to commend themselves to God by obeying the law of Moses—"law righteousness."
- The Deuteronomic (covenant) blessings rest on believing Gentiles because they trust in Christ—"faith righteousness."
- Christ is the end of the law of Moses; therefore everyone can receive God's righteousness by faith in Christ.

the Torah (non-Christian Jews) remain under the Deuteronomic curses. This ironic contrast surfaces when one observes the parallels in 9:30–10:4:

A The acquisition of righteousness (9:30)
  B Israel's failure to obey the law (9:31)
    C Israel's misunderstanding of the law (9:32–33)
A′ The acquisition of salvation (righteousness) (10:1)
  B′ Israel's failure to obey the law (10:2)
    C′ Israel's misunderstanding of the law (10:3–4)

With regard to the first parallel (9:30; 10:1), both verses speak of the acquisition of the righteousness of God or salvation. The former attests to the ironic fact that

Synagogues provided a setting where Jews could read, teach, and discuss the law, pursuing it as the way of righteousness (Romans 9:31). Archaeological remains of the synagogue at Ostia, Italy (the ancient port of Rome), reveal two building periods, the earliest dated to the first century AD. Synagogues were the places for Jews to gather and helped them maintain their identity while surrounded by Greco-Roman culture.

Gentiles, who do not pursue God's righteousness via the Mosaic law, have actually received that righteousness by faith (implied: faith in Christ). The latter expresses Paul's deep desire that Israel also receive God's salvation or righteousness (implied: like the Gentiles already have).

The second parallel (9:31; 10:2) addresses Israel's failure in attempting to obey the Torah. The first parts of both verses speak of Israel's commitment to keep the law ("pursued the law as a way of righteousness" [9:31]; "they are zealous for God" [10:2]). The second parts of both verses lament Israel's failure to achieve that objective ("have not attained their goal" [9:31]; "their zeal is not based on knowledge" [10:2]).

The third parallel (9:32–33; 10:3–4) exposes Israel's misunderstanding of the law. Both texts present two aspects of that confusion—one general, the other specific. In general, Israel failed to perceive that the divine intent was that the law be pursued by faith, not by one's meritorious works (compare 9:32 with 10:3). More specifically, Israel perpetuates that mistake in its rejection of Jesus Christ, who is the fulfillment of the law and the only means of acquiring God's righteousness (compare 9:33 with 10:4).

Paul concludes his argument in 9:30–10:4 by explicitly contrasting obedience to the law (compare Rom. 10:5 with Lev. 18:5) with the righteousness that comes by faith in Christ (compare Rom. 10:6–8 with Deut. 30:12–14). In doing so, he essentially reverses the Deuteronomic curses and blessings by replacing nomism with fideism (law with faith) and particularism with universalism (salvation for the Jews with

salvation for all who believe). These are the two results that proceed from Paul's severance of wisdom (Christ) and the Torah.[1] Such a reading of 9:30–10:4 to the effect that Paul portrays the law negatively, however, does not sit well with some modern scholars. Interpreters such as James Dunn view this passage as refuting only Jewish nationalism (circumcision, Sabbath, and dietary legalism), not the law per se.[2] In other words, they allow for a more positive understanding of the Torah in this passage. Thomas Schreiner, however, provides a formidable critique of this newer approach. First, the "works" that Paul mentions in 9:32 should not be restricted to Jewish nationalist markers. In fact, none of those badges are even mentioned in the passage or its context.[3] Second, to distinguish the nationalistic righteousness of the Jews from their observance of the law creates a false dichotomy. The Jews felt superior to Gentiles, not only because of their birth, but also because of their perceived obedience to the Torah. Third, the words *hē idia dikaiosynē* ("their own righteousness") in 10:3 refer to righteousness born out of works in the broad sense, an interpretation confirmed by the parallel text, Philippians 3:9: "not having a righteousness of my own that comes from the law, but that which is through faith in Christ." These criticisms combine to refute a positive rendering of the Torah in 9:30–10:4.[4]

As we noted above, in 10:4 Paul reverses the Deuteronomic curses and blessings. Christ brought an end to the law by taking upon himself at the cross its curses (cf. Gal. 3:10–13), so that those whose faith is in him can experience justification—that is, the covenantal blessings. In this, Paul replaces nomism with fideism. Moreover, the gift of salvation is available to both Jew and Gentile, indicating the universal scope of the apostle's message. For further discussion of 10:4, see the third item in the "Additional Insights" section.

10:5 *the righteousness that is by the law.* As noted in the "Additional Insights" section regarding 10:4, so too with regard to 10:5 two basic interpretations emerge concerning the Torah—one positive, the other negative. The traditional exegesis of this verse is that Paul is using Leviticus 18:5 negatively to warn people about attempting to achieve righteousness by obeying the law. That is, anyone who intends to find acceptance before God by following the law had better be prepared to obey it perfectly or suffer its curses for disobedience. But, of course, no one is capable of fulfilling the law, for all are affected by sin (see Rom. 3:20; 7:5–11). Nor does one need to obey the Torah, for Christ's coming has spelled the end of that approach in the divine program (10:4). Rather, what is needed to acquire God's righteousness is faith in Christ, as he is revealed in the kerygma (preaching of the gospel) (10:6–8). This is the way to life and the Deuteronomic blessings.

More recently, however, a positive rendering of 10:5 has been offered by some scholars,[5] claiming that it describes the obedience of faith. According to this approach, the doing of the Torah is essential if one is to have life, and this is compatible with faith in Christ (10:6–13). Thus, the *de* in 10:6 should be translated "and," not "but," indicating continuity between doing the law (10:5) and faith in Christ (10:6–8). Consequently, this viewpoint argues that Paul interprets Leviticus 18:5 positively.

Schreiner's criticisms of this approach, however, render the tertiary usage of the law in 10:5 untenable.[6] First, to posit such a view of the law in 10:5 would mean that Paul has radically reversed his negative portrayal of it in 9:30–10:4, something that surely would confuse his readers. Second, similar to the first criticism, the contrast between doing the law and believing in Christ pervades 9:30–10:3. For Paul suddenly to shift gears and describe the doing of the law in positive terms seems very awkward and ultimately self-refuting to the apostle's argument in Romans that salvation is by faith alone. Third, the parallel between 10:5 ("righteousness that is by the law") and Philippians 3:9 ("not having a righteousness of my own that comes from the law") is too close to be denied. Since the latter is negative in connotation concerning the law, it stands to reason that so is the former. Fourth, Paul's negative employment of Leviticus 18:5 in Romans 10:5 would be consistent with his pejorative usage of Leviticus 18:5 in Galatians 3:13,[7] which warns that following the law, ironically, invokes the Deuteronomic curses.

Theological Insights

At least two truths meet the reader of Romans 9:30–10:5. First, these verses, like 9:1–29 before them, deal with the problem of Israel's unbelief in their Messiah. Paul's immediate explanation in 9:1–10:5 for that anomaly is that Israel "got hung up" over the works righteousness of the law and consequently rejected the only way to God's righteousness: faith in Jesus Christ. This is why the majority of Jews are rejecting Christ, while many Gentiles are accepting him. Paul's long-range explanation of the problem of Israel's unbelief is that God intends that the Gentiles' acceptance of Israel's Messiah will make the Jews jealous and convert them at the end of history (see chap. 11). Second, such a mass conversion of the Gentiles to Christ is the obedience of faith (recall 1:5), the end-time conversion of the Gentiles. But such a happening is, surprisingly, occurring before the restoration of Israel (cf. 10:19–20; 11:25–27). In the meantime, the new-covenant blessing of life belongs to Christian Gentiles, while the covenant curse of spiritual death pertains to non-Christian Jews.

Teaching the Text

A broad message comes to mind relative to Romans 9:30–10:5. One could take a general approach to 9:30–10:5 by emphasizing it as the human responsibility side of election, while 9:1–29 reflects the divine side of election. Both, I think, are true. There is mystery though harmony. A view that is being championed these days claims to harmonize divine sovereignty and human responsibility. It is known as Molinism. Over three hundred years after Thomas Aquinas, a Spanish Jesuit of the Counter-Reformation, Luis de Molina (1535–1600), advanced Aquinas's compatibilist theory of divine sovereignty and human responsibility with his theory of middle knowledge (*scientia media*). According to Molinism, there are three types of God's foreknowledge. The first level is natural knowledge. God knows all possible worlds and all things that humans can do. The third level is actual knowledge. God knows what actually will happen in the real world. This is determined by God's free and sovereign choice. In between these two levels is a second level, middle knowledge. God knows what humans would do in any given set of circumstances; that is, God knows counterfactuals (note, e.g., Matt. 11:23: "For if the miracles that were performed in you had been performed in Sodom, it would have remained to this day").

Thus, God's sovereignty applies to his knowledge, which leaves room for human choice. Molina's concept of middle knowledge appears to harmonize divine sovereignty and human responsibility because it enables God to exercise providential control of free creatures without abridging the free exercise of their wills. By virtue of his knowledge of counterfactuals of creaturely freedom and his freedom to decree that certain circumstances exist and certain free creatures be placed in those circumstances, God is able to bring it about indirectly that events occur that he knew would happen as a direct result of the particular decisions that those creatures would freely make in those circumstances. In other words, out of all the possible worlds that God could have created, he created a world that best predisposed humans to make the right decisions for life and eternity.

Illustrating the Text

To be the "chosen people" does not preclude the need to confess Jesus as Savior.

Personal Stories: Dr. Michael Rydelnik, a professor of Jewish studies at Moody Bible Institute and the son of Holocaust survivors, tells the story of his Jewish father. When his father, who had severed all ties when Michael became a Christian, died in 1996 in

Israel, Michael questioned the theology he had learned that "apart from conscious faith in Yeshua [Jesus], all people, including my father, would be lost for eternity."[8] Rydelnik knew that if admission to heaven could be earned by suffering, his father should be there. He had lost his first wife, five sons, and an adopted daughter to the ovens at Auschwitz. He had also suffered terribly in several concentration camps. He later would lose a second wife in childbirth, and a two-year-old daughter by his third marriage drowned in Berlin. Rydelnik's father and his third wife moved to America; twenty years later, that wife and his son Michael and two daughters came to faith in Jesus Christ. The elder Rydelnik then disowned them and moved to Israel. Among the conclusions Dr. Rydelnik draws are these: "Jewish people, in fact all people, are lost without faith in Yeshua as their Redeemer," and "Jewish people and Gentiles must have conscious faith in Yeshua to experience God's forgiveness and receive the promise of life in the world to come."[9]

God is behind everything, yet we have free will to accept or reject God's offer.

Literature: *The Brothers Karamazov*, by Fyodor Dostoyevsky. Chapter 5 of book 5 of this renowned novel (1880), "The Grand Inquisitor on the Nature of Man," has led to the conversion of more than one prominent personality and can be read coherently with the background of chapter 4. A story within a story, it includes a profound defense from an agnostic's mouth of a Christ who will neither manipulate nor be manipulated but who seeks the free love of individuals. Ivan, the agnostic brother, says about

Christ, "You desired the free love of man, that he should follow you freely, seduced and captivated by you. Instead of the firm ancient law, man had henceforth to decide for himself, with a free heart, what is good and what is evil, having only your image before him as a guide."[10]

Literature: *The Great Divorce*, by C. S. Lewis. In chapter 11 of this book (1945) is a well-known account in which a "little red lizard" riding on the ghost's shoulder represents lust. What becomes clear is that the ghost must choose whether or not to accept an angel's offer to kill the lizard. The ghost makes several excuses, including that the lizard is asleep and bothering no one, and that the process will cause too much pain. In desperation, he tries to manipulate the angel, but the angel insists the ghost must ask him to do it, bringing his will into submission.

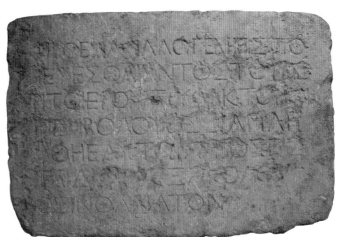

This inscription from the first century AD forbids Gentiles in the temple courtyard. Those who entered could be punished with death. It was posted on the fence that separated the Court of the Gentiles from the temple area on the temple mount in Jerusalem. Though Gentiles were once excluded from God's presence in the temple, now all can be saved through belief in Jesus Christ.

Romans 9:30–10:5

Deuteronomic Background | Zealotry | *Telos*

Here we return to two background concerns and a further exegetical matter.

1. James Scott identifies the Deuteronomic underpinning of Romans 9–11 by applying to this text the sixfold description of the Deuteronomistic tradition developed by Odil Steck.[1] To summarize: Israel has been disobedient to the law of God throughout history (Rom. 9:31; 10:21; cf. chap. 2). God has sent his prophets to call Israel to repentance, but Israel has repeatedly rejected them, including Paul himself (11:2–5; 10:16; cf. 15:31). The Deuteronomic curses now rest on Israel in the form of foreign oppression (9:1–3; 10:3; 11:1, 5, 10, 16–25; cf. 2:6–8; 3:5). It is still possible for Israel to repent (9:22; 10:16, 19; 11:11, 14; cf. 2:4–5). One day Israel will indeed repent and be restored (11:26–27). To this I would add that Paul reverses the Deuteronomic curses and blessings in Romans 9:30–10:21. We see, then, that the covenant structure as well as the Deuteronomic background are deeply imprinted upon Paul's letter to the Romans, thus justifying our proposed outline for the book as a whole (see "The Genre/Outline of Romans" in the "Introduction to Romans," above).

2. Zealotry was an important part of Israel's heritage. The classic examples were those who were prepared to use the sword to maintain Israel's commitment to the Torah and purity as expressed by being set apart from the Gentiles.[2] "Zeal for the law" became the watch cry of the Macca-bean revolt against Antiochus IV Epiphanes begun in 167 BC (1 Macc. 2:26–27, 50, 58; 2 Macc. 4:2). In AD 66, the Zealot movement incited Israel to revolt against Rome. Similarly, zeal for the ordinances (of the law) characterized the Essenes (e.g., 1QS 4.4; 9.23; 1QH^a 6.14), although their zeal was directed toward spiritual rather than physical warfare.[3] Moreover, Paul in his pre-Christian days seems to have imbibed the zealot spirit of his Jewish ancestors. I have argued elsewhere that Rabbi Paul walked in the circle of writers of such Jewish works as Sirach, Baruch, and *Psalms of Solomon*. These writings are strongly nationalistic and nomistic in perspective. One perceives in them a zealot attitude toward the law and Gentiles. That is to say, if Jews were going to take the law of Moses seriously they would need to expel Gentiles from the land of Israel because their failure to follow the Torah made the land ritualistically unclean, thereby polluting Palestine. But what a change in Paul's perspective after his conversion to Christ! Paul parted company with such zealous regulations, such that now Paul argued that the Torah was finished in the plan of God. And if that were so, then Gentiles were now invited to know God through faith in Christ, not the rituals of the law. No doubt, Paul's about-face regarding the Torah and Gentiles incited zealot-minded Jews to oppose him. Indeed, his letters to the Galatian, Roman, and Philippian churches signal as much.

3. Here I delve more deeply into the nuance of the word *telos* (10:4). Basically, two interpretations of this word have been proposed: "termination" and "goal" (some suggest a hybrid of the two).[4] Referring to the "termination" of the law is more negative, while the "goal" of the law sounds more positive, implying the continuation of the Torah in the lives of believers.

Those who opt for the second approach point to two key considerations. First, the word *telos* has a degree of ambiguity,[5] which allows for the meaning "goal." Second, *telos*, along with *katelaben* ("attained" [9:30]) and *ephthasen* ("arrived" [9:31]), calls forth race imagery,[6] suggesting the meaning of "goal" or "winning post."[7]

Those who see in *telos* the idea of termination or end counter with two points. First, in the New Testament *telos* normally conveys a temporal meaning (see especially 1 Cor. 1:8; 10:11; 15:24; 2 Cor. 3:13; 11:15; Phil. 3:19).[8] Second, although Paul uses race imagery, surely *telos* as a goal signifies the finish line. In addition to these criticisms, a third consideration is in order. If indeed 10:5 portrays the law negatively, consistency dictates a similar rendering in 10:4. Indeed, the connecting word between 10:4 and 10:5, *gar* ("for, since"), seems to link the negative statement in 10:4 with a similar remark in 10:5.

The Reversal of the Deuteronomic Curses and Blessings: Righteousness by Faith

Big Idea *Paul continues in 10:6–21 his reversal of the Deuteronomic curses and blessings. The former have fallen upon disobedient Israel, while the latter belong to believing Gentiles.*

Understanding the Text

The Text in Context

This unit addresses the last three sections of Romans 9:30–10:21: 10:6–8; 10:9–13; and 10:14–21.

The theme of 10:6–8 is the nearness of the gospel. It outlines thus:

1. Righteousness by faith versus the law (10:6a)
2. Righteousness by faith is in the gospel (10:6b–8)

The theme of 10:9–13 is the assurance of salvation. It divides into two parts:

1. The steps to salvation (10:9–10)
2. The scope of salvation (10:11–13)

The theme of 10:14–21 is the steps of salvation. It answers two questions:

1. What are the steps of salvation? (10:14–15)

   a. A preacher is sent to declare the good news
   b. The good news is heard
   c. The good news is believed
   d. The individual calls on the name of the Lord (cf. 10:12–13)

2. What has actually happened? (10:16–21)

   a. Israel has not believed the good news of restoration in Christ
   b. Gentiles have believed the good news of restoration in Christ

Note also that 10:19–20 forms an *inclusio* with 9:30: Gentiles believe the gospel and enjoy the blessings of the covenant.

Historical and Cultural Background

1. Many commentators argue that Romans 10:6–8 plays off of a prized equation in Second Temple Judaism: God's wisdom is embodied in the Torah (Deut. 30:12–14;

Bar. 4:1; cf. Philo, *Posterity* 84–85; *T. Neof.* on Deut. 30; also expressed in the Dead Sea Scrolls). The upshot of Paul's argument in Romans 10:6–8 is that Christ is the wisdom of God who has replaced the law as the means to God's righteousness.[1]

2. Paul's midrash (commentary) on Deuteronomy 30:12–14 in Romans 10:6–8 is reminiscent of the *pesher* method of commenting on the Old Testament in the Dead Sea Scrolls. That literature quotes an Old Testament text and then says "that is" or "this means that" (which is the translation of the Aramaic word *pesher*), offering an eschatological reading of that text. In other words, the Qumran new-covenant community applied the Old Testament prophecies about the remnant to itself as the people of God in the end time (see, e.g., their *pesharim* on Habakkuk, Nahum, Isaiah).[2] Paul does something similar in Romans 10:6–8. He quotes Deuteronomy 30:10–12, and then he applies it to Christ, the wisdom of God who has replaced the Torah, by introducing the quotation with "that is" (vv. 6b, 7b, 8b).

3. Once again the key background to a Romans passage is the Deuteronomistic tradition. This Old Testament setting heavily influences Romans 10:14–21. Thus, (a) God sent his prophets to call Israel to repentance (Rom. 10:14–15, 18); (b) but Israel persisted in their sin of unbelief (Rom. 10:16, 18, 21); (c) therefore God judged Israel by sending that nation into exile (the covenant curses; compare Rom. 10:16, 18, 21 with the exilic setting of Isaiah 52:7; 53:1 and the prophecy of Deut. 32:21); (d) but if Israel repents, God will restore them (Isa. 52:7); yet it is the Gentiles who repent that are being restored

Key Themes of Romans 10:6–21

- Those who try to obey the law to obtain righteousness before God must follow it perfectly (according to Lev. 18:5).
- The gospel is near to each of us. Therefore, everyone has the responsibility to believe.
- Salvation involves believing Jesus Christ the Lord and confessing him to others.
- Paul spells out the order of salvation: a preacher declares the good news; it is heard and believed; the individual calls upon the name of the Lord and is saved.
- However, Israel has heard but not believed the gospel, while Gentiles have heard and believed.
- The Deuteronomic tradition is the key theme that informs Romans 10:14–21, but it is reversed: Jews have rejected the good news and therefore suffer the covenant curses, while Gentiles accept the gospel and therefore enjoy the covenant blessings.

to God—the covenant blessings (Isa. 65:1; cf. Deut. 32:21).

Interpretive Insights

10:6–8 *the righteousness that is by faith.* Earlier I discussed this passage with reference to the identification of wisdom. Here I wish to make two further comments. First, 10:6–8 contrasts the righteousness that is from faith with 10:5 and the righteousness of the law. We may summarize this antithesis accordingly: the Mosaic law had promised life to those who observed its precepts (Lev. 18:5). However, an ominous note is sounded in Leviticus 26:14–39, where already there is the anticipation that Israel will fail to keep the stipulations of the covenant. Surely Paul, like much of Judaism, was aware of that eventuality. In other words, although Leviticus 18:5 held out the theoretical possibility of obeying the law, in practice it didn't deliver on its promise of life for those who attempted to keep the divine commandments, because they failed to keep it fully. In reality, no one can perfectly obey the Torah. A different picture emerges, however, in Romans 10:6–8, where the righteousness that comes through faith speaks. That message of justification is that salvation is available to all (10:6–8) through faith in Christ (10:9–13). This contrast between faith and law surely casts the latter in a negative, not positive, light in 10:6–8.

Second, Paul's midrash on Deuteronomy 30:12–14 (cf. Bar. 3:29–30; see "Historical and Cultural Background," above), whereby he replaces the law with wisdom, serves to contrast the two. That is, divine righteousness comes not through the Torah but rather through Christ, God's preexistent, now incarnate wisdom. In effect, then, Paul's interpretive technique serves to disassociate wisdom from the law, with two results: he replaces nomism with the principle of faith alone, and particularism with universalism.

I conclude my comments on 10:6–8 by noting that even Moses himself, according to Paul, apparently had doubts that Israel would achieve God's righteousness by obeying the law. Thus, if Leviticus 18:5 (see Rom. 10:5) and Deuteronomy 30:12–14 (see Rom. 10:6b–8) dictate that Israel needed to obey the law in order to have the covenantal blessing of life, then in Deuteronomy 9:4–5 (see Rom. 10:6a: "Do not say in your heart") Moses already warned the Israelites not to think that it was their righteousness via the law that won them the land of Canaan. It was only God's mercy and power that accomplished that. This reminds us of how different the Abrahamic and Mosaic covenants were. The former was based on grace, whereas the latter could easily lead to a works-based salvation. It seems that Moses himself early on became aware of the spiritual impotence of the Torah.

10:9–10 *declare with your mouth, "Jesus is Lord," and believe in your heart.* Verses 9–10 provide an overview of the steps to salvation (see 10:14–15). First, the sinner must believe that Jesus is Lord. That is, the sinner must believe that God raised Jesus from the dead as proof that the cross was atoning (recall 4:24–25). Second, the individual then must publicly confess Jesus as Lord. If, as many commentators suggest, the pronouncement "Jesus is Lord" was made at the time of one's baptism, then Paul would be saying that salvation is first a matter of believing in the heart and then making that profession public through baptism (cf. Acts 2:38; Rom. 6:1–14; Col. 2:12; Titus 3:5; 1 Pet. 3:20–22).[3]

HE IS NOT HERE—
FOR HE IS RISEN

The Garden Tomb is a site near the Damascus Gate of the Old City of Jerusalem that many believe to be the garden and sepulcher of Joseph of Arimathea. Whether it is authentic or not is up for debate, but the site itself creates a reverent and meaningful atmosphere for visitors to reflect on Jesus' death, burial, and resurrection. Visitors can enter the tomb and, when turning around to exit, see a sign reminding them "He is not here—for he is risen."

10:11–13 *"Everyone who calls on the name of the Lord will be saved."* Here Paul provides the assurance of salvation. Quoting Isaiah 28:16 in 10:11, which assures Jews that if they trust God, he will vindicate them at the judgment, Paul applies that hope to Christians because of their faith in Christ. Such an assurance is for anyone—Jew or Gentile—for God is the same Lord of both (cf. Rom. 3:29–30). Indeed, everyone who trusts in Christ will be saved, which is Paul's adaptation of Joel 2:32. And not to be overlooked in this discussion is the fact that the setting of Joel 2:32 is the promised Spirit and restoration, which are now fulfilled in Christ.

10:14–15 *How, then, can they call on the one they have not believed in?* Verses 14–21 specify the steps in the process of salvation just mentioned in 10:12–13. I have already laid out the logical order of those steps in the outline above. Here we follow the exegetical order, which, through a series of rhetorical questions, reverses the process:

> How can they call on the Lord for salvation (cf. vv. 12–13) if they have not *believed* in the Lord? (v. 14a)
>
> But how can they believe in one they have not *heard*? (v. 14b)
>
> And how can they hear if someone is not *sent*? (vv. 14b–15)

The Isaiah 52:7 quotation recalls God's promise to restore Israel out of exile (the covenant curses). This good news is, according to Paul, spiritual restoration in Christ, the blessings of the new covenant (cf. Rom. 1:1–2, 16).

10:16–21 *not all the Israelites accepted the good news.* Verse 16 interrupts the flow of thought of 10:14–15, signaling that Israel did not accept the good news of restoration, neither during Isaiah's day (see Isa. 53:1) nor during Paul's day. This is because Israel rejected the Suffering Servant in Isaiah's day (compare Isa. 53:1 with Isa. 52:13–53:12) and now Jesus the ultimate Suffering Servant. Such ominous news of Israel's rejection is picked up again in 10:18. But there is a positive note in 10:16 that anticipates 10:19–20. The proper response to the good news is to accept it or obey/believe (*hypēkousan/episteusen*) it. This combination of obedience/faith brings to mind the obedience of faith of the Gentiles mentioned in Romans 1:5 and developed in Romans thereafter. Paul will turn to that subject again in 10:19–20. Verse 17 specifies the object of the believer's faith: the word, or the gospel, of Christ.

In 10:18 Paul uses the language of natural revelation to say that the gospel has gone all over the world (the Roman Empire?) (cf. Ps. 19:4). Thus, Jews have had ample opportunity to hear and believe that good news. Ironically, however, it is Gentiles, not Jews, who have believed the gospel of Christ, just as Deuteronomy 32:21 (see Rom. 10:19) and Isaiah 65:1 (see Rom. 10:20) predicted. In accepting the gospel, Gentiles are participants in the blessings of the new covenant. This is the obedience of faith, the end-time conversion of the Gentiles. Indeed, such mass conversion of the Gentiles not only precedes Israel's restoration but also participates in that restoration before Israel does (cf. Rom. 11:25–27). Lamentably, however, unbelieving Israel continues to dig in its heels against the gospel (cf. Isa. 65:2). Consequently, the covenant curses continue to fall on Israel in its spiritual exile from God.

Theological Insights

Three theological insights surface in Romans 10:6–21. First, righteousness by faith is the only way to please God (10:6–8). Second, righteousness by faith provides assurance of salvation (10:9–13). Third, Romans 10:14–21 still provides powerful motivation for evangelism and mission work today. Missionaries must go to preach the good news to those who have never heard.

Teaching the Text

Romans 10:6–21 provides excellent material for a message on missions, especially 10:12–15 with its steps to salvation, which are straightforward. Someone goes to a people group and preaches the gospel to them; those people hear the gospel and believe it, resulting in calling on the name of the Lord, which in turn results in their salvation (10:14–21). But this has sparked an age-old debate: do the lost have to actually hear the gospel and respond to it in order to be saved?

The numerous answers to this question can be reduced to three. The "exclusivist" answers yes to that question. No one can come to God in any way other than the gospel of Jesus Christ. Simply responding to natural revelation alone—believing from creation and conscience that there is a God—without hearing and accepting the special revelation of the gospel is insufficient for salvation. The "inclusivist" answers no to the question. A person who responds to whatever light he or she has—general revelation, not special revelation—and believes it (that there is a God) and thereby lives a moral life is accepted by God, apart from the gospel. This is often labeled the "anonymous Christian" view. The "universalist" goes even further than the inclusivist, saying that Jesus' death and resurrection were so effective that they saved all people without them having to trust in Christ or even hearing the gospel at all. But from Romans 10:14–21 it seems clear that the "exclusivist" view has the most biblical support, though sometimes God may reveal Christ to the lost through dreams and visions apart from human contact.

Illustrating the Text

We have powerful motivation for missions and evangelism.

Biography: The recent death of Ralph Winter (1924–2009) reminds us of his strategic emphasis on reaching not simply every nation with the gospel but also every people group. Winter founded the U.S. Center for World Mission and, soon after, the William Carey International University without financial backing at the time and only one hundred dollars to begin. Winter said, "We were willing to fail because the goal we sensed was so urgent and strategic." However, the center did not fail, and it has trained thousands of missionaries and support personnel and worked tirelessly to bring the vision of reaching hidden peoples to the wider church. In 2005 *Time* magazine included Winter as one of the twenty-five most influential evangelicals. In 2008 the North American Mission Conference gave him the lifetime service award. "No doubt Winter will take greater pleasure in meeting the men and women from every tribe, tongue and nation who praise the name of Jesus in glory—all because of his passion to spread Christ's message."[4]

Biography: David Brainerd. A great missionary statesman, Brainerd (1718–47) worked among the American Indians. He was powerfully motivated to evangelism. He suffered all kinds of distresses, including both physical discomfort and emotional discouragement, but continued his work because of his calling. Having waited long for revival among the Native Americans, Brainerd finally saw it. In his journal, he wrote, "It was very affecting to see the poor Indians, who the other day were hallooing and yelling in their idolatrous feasts and drunken frolics, now crying to God with such importunity for an interest in His dear Son."[5]

Anyone who believes on and confesses the Lord Jesus Christ will be saved.

Biography: Christopher Hitchens and Peter Hitchens are brothers: one is an atheist, the other a Christian. After Peter regained his Christian faith, he wrote a book entitled *The Rage against God: How Atheism Led Me to Faith*. His older brother, Christopher, became famous as an acerbic advocate for atheism and wrote *The Missionary Position: Mother Teresa in Theory and Practice* and his bestseller, *God Is Not Great: How Religion Poisons Everything*. Peter understands that logic; as a teen, he burned his Bible and rebelled against everything that he had been taught was good, right, and holy. But in time, he stopped avoiding churches and great religious art, leaving himself open to unsettling messages from the past. While gazing at a fifteenth-century painting of the last judgment, he was moved. "These people did not appear remote or from the ancient past; they were my own generation. Because they were naked, they were not imprisoned in their own age by time-bound fashions," says Peter. "On the contrary, their hair and the set of their faces were entirely in the style of my own time. They were me, and people I knew. I had a sudden strong sense of religion being a thing of the present day, not imprisoned under thick layers of time. My large catalogue of misdeeds replayed themselves rapidly in my head." Then came the oaths of his wedding rites and the baptisms of his formerly atheistic wife and their daughter. A fellow journalist heard that Peter Hitchens had returned to church and, with "a look of mingled pity and horror," bluntly asked, "How can you do that?"[6]

On its website, the U.S. Center for World Mission describes itself as "a mission agency that helps to improve strategic decision-making and practice on the frontiers of mission, surmounting the barriers that hinder God's kingdom from coming among all peoples." The heart of its mission and vision is "a church for every people." (http://www.uscwm.org/index.php/about/)

Exile for National Israel, Restoration for Spiritual Israel

Big Idea *Paul juxtaposes two types of Israel: national Israel (11:7–10) versus spiritual Israel (11:1–6). The former remains in exile and under the covenant curses, but the latter as the remnant is enjoying the long-awaited restoration of Israel as well as the covenant blessings.*

Understanding the Text

The Text in Context

Romans 11 moves from Paul's day to a day in the future when national Israel will convert to Jesus the Messiah. At that time, national Israel will, for the first time, become spiritual Israel. Paul therefore provides three reasons why God is not finished with ethnic Israel. First, Israel's rejection of Christ is only partial (11:1–10). Not all of Israel has rejected Christ. There is a remnant of Israel that has accepted Christ. Second, Israel's rejection of Jesus the Messiah actually serves a merciful purpose. It has made room for the Gentiles' conversion in the present (11:11–24). Third, Israel's rejection of the Messiah is only temporary. The day will come when ethnic Israel will accept Christ (11:25–32). The thought of all of this causes Paul to burst forth in praise of God's wisdom in 11:33–36.

In Romans 11:1–10 Paul contrasts national Israel with the remnant, spiritual Israel:

1. Spiritual Israel (the remnant) is the true restoration by God's grace (11:1–6).
2. National Israel is still in exile from God because of their works or attempts to keep the law (11:7–10).

Historical and Cultural Background

The main background of Romans 11:1–10 is the Elijah narrative in 1 Kings 18–19. There we read about Elijah's defeat and destruction of the prophets of Baal (the storm-god and head of the Canaanite pantheon of deities) and about Jezebel, King Ahab's wife, and her threat to kill Elijah in retribution for his actions. Elijah flees for his life to Mount Horeb, where God assures him that a faithful group of seven thousand Jews have not bowed to Baal.

These are the faithful remnant, and God will accomplish through Elijah and them his purposes for Israel.

Interpretive Insights

11:1–4 *Did God reject his people? . . . "I have reserved for myself seven thousand."* Romans 11:1–10 provides the first reason that God has not abandoned Israel or, to put it another way, why God is not finished with Israel: not all of Israel has rejected Christ. Verses 1–4 assure the reader that God has always had a remnant—Jews faithful to God. Two examples are provided. The first is Paul himself, who is an Israelite, a descendant of Abraham, and from the tribe of Benjamin. These credentials show that Paul is Jewish, and, as a Christian, he is one of the remnant. Indeed, the first believers in Jesus were Jews and therefore also constituted the remnant. The second example that Paul provides is the remnant in the Old Testament—Elijah and the seven thousand who remained faithful to Yahweh when the rest of Israel acquiesced to the worship of Baal (compare 11:3–4 with 1 Kings 19:10, 14, 18).

11:5–6 *there is a remnant chosen by grace . . . it cannot be based on works.* Verses 5–6 make clear that the salvation of the "remnant" (*leimma*) is based on God's grace,

Key Themes of Romans 11:1–10

- God has not abandoned his covenant people, spiritual Israel, the remnant.
- But for the time being, national Israel remains outside the covenant blessings.

not works (of the Torah). Paul said something similar in 4:1–5, where he made the point that God is no one's debtor. In other words, God's acceptance of Abraham and the Old Testament remnant was based on grace. Likewise, in Paul's day, the salvation, or restoration, of the remnant happens because they have accepted Christ rather than obeyed the law as the means to justification.[1]

11:7 *What the people of Israel sought so earnestly they did not obtain.* Paul paints a dim picture of national Israel that makes it clear that they are not a part of the remnant. This foreboding reality goes all the way back to the Old Testament. In 11:7 Paul says that national Israel is not a part of the elect (the remnant), because their heart has been hardened. Here the verb *epōrōthēsan* ("were hardened") is a "theological passive": Israel was hardened to God by God! As we will see, Paul provides proof of this by quoting from the threefold division of the Hebrew Bible: the Law, the Prophets, and the Writings.[2]

11:8 *"God gave them a spirit of stupor, eyes that could not see and ears that could not*

The traditional location of Elijah's contest with the prophets of Baal is on Mount Carmel, where the Mukhraqa monastery now stands (pictured here). It was after the magnificent show of God's power that Elijah fled from Jezebel's wrath. The discouraged Elijah headed to Mount Horeb, where God revealed to him that a loyal remnant still existed, ones who had not "bowed the knee to Baal" (Rom. 11:4).

hear." In verse 8 Paul quotes from the Law, at Deuteronomy 29:5, to demonstrate that God induced a spiritual stupor on Israel such that they really neither saw nor heard the truth concerning God. The Deuteronomic setting was Moses' speech to Israel before they crossed over into the promised land. Deuteronomy 29 is a part of the covenant blessings and curses. Moses hoped Israel would obey the law and enjoy the covenant blessings. But Moses suspected that Israel would not do so. God would dull Israel's heart to the law, and consequently the nation would experience the covenant curses. Paul also draws upon the Prophets, at Isaiah 29:10, which shows that Moses' and Isaiah's worst fear has come true. Israel is spiritually blind to God's law, and that is why they are about to be judged and sent into exile—the covenant curses.

11:9–10 "*May their table become a snare . . . and their backs be bent forever.*" Here Paul quotes from the Writings, at Psalm 69:22–23. The reference is to King David's enemies, who one day will be judged by God for betraying David. Psalm 69 played a prominent role in the early Christians' understanding of Jesus (cf. Mark 3:21; 15:23; Luke 13:35; John 2:17; 15:25; Acts 1:20; Rom. 15:3; Phil. 4:3; Rev. 3:5; 16:1). The nuance here is that Jesus, the true Davidic king, has been betrayed by his people Israel. Consequently, God has cast a spiritual spell of unbelief upon national Israel that has resulted in the heaping upon them of the covenant curses—subjection to the Roman Empire and spiritual exile from God.[3]

Theological Insights

Several theological insights open to us in Romans 11:1–10. First, salvation is by God's grace, not human effort. Second, God's sovereign choice to dull Israel to the things of God, in the context of 11:1–10, probably refers to the nation, not to individuals as 9:6–29 did. Third, Israel's rejection of the law, killing of the prophets, and subsequent exile and judgment, along with the remnant's restoration, constitute the key themes of the Deuteronomic tradition. Fourth, God has always had a faithful few—a remnant—who have stood for him against the majority who do not. Fifth, the fact that not all of Israel has disobeyed God indicates that Israel's rejection of Christ is partial. And one day national Israel will embrace its Messiah (see 11:11–15, 25–27).

Teaching the Text

This is a good opportunity for a lesson on the "remnant," since Paul uses that word in 11:1–10. Although appearing in a wide variety of texts and contexts, the central idea of the remnant concept or theology is that in the midst of seemingly total apostasy and the consequential terrible judgment and/or destruction, God has always had a small, faithful group that he delivered and worked through to bring blessing.

Early allusions to the idea of a remnant are introduced in the book of Genesis. Noah and his family (Gen. 6–9) are the remnant that is saved during the flood, when all other people are destroyed in judgment. Likewise, in Genesis 45:6–7 Joseph declares to his brothers, "For two years now there has been famine in the land, and for the next five years there will be no plowing and reaping. But God sent me ahead of you to preserve for you a remnant on earth and to save your lives by a great deliverance."

The remnant theme surfaces in several other places in the Old Testament. For example, when Elijah complains to God that he is the only faithful one left, God corrects him by pointing out that he has maintained a remnant of seven thousand faithful ones in the midst of national apostasy (1 Kings 19:10–18).

The Old Testament prophets continue the remnant theme (see, e.g., Isaiah, Jeremiah, Ezekiel, Joel). The prophets proclaim that since Israel/Judah has broken the covenant, and since they refuse to repent and turn back to God, judgment is coming. This judgment takes the form of terrible foreign invasions and destruction, followed by exile from the land. Thus, the southern kingdom of Judah was destroyed and exiled by the Babylonians in 587/586 BC. Yet the prophets also prophesy hope and restoration beyond the judgment. They declare that many will be destroyed in the judgment, but not all. They prophesy that a remnant will survive, and that God will work through the remnant to bring blessings and restoration. Usually the remnant is identified as those who go into exile but who likewise hope to return to the land. The reestablishment of the remnant often is connected with the inauguration of the messianic age.

The remnant theme continues into the New Testament, but it is not nearly as prominent there as it is in the Old Testament prophets. The term "remnant" does not occur in the Gospels, although the idea is implied in several texts. Thus, in Matthew 7:13–14 Jesus states, "For wide is the gate and broad is the road that leads to destruction, and many enter through it. But small is the gate and narrow the road that leads to life, and only a few find it." Likewise, in Matthew 22:14 Jesus summarizes his preceding parable by stating, "Many are invited, but few are chosen."

In Romans 11 Paul is much more explicit. Not only does he use the term "remnant," but also in 11:2–5 he connects his argument specifically to the remnant idea in 1 Kings 19:18 ("I have reserved for myself seven thousand" [11:4]). Paul is pointing out the similarities between the apostasy in Israel in 1 Kings 19 and the parallel rejection of the Messiah by Israel during Paul's day. In both cases the nation has rejected God's word and his salvation plan. But in both situations, even though the nation as a whole has rejected God, God maintains a faithful remnant. Paul also underscores that the remnant is established by God's grace. Thus, in 11:5 Paul explains, "So too, at the present time there is a remnant chosen by

When Israel broke the covenant with the Lord by worshiping other gods, God sent judgment in the form of the Assyrian army and then the Babylonian army. Cities were captured and their residents killed or sent into exile, as shown in this battle scene of Sennacherib's successful victory over the city of Lachish (700–692 BC). Yet God preserved a small remnant who remained in the land or returned from exile, through whom he would restore the nation of Israel and bring blessing.

grace." In the early church, that remnant consisted of Jewish Christians, like Paul himself. And, to the degree that the church as a whole inherited the promises to Israel, it too could be included in the category of remnant (see again Rom. 11:11–24; cf. 1 Pet. 2:5–10; Rev. 7; 14). Indeed, Paul hoped that the conversion of Gentiles to Christ might make his Jewish compatriots jealous so that they might "take back" their Messiah (compare Rom. 11:11–12 with vv. 25–36). In that case, national Israel would become the spiritual remnant for the very first time in Israel's history, because "all Israel" would be saved. That is, national Israel and spiritual Israel would be one.

Another way to grasp the idea of the remnant as it unfolds throughout the Bible is to think of it in the shape of an hourglass: starting wide, then narrowing, then widening again. God created the entire world to be in fellowship with him, only to have his creation spurn that offer. To rectify this problem, God called out Abraham from paganism in order to make of him a new people, Israel, to worship God and declare him to the nations. Alas, Israel in time disobeyed God's law, just as the nations of the world had disobeyed God by worshiping other gods. However, the purpose of God was not thereby thwarted, for he raised up for himself a remnant, a faithful few who remained true to him—for example, Elijah and the later returnees to Israel. However, by the end of the Old Testament the hopes of Israel now rested upon one individual, the Messiah, who would turn the hearts of Jews back to God and convert the nations of the earth to the one true God. As it turns out, Israel's rejection of God throughout the Old Testament actually carried along the plan of God as it narrowed its focus, culminating in the expectation of the one Messiah. But, with the advent of Jesus Christ, the focus of God now widened, beginning with the apostles (the beginnings of the remnant in the New Testament), and expanding to include the church (the replacement of Israel, however temporary that may be); and one day it will encompass the world (which will bring the revelation of God full circle).

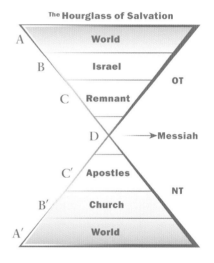

The **Hourglass of Salvation**

Illustrating the Text

A remnant of Israel is chosen by grace.

Biography: Many people are unaware that prominent Jewish believers in Jesus have lived their faith openly and still do. One such example is the great musician Felix Mendelssohn (1809–47), conductor and prolific composer. Mendelssohn's grandfather was an important Jewish philosopher, but his father, not wanting Felix and his siblings to be shunned or worse for being Jewish, had them undergo Christian baptism. Mendelssohn embraced the Christian faith and was a disciplined, devoted Christian the rest of his life. Many people are familiar with his renowned oratorio *Elijah*, but few seem to know that he also composed an oratorio called *St. Paul* and was rigorous in making sure that the scriptural wording was accurate because the Bible was such an important part of his life. Patrick Kavanaugh, in his book *The Spiritual Lives of Great Composers*, gives more detailed information about Mendelssohn.

Personal Stories: Old Testament and Semitics scholar Charles Feinberg (1909–95) tells an interesting story about a Church of England clergyman who attended an early-morning prayer meeting on behalf of Israel in an East London Jewish mission. Coming out of the meeting, he met a fellow clergyman, who had attended a service commemorating the conversion of Saint Paul. As they conversed, they told one another about where they had been. The minister who had been at the Saint Paul service expressed surprise that his fellow minister believed in the possibility of Jews being converted. "Who was St. Paul?" asked the

Jewish sympathizer. The skeptical minister answered with hesitation, "I suppose you would consider him a converted Jew." "What music did they play at the service?" asked the other minister. "Why, Mendelssohn's 'St. Paul,' of course." "Who was Mendelssohn?" "Why, a German." "He was a converted Jew." As Feinberg notes in conclusion, "This man did not believe in converted Jews, and yet he had been in a church dedicated to the memory of a converted Jew; he had attended a service in honor of this Jew's conversion; he had listened to music composed by a converted Jew." He also notes that "uncounted is the number of those who have through the centuries received the Messiah in Israel, to the saving of their souls and obtaining eternal life."[4]

Seeking is not enough; even Jews require God's sovereign grace to succeed.

Quote: C. S. Lewis is the source of many powerful quotes about God's relationship to the Jewish people, about their relationship to the Gentiles, and about God's active grace and initiating power in saving both. Particularly useful in finding these quotes is Janine Goffar's 1995 book, *The C. S. Lewis Index: A Comprehensive Guide to Lewis's Writings and Ideas*.

This statue of Felix Mendelssohn stands across from St. Thomas Church in Leipzig, Germany. It is a reconstruction of a statue originally created by Werner Stein in 1892, which stood atop a monument in Mendelssohn's honor. In 1936 the Nazis removed it because of Mendelssohn's Jewish heritage, and it was presumably destroyed. The new statue was dedicated in 2008.

The Kindness and Sternness of God

Big Idea *Israel's rejection of Jesus as Messiah is the occasion for God to show mercy to the Gentiles. Their conversion, Paul hopes, will stir Jews to jealousy and thus to accept their Messiah. God is showing kindness to Gentiles but sternness to Jews who have not accepted the Messiah. In the future, however, God will show kindness to Israel but sternness to Gentiles who fall into unbelief.*

Understanding the Text

The Text in Context

Romans 11:11 picks up the theme of 11:1. Has God finished with Israel? Verses 1–10 provided Paul's first answer to that question: no, because not all of Israel has rejected the Messiah; that is to say, the remnant has accepted the gospel. Now 11:11–24 provides a second reason why God is not done with national Israel: Israel's unbelief has allowed the Gentiles the opportunity to accept Christ, which in turn, Paul hopes, will make Jews jealous to "reclaim" their Messiah, Jesus. Romans 11:11–24 divides into two parts:

1. The twofold result of Israel's rejection of Jesus (11:11–16)
   a. The conversion of the Gentiles (11:11a, 12a, 15a)
   b. The subsequent conversion of Israel (11:11b, 12b–16)

2. Warning to the Gentiles not to look down on Jews (11:17–24)
   a. Christian Gentiles are indebted to the Jewish heritage (11:17–18)
   b. Gentiles were grafted into the people of God because of Israel's unbelief, not because Gentiles are superior (11:19–21)
   c. God's present kindness and sternness can be reversed in the future (11:22–24)

Historical and Cultural Background

1. The first relevant background information comes from horticultural practices. Paul's argument in 11:11–24 presumes that the olive tree is the one people of God, with the patriarchs representing the root/trunk of the tree. Jews are the natural branches of that tree that have been broken off because of unbelief. Gentile Christians are the wild branches grafted into the tree. Nor-

mally, the opposite occurs in horticulture: a healthy, productive branch is grafted into a wild, unproductive tree to bring health to it. But Paul's reversal of that process—a wild or uncultivated branch is grafted into a healthy tree—is attested in Israel.[1]

2. Paul has good reason for his condemnation of anti-Semitism: it was widespread in his day.

Interpretive Insights

11:11–16 *their rejection brought reconciliation to the world*. Verses 11–16 present the twofold result of Israel's rejection of their Messiah. The first is the conversion of the Gentiles. Three synonymous phrases are used to describe this conversion: Israel's stumbling/fall/transgression brought salvation to the Gentiles (11:11a); Israel's transgression/loss resulted in riches (spiritual blessings of salvation [cf. the riches of God's mercy and grace in Rom. 2:4; 9:23; 11:33; Eph. 1:7, 18; 2:7; 3:8; Phil. 4:17; Col. 1:27]) for the world/Gentiles (11:12a); Israel's rejection resulted in Gentiles being reconciled to God through Christ (11:15a). That the Gentiles would convert to the true God in the end time was a part of Jewish

Key Themes of Romans 11:11–24

- The present unbelief of Israel relative to the gospel has become the occasion for the Gentiles to accept Christ.
- But in the future, Israel, stirred by jealousy, will accept their rightful Messiah, Jesus.
- There is no room whatsoever for anti-Semitism among Christians.
- God is fair: in the Old Testament he showed kindness to Israel but sternness to Gentiles, while in the present he is showing kindness to Gentiles but sternness to Israel. God's response depends on belief.

expectation (Isa. 2:2–3a; 56:6–7; 60:1–7; Tob. 13:11–13; 14:6–7; *T. Zeb.* 9.8; *T. Benj.* 9.2; *Sib. Or.* 3.767–95; *Pss. Sol.* 17.26–46). But what was not expected was that the conversion of the Gentiles would take place before the restoration of Israel. Paul calls this a "mystery" in Romans 11:25. Moreover, this end-time conversion of the Gentiles Paul understands to be "the obedience of faith" (Rom. 1:5).

The second result of Israel's rejection of Jesus the Messiah directly proceeds from the first. The conversion of the Gentiles, Paul hopes, will stir the Jews to jealousy to "reclaim" their Messiah (11:11b, 12b–16). Verse 12 contains a *qal wahomer* argument

Olive trees were very common and valuable trees in the Mediterranean region, and Paul's audience would have been familiar with their characteristics and the horticultural practices needed to care for them. The olive tree in its wild state produces small and inferior olives, which is why productive branches are grafted onto wild stock in order to create cultivated varieties producing a bountiful harvest of fruit.

(in this case, a "greater to lesser"; see the sidebar in the unit for Rom. 4:1–8):

> Greater: Israel's transgression/loss means salvation to the Gentiles.
>
> Lesser: How much more, then, will Israel's fullness/conversion to Christ bring riches to the world.

The terms "loss" (*hēttēma*) and "fullness" (*plērōma*) have the same ending, creating an aural parallel. Since *plērōma* in 11:25 means "full number," probably it means the same in 11:11: the full number of the Gentiles to be saved (11:11) and the full number of Jews to be saved (11:25). The implication is that the believing number of the remnant plus the nation of Israel to be converted to Jesus in the end time totals the full number of Jews destined for salvation (see again 11:25–27). What Paul means by greater "riches" for the world (11:12) is not stated until 11:15: life from the dead or the resurrection of humanity at the end of the world.[2]

Verses 13–14 contain a parenthetical remark by Paul. His ministry to the Gentiles is designed to make Jews jealous that Gentiles are accepting Christ and therefore motivate Jews to "take back" their rightful Messiah. We see two things from this statement. First, Paul longs for his compatriots to come to Christ (cf. 9:1–3; 10:1). In no way is Paul anti-Semitic. Second, though it is debated, Paul apparently perceived his ministry—to convert the Gentile world as a catalyst for Israel's restoration—as apocalyptic in orientation. His apostleship, he hoped, would bring about the return of Christ (recall my remarks in the introduction, and see my comments to follow on Rom. 15:22–29).

Verse 15 provides another *qal wahomer* argument in a restatement of 11:12: Israel's rejection is the reconciliation of the world (greater); Israel's acceptance will be life from the dead (lesser).

Most likely, we are to interpret "life from the dead" as referring to the resurrection of the dead that will occur at the parousia, the return of Christ (cf. Matt. 25:31–46; Rom. 8:11, 23; 1 Cor. 15:22–24; Phil. 3:1–10; 1 Thess. 4:16; Rev. 20:4–6), which will include the restoration of Israel.

The illustration in 11:16—the firstfruits of the dough being holy ensures that the whole batch will be holy—draws on Numbers 15:17–21, although the Numbers text does not mention the firstfruits making the batch holy. James Dunn suggests that this latter principle was derived from the idea that the temple conveyed holiness to all of Jerusalem (cf. Neh. 11:1, 18; Isa. 11:9; 48:2; 66:20; Jer. 31:23, 40; Ezek. 20:40).[3] Most likely, Paul means in 11:16 that the

The grafting of an olive tree on the Mediterranean island of Mallorca

patriarchs (beginning with Abraham) convey to Israel the blessings of the covenant with God (cf. 11:28). In other words, God's promise to the patriarchs ("the firstfruits") ensures that Israel ("the whole batch") will be holy one day.

11:17–18 *You do not support the root, but the root supports you.* In 11:17–24 Paul warns Christian Gentiles not to look down on Israel because of their present unbelief. The apostle to the Gentiles supplies three reasons for this warning. Verses 17–18 provide the first of these: Christian Gentiles are indebted, even dependent, on the spiritual heritage of the Old Testament people of God. Paul uses his now famous analogy to illustrate the point. Gentile Christians are wild olive branches; Jews are the natural branches; the patriarchs and the covenant with God are the root. Thus, the patriarchs and Israel precede Christian Gentiles as the people of God. Gentiles only recently have become united with the one people of God.[4]

11:19–21 *they were broken off because of unbelief, and you stand by faith. Do not be arrogant.* The second reason for Paul's warning to Gentile Christians not to look down on Israel is stated in 11:19–21: Israel was broken off from the tree—the people of God—because of unbelief, not because the Gentiles are superior. This prideful attitude of the Gentile interlocutor in 11:19 is ironically similar to the arrogant attitude of the Jewish interlocutor back in Romans 2. But no, says Paul, it was Jewish unbelief that made room for Gentiles to come to faith. It is only by faith, not works, that Gentile Christians have been grafted into the people of God (cf. 11:5–6). Indeed, if Gentile Christians abandon their trust in

Christ, they too, like Israel, will be cut off from the people of God.[5]

11:22–24 *Consider therefore the kindness and sternness of God.* Paul gives a third reason why Gentile Christians should not look down on unbelieving Jews: the kindness and sternness of God. Thus, in the present God is kind to Christian Gentiles but stern toward unbelieving Jews. But in the future God will be kind to Israel if they come to faith in Christ but stern to Gentile Christians if they do not remain in faith. Verse 24 concludes Paul's third reason with another *qal wahomer* argument: if God grafted the wild branches (Gentiles) into the tree of the people of God (greater), how much more will God regraft the natural branches (Jews) into the tree of the people of God, assuming that they accept Christ (lesser).[6]

Thus, 11:11–24 issues a serious warning to Gentile Christians: do not look down on Jews. Paul hopes by this warning and his later comments in chapters 14–15 to bring unity to Gentile and Jew in the congregations at Rome.

Theological Insights

Several truths emerge in Romans 11:11–24. First, God is fair. In the present he shows sternness to the Jews and kindness to the Gentiles; in the future, he will show kindness to Israel and, potentially, sternness to Gentiles; all of this is of course based on one's response to Christ. Second, there is only one people of God, those in the Old Testament and the New Testament eras whose faith is in God, apart from works. Third, there is no place for anti-Semitism in the world, and certainly not among Christians. The persecution of Jews throughout history, including the Holocaust, should be a stark reminder to the church of the horrors that anti-Semitism breeds. Fourth, for that matter, there should be no prejudice of any kind in the church.

Teaching the Text

Perhaps the best way to preach/teach Romans 11:11–24 is to divide it into two messages. The first sermon is "The Twofold Result of Israel's Unbelief: The Conversion of the Gentiles and the Jealousy of Israel" (11:11–16). The second message is "Dear Gentile Christians: Don't Look Down on Unbelieving Jews" (11:17–24), with the three reasons that Paul gives: the Christian Gentiles owe much to Israel's spiritual heritage (11:17–18); Israel was removed from the people of God because of unbelief, not because Gentiles are superior (11:19–21); and the kindness and sternness of God (11:22–24). The second message is self-explanatory, so the teacher might expand upon the two points under the first message. Thus, Israel's unbelief is bringing about the conversion of the nations. This needs some unpacking as follows. What would have happened if the nation of Israel had accepted Jesus' offer to be their savior? It is possible, perhaps probable, that Israel then would have enthroned Jesus as their king in Jerusalem and not have crucified him. And that would have restricted the message of God's salvation to mostly Jews. And the result of that would have been a return to Old Testament Israel's state of theocracy. But, of course, such an answer is no more than hypothetical because in fact the Jewish leadership in Jerusalem in league with the Romans rejected Jesus and masterminded his demise. For this reason, the gospel of Christ is without geographical boundary. But one day Israel will indeed accept Jesus as the Messiah, thanks to the Gentiles' conversion to Christ.

Illustrating the Text

Israel's unbelief resulted in the Gentiles' conversion and Israel's jealousy.

Theological Book: *Not the Way It's Supposed to Be*, by Cornelius Plantinga Jr. Author, profes-

Israel's spiritual heritage is reflected in the genealogy of Jesus, illustrated by this beautiful mosaic dome in the Chora Monastery, now Museum, in Istanbul, Turkey. Christ Pantocrator is at the center. Surrounding him are Old Testament figures depicting ancestors from Adam to Jacob. The lower ring then includes the twelve sons of Jacob.

sor, and minister Cornelius Plantinga observes, "Envy wants to remove somebody's good; jealousy wants to protect the good it already has (sometimes justly)." One could use these words to address the jealousy/envy of Israel.[7]

The Jews are God's chosen people, so Gentiles should show them love and respect.

History: Many stories of Gentile love for the Jews in hard times exist. Outside Yad Vashem, the Holocaust museum in Jerusalem, a garden of trees is planted in honor of "righteous Gentiles," those who risked a great deal to protect Jews, especially during the Holocaust. One of the trees planted there is in honor of Oskar Schindler, who helped to save hundreds of Jews from the gas chambers of Nazi Germany.

Film: *Weapons of the Spirit.* This award-winning documentary (1987) is the stirring account of the villagers of Le Chambon in France, many of them descendants of French Huguenots, the first Protestants in Catholic France, who remembered their ancestors' persecution and also believed the biblical injunction to love one's neighbor as oneself. Led by their pastor, André Trocmé, the people of this village defied the Nazis and took in thousands of Jews, giving them safe haven. Not a single Jew who came to them was turned away, and about five thousand Jews were saved. The villagers never spoke of it until later, and even then reluctantly, viewing their acts simply as the human and Christian thing to do.

The Mystery and Mercy of God

Big Idea *Paul merges two grand themes: mystery and mercy. The mystery of God is that the end-time conversion of the Gentiles will occur before the restoration of Israel, the reverse order of the Old Testament prophecies. God's mystery involves his showing mercy to both Gentiles and Jews in these last days.*

Understanding the Text

The Text in Context

Romans 11:25–32 is the grand conclusion to chapters 9–11, showing that God has not cast off Israel, all the while showing mercy to the nations. Romans 11:25–32 divides into two interrelated themes:

1. The Mystery of God (11:25–27)
   a. Definition of the mystery (11:25a)
   b. Delineation of the mystery (11:25b–26a)
      i. Hardening of Israel
      ii. Fullness of Gentiles
      iii. Restoration of Israel
   c. Date of the mystery (11:26b–27)
2. The Mercy of God (11:28–32)
   a. Problem for mercy (11:28–29)
   b. Procedure of mercy (11:30–31)
   c. Plan behind mercy (11:32)

Historical and Cultural Background

While not specifically historical and cultural background, there is a theological debate that has raged over Romans 11:25–27: dispensationalist versus covenantalist theology. Table 1 highlights the differences between these two venerable evangelical traditions.

Table 1: Dispensationalism versus Covenantalism

Dispensationalism	Covenantalism
Church ≠ Israel	Church = Israel
Literal fulfillment of Old Testament prophecy (premillennial)	Symbolic fulfillment of Old Testament prophecy (amillennial)
Seven dispensations	Two covenants
Innocence	Works
Conscience	Grace
Civil government	
Mosaic	
Church	
Tribulation	
Millennium	

Dispensationalism believes that God has not finished with Israel. Indeed, after the rapture of the church to heaven, God will use the great tribulation to bring ethnic Israel to faith in Christ. Then Christ will return to establish his millennial kingdom of one thousand years on earth in Jerusalem. Covenantalism, or Reformed theology, believes to the contrary that God has permanently replaced Israel with the church (though some within this camp believe that Jews will convert to Jesus Messiah at the end of history). Furthermore, the millennial kingdom is now, as is the great tribulation. The church as the manifestation of the kingdom of God will suffer the great tribulation until Christ returns to make a new creation.

Interpretive Insights

11:25–27 *I do not want you to be ignorant of this mystery . . . all Israel will be saved.* Three points can be made about this mystery: the definition (11:25a), the delineation (11:25b–26a), and the date (11:26b–27).

First, the definition of "mystery" (*mystērion*) comes from Jewish apocalyptic circles. A mystery is an end-time event that God reveals to the prophetic seer (e.g., Dan. 2:18–19, 27–30; *1 En.* 41.1; 46.2; 103.2; *2 En.* 24.3; *4 Ezra* 10.38; 12.6–38; 1QS 3.23; 4.18; 9.18; 1QHᵃ 9.21; 10.13). This background, rather than the mystery religions, informs Paul's use of the term "mystery" (e.g., Rom. 16:25–26; 1 Cor. 15:51–52; 2 Thess. 2:7). The mystery in Romans 11:25–27 is that Israel's spiritual hard-heartedness is the occasion for the conversion of the Gentiles, after which Israel will be restored to God by embracing Jesus the Messiah.

Second, in 11:25b–26a this mystery is delineated in three stages. The first stage is the present spiritual blindness of Israel to Jesus the Messiah. Israel's spiritual hardening is partial because, as we saw back in 11:1–10, there is a remnant of Jews that has accepted Christ.

- The mystery of God is an end-time event that God shared with Paul, in this case concerning the occurrence of the conversion of the nations before the restoration of Israel.
- That mystery is unfolding in these last days in three steps: the spiritual hardening of Israel's heart; the conversion of the Gentiles; the restoration of Israel.
- The purpose of God's mystery is to demonstrate his mercy to both Gentiles and Jews.

In the second stage, Israel's rejection of Christ has given the Gentiles the opportunity to accept Jesus. This will continue until the full number (*plērōma*) has come in. Three comments about this "fullness of the Gentiles" can be offered. First, the conviction that God elected a certain number of people to enter his kingdom was pervasive in first-century Judaism and early Christianity (*2 Bar.* 23.4; 30.2; 75.6; *4 Ezra* 4.36–37; *Apoc. Ab.* 29.17; Rev. 6:11; 7:4; 14:1; *1 Clem.* 2.4; 59.2; *5 Ezra* 2.40–41). Second, the Old Testament predicts that in the end time Gentiles will make a pilgrimage to Jerusalem to worship God and venerate Israel (Ps. 22:27; Isa. 2:2–3; 56:6–8; 60:2; Mic. 4:2; Zeph. 3:9; Zech. 2:11; 14:16; Tob. 13:11; 14:6–7; *Pss. Sol.* 17.34; *Sib. Or.* 7.710–20, 772–75; *T. Zeb.* 9.8; *T. Benj.* 9.2; cf. Mark 11:17; Isa. 56:17; 12:9). There is a contrast here. Luke 21:24 says that the time of the Gentiles began with the destruction of Jerusalem (AD 70), but it will end with the fullness of the Gentiles entering into Jerusalem to praise God and venerate Israel (Rom. 11:25–26). Third, "entering in" (*eiserchomai*) draws on the Jesus tradition about entering into the kingdom of God (e.g., Matt. 5:20; 7:21; 19:17; Mark 9:43, 45, 47; 10:15, 23–25; John 3:5).

The third stage of Paul's mystery is that "all Israel will be saved" (11:26a). This last idea calls for extended comment. Three hermeneutical problems are raised by verse 26.

1. What does "Israel" mean? If it indicates spiritual Israel, then the referent would include Gentiles as well as Jews, and thus Paul is not necessarily saying that national Israel will be restored to God. But the "spiritual Israel" view is unlikely, seeing that the other ten times "Israel" is used in Romans 9–11 (9:6 [2x], 27 [2x], 31; 10:19, 21; 11:2, 7, 25) refer to ethnic Israel. For 11:26 to posit a different meaning is unlikely.[1]

2. What do the words "and thus [my translation of *kai houtōs*] all Israel will be saved" mean? Some take the phrase as temporal, "and then," meaning that after the spiritual hardening of Israel and the fullness of the Gentiles, then all Israel will be saved.[2] But a temporal rendering of *kai houtōs* is rare in Paul's writings. Most, therefore, take the phrase comparatively,

meaning "and so" or "and in this manner" and referring to the immediate context of 11:25. Some of these interpreters go on to suggest that 11:26 refers to the remnant (including both Jew and Gentile—i.e., the church), thereby ruling out any future conversion of national Israel.[3] It is preferable, however, to take the antecedent of 11:26 as the Gentiles coming into the community of faith, which, when completed, turns Israel to Jesus the Messiah. The future tense "will . . . be grafted" (11:24) and "will be saved" (11:26) supports this conclusion.[4] On this reading, 11:26 refers to an event that will witness a national turning of Israel to Christ.

3. What does "all Israel" mean? Three main possibilities surface: (a) Some Covenantal/Reformed theologians take the phrase to indicate spiritual Israel, the elect of God, including both Jewish and Gentile Christians (i.e., the church). But C. E. B. Cranfield sufficiently refutes this perspective by exposing its problem. To say that the church will be saved is

At the time Paul was writing his letter to the Roman believers, Marcus Antonius Felix was the Roman procurator of Judea and in charge of Jerusalem. Nero would replace him with several other administrators, and in AD 64 Gessius Florus was appointed to the post. He proceeded to institute policies that created tensions between the Greek and Jewish populations of Jerusalem, which led to formal rebellion by the Jews in AD 66. Known as the First Jewish Revolt, the uprising was crushed by the Roman siege of Jerusalem in AD 70 by Titus. Jerusalem was attacked and much of the city, including the temple, was destroyed. An arch was erected at the southern entrance to the Roman Forum to celebrate this victory. This relief on the arch shows items taken in plunder from the temple in Jerusalem, including silver trumpets, the table for the bread of the Presence, and a menorah.

redundant. (b) Dispensationalists take the words to refer to national Israel, Israel as a whole, though not necessarily every individual Israelite. The phrase "all Israel" is used elsewhere to refer to the nation but without necessarily including every Jew (see 1 Sam. 7:2–5; 25:1; 1 Kings 12:1; 2 Chron. 12:1–5; Dan. 9:11; cf. *b. Sanh*. 10.1). (c) The most recent theory, proposed by Bruce Longenecker, is that of unified Israel, which builds on the second possibility. He writes,

> Instead, in 11.26 Paul is thinking exclusively of an ethnic entity, and moreover, of that entity as a whole. Throughout 9–11, Paul draws out the disparate courses of two groups—believing and unbelieving—within ethnic Israel. By the inclusive "all" in 11.26, he joins both groups together. Thus Paul looks forward to the time when not only the remnant of Israel who have believed but also those of Israel who have strayed from the course of their unbelief will be saved. When Paul speaks of "all Israel" in 11.26, what he has in mind is an ethnic group whose members at present are schismatically divided. In this sense, his point is not so much that all *Israel* will be saved, but that *all* Israel will be saved.[5]

In other words, "all Israel will be saved" refers to the future event of the nation of Israel's conversion to Jesus as the Messiah, which will unite it with those Jewish Christians (spiritual Israel) throughout the period of the church. Truly, all Israel, united Israel, will for the first time be saved.[6]

We should note that Paul's collection of the Gentiles' offering in order to help the poor saints in Jerusalem (Rom. 15:25–29; 1 Cor. 16:1–4; 2 Cor. 8–9) probably also conveys the apostle's eschatological perspective. The Old Testament underpinning of this action undoubtedly proceeded from the Jewish expectation of an eschatological conversion and pilgrimage of the Gentiles to Zion (compare Rom. 9:25–27; 15:16–33 with Isa. 45:15; 60:15–17; Mic. 4:13; Tob. 3:11; 1QM 12.13–15). Only at that time would the union between Jews and Gentiles be complete.

I conclude my comments on the delineation of the mystery by noting that Paul reverses the Old Testament expectation from restoration of Israel followed by conversion of Gentiles to conversion of Gentiles followed by restoration of Israel.

Third, 11:26b–27 gives the occasion of the mystery. There Paul quotes Isaiah 59:20–21 LXX. That text envisions that God will send Israel out of exile into the restoration of their land and the renewal of the covenant. Paul interprets the passage to predict that Jesus Christ will return to earth from heaven (Zion) to convert Israel to himself and establish with that nation the new covenant. For Paul, then, the true restoration of Israel will occur at the parousia, the return of Christ.

11:28–29 *they are enemies for your sake . . . loved on account of the patriarchs.* Here Paul draws a contrast: according to the gospel, the Jews are enemies for the sake of the Gentiles, while according to election, the Jews are beloved because of the patriarchs. Paul presents the problem that faces the mercy of God vis-à-vis Israel: Israel is beloved because of the divine promises to the patriarchs and therefore is God's elect (9:4–5); yet Israel is an enemy of God because they have rejected the Messiah. But already Paul has supplied the solution to the quandary of Israel's unbelief: it has allowed the Gentiles to come to Christ, and in the future, Israel itself will come to Christ.

11:30–31 *have now received mercy . . . may now[7] receive mercy.* Here Paul spells out the procedure according to which God's mercy has been and will be dispensed, as shown in table 2. God showed sternness to Gentiles in the past but shows them mercy in the present, while God is showing sternness to Israel in the present but will show them mercy in the future (cf. 11:11–24).

Table 2: The Procedure by Which
God's Mercy Is Dispensed

	Past	Present	Future
Gentiles (11:30)	Disobedient	Mercy	
Jews (11:31)		Disobedient	Mercy

11:32 *that he may have mercy on them all.* God's plan has been to convict both Gentiles and Jews of their sin in order to drive them to the mercy of the gospel (cf. Gal. 3:19–25).[8]

Theological Insights

Several theological insights meet us in Romans 11:25–32. First, God is fair; he is merciful to both Gentiles and Jews. Second, God uses the law to expose sin for the good purpose of leading people to the gospel. Third, God has a plan for history that will culminate in the return of Christ and the full establishment of his kingdom.

Teaching the Text

Romans 11:25–32 divides nicely into two sermons/lessons: the mystery of God (vv. 25–27) and the mercy of God (vv. 28–32). The first lesson could follow Paul's threefold comment on the mystery, which I explicated above: its definition, delineation, and date. The second sermon could simply follow the suggested outline that I offered for 11:28–32: the problem for mercy, the procedure of mercy, and the plan behind mercy.

Concerning the first sermon/lesson, a mystery, for Paul, usually is an apocalyptic event now revealed to him, the apostle of the end time, in this case the mystery of Israel's conversion to Jesus as the Messiah. The catch is that the nations will first come to Christ, and then Israel's restoration to God will occur via their trust in Jesus. God's ways are not our ways, nor are his thoughts our thoughts; so a divine twist in the story of salvation should not be surprising to the people of God. The delineation reflects that mystery, as we saw above: presently Jews as a group have rejected their Messiah. This allows for the current conversion of the Gentiles, and then the restoration of Israel will transpire. And the date of Israel's change of heart regarding Jesus will occur in and around the events of his return.

Concerning the second sermon/lesson, the problem of Israel's belief looms large in the New Testament. Jesus' answer to that quandary was to view Isaiah 6:9–10 as a prophecy of Israel's future rejection of God and his Messiah (compare Isa. 6:9–10 with Mark 4:11–12). Paul probably taps into that prophecy here in Romans 11:25–27. God's procedure in all of this is to show mercy to Gentiles now just as he showed mercy to Jews in the past. Thus, the overall plan of salvation history is that one people group's rejection paves the way for the other's salvation. In other words, rejection of the gospel does not take God by surprise; indeed, he uses such rejection to advance his kingdom.

Illustrating the Text

We must respect the mystery of God.

Bible: Historical events in Scripture demonstrate the intersection of heaven and earth. In Genesis 18 Abraham entertains heaven in human form outside his tent. In 2 Kings 6 Elisha asks Yahweh to open his servant's eyes to see the angelic army surrounding the physical Syrian army. Supernatural battles keeping God's messengers from delivering a message are recorded in Daniel 10. Philip's inexplicable transfer from one location to another for evangelism is found in Acts 8. And in Jude 5–16 Satan's contention for Moses' body with the archangel Michael (v. 9), which is used as an example of worlds colliding.

Quote: Writer Flannery O'Connor (1925–64) believed that Southern authors were "Christ-haunted"—by implication, a better way to be. She said,

> We find that the writer has made alive some experience which we are not accustomed to observe every day. . . . If the writer believes that our life is and will remain essentially mysterious, if he looks upon us as beings existing in a created order to whose laws we freely respond, then what he sees on the surface will be of interest to him only as he can go through it into an experience of mystery itself. . . . Such a writer will be

Jewish apocalyptic literature, including among the Dead Sea Scrolls, use the word "mystery" as a technical theological term meaning an end-time event that God reveals to the prophetic seer. Shown here is a fragment from the *Rule of the Congregation* (1QSa), records rules for behavior in the congregation of Israel in the "last days."

interested in what we don't understand rather than in what we do.[9]

The mercy of God is an unending reality.

Bible: The greatest display of mercy in the Old Testament is that of David to Mephibosheth in 2 Samuel 9. The customary practice of victorious kings was to kill the descendants of the vanquished ruler. Mephibosheth anticipated his own death. Not only did David let the man live, but also, in an extraordinary act of mercy, he gave him a place at his table.

Bible: Jesus' parable of the unmerciful servant (Matt. 18:23–35) is one of the strongest literary statements concerning God's mercy toward Israel and Israel's rejection of salvation for the Gentiles.

The Divine Plan of Salvation

Big Idea *Paul offers a hymn of praise to God for his plan of salvation.*

Understanding the Text

The Text in Context

Romans 11:33–36 is a hymn of praise to God's plan of salvation; it consists of three strophes:

1. Three characteristics of God's plan: riches, wisdom, knowledge (11:33)
2. Three rhetorical questions about God's plan (11:34–35)
   a. Who has known the mind of the Lord? (11:34a)
   b. Who has been the Lord's counselor? (11:34b)
   c. Who has given to God that God should repay? (11:35)
3. Doxology to God's plan (11:36)

Note the chiastic structure of 11:33–35:

A Riches (11:33)
   B Wisdom (11:33)
      C Knowledge (11:33)
      C′ Who has known the mind of the Lord? (11:34a)
   B′ Who has been the Lord's counselor? (11:34b)
A′ Who has given to God that God should repay? (11:35)

Historical and Cultural Background

1. Romans 11:33 is rooted in Jewish apocalypticism. Thus, for example, *2 Baruch* 14.8–9 raises questions similar to those Paul raises in 11:33 with regard to the destiny of God's people during their exile (see also *1 En.* 63.3; 93.11–14; *4 Ezra* 4.21; 5.36–40; 8.21). Moreover, the apocalyptic nuance of *mystērion* (11:25) continues to influence Paul in 11:33: the undiscoverable wisdom of God's salvation history has been revealed to Paul, the apocalyptic seer (cf. Dan. 2:20–23).

2. Jewish wisdom traditions inform Romans 11:33–35, particularly the notion that God's wisdom was revealed to Israel in the form of the Torah (Sir. 24:23; Bar. 4:1).[1] Indeed, A. T. Hanson has argued convincingly that the two Old Testament texts quoted by Paul in 11:34–35—Isaiah 40:13 and Job 41:11—were connected in rabbinic literature to say that the Torah is none other than God's preexistent wisdom.[2] I have argued elsewhere that Paul well knew this connection between Isaiah 40:13 and Job 41:11 and made use of it here

in Romans 11:34–35.[3] But Romans 11:33–35 begs to disagree, arguing instead that the Torah is finished in God's plan of salvation (cf. Rom. 10:4) because Christ is God's preexistent wisdom (cf. Rom. 10:5–8).

3. Romans 11:36 shares the language of Stoicism, "for from him and through him and to him are all things" (Pseudo-Aristotle, *Cosmos* 6; Seneca, *Mor. Ep.* 65.8; Marcus Aurelius, *Medit.* 4.23). Hellenistic Judaism borrowed Stoic language in praise of the one true God (Philo, *Spec. Laws* 1.208; *Cherubim* 125–56). Paul continues the Hellenistic Jewish pattern, except that he applies the language to both God and Christ elsewhere (1 Cor. 8:6; Col. 1:16–17). Indeed, Paul probably applies that language to God and Christ here in Romans 11:36.[4]

Interpretive Insights

11:33 *Oh, the depth of the riches of the wisdom and knowledge of God!* Romans 11:33–36 appropriately concludes Paul's overview of salvation history in chapters 9–11, the driving force of which is God's mercy. Verse 33 is the first strophe in Paul's hymn

Romans 11:36 shares the language of Stoicism. Marcus Aurelius asserts, "Everything is fruit to me which your seasons bring, O Nature: from you are all things, in you are all things, to [*eis*, "into"] you all things return" (*Medit.* 4.23; trans. George Long). Photo shows bust of Marcus Aurelius (AD 161).

Key Themes of Romans 11:33–36

- The content of God's plan of salvation history is that he is fair in showing both wrath and mercy to Jew and Gentile alike. Such a plan defies human comprehension.
- God's plan of salvation is accomplished through Jesus Christ, the wisdom of God, not through the law of Moses.
- The participants in God's plan of salvation are those whose faith is in Christ.

to God's plan; it contains a threefold description of that plan: "riches," "wisdom," and "knowledge." To think that God's mercy through Christ is being shown to Gentiles in the present and to Jews in the future is breathtaking. Indeed, this was his plan all along, beginning in the Old Testament and culminating at the parousia, the return of Christ. No human could have figured that plan out; only God could reveal that to his own, through his point man, the apostle Paul, an apocalyptic seer.

11:34–35 *"Who has known the mind of the Lord?" . . . "Who has ever given to God?"* Verses 34–35 constitute the second strophe, which raises three rhetorical questions about God's plan. As we noted above, Paul's composite quotation of Isaiah 40:13 and Job 41:11 in 11:34–35 serves to sever the Torah from wisdom. Christ, the preexistent wisdom of God, has fulfilled and terminated the law of Moses (see sidebar). It is interesting that Isaiah 40:13 begins the second half of the book of Isaiah. Isaiah 1–39 predicts judgment and exile—the covenant curses—upon Israel for their disobedience to Yahweh. But Isaiah 40–66 predicts that Israel will repent and turn back to the Torah and God in the future.

This will be the restoration of the covenant blessings. With this as the subplot to 11:34–35, we see how Paul, to the contrary, hints that Israel's future restoration will come because they obey Christ, not the Torah. Indeed, the chiastic structure of 11:32–35 (see above) suggests that this theme of the restoration of Israel through Christ the wisdom of God, not the law, undergirds the divine plan of salvation history.

11:36 *For from him and through him and for him are all things.* Fittingly, Paul concludes the hymn of 11:33–36 with a doxology to God. All things, especially the plan of salvation, originated in God and were implemented through him and for his glory. And Jesus Christ was the means for doing so. Thus, the plan of salvation is based not on the works of the law or any human merit, but rather on God's grace through Christ, who is God's riches, wisdom, and knowledge.

Theological Insights

At least three theological truths meet us in Romans 11:33–36. First, this text concludes chapters 1–11. Romans 1:1–15 is the preamble, identifying God through Christ as the author of the gospel of salvation. Romans 1:16–17 is the historical prologue, announcing that God's restoration of the covenant blessings is provided for in the gospel of Christ. Romans 1:18–4:25 replaces the law of Moses as the stipulation of the old covenant with faith in Christ as the stipulation to enter into the new covenant. Romans 5–8 records the ironic fact that it is Gentile Christians who are enjoying the covenant blessings, but Romans 9–11 laments the reality that the covenant curses abide on Israel because of their rejection of Jesus the Messiah, which itself has been spawned by the law. But in 11:25–32 Paul reveals that the conversion of the Gentiles

is designed by God to stir Israel to jealousy and thus drive them to embrace Christ in the end time. No wonder Paul offers a hymn of praise to God's plan of salvation history in 11:33–36. Second, God is holy and merciful. And ultimately, it is Jesus Christ who has met the holy standard of God so that he can pour out his mercy on sinners. Third, good theology (like that of Rom. 1–11) should always lead to worshiping and glorifying God (11:33–36).

Teaching the Text

An effective message on Romans 11:33–36 could be entitled "The Divine Plan of Salvation," and it would follow the three-point outline of the chiastic structure of 11:33–35, relating each point to Christ. First, Christ, not human merit, is the basis of God's riches of grace. That Paul has Christ in mind in 11:33, 35 is clear in the way that elsewhere the apostle associates

Christ the Preexistent Wisdom of God

According to Martin Hengel, it was Jesus' exaltation as the Son of Man and the Son of God through the resurrection that prompted the early church to transfer the predicates of wisdom to him, especially the attribute of preexistence. Hengel describes this process:

> After the introduction of the idea of pre-existence it was natural that the exalted Son of God also attracted to himself the functions of Jewish Wisdom as a mediator in creation and salvation. Even the pre-existent Wisdom, which was connected with God in a unique way, could no longer be regarded as an independent entity over against the risen and exalted One and superior to him. Rather, all the functions of Wisdom were transferred to him, for 'in him are hid all the treasures of wisdom and knowledge' (Col 2.3). Only in this way was the *unsurpassability and finality of God's revelation* in Jesus of Nazareth expressed in a final, conclusive way.[a]

For Hengel, the logical consequence of all of this, especially as reflected in Paul's writings, was the shattering of the connection between wisdom and law:

> If, however, the Son of God entered into the all-embracing function of Wisdom as mediator, then the function of the Torah, which was identified with Wisdom, was also completely shattered. For the Jews the Torah had an authoritative, ontologically based function in the ordering of the world and in salvation. Paul, the former Pharisee and scribe, drew the ultimate radical consequences here. If others before him pondered as to what changes were brought about in the Torah through the interpretation of the true will of God in the message of the Messiah Jesus, his characteristic statement 'Christ is the end of the law to every believer for righteousness' (Rom 10.4) expresses in a fundamental way, against the claim of the Torah, the unique soteriological function of the crucified and risen One as the all-embracing, final, eschatological revelation of God. Not just Moses, but the Christ of God alone mediates salvation.[b]

[a] Hengel, *Son of God*, 113.
[b] Hengel, *Son of God*, 115.

The Roman Forum contained many temples where pagan worship occurred. From left to right the columns mark the remains of the following temples: in the left foreground, the Temple of Vespasian and the Temple of Saturn; in the right background, the Temple of Antoninus and Faustina and the Temple of Vesta. Roman worship was very practical, serious, and ritualistic, seeking to placate all gods so that none were offended and that petitions would be granted and the god's favor bestowed. The few hymns that we have reflect that practicality. Their structure consists of an invocation, a section of praise to the god—which might include recalling the god's power, mighty deeds, and previous acts of blessing—and then perhaps a petition. One example is the hymn to Diana by Catullus, written in the first century BC.

Christ with the spiritual riches of God (e.g., Eph. 1:3–10; Phil. 4:19; Col. 1:27). In other words, God's riches of salvation are poured out on sinners through the grace of God according to his riches in Christ Jesus. Second, Christ is the wisdom of God, the means of salvation history, according to 11:33–34. Recall the hourglass illustration concerning the remnant of God's people in the Bible (see the "Teaching the Text" section for Rom. 11:1–10). In that diagram, the Old Testament story narrowed from the creation of the world, to the calling out of Israel, to the faithful few who followed Yahweh, to the prophetic expectation of the Messiah and then expanded the plan of God from the twelve disciples, to the church, to the world. Third, Christ is the knowledge of God, the ultimate revelation of his mysterious ways, according to 11:33–35. In Colossians Paul says that Christ is the fullness of the knowledge of God (1:27), and Paul goes even further by asserting that Christ is the fullness of God himself (2:9). To put it another way, the key to the meaning of life is Jesus Christ. Whereas once that honor might have been accorded to the law, now it belongs exclusively to the Son of God.

Illustrating the Text

The seeking mind must turn to the heart's praise.

Hymn Text: "God Moves in a Mysterious Way," by William Cowper. A renowned poet and hymnist, Cowper (1731–1800) spent a great deal of his life in deep, chronic depression, even experiencing suicidal thoughts. Nevertheless, he left us many great hymns, among them "God Moves in a Mysterious Way," which seems an appropriate illustra-

tion to use at the end of verses from Romans that discuss the hard mystery of God but conclude with a hymn of adoration. Indeed, one cannot help but wonder if Cowper had Romans 11:33–36 in mind when he wrote, in the second stanza, "Deep in unfathomable mines / Of never failing skill / He treasures up his bright designs / And works His sovereign will."

Christ is the basis of God's riches of grace, not human merit.

Bible: Hosea. The book of Hosea relates the story of Hosea and his wife, Gomer. Hosea is faithful to his unfaithful wife and forgives her and reconciles with her despite her frequent willful abandonment of him and her family for adulterous activities. Hosea is an evocative illustration of God's grace. He is only able to do what he does because of the grace with which God infuses his spirit in order to bring about such obedience to God's will. There is nothing in Gomer that merits a single action of Hosea; she is the recipient of pure grace.

Christ is the knowledge of God, the ultimate revelation of his mysterious ways.

Science: Using words such as "infinite," "mystery," and "wonder," Maria Spiropulu, a University of Chicago experimental physicist, says, "Our view of things has changed tremendously in the last five years. We are being totally surprised by what we observe in nature." Apparently, something unknown that exerted a great gravitational force keeps galaxies bound together. Scientists call it "dark matter," and although we can measure its presence, we can neither see nor feel it. Theoretical physicist David Gross says

that scientific "string theory" can explain all the particles and forces that we see as vibrations of the same object. "So, instead of having dozens of particles," he says, "you have one string. We don't know whether it really works yet. But it has this wonderful feature of unifying everything."[5] Science can demonstrate for us the beauty and joy that come from explaining what was once unexplainable, as well as the way new knowledge can illumine reality in new and sometimes unexpected ways.

Though it was unknown a century ago, scientists now assert that dark matter plays a central role in the composition of the universe. Though it cannot be seen, its gravitational force does distort the light of stars and galaxies, producing visible evidence of its existence. This photograph, from the Hubble Space Telescope, shows a "ring" of dark matter around a distant galaxy cluster.

Romans 11:33–36

Witnesses of the New Covenant

Big Idea *Paul challenges believers to be witnesses of the new covenant by distancing them-selves from this age and by being transformed in their minds so that they can fulfill the will of God.*

Understanding the Text

The Text in Context

Romans 12:1–2 is, in genre, parenetic (ex-hortational) material. The basis of Paul's challenge to the Roman Christians (and us as well) is the mercy of God—that is, the blessings of the new covenant delineated in 3:21–11:36: justification, sanctification, glorification, and so forth. Thus, the indica-tive is the basis of the imperative. In light of those mercies, Paul challenges believers to live out the will of God. God's will is spelled out in 12:3–15:33: using one's spiri-tual gifts for the body of Christ (12:3–8); being a witness of Christ to society even if persecuted for doing so (12:9–21); obeying the government (13:1–7); living in the light of the imminent parousia (13:8–14); accept-ing one's fellow Christians (14:1–15:13); and supporting evangelism and missions (15:14–33). Thus, 12:1–2 introduces the theme of 12:3–15:33: commit to being wit-nesses of the new covenant. Romans 12:1–2 is easily outlined:

1. The basis of commitment (12:1a)
2. The act of commitment (12:1b)
3. The means of commitment (12:2a)
4. The result of commitment (12:2b)

Historical and Cultural Background

1. The first facet of the historical and cultural background is eschatological in nature. Paul refers to this "age" (*aiōnos*) in 12:2, with reference to this present evil age. He exhorts Christians not to be "con-formed" (*syschēmatizō*) to this age but rather to be "transformed" (*metamorphoō*) by the "renewing" (*anakainōsis*) of the mind. The latter injunction—transformed/renewing—alludes to the age to come, as many commentators recognize. So believers are to daily break with this age by renew-ing their commitment to the age to come.

2. Romans 12:1 is chock-full of sacri-ficial language, as many commentators also recognize: "offer your bodies as living sacrifices"; "holy and pleasing to God"; this is the Christian's "spiritual/reasonable worship" (*latreia*). But I suggest that the concept behind this sacrificial language is the "witness" component of the covenant format. Note the following connections between 12:1–2 and the covenant.

(a) "Mercies" (NIV: "mercy") translates the Greek *oiktirmoi*, which in the LXX often translates the Hebrew *rahamim*. In the Old Testament, this Hebrew word is used at times to refer to God's covenant mercy with Israel (e.g., Deut. 13:17 [13:18 MT]; Ps. 51:1 [51:3 MT]; Isa. 47:6; Jer. 42:12).

(b) As James Dunn notes, the mention of renewing one's mind is parallel to Jeremiah 31:31–35 and Ezekiel 36:26–27—that is, the obedience of the new covenant wrought by the Holy Spirit.[1]

(c) Furthermore, Douglas Moo calls attention to the covenantal nuance of doing the "will of God" (12:2), identifying this as the ethic of the new covenant.[2]

(d) The sacrificial language of 12:1 takes on new meaning as we see it through the lens of the covenant. Moses sprinkled the blood of the sacrificed bulls on the people of Israel as a sign that they accepted the terms of the covenant with Yahweh (Exod. 24:1–8). Moreover, in the covenant renewal service recorded in Joshua 24, the children

Key Themes of Romans 12:1–2

- The mercy of God is the basis of Christian sanctification and service.
- The Christian ethic consists of doing the will of God by making a break with this present age and aligning oneself with the age to come.
- God's will is in the best interest of his people.

of Israel reaffirmed their acceptance of the covenant with Yahweh by pledging to serve him alone and to thereby be "witnesses" of the covenant (Josh. 24:22–27). Rather than appealing to other gods, Joshua appeals to the Hebrews to be witnesses of their covenant with the true God.

(e) Indeed, Romans 11:26–27 (quoting Isa. 59:20–21) asserts that at the parousia, Israel's sins will be removed and God will renew his covenant with them.

I suggest, then, that in 12:1–2 Paul exhorts Christians to accept the terms of the new covenant: obey God with a renewed mind. This is what he means by challenging them to be living sacrifices. The blood of Christ, the perfect sacrifice, has cleansed them and incorporated them into the new covenant (recall 3:21–31). Now they must give witness to that covenant by being obedient to God.

3. I suggest that Adam theology is at work in 12:1–2. Paul challenges Christians to worship God with a renewed mind rather than conforming to this evil age begun by Adam that perverts worship of the Creator into worship of the creation and that ruins one's mind. It is only reasonable

Sacrifices were a necessary part of worship in the Roman world. This Roman relief shows a bull being led for sacrifice (early second century AD).

Romans 12:1–2

that they worship God (compare 12:1–2 with 1:21–25).[3] The three preceding interlocking traditions are summarized in table 1.

Table 1: Summary of Three Interlocking Traditions

Eschatology	This age	The age to come
Adam	First Adam—catalyst for perverted worship	Last Adam—engenders true worship
Covenant	Failed witnesses of the old covenant	True witnesses of the new covenant

Interpretive Insights

12:1 *offer your bodies as a living sacrifice . . . your true and proper worship.* At the beginning of this verse the "therefore" (*oun*) connects 12:1–2 with what precedes (3:21–11:36). Paul can exhort the readers because he is their apostle. Paul's challenge is that the Roman Christians (and all believers) present their bodies to God as a living sacrifice. Three words call for comment here. First, by his use of the verb "offer" (*parastēsai*), Paul is not suggesting that we offer our bodies only once to God. Instead, as the verbs in 12:2 indicate,

"offer" is a continual action, a daily occurrence. Second, "bodies" includes the whole person. Third, "living sacrifice" might mean a live versus a dead sacrifice. But more likely it is "living" in a spiritual dimension—those alive spiritually in Christ.

Just as the Old Testament sacrifices were to meet the divine requirements, so should Christians present themselves as a sacrifice, "holy and pleasing to God." That is, the Christian should live a holy life that pleases God. *Logikos* is translated as "spiritual" in the NRSV. This is true, but the word *logikos* has a long history in Greek philosophy and in Hellenistic Judaism as meaning "reasonable," in the sense of appropriate or suitable.[4] Thus, Paul declares in 12:1 that it is most appropriate that believers worship God by being living sacrifices for him because of God's mercies to them.

For residents of Rome, being conformed to this age meant participating in the pagan religious system of the day. The Roman Pantheon, the remains of which are shown here, was originally commissioned by Marcus Agrippa in the first century BC. After a fire, it was rebuilt by Hadrian in AD 126 and dedicated as a temple and place of sacrifice to all the Roman gods whose statues filled the interior niches. In the seventh century AD it was converted to a Roman Catholic Church, today known as the church of Santa Maria ad Martyres.

As I mentioned above, the "mercies of God" tap into the covenant blessings described in 3:21–11:36: justification, sanctification, and glorification, and so forth. Indeed, chapters 9–11 are devoted to the theme of the mercy of God in salvation history, for both Gentile and Jew. Therefore, I suggest that 12:1 is analogous to the covenant ceremony in Exodus 24:1–8 and Joshua 24. Christians are to accept the terms of the new covenant by dedicating themselves to God as living sacrifices. Christ died for them; now they must live for him. Thus, 12:1 contains the basis of Christian commitment (the mercies of the new covenant) and the ongoing act of commitment (become living sacrifices to God). This is what it means to be a living sacrifice for God and thereby to be witnesses of the new covenant.

12:2 *be transformed by the renewing of your mind . . . to test and approve what God's will is.* This verse gives the means and result of commitment to Christ. The means for doing so is not to be conformed (*syschēmatizō*) to this age but rather to be transformed (*metamorphoō*) to the age to come (implied) by the renewing (*anakainōsis*) of the mind. The two verbs are imperatives. While older scholarship distinguished these verbs as outward conformity and inward transformation, recent scholarship rightly rejects such a distinction. Rather, both verbs suggest a total commitment. Thus, Christians should continually reject this age in favor of the age to come. "Renewing" (*anakainōsis*) is similar to *kainos* ("new") with reference to the age to come (2 Cor. 3:6; 5:17; Gal. 6:15; Eph. 2:15; 4:24). The renewed mind is, in effect, the renewed heart of obedience envisioned by the new covenant. The result of being a living sacrifice is that the Christian discovers and does the will of God (12:2b). "Test and approve" translates *dokimazō*, not in the sense that God needs our approval for his will to be good, but rather that we experience in practice that his will is good. The will of God is worth discovering, for it is good, acceptable, and perfect. God's will, the ethic of the new covenant, steers the right path between legalism and libertinism. In other words, for the Christian, God's will is no longer dictated by the Torah but is instead found in Spirit-guided discernment.

Theological Insights

Several theological insights can be culled from Romans 12:1–2. First, Christian commitment is based on God's mercy. The imperative proceeds from the indicative. Second, serving Christ is a sacrifice; it means a daily decision to part company with this age and to align oneself with the age to come, the kingdom of God. Third, the key to it all is to continually renew one's mind to think the thoughts of God. Fourth, doing the will of God is worth the effort, for God's will is the only way to go.

Teaching the Text

I would preach/teach Romans 12:1–2 by following the four points of the outline above: the basis, act, means, and result of commitment to Christ. First, the basis of our Christian commitment is the mercy of God. Lives lived in dedication to God should be motivated by what he has done for us in Christ. Otherwise, sanctification, like justification, can become legalistic in orientation. In the early part of my pastoral ministry I was involved in a well-intentioned but Pharisaic-like church that focused on outward appearance, not on the motivation of one's heart. How liberating it was for me to move out of that overly strict tradition and enter into a loving and irenic church, one in which I and my fellow congregants grew spiritually.

Second, the act of our commitment to Christ involves the totality of our being. In Paul's mind, such a commitment quite possibly paralleled Old Testament Israel's renewal of the covenant ceremony. On a different note, the last twenty years has witnessed a debate among evangelicals as to whether a person accepts Jesus as Savior only, or as Savior and Lord. In light of the analysis offered above, I suggest that one comes to Jesus as Savior and Lord, but that Christ's lordship over our lives is progressive; hence the need to daily dedicate ourselves to God afresh and anew.

Third, the means for doing so is to fill our minds with the word of God through daily devotions. Such a devotion time, I suggest, is best cultivated by studying and applying one book of the Scripture after another. I began that practice as a teenager, and it has made all the difference in the world for my spiritual progress.

Fourth, the result of daily commitment to God in Christ through the power of the Holy Spirit is that we as Christians discover and do the will of God, which is God's perfect plan for us.

Illustrating the Text

Real worship is the offering of our everyday lives to God.

Poetry: "The Altar," by George Herbert. The Welsh-born Herbert (1593–1633) was a gifted poet, writer, and orator educated at Cambridge who, having once had aspirations toward a courtly life, eventually became a country parson. Few individual lives exemplify such holiness and devotion. He had single-mindedness of purpose toward God, shown in all that he did and wrote. His well-known poem "The Altar" is an example of such devotion and reflects well the themes of sacrifice, worship, transformation, and renewal found in Romans 12:1–2. Refer also to other poems he wrote, to his sermons, and to his biography.

Essay: "Tremendous Trifles," by G. K. Chesterton. In this essay/story Chesterton (1874–1936) argues for attention to the ordinary events of the everyday, for the power to see wonder in what lies around us instead of always having to look beyond. As he wrote, "The object of my school is to show how many extraordinary things even a lazy and ordinary man may see if he can spur himself to the single activity of seeing."

Real worship demands a radical change of the inward personality.

Literature: *The Voyage of the Dawn Treader*, by C. S. Lewis. In chapter 6, a captivating section of this third book of The Chronicles of Narnia, Lewis paints this process of change as the "un-dragoning" of the character Eustace, one that will force him to shed

The Altar
by George Herbert

A broken ALTAR, Lord thy servant rears,
Made of a heart, and cemented with teares:
Whose parts are as thy hand did frame;
No workmans tool hath touch'd the same
A HEART alone
Is such a stone,
As nothing but
Thy pow'r doth cut.
Wherefore each part
Of my hard heart
Meets in this frame,
To praise thy Name:
That if I chance to hold my peace,
These stones to praise thee may not cease.
O let thy blessed SACRIFICE be mine,
And sanctifie this ALTAR to be thine.

his pride and unbelief. Eustace starts out as a selfish young boy who only values facts and so will not listen to his cousins when they talk about Narnia. One day, however, he is "pulled" into Narnia and forced into the company of people who understand that selfishness is a joyless way to live. Eustace becomes a dragon—a lonely creature that feeds off other dragons, animals, and human beings—as he insists on "greedy, dragonish thoughts in his heart." In time, he feels the horror of his monstrous self and begins to weep. Eustace, wearing dragon scales instead of clothes, begins to scratch himself, only to find more dragon skins underneath. Desperately he claws at himself, only to find still another layer. Aslan then offers to undress him, and proceeds to dig his claws into Eustace deeply until, the pain being so intense, Eustace thinks that his heart is penetrated. After Aslan throws Eustace into a crystal-clear pool, the boy sinks into the pure water and discovers that he has turned back into a boy. His pride is gone. He is ready to worship Aslan.

Literature: *Paradise Lost*, by John Milton. In book 1 of this epic poem Milton (1608–74) provides a vivid view of the pride that led to Satan being cast out from heaven, and drove him to deceive "the mother of mankind" and even to claim that it is "better to reign in hell than serve in heaven." It serves as a warning and illustrates what this passage in Romans calls the Christian to be.

Romans 12:1–2

Service in the New-Covenant Community

Big Idea *Paul's challenge to believers in 12:1–2 to become living sacrifices to God is given specific content in 12:3–8. Believers are to serve one another in the new-covenant community. This service takes the form of using one's spiritual gifts to minister to others in the body of Christ.*

Understanding the Text

The Text in Context

Romans 12:3–8 provides one practical way Christians are to be living sacrifices for God: serving others in the new-covenant community through the exercise of spiritual gifts. Romans 12:3–8 can be outlined as follows:

1. The authority behind Paul's exhortation (12:3a)
2. The content of Paul's exhortation (12:3b)
3. The context of Paul's exhortation (12:4–5)
4. The outworking of Paul's exhortation (12:6–8)

Historical and Cultural Background

1. Paul's exhortation to Christians to serve one another is rooted in the Old Testament covenant, especially its stipulation.

Not only was Israel expected to keep the law of Moses as the stipulation of the covenant, but also a part of that requirement involved serving fellow Jews, covenant brothers and sisters. This is why the Old Testament prophets often thundered forth against Israel: Israel sins against God by not treating fellow believers rightly (see the classic illustration in Mic. 6:1–7:7). Hence the emphasis on social justice by the prophets.

2. Paul's analogy of the body of Christ in 12:4–5 has been much discussed in terms of its background (cf. 1 Cor. 12:12–28; Eph. 4:7–16; Col. 1:18). Seven theories can be delineated (see the "Additional Insights" section after this unit).

3. As a third piece of historical-cultural data, I offer some introductory comments about Paul on the subject of spiritual gifts. There are three key texts on the subject in his writings: Romans 12:3–8; 1 Corinthians 12–14; Ephesians 4:7–16. Several general observations can be made concerning the

gifts. (a) The word for "gift" (*charisma*) refers to an endowment to believers by God's grace, which is to be used for his glory and the good of others (Rom. 12:3–8; Eph. 4:7–16). (b) The gifts are distributed to believers by the Spirit; they are "Spiritual" gifts (1 Cor. 12:10–11; 14:1). (c) Every believer possesses at least one gift (1 Cor. 12:7; Eph. 4:7). (d) It is through the diversity of the gifts that the body of Christ matures and is unified (Rom. 12:4; 1 Cor. 12:12–31; Eph. 4:7–18). (e) Spiritual gifts are eschatological in nature and, in particular, are stamped by the "already but not yet" dialectic. The gifts are a sign that the *eschaton* has already dawned, but they should be exercised in love, which is itself eternal and therefore belongs to the consummation of the age to come. (f) A glance at the lists of spiritual gifts in the three key texts above reveals that they do not disclose all the spiritual gifts available to the body of Christ. The lists both differ and overlap.

Key Themes of Romans 12:3–8

- The body of Christ is both unity and diversity; indeed, the latter contributes to the former.
- God has distributed spiritual gifts to his people to be used in serving one another.
- With each gift comes divinely proportioned faith to use it.

Interpretive Insights

12:3 *by the grace given me I say . . . : Do not think of yourself more highly than you ought.* This verse contains the authority behind Paul's exhortation in 12:3–8 and the content of that exhortation. Paul is the apostle to the Gentiles, commissioned to be so by the sheer grace of God. This divine authority empowers Paul to make requests of the Roman believers (12:3a). The content of Paul's exhortation is this: the members of his audience should not have an exaggerated opinion of themselves (12:3b). In the Greek text there is a clever play on the word *phroneō* ("to think"): the Roman believers should "think" (*phroneō*) of themselves not with "lofty thought" (*hyperphroneō*) but rather with "sensible thought" (*sōphroneō*). The last term was used in the Greek world in contrast to that despised trait called *hybris* ("pride"). The reason why Christians should not be arrogant is that God has distributed to each

From an original statue in the Art Collection of Villa Albani, Rome (first to fifth century AD), this cast replicates the bust of Aesop, the famous Greek writer of fables who lived in the sixth century BC. Of relevance to Romans 12 is his fable, "The Belly and the Members." In this fable the members of the body decide to go "on strike" because they feel that the belly is getting all of the food while doing none of the work. As a result, the body goes hungry and grows weak until the members realize that the belly was doing necessary work after all. While Paul is probably not referencing this fable in his analogy of the church as a body, it was not new imagery and may have been familiar to his audience.

believer the measure, or quantity (*metron*), of faith that it takes to use their respective gifts.[1]

12:4–5 *in Christ we, though many, form one body.* Verses 4–5 explain the context of Paul's exhortation for Christians not to be haughty in the usage of their spiritual gifts: the body of Christ. We examined earlier the notion that Christ is the last Adam, whose body is the corporate people of God (see the units on 5:12–14; 5:15–21). Verses 4–5 assume the obvious, that the human body consists of many members, each with its respective function, but then add the profound truth that Christ's body, the church, is composed of many members, each with its own spiritual function.

12:6–8 *We have different gifts, according to the grace given to each of us.* Verses 6–8 give more detail regarding Paul's exhortation in that they record the outworking of spiritual gifts in the body of Christ. Verse 6a indicates that spiritual gifts (*charisma*) are grace (*charis*) gifts (*dotheisan*, "given"). Moreover, God in his wisdom measures or distributes those gifts to believers as he wills (*diaphora*, "different") as well as supplies the needed faith to exercise them.[2] Other than the opening participle in 12:6, "having" (*echontes*), there is no verb in 12:6–8, which is reflected in the NRSV translation, whereas the NIV supplies the likely intended verbs ("prophesy," "serve," "teach," etc.).

Seven gifts are listed, with no intended symbolism accompanying that number here. Whoever has the gift of prophesy (*prophēteia*) should use it according to the faith given by God (12:6b). Prophecy was treasured in the early church (1 Cor. 12:28; 14; Eph. 2:20; 4:11). The prophets spoke spontaneously to the gathered congregation as the Spirit gave them utterance. The church was then supposed to evaluate that prophecy to see if it squared with apostolic teaching (1 Thess. 5:19–22). Prophecies could be predictive (Acts 21:10–11) or declarative, speaking the word of the Lord for a specific congregation (1 Cor. 14:29–33). Service (*diakonia*) probably has to do with rendering financial and material assistance. Perhaps the first deacons are in view here (cf. Acts 6:1–7). The gift of teaching (*didaskalia*) involved explaining the Old Testament in light of the arrival of the Messiah, passing on the sayings and works of Jesus (see Rom. 12:9–21),

One of the spiritual gifts Paul mentions in Romans is the gift of teaching. Ambrose and Augustine are honored as two of the original four "great doctors" of the Western church for their contribution to the church as teachers of theology and doctrine. This scene on a Cambridge altarpiece by Simone Martini (AD 1320–25) shows Ambrose and Augustine on either side of Michael, the archangel.

and teaching catechetical material.[3] The content of the teaching probably was based on the apostles' doctrine (cf. Acts 2:42). *Paraklēsis* is the gift of exhortation or encouragement to apply God's truth to one's life. The fifth spiritual gift that Paul mentions here is generosity (*haplotēs*) in giving with reference to the tangible needs of others. The gift of leadership comes next. The *proistamenos* is an appointed leader in the church, whether elder or deacon (1 Thess. 5:12; 1 Tim. 3:4, 5, 12; 5:17) or deaconess (Rom. 16:1). The seventh spiritual gift is to have cheerfulness (*hilarotēs*) when showing mercy to others.

Theological Insights

Several truths surface in Romans 12:3–8. First, God has distributed spiritual gifts to every believer. Second, God gives the faith needed to exercise those gifts. Third, because spiritual gifts are rooted in God's grace, there is no room for arrogance or feelings of inferiority among Christians. Fourth, spiritual gifts are to be used for others, especially the new-covenant community. Fifth, diversity of spiritual gifts brings unity to the body of Christ.

Teaching the Text

A couple of approaches could be taken to preaching or teaching Romans 12:3–8. One could follow the four-point outline offered above: the authority, content, context, and outworking of Paul's exhortation. Or, one might provide a list of the spiritual gifts that Paul mentions in 1 Corinthians 12–14; Romans 12:3–8; Ephesians 4:7–16 and, after explaining each of the gifts, allow the audi-

ence members to identify what might be their respective gifts. Below I gives some details for doing the latter.

An apostle, technically, was one of the twelve apostles of Jesus, also including Paul. However, the word "apostle" could be used more generically of someone sent by the Lord to preach the gospel. This latter sense could encompass missionaries.

A prophet is directly inspired by the Spirit to give a word from God. It seems that in the worship services of the early church prophecy was an integral part of God's revelation to his people. "Discernment of spirits" refers to the gift whereby someone had the ability to detect demonic activity in the life of an individual or to sense false teaching. It also could be associated with discerning the message of the prophets to ensure that the proclaimed word was in keeping with the gospel. Today, churches differ in their opinion as to whether God still speaks through prophets or whether God speaks only through the Bible.

A teacher is adept at explaining biblical doctrine. In New Testament times, teaching, like preaching, was devoted to poring over the Old Testament to see how Jesus fulfilled its messianic predictions. A "word of wisdom/knowledge" is a gift whereby the Lord instructs someone in how to address a particular problem in a church, perhaps in the worship setting. These gifts are sometimes thought today to be associated with those well trained in interpreting and applying the Scriptures.

A pastor both teaches and preaches, all the while shepherding the congregation toward spiritual maturity.

An evangelist is especially successful at winning others to Christ. But this particular calling does not eliminate the mandate of the Great Commission that all believers be witnesses to Christ as well.

An exhorter is someone in the body of Christ who is good at challenging and encouraging believers to greater heights in their spiritual growth.

A person with the gift of faith has a vision of God's plan for a church or perhaps has unusual faith in God's healing ability. The gift of miracles is possibly related to this last gift. Healing is similar to the previous two gifts, except that healing seems to focus on human need.

The gift of tongues, according to Acts 2:1–8, is a supernatural ability to speak in a human language not known by the speaker. However, according to 1 Corinthians 14, tongues is a supernatural ability to utter ecstatic speech intelligible to God. The gift of interpretation allows a person empowered by the Spirit to translate this ecstatic speech in the worship setting of the church. Indeed, Paul insisted that such interpretation should accompany ecstatic speech so that the congregation could understand and unbelievers would not misconstrue ecstasy as insanity (compare Acts 2:13 with 1 Cor. 14:23).

The gift of ministry is possibly applied to someone who serves the Lord and people behind the scenes in both physical and spiritual ways. Administration is the ability of Christians to provide leadership for local congregations. Being a ruler may involve the same gift just mentioned, though with a focus on the leaders themselves. Being a helper may involve the same gift as ministry—that is, it may refer to those who prefer not to be in the limelight as they quietly serve the church. Mercy is a gift well suited to those believers called to serve in the medical field. Giving refers to those Christians who possess an exceptional ability to make money and give a portion of it back to the Lord; this is to be distinguished from the responsibility of every Christian to give a portion of their income to the Lord.

One of the spiritual gifts Paul mentions in Romans is the gift of mercy. In other letters Paul more specifically mentions the gift of healing. This relief (ca. AD 1400) shows the Saints Cosmas and Damian treating the sick or injured, be it man or animal. These twin brothers were early Christian physicians martyred for their faith under Diocletian. In the Eastern Orthodox Church they are revered as unmercenary physicians because they took no payment for their work, practicing their healing ministry because of their love of God and desire to care for people.

Illustrating the Text

Every believer has spiritual gifts and can exercise them by faith.

Story: "Modern Hexameron: *De Aranea*," by Walter Wangerin. In this little story Wangerin, who was noted earlier in the commentary (see the "Illustrating the Text" section under Rom. 1:8–15), writes about the life habits of a mother spider.[4] Wangerin shows how even this lowly creature, which we tend to despise, uses her native gifts to give life to her offspring at the cost of her own.

Recalling that our spiritual gifts are from God prevents arrogance and inferiority.

Apologetics: *Mere Christianity*, by C. S. Lewis. In chapter 8 of book 3 Lewis identifies pride as the worst of all sins and asserts, "Pride has been the chief cause of misery in every nation and every family since the world began." In the same section he also asserts that the solution to pride is not to be a "greasy, smarmy person who is always telling you that, of course, he is a nobody." Instead, the truly humble person will be cheerful, giving little if any thought to self at all, one way or the other. The author emphasizes much the same thing in story form in *The Screwtape Letters*.

Poetry: "I'm Nobody! Who Are You?," by Emily Dickinson. In this very short poem of only eight lines, Dickinson (1830–86) addresses the narcissism all too prevalent in society while indicating the opposite extreme as a potential problem.

I'm nobody! Who are you?
Are you nobody, too?
Then there's a pair of us—don't tell!
They'd banish us, you know.

How dreary to be somebody!
How public, like a frog
To tell your name the livelong day
To an admiring bog![5]

The diversity of gifts among believers brings unity to the body of Christ.

Film: *Places in the Heart*; *It's a Wonderful Life*. These films have wide appeal, and both illustrate beautifully the concept of individuals in communities responding in varied ways to the sadness and tragedy in the lives of their members, each one giving what he or she can to resolve the needs. In *Places in the Heart* (1984), set in Texas in 1935, a widow tries to keep her farm together with the help of, among others, a blind man and an African American man during the Great Depression. The movie ends as it opens, in church with church music playing. The minister reads 1 Corinthians 13. As the choir sings, communion is passed from person to person, and we see characters both alive and dead sharing in fellowship. In *It's a Wonderful Life* (1946), a man who has helped many others gets into deep financial trouble when his uncle misplaces a large sum of money. The movie ends with the entire community coming to his aid, each person contributing a lot or a little to repay the lost money. Certainly, what happens in these communities serves as a metaphor for the Christian community.

The Background of Paul's Body Imagery

As noted in the "Historical and Cultural Background" section, the background of Paul's analogy of the body of Christ in Romans 12:4–5 has been much discussed. There are seven basic theories.

1. Eduard Schweizer called attention to the political view, which compares the body of Christ with the Greek idea that associates a gathered political group of people with a human body (see Livy, *Hist*. 2.32).[1] While this view explains the parallel (community = body), it leaves unanswered the question of why Paul speaks of the "body *of Christ*" (e.g., 1 Cor. 12:27).[2]

2. Wilfred Knox argued that the notion of the body of Christ and its individual members originated in "the Stoic commonplace of the state as a body in which each member had his part to play."[3] But, like the political theory, this suggestion cannot explain why Paul calls it the "body *of Christ*." Ernest Best points out in this regard that the comparison is not between the body and its members, but rather between the members as members of the body of a person.[4]

3. Lucien Cerfaux claimed that the idea of the body of Christ originated in the church's celebration of the Lord's Supper.[5] But this theory, which equates the body of Christ with the bread of Christ, is based on the assumption that Paul's teaching on the Eucharist is borrowed from the mystery religions' belief that partaking of the meal of the deity was tantamount to being united with the god.[6]

4. Rudolf Bultmann popularized the position that gnosticism informed the Pauline concept of the body of Christ. That view promoted the "primal man" myth, a teaching identifying individuals as pieces of an original cosmic, heavenly man, who, upon his fall to earth, disintegrated into myriads of human bodies. On recollecting their original spiritual state, however, those individual pieces are ultimately regathered into the one primal man.[7] Few scholars today, however, date that myth to the first century AD.

5. James Dunn roots the body-of-Christ concept in the charismatic worship of the early church. As believers gathered for worship and as God manifested himself through the *charismata* (spiritual gifts), the people sensed themselves to be a corporate body, unified in Christ.[8] This suggestion is too generic, however, especially since two other ideas better explain the phrase.

6. W. D. Davies insightfully argues that the Jewish apocalyptic/rabbinic concept of the corporate body of Adam is the best antecedent to the notion of the body of Christ.[9] He writes, "Paul accepted the traditional Rabbinic doctrine of the unity of mankind in Adam. That doctrine implied that the very constitution of the physical body of Adam and the method of its formation was symbolic of the real oneness of mankind. In that one body of Adam . . . [all people] were brought together as male and female."[10] There is much to commend

this view, especially since many interpreters see Adam behind the Pauline passages on the body of Christ (compare 1 Cor. 12 with 1 Cor. 15:44–49; Rom. 12:4–5 with 12:1–2; 5:12–21; 7:7–13; 8:17–25; Col. 1:18 with 1:15; Eph. 4:7–16 with 1:15–23; 5:22–33). The major objection is that there is no explicit mention of the "body of Adam" in the Jewish literature contemporaneous with Paul. But this objection can be adequately met by the next theory.

7. A. J. M. Wedderburn proposes that the roots of the idea of the body of Christ stem from the ancient Hebrew belief that one person represents many, and many are incorporated in the one (Gen. 12:1–3; compare Gen. 14:17–20 with Heb. 7:4–10; Josh. 7:16–26).[11] This reciprocal relationship takes one a long way toward understanding the body of Christ, and it is commensurate with the Adamic theory that the first man is the representative of the fallen human race (Rom. 5:12–21). If so, then the church, the corporate body of Christ, is none other than the eschatological Adam (1 Cor. 15:45), the new humanity of the end time, which has now appeared in human history.

The Background of Paul's Body Imagery

The New-Covenant Ethic of Love

Big Idea *Paul, like Jesus, says that the new-covenant ethic is love. The thesis here is simple: love sincerely. Love should be shown toward God, fellow believers, and even nonbelievers who persecute Christians. Thus, Paul's ethic continues the radical call by Jesus to his disciples to love one another. To love others is to sacrificially accept the new-covenant stipulation to love.*

Understanding the Text

The Text in Context

Romans 12:9–21 continues the theme of being a living sacrifice (12:1–2) by loving others. Romans 12:9 and 12:21 form an *inclusio* for the intervening verses: to love is to avoid evil and cling to good. Although a sequential outline is difficult to identify in 12:9–21, a topical outline does emerge:

1. Love God (12:11–12)
2. Love one's fellow Christians (12:10, 13, 15, 16)
3. Love one's enemies (12:14, 17–21)

Historical and Cultural Background

1. Verse 13b mentions the importance of hospitality in the early church. Third John 5–8 shows how important hospitality was in the early Christian centuries for the spreading of the gospel. There were inns, but these were of ill repute; most travelers preferred to find lodging with friends, relatives, and acquaintances or those to whom they bore letters of introduction and recommenda-tion (see Matt. 10:9–13; 2 Cor. 3:1; Heb. 13:1–2).

2. Paul speaks of persecution in 12:14, 17–21. Up until AD 64–67, there was no real imperial harassment of the early Christians. Nero changed that, however, with his perse-cution of Christians in Rome, a prec-edent followed by Domitian after him (AD 81–96).

3. Several traditions inform Romans 12:9–21. The first is Jewish wis-dom.[1] The sec-ond is Jesus' teachings in the Sermon on the Mount/Plain.[2] The third, I sug-gest, is the cov-enant. Jesus' new-covenant command to love one another resonates throughout this passage. Moreover, the "two ways" tradition (see

Deut. 30:15–20)—choose good or choose evil—is echoed in 12:9, 21. Indeed, the entire passage is about manifesting good by loving God and others and avoiding evil by renouncing selfishness and revenge (in 12:19 Paul quotes Deut. 32:35, about vengeance belonging to God).

Interpretive Insights

12:9 *Love must be sincere.* In the New Testament the word *agapē* can express the highest form of love: God's commitment to his children (Rom. 5:5, 8; 8:39; cf. 8:35). Verse 9 says that Christians are to pass that love on to others.[3] (Although the verb *agapaō* can also be used of selfish love in Paul's writings and elsewhere [see 2 Tim. 4:10; cf. 1 John 2:15], the context of *agapē* here is that of altruistic love.) To love others is to cling to what is good. Not to do so is to give place to selfishness, revenge, and evil. The latter is to be hated.

12:10–12 *Be devoted to one another in love.* Verse 10 is the first of a number of verses in this paragraph that focus on loving other Christians. The *phil-* root, used twice here—in brotherly love (*philadelphia*) showing family affection (*philostorgoi*) to one another—refers to familial love.[4] Christians are to treat each other as brothers and sisters in the family of God. Verse 10b is translated either, "showing the way to one another in honor," or "Honor one another

Sculptured head of Emperor Nero from the Julian Basilica, Corinth, AD 60. Nero was emperor of Rome from AD 54 to 68. The historical record of his reign is filled with contradictions, but there is no doubt that Nero ordered the horrific persecution of Christians during the last years of his rule.

- The central theme is the new-covenant ethic of love.
- Christians should love God.
- Christians should love their fellow Christians.
- Christians should even love non-Christians who persecute them.

above yourselves." The second translation is thought by some to ironically breed pride—outdo one another in showing love. But that need not be the case. Moreover, the latter translation is parallel to Philippians 2:3 ("in humility preferring others as more excellent than yourselves"). So the second translation is probably correct. Paul's command here to "honor others" (especially the Christian family) above oneself is a healthy corrective to the natural self-centeredness that plagues us all, but it does not rule out self-respect.

12:11 *Never be lacking in zeal, but keep your spiritual fervor.* Verses 11–12 focus on loving God. It is true that "zeal" and "spiritual fervor" should characterize the Christian's love for fellow believers, but even that is ultimately an act of service to the Lord. Such zeal for serving the Lord comes from being energized by the Spirit. Behind "keep your spiritual fervor" is the verb *zeō*, which means "to bubble, boil." The "bubbling up, boiling over" work of the Holy Spirit in the human spirit is the key to being faithful to the Lord.

12:12 *Be joyful in hope . . . faithful in prayer.* Verse 12 is also God-directed: during trials, Christians should place their hope in God. Indeed, it is prayer that reminds God's children of their destiny (hope) when they are experiencing the furnace of affliction. The early church was devoted to prayer (Luke 18:1; Acts 1:14; 2:42; 6:4; 1 Thess. 5:17; Eph. 6:18; Col. 4:2).

Romans 12:9–21

12:13 *Share with the Lord's people who are in need. Practice hospitality.* Verse 13 returns to loving others, particularly the family of God. Two acts of love are specified: share with God's people in need and be hospitable. The early Christians wonderfully demonstrated charity to one another and beyond to the watching world. Regarding hospitality, the progress of the gospel depended on Christian homes being open to itinerant missionaries.

12:14 *Bless those who persecute you . . . do not curse.* Verse 14 focuses on the need for Christians to love nonbelievers, even those who persecute the church. We noted above the stages of persecution of early Christianity by the Roman government. But such persecution also came from Jews who opposed the gospel, as Acts and the letters

In Romans 12:15, Paul tells the believers to "mourn with those who mourn." The mythological story of the death of Meleager is told in a panel from a Roman sarcophagus dated to the second century AD, which captures the grief of those that remain behind.

of Paul illustrate. But, rather than to retaliate, Paul challenges believers to bless their persecutors, not curse them. Two traditions inform this command: Jesus' teaching (Matt. 5:44; Luke 6:27–28) and the covenant. Regarding the covenant, James Dunn points out that blessing those who persecute is an advance beyond the attitude of the Old Testament (Gen. 12:3; 27:29; Num. 24:9; cf. 1QS 2.10; Matt. 5:38–44).[5] The *lex talionis*—the law of proportion-

ate judgment ("Only an eye for an eye and a tooth for a tooth")—is taken to a new and different level by Jesus and Paul. When persecuted, the Christian is to respond not in kind (curse them) but in love (bless them). The new covenant's stipulation of love eclipses the old covenant's law of retaliation.

12:15 *Rejoice with those who rejoice; mourn with those who mourn.* Verse 15 uses Greek infinitives to express admonitions to love fellow Christians: *chairein* ("rejoice") and *klaiein* ("weep"). Rejoicing with those who rejoice and weeping with those who weep are tangible ways to love the family of God. One might find it odd that Paul should first command Christians to rejoice with others. But, as John Chrysostom observes, such rejoicing is harder because it "requires a very noble soul, so as not only to keep from envying, but even to feel pleasure with the person who is in esteem" (*Hom. Rom.* 22).[6]

12:16 *Live in harmony . . . Do not be conceited.* Verse 16a returns to participles to express commands: living in harmony and not being proud.[7] Humility and harmony go hand in hand, while pride and conceit breed division. With these thoughts, Paul may be broaching the subject of unity among Jews and Gentiles in the Roman congregations (see Rom. 14–15). One way to diffuse pride is to associate with less fortunate people (12:16b).[8] This is what Jesus was noted for, and so too should his followers be.

12:17–21 *Do not repay anyone evil for evil . . . but overcome evil with good.* Paul here focuses on how Christians are to respond to those who persecute them. He begins by cautioning Christians not to repay evil for evil (cf. Matt. 5:38–39, 44–45; Luke 6:29, 35). Not exacting revenge is an honorable response even in the eyes of the world. Verse 18 adds a realistic note encouraging believers to be at peace with others whenever they can ("if it is possible"). This leaves open the possibility that believers cannot be at peace with their enemies all the time. Thus, for example, one cannot compromise the gospel to keep peace.

Verses 19–20 offer contrasting instructions. According to 12:19, Christians should leave their persecutors to the Lord (quoting Deut. 32:35, which speaks of God's judgment on the nations that hurt Israel).[9] But 12:20 challenges Christians that while God is to avenge injustice perpetrated against them, believers are to love their enemies, in tangible ways: feeding them and giving them drink (quoting Prov. 25:21–22). These acts of kindness will "heap burning coals" on the heads of the Christians' enemies. The most common view of this is that Christians' loving actions will create in their persecutors burning shame and remorse. Verse 21 seems to confirm this interpretation: showing love overcomes evil with good—the good actions of the believer, but also the good response (hopefully) of the enemy in terms of repentance. Moreover, 12:21 returns us to 12:9: love consists in

Romans 12:9–21 as Parenesis

The purported genre of Romans 12:9–21 is parenesis (admonition). Parenesis, found in both Greek and Jewish writings, is characterized by stringing together general admonitions culled from various sources with a lack of concern for sequence of thought or development of a single theme.[a] In 12:9–21 Paul does string together admonitions and does draw on various sources. But, unlike many ancient examples of parenesis, this passage has an overarching theme—love—and it relates the admonitions to a specific audience. Therefore, one should label the genre of 12:9–21 as parenesis only with these caveats in mind.

[a] See Dibelius, *Fresh Approach*; see also Dibelius, *James*, 3–11.

doing good and avoiding evil. This is the new-covenant ethic of love.

Theological Insights

Several theological insights greet the reader of Romans 12:9–21. First, the key characteristic of the Christian life is love, toward God, the family of God, and even one's enemies. Second, if the perpetrators of harm upon Christians do not repent, God will avenge his children. But that task belongs to God, not to Christians. Third, 12:9–21 delineates how love is to be shown: (a) love toward God expresses itself in devotion; (b) love toward others, especially believers, is demonstrated by selflessness; (c) love toward enemies is shown not by retaliating, but by caring for them with deeds of kindness. This type of threefold love brought great success to the early church and will do so to the modern church as well.

Teaching the Text

Perhaps the best approach to Romans 12:9–21 is topical. Thus, a sermon title could be "The New-Covenant Commandment to Love": love God (12:11–12); love the family of God (12:10, 13, 15, 16); love your enemies (12:14, 17–21).

First, the Old and New Testaments both admonish believers to love the Lord their God supremely. In fact, to put anyone or anything before him is idolatry.

Second, 12:13a admonishes believers to share with those in need, whether Christians or nonbelievers. That the early Christians did so magnificently is documented by Adolf von Harnack in a chapter entitled "The Gospel of Love and Charity."[10] Harnack lists at least ten acts of charity by early Christians: (1) alms, (2) support of teachers and officials, (3) support of widows and orphans, (4) support of the sick, the infirm, and the disabled, (5) care of prisoners and people languishing in the mines, (6) care of poor people needing burial, and of the dead in general, (7) care of slaves, (8) care of those visited by great calamities, (9) furnishing work, and insisting upon work,

and (10) care of brothers and sisters on a journey (hospitality), and of churches in poverty or any peril.

Third, loving our enemies is easier said than done, but it is nonetheless the way of the follower of Jesus. Only heaven will reveal how many Christians have sincerely prayed, "Father, forgive them, for they know not what they do."

Illustrating the Text

Love is shown in devotion to God and selflessness toward other believers.

Biography: Many biographies have been written about the artist Vincent van Gogh (1853–90). His troubled life even became the subject of Don McLean's popular song "Vincent," the first line of which, "Starry, starry night," is borrowed from the title of one of van Gogh's paintings. A film, *Lust for Life* (1956), was also made about him.

Van Gogh began his life wanting to teach the Bible to poor and working-class people. In London he went to the darkest parts of the city, to the poorest inhabitants. He read his Bible daily, wanting to know it well. After getting some theological education, he took a post as a missionary in a desperately poor coal-mining town in Belgium, choosing to share the squalid living conditions of the miners. He lived among them, visiting the sick and bringing spiritual consolation. He was fanatical in his zeal and self-denial, but consequently those who sent him dismissed him for "undermining the dignity of the priesthood." After this, he became an artist, his paintings reflecting his love for the common people, the poor, and the suffering.

Love toward one's enemies is shown through kindness and forgiveness.

History: To better understand the Roman persecution of early Christianity, read Pliny the Younger's letter to Emperor Trajan (ca. AD 113), written while he was governor of Bithynia, which spells out how he interrogated Christians.

Quotation: Nelson Mandela. Mandela spent twenty-seven years in jail as a result of his attempts to end apartheid in South Africa. He was released in 1990. In 1994 he was elected president of the country in the first open election, and his mission to end apartheid continued. Mandela said, "If there are dreams about a beautiful South Africa, there are also roads that lead to their goal. Two of those roads could be named Goodness and Forgiveness." Here is a powerful example for Christians to aspire to in forgiving others for the sake of Christ.

True Story: Ruby Bridges was the first African American child to attend an all-white elementary school in the South. Robert Coles, child psychiatrist and author, tells of her in his book *Children of Crisis* (1967), and her story has also been published as a children's book entitled *The Story of Ruby Bridges* (1995), written by Coles and illustrated by George Ford. Ruby was one of the black children who, in the face of abusive, even potentially violent resistance, began the process of school desegregation in New Orleans. Day after day, Ruby was ushered to and from school alone while onlookers taunted her. Coles was deeply troubled by the calmness of the child, and when he visited the family, Ruby's mother told him that Ruby prayed every night for the mob that threatened and harassed her. When he asked the parents why they would ask this of Ruby, they were perplexed and answered that this was what a person is to do, that it was the Christian thing to do.

One of Rome's most famous archaeological landmarks, this Roman amphitheater known as the Coliseum was built over a thirty-year period and was finally completed during the reign of Domitian, long after Paul's death. It could seat 45,000 people, who watched gladiator spectacles such as combat, mock sea battles, and wild animal hunts. Domitian ruled from AD 81 to 96. He was a good administrator and successful military commander but was unpopular with the senate. He reinstituted strict rules for religious practice. Those that were associated with Jewish beliefs, which included Christians, were persecuted. This is just one example of a time in church history when the words of Paul in this passage regarding the attitude and action of Christians toward their enemies would be challenging to put into practice.

Romans 12:9–21

God and Government

Big Idea *Paul declares that government is a divine institution, and so Christians should submit to its authority. He provides two reasons why believers should do so: fear of punishment for wrongdoing, and obedience for conscience's sake. The specific form that this submission should take is paying taxes. Thus, obeying the authorities is another expression of being a living sacrifice to God.*

Understanding the Text

The Text in Context

Even though Romans 13:1–7 is a part of general Christian exhortation (cf. 1 Tim. 2:1–3; 1 Pet. 2:13–17) and therefore transcends the immediate context, it is connected to 12:9–21 and 13:8–14 and even to the churches at Rome. Thus, while 12:9–21 requires that Christians love others, including their persecutors, 13:1–7 makes clear that God avenges those who wrong Christians and others through the government. The believer can find solace in that thought. Moreover, 13:8–14 makes much of the dawning of the age to come (see my comments in that unit); Christians continue to live in this age as well and therefore must obey the ruling authorities. And Paul no doubt knew that the city of Rome was becoming impatient with the emperor and the senate because of the strain of taxation, so the apostle encourages Christians not to join the chorus of complaining, but rather to pay their taxes.

Romans 13:1–7 unfolds in this way:

1. The divine establishment of government (13:1–5)
   a. The divine authority of government (13:1–2)
   b. The responsibility of government (13:3–4)
      i. Promote good behavior (13:3–4a)
      ii. Punish bad behavior (13:4b)
   c. Summary (13:5)
2. Human responsibility to government (13:6–7)
   a. Specifically to pay taxes (13:6–7a)
   b. Generally to be respectful (13:7b)

Historical and Cultural Background

Two key items inform Romans 13:1–7: the Jewish tradition of respecting the government, and Roman taxation.

1. The Old Testament anticipates Romans 13:1–7 in its recognition that no

human ruler wields power except through God's appointment (Prov. 8:15–16; Jer. 27:5–6; Dan. 2:21, 37–38; 4:17, 25, 32; 5:21; Isa. 41:2–4; 45:1–7; cf. Wis. 6:1–3; Sir. 4:27; Josephus, *J.W.* 2.140). This applies to leaders of other nations, from Nebuchadnezzar (Dan. 4:17) to Cyrus (Isa. 45:1). Therefore, Jews prayed and sacrificed to God on behalf of the Roman emperor. Still, however, whenever foreign rulers occupying Israel demanded that Jews disobey God, Israel revolted. The most famous examples are the Maccabean revolt against Antiochus IV Epiphanes in 167 BC and the revolt against Rome in AD 66. It may be that the latter, spurred by the Jewish Zealot party in Jerusalem, was already voicing its protests in the mid- to late 50s. Paul, however, cautions the Roman Christians against following suit.

2. Paul's command that Christians pay their taxes calls for comment. Romans 13:7 uses two words found in extrabiblical documents for taxes—*phoros* and *telos* (Josephus, *Ant.* 5.181; 12.182; see *TDNT* 9:80–81; BDAG, s.v. *teleō* 3). The former corresponds to the Latin term *tributum*, while the latter corresponds to *vectigalia*. *Tributum* refers to the Roman direct tax, which included property and poll taxes. *Vectigalia* refers to the indirect tax, which covered customs, duties, toll taxes, and fees for various services. We know from the Roman historian Tacitus (*Ann.* 13) that the masses reached a boiling point in AD 58 about exorbitant tax rates, so much so that the emperor Nero considered

dropping the indirect tax, although he decided against doing so. So Paul's letter to the Roman churches tried to keep Christians out of the debate by instructing them to pay their taxes.

Interpretive Insights

13:1–2 *Let everyone be subject to the governing authorities . . . what God has instituted.* Verses 1–5 make it clear that government is ordained by God and therefore is a divine institution, like the family and church, essential to the fabric of society. Therefore, everyone (*pasa psychē*) must obey the government.[1] This means both Christian and non-Christian, for without some structure of government, anarchy and violence will ensue. "Be subject" (*hypotassō*) conveys the idea of getting in one's place in a hierarchal role, in this case placing oneself under the government. "Authorities" (*exousiai*) refers to secular authorities—government. Oscar Cullmann popularized the view that the authorities here are spiritual beings who rule

- Government is divinely ordained.
- Christians should obey the governing authorities because they have been appointed by God.
- Christians should pay taxes to the government.
- Not to obey the government is to invite punishment.

Antiochus IV Epiphanes, whose face is shown on this coin, took his frustrations with Rome out on the Jews. He ordered a Sabbath attack on the city of Jerusalem that resulted in the death or enslavement of most of its Jewish inhabitants. The city walls were destroyed and pagan sacrifices offered at the temple, which was newly dedicated to Zeus. All Jewish religious practices were prohibited. This led to the Maccabean revolt in 167 BC, which was successful in ending the Jewish persecution and restoring the temple to its rightful use.

secular authorities, and because Christ has defeated these spiritual beings, Christians need obey them only as long as they recognize their submission to Christ.[2] Two facts, however, refute such a theory. First, when Paul speaks of spiritual beings, he always combines "authorities" with "rulers" (*archai*), but in Romans 13:1–7 he only uses "authorities." Second, nowhere does Paul encourage believers to submit to spiritual beings, precisely because Christ has defeated them (Col. 2:15).

13:3–4 *For rulers hold no terror for those who do right . . . But if you do wrong, be afraid*. In 13:3–4 Paul lists two responsibilities that God has entrusted to government. First, according to 13:3–4a, government exists to promote good behavior. Such ethical behavior and good citizenship comes, stated negatively, because those who disobey the government disobey God and therefore will be judged accordingly. So to avoid such punishment, Christians are admonished to submit to the powers that be. Indeed, according to 13:3b–4a, doing what is right will be rewarded by the authorities. This is to state the matter positively. No doubt Paul implies that since God has put government in place to maintain order in society, it is God who punishes the criminal and praises the law-abiding citizen through the secular rulers. In promoting good behavior, an official acts as God's "servant" (*diakonos*).

In addition to motivating good behavior among citizens, government has a second responsibility: to punish criminals (13:4b). "Bear the sword" may refer to the Roman *ius gladii*, the authority of government to inflict death (see Tacitus, *Hist*. 3.68). But, according to A. N. Sherwin-White, this practice seems to have been confined to the power of Roman provincial governors to condemn to death Roman citizens serving in the military.[3] Therefore, "bear the sword" would not be relevant to most Roman Christians, who were not Roman

During the first century AD the Roman senate acted as an advisory body to the emperor. Made up of wealthy, influential individuals, its power and prestige were controlled by the emperor, who granted it authority to create legislation and make judicial rulings. The senate managed the public treasury of Rome and governed the senatorial provinces. Shown here is the Roman Forum, the center for religious and political affairs. The Curia, where the senate met for official business, is the square building near the center top of the photo (see also inset). Paul tells his audience to be in submission to the government authorities.

citizens serving in the military. Paul, then, probably is referring to the divine right of government to punish crime in general. And it may well be that Paul's Old Testament background led him to include in "bear the sword" the right to inflict capital punishment (cf. Gen. 9:6), though this could be debated. In meting out punishment, the governmental official again is called a "servant" (*diakonos*) by Paul.

13:5 *not only because of possible punishment but also as a matter of conscience.* Verse 5 summarizes 13:1–4. Government is ordained by God to punish criminals, and this should motivate Christians to obey. More than this, Christians should obey government for conscience's sake: to submit to government is to submit to God.

13:6–7 *If you owe taxes, pay taxes; . . . if respect, then respect.* Verses 6–7 list two responsibilities incumbent upon Christians (and, for that matter, upon all citizens) to secular rulers. The first is specifically paying taxes, whether direct or indirect taxes (recall my earlier comment in this regard). Paul once again indicates that secular authorities are God's "servant" (but this time the word is *leitourgos* not *diakonos*). *Leitourgia* (from which we get the word "liturgy") is a cultic term in the LXX for service to God in the temple. Taxes, in part, pay the salaries of governmental officials, which, Paul implies, has God's approval (note the connection between taxes and officials devoting themselves full time to their jobs, though Paul's intention in the latter description may mean officials devote themselves to governing in general). I mentioned above that both direct taxes (*phoros*) and indirect taxes (*telos*) are intended by Paul. Paul probably focused on taxes because

this is the most obvious symbol of a government's rule over its people. In this, Paul had Jesus' divine stamp of approval: "Give back to Caesar what is Caesar's" (Mark 12:17; Matt. 22:21; Luke 20:25).

The second responsibility that Christians and all citizens have toward their political authorities is to show them honor and respect in general. After all, our officials, especially those in the line of fire, place themselves in harm's way to protect us. Thus we owe them, as well as the God who appointed them, the utmost in honor and respect.

But what should a Christian do when the government requires disobedience to God? Peter's answer is clear, and Paul's actions agree: we must obey God rather than human beings (Acts 5:29). But some cases are not so straightforward. Should we pay taxes to a government that supports abortion clinics? Should Christians go to war in defense of their country? Should the church support the death penalty? The answers to these quandaries and others will depend on the individual conscience. However, any believer who feels compelled to break the law in the name of justice and the Christian faith should do so nonviolently and be prepared to face the consequences for civil disobedience. At least that is what I suspect Paul would say on the matter.

Theological Insights

Several theological truths are contained in Romans 13:1–7. First, government is a divine institution. Second, this is the case even for unjust governments, since not to have any form of rule is to breed anarchy and political disaster. Third, Christians are to support their governments by paying taxes and showing respect to their officials. Fourth, if, however, a political regime demands that Christians disobey God, they must respectfully refuse to do so in a nonviolent way and be prepared to suffer the consequences.

Teaching the Text

The two-point outline offered above nicely covers Romans 13:1–7: "The Divine Establishment of Government" (vv. 1–5) and "Human Responsibility to Government" (vv. 6–7). But we probably should also consider a third point: is there a time when Christians should oppose their government?

Paul is clear in 13:1–5 that political authorities are ordained of God. And happy is the nation whose philosophical assumption and legal commitment is that government should be run by and for the people. But such a blessed notion is only a rather recent development in governmental theory (ancient Greece deserves some credit for that process). Paul wrote his words

This Roman sestertius coin shows the image of Emperor Nero. The emperor controlled the imperial treasury, which paid all the expenses associated with administrating and controlling the imperial provinces. Taxes were the main source of income for the Roman Empire during the first century AD and were levied on these provinces that Rome had conquered. There was the annual fixed rate property tax known as the *tributum soli* (1 percent in Syria during the New Testament era) and the annual *tributum capitis*, or head tax, levied on individuals within a certain age range (one denarius, as recorded in the Gospels). Rome also raised money through sales taxes; inheritance taxes; road, bridge, and harbor tolls; and customs fees on imports and exports. Paul instructs his readers to pay their taxes.

(ca. AD 55–57) during the reign of Emperor Nero (AD 54–68), whose first five years were good years for the Roman Empire. After that, however, it was all downhill for Nero and those whom he harassed and tortured. It could be argued, then, that since Paul penned his letter to the Roman churches during Nero's good years, the apostle's command to be obedient to the government was retractable. Yet when Peter wrote his letter to the same Roman churches sometime between AD 64 and 68, at the height of Nero's atrocities, he essentially repeated Paul's words to obey the government if at all possible (1 Pet. 2:13–17). And Paul himself continued to call for the church to honor and pray for the king and his magistrates right up until his death (see 1 Tim. 2:1–3). All this is to say that the immoral condition of a government does not revoke the apostolic call for Christians to obey their governments (though see my comments below).

According to Paul's second point in 13:6–7, believers are to respect authorities and pay their taxes. Obviously without the latter government could not survive. Concerning the former, followers of Jesus would do well to remember that civic authorities—police officers, firefighters, soldiers, and so forth—often place themselves in harm's way to protect their citizens. That should certainly count for something when speaking of those who are in authority over us.

Nevertheless, ours is not a perfect world, and governments can become a part of the problem instead of part of the solution. What should the Christian do in this case? Paul, Peter, and John offer some inspired guidance in that matter. Paul would say that we should pray for our officials and respect them even if they do us wrong. Peter would say that if Christians are commanded to disobey God, they should respectfully disagree and obey God. And John's apocalypse reinforces Peter's stance, reminding the church that Jesus, not Caesar, is Lord. This is about the best that believers can hope for until the parousia and the establishment of the only perfect rule.

Illustrating the Text

Government is a divine institution, so we must pay taxes and respect officials.

Bible: Use the story of Daniel. Daniel 6:4 says: "Then the presidents and the satraps sought to find a ground for complaint against Daniel with regard to the kingdom, but they could find no ground for complaint or any fault, because he was faithful, and no error or fault was found in him" (ESV). What is clear here is that Daniel was respectful in his attitude toward and compliance with the established expectations and leaders of the kingdom he found himself in.

Literature: *The Green Mile*, by Stephen King. The main character in this novel (1996), John Coffey, an inmate on death row who possesses extraordinary powers of healing, always shows respect to the officials in jail even though he endures great hardship and suffering and goes to his death falsely charged. A film version was made in 1999.

If a regime demands disobedience to God, we must refuse nonviolently and accept the consequences.

History: "Letter from Birmingham Jail," by Martin Luther King Jr. Few documents illustrate as powerfully the loving refusal to cooperate with wrongs perpetrated by the government as this letter written on April 16, 1963. This response to a published statement critical of King by eight white clergymen from Alabama was fashioned under hard circumstances. Lacking writing paper, he scribbled in the margins of a newspaper page. An aide smuggled the newsprint out of the jail. Not only did King work within the parameters of the law, but also he held peaceful rallies against racial discrimination. The letter is literary, full of rich metaphors and compelling illustrations, a sermonic piece that leaves any reader with conviction and a better understanding of the role of courage in the Christian's life. Passages of this letter could be read out loud; it is a memorable and quotable piece.

Ethics and Eschatology

Big Idea *Ethics and eschatology go hand in hand. Because the age to come has dawned, Christians participate in the new covenant; but because the present age continues, Christians must love others and not cater to the flesh. Indeed, the dawning of the age to come in Christ empowers believers to love others in the present age. The Old Testament law could not accomplish this.*

Understanding the Text

The Text in Context

Romans 13:8–14 resumes Paul's discussion about Christian love in 12:9–21. At the same time, 13:8–14 anticipates Paul's challenge to the Roman Christians to love one another in 14:1–15:13.

Romans 13:8–14 divides into two sections: the ethic of love (vv. 8–10) and the dawning of the eschaton (vv. 11–14). The two paragraphs are closely related: love is the power of the age to come, the stipulation of the new covenant; only it, not the law, can overcome the flesh of this present evil age.

I outline these two sections in this way:

1. The ethic of love (13:8–10)
   a. The fulfillment of the law and the presence of the new covenant (13:8, 10)
   b. Love is the fulfillment of the law in the way it treats one's neighbor (13:8–10)

2. The dawning of the age to come (13:11–14)
   a. The indicative of the age to come (13:11–12a)
   b. The imperative needed for the present evil age (13:12b–14)

Historical and Cultural Background

Several traditions inform Paul's ethic and eschatology in 13:8–14.

1. Jesus' reduction of the law to loving God and loving one's neighbor informs Paul's command to love others (see Lev. 19:18; Mark 12:29–31; Matt. 22:37–39; Luke 10:27–28).

2. Paul's language about taking off and putting on clothing is thought by many to allude to early Christian baptism.[1]

3. Romans 13:11–14 is thoroughly immersed in Jewish apocalypticism. Evald Lövestam points to a number of Jewish eschatological texts that undergird the passage.[2] I would add to Lövestam's discussion that the texts he lists are informed by an

apocalyptic reading of the Deuteronomic tradition, especially the pattern of sin, exile, and restoration that composes the story of Israel (see "The Theme of Romans" in the introduction). Thus, for example, Amos 5:18, 20 reverses the meaning of the day of the Lord for Israel, ascribing to it darkness and exile (Deuteronomic curses) because of their sin, not light and deliverance. One day, however, Israel will repent and obey the Lord, resulting in restoration and salvation (Deuteronomic blessings [Amos 9:13–15]). Similarly, Isaiah 60:19–20 envisions the lifting of God's judgment upon Israel (Deuteronomic curses) and the subsequent restoration to the land, along with newfound obedience to God. It does so by employing the imagery of light and glory (Deuteronomic blessings [see Isa. 60:21–22]).[3]

I suggest that the preceding background sheds significant light on the Jewish underpinning of Romans 13:8–14: it is consonant with the hope that obedience to the Torah in this age (13:8–10) will bring about the age to come and the Deuteronomic blessings (13:11–14). Paul, however, reverses that tradition: only those whose faith is in Christ, not the law, and who thereby live a life of love (13:8–10) are participants in the Deuteronomic blessings of the age to come. This is what it means to put on Christ (13:14a). In doing so, Christians provide no opportunity for the flesh (13:14b). It is possible that because of the polemical nature of 13:8–13 (Paul

Key Themes of Romans 13:8–14

- The age to come and the new covenant have dawned.
- The ethic of the new covenant is love, which overcomes the sinfulness of the flesh in this age, something that the law could not do.
- Love fulfills the Old Testament law.

extricates his gospel from the charge of libertinism), and because elsewhere in Romans Paul states that the law is no match for the flesh since it actually stirs up sin (3:20; 4:15; 7:7–11; 8:3), we are to understand Paul as saying in 13:14b that following the Torah is not the way to overcome the sinful nature (against the Judaizers). In reality, attempts to follow the Torah bring about disobedience and the Deuteronomic curses. If so, Paul's reversal motif in 13:8–14 becomes clear: faith in Christ (who already obeyed and thereby terminated the Torah) brings the Deuteronomic blessings; but efforts to pursue the law in one's own power do not lift the Deuteronomic curses.

Known today as San Giovanni in Fonte, or the Lateran Baptistery, this ancient octagonal building was constructed in the fourth century AD by Constantine the Great. The walls are all that remain of the original structure. It housed the first baptistery of Rome.

Interpretive Insights

13:8–10 *whoever loves others has fulfilled the law . . . love is the fulfillment of the law.* Verses 8–10 present the ethic of love. The key concept in this paragraph, that love is the fulfillment of the law, forms an *inclusio* (13:8, 10). Douglas Moo rightly points out that "fulfill" means for Paul the eschatological completion of the law, which was accomplished in Christ (as I argued above).[4] Christians, therefore, because they are in Christ and disseminate his love, need not worry about any other commandment. Romans 13:10b forms an *inclusio* with 13:8b and should be read in the same light: the Christian who loves, and who therefore does what the law requires (8:9–10a), has brought the Torah to its culmination. In other words, the new covenant has arrived, and its ethic is love.

But how does this relate to those commandments that Paul mentions in 13:9? There are three views. First, there is the traditional, or Lutheran, view stated above with reference to Moo. The law is finished in Christ. The Christian therefore is not obligated to any part of the law, certainly not the civil and ceremonial aspects, and not even the moral aspect—the Ten Commandments. Rather, the love of Christ flowing through the believer fulfills all that the law ever intended (though Moo perhaps allows for the continuing role of the law in the Christian life in light of human sinfulness). Second, there is the Calvinist view, which says that the Ten Commandments should function as a gauge of the Christian's behavior. This is often called the "third use" of the law.[5] Third, James Dunn approaches 13:8–10 from the New Perspective on Paul. The curse of the law has been lifted in Christ so that now believers can obey the law in the power of the Spirit and guided by love.[6] The last two views seem to miss the eschatological significance of Paul's statements in 13:8, 10 (love fulfills the law): Christ is the end of the law.

Verses 9–10 state Leviticus 19:18 positively, "love your neighbor as yourself," and negatively, "love does no harm to its neighbor." The latter reminds one of the negative Golden Rule in Judaism (see Tob. 4:15; Sir. 10:6; *Let. Aris.* 168, 207).

13:11–14 *The hour has already come . . . clothe yourselves with the Lord Jesus Christ.* These verses attest to the overlapping of the two ages in Paul's theology. Verses 11–12a emphasize the indicative aspect of salvation: by virtue of the Christ event, the age to come has drawn near and, with it, the

Members of the community at Qumran referred to themselves as "the children of light," and in their Dead Sea Scrolls manuscript known as the *War Scroll* (fragment shown here) the writer prophesies a conflict between Sons of Light and the Sons of Darkness. Paul uses similar terminology when he tells the Roman believers to "put aside the deeds of darkness and put on the armor of light" (Rom. 13:12).

salvation of believers. Three temporal clues in 13:11 confirm this to be the case: (1) the word "time" (*kairos*) is one of Paul's choice terms for referring to the dawning of the eschaton (cf. Rom. 3:26; 5:6; 1 Cor. 7:29); (2) the words "already the hour" (*hōra ēdē*) convey a definite eschatological overtone, drawing their inspiration from Daniel's idea that God has appointed a time for fulfilling his promise of the arrival of his kingdom (Dan. 8:17, 19; cf. 1 John 2:18; Rev. 3:3, 10); (3) the words "our salvation is nearer now than when we first believed" are full of eschatological language. "Now" (*nyn*) refers to the presence of the age to come (cf. Rom 3:21; 5:9; 2 Cor. 6:2), and "salvation" (*sōtēria*) refers to the Christian's redemptive wholeness and spiritual deliverance, a process begun by faith and soon to be culminated at the parousia. This salvation has drawn "nearer" (*engyteron*), a term recalling Jesus' proclamation of the arrival of the kingdom of God, the age to come (Mark 1:15; 13:28–29; cf. James 5:8; 1 Pet. 4:7).

These temporal terms, then, indicate that salvation and the end time have already dawned for the believer. However, the salvific message of 13:11–12a occurs in the context of this present age; hence Paul's emphasis in 13:12b–14 on the necessity for Christians to live holy lives. It is clear that, for the apostle, eschatology forms the basis for Christian ethics. Accordingly, two general commands are issued: Christians are to put off the deeds of darkness and put on the weapons of light. This respective shedding of unrighteousness and donning of righteousness reflect the ongoing struggle that believers experience because they live in between the two epochs. The metaphor

The Delay of the Parousia

In the past, numerous New Testament scholars claimed that Jesus taught he would return in the lifetime of his disciples, which did not occur. This supposedly greatly unsettled the early church. That phenomenon is called the "delay of the parousia." But two pieces of evidence dispute the claim that the delay of the parousia was a pervasive problem for early Christians. (1) Jesus allowed for a delay in his return (see the parables of the faithful servant, the ten virgins, and the talents in Matt. 24:45–25:30). (2) The "already but not yet" eschatological tension encouraged the early church.

Even though Christ did not return in the first generation, the early church saw his first coming as eschatological. That is, the first coming of Christ inaugurated the signs of the times and the age to come (e.g., antichrist, great tribulation, apostasy, cosmic upheaval, arrival of the Spirit). Because the signs of the times were already set in motion in the first century AD, the New Testament church focused its attention more on the Son than on the signs. What remained in history was but the coming intensification and culmination of those signs of the times that were already initiated and thereby ensured Christ's return. Thus, the early church seemed to view the second coming of Christ as an apt epilogue to his first coming.

of the conflict between darkness and light brings to mind the eschatological battle between the unrighteous and the righteous envisioned in the Qumran literature (1QM 1.1, 8–14; 13.5–16; see also 1QS 1.9–10; 3.24–25; 4.7–13), as well as 1 Thessalonians 5:1–9.[7]

Moreover, 13:11–14 should not be isolated from the earlier discussion of 13:8–10, for the former refers back to the love command in the latter: do this (fulfill the law by love), knowing that the eschaton has dawned (13:11–14). That connection is important because it provides the overarching logic of 13:8–14, which is that Paul is answering the polemics of his Judaizing opponents. Freedom from the law does not lead to licentious living; rather, Christian love alone provides victory over the flesh (11:14). This understanding accentuates the fact that, as far as the Christian is concerned, the law is terminated and now is replaced by love. The Torah, therefore, does not govern the Christian experience; rather, it is the new-covenant stipulation of love that does so.

Theological Insights

Several truths based on Romans 13:8–14 impact the Christian. First, the only debt that the believer owes is to love God and others. Paul's command in 13:8–10 cannot be understood to prohibit, in our time, the (prudent) use of credit cards, mortgage, and so forth. Rather, it makes the point that loving others is an ongoing obligation for believers. Second, the Christian is under love, not law. But, as the Sermon on the Mount shows, loving others is more demanding and radical than the Torah itself. Only the power of the Holy Spirit can accomplish such behavior. Third, the power to love is available to the Christian because the age to come, the new covenant, and the kingdom of God (all similar concepts) have dawned. Thus, Christians love others (13:8–10) and God by pleasing him with holy lives (13:11–14).

Teaching the Text

I would use the title of this unit, "Ethics and Eschatology," and the accompanying outline to teach or preach Romans 13:8–14. The basic point to be made is that eschatology—the dawning of the age to come—gives Christians the power to love God and others and thus the strength not to embrace an escapist mentality relative to this age. Regarding ethics, I noted above that 13:8–10

indicates that living a life of love for God and others fulfills the Old Testament law and even exceeds its requirements. So there is no room for licentiousness in the Christian life or for a cavalier attitude toward sin. And the power to live such a supernatural life of love has dawned in the person of Christ, who by his Spirit indwells his people (13:11–14). Yet we might also look again at Paul's comments about ethics and eschatology from a slightly different perspective. Ethics obviously focuses on the here and now, while eschatology finds its ultimate fulfillment at the return of Christ. Assuming that to be the case, we can also detect that 13:8–14 offers a healthy balance toward life and eternity in the following ways.

If we as Christians focus only on ethics—the here and now—by trying to bring utopia to earth only through voting, social justice, transforming the structures of society with the gospel, and so forth, then probably we are in for a big disappointment. Theologians have tried to do that for centuries, from those who first legalized Christianity, to the Crusaders of the Middle Ages, to the theonomists of the twentieth century, to liberation theologians past and present. And all of them without exception have failed in their laudable attempts to usher in the kingdom of God through human effort. What is needed here is the humble recognition that only God himself will bring his kingdom to this planet.

But, on the other hand, if the church loses sight of its divine calling to be the salt and light of the earth by becoming obsessed with the date of the second coming or other eschatological phenomena, it will become so heavenly minded that it will be no earthly good. Therefore, Paul offers precisely the right balance to the church in 13:8–14: it should concentrate on preaching the gospel and loving others (ethics), all the while knowing that the final resolution awaits the return of Jesus Christ (eschatology).

Illustrating the Text

Our continuing debt is to love others.

Literature: *Les Misérables*, by Victor Hugo. In a well-known scene from this novel (1862), which has been made into a Broadway play and adapted for film, the escaped convict Jean Valjean is taken in by Bishop Myriel and given dignity and shelter. Nevertheless, Valjean steals the bishop's silverware and escapes. When he is captured, the bishop protects Valjean, saying he had given the silverware to him and in fact wondered why Valjean had left the candlesticks. This act of love profoundly changes Valjean's life forever, and he becomes a great force of love and generosity for the rest of his life.

Understanding eschatology, we must stop sinning and behave decently.

History: In his masterful book on New Testament eschatology, *Christ and Time*, Oscar Cullmann compared the first and second comings of Christ to D-Day and V-E Day of World War II. Just as D-Day marked the beginning of the end for the Axis armies, so too the death and resurrection of Jesus signaled the victorious invasion of the age by the kingdom of God. Even after D-Day, however, there was another year of war and death before the final victory. So too, even after the triumph of Jesus' resurrec-

Augustine of Hippo (AD 354–430), one of the greatest theologians of all time, was profoundly influenced by Paul's letter to the Romans. The painting shown here is by Antonello da Messina (AD 1472–73).

tion, spiritual warfare will continue to be the lot of God's people until the parousia. The outcome of the battle, however, is not in doubt; the Christian is on the victor's side.

Church Fathers: Augustine, in his *Confessions* (AD 397–98), reveals how he experienced his conversion to Christ by meditating on Romans 13:13–14 (*Conf.* 8.12.29). The challenge of Paul to put on the Lord Jesus Christ and make no provision for the flesh (the sinful nature) empowered Augustine to break with his past immorality and commit his life to Christ and his kingdom.

"Weak and Strong" Should Get Along

Big Idea *Romans 14:1–15:13 forms a unit unto itself containing Paul's plea for the Roman Christians to get along—specifically, that the weak and the strong in faith would accept each other in Christ. Romans 14:1–12 begins the discussion with a twofold exhortation (vv. 1–3, 10–12) grounded in a theological explanation (vv. 4–9).*

Understanding the Text

The Text in Context

In the past, some scholars have contended that Romans 14:1–15:13 is parenetic material that Paul includes in his letter at this point but that has no real connection to the churches at Rome.[1] According to this view, Paul rewrites and generalizes his earlier instructions in 1 Corinthians 8:1–11:1 in Romans 14:1–15:13.[2] To be sure, there are similarities between Romans 14:1–15:13 and 1 Corinthians 8:1–11:1: both address the "weak" (in faith); both center on the controversy of whether Christians should abstain from certain foods; both admonish believers in their decisions regarding that matter not to become stumbling blocks to their fellow believers.[3]

Most interpreters today argue instead that Romans 14:1–15:13 focuses on a divisive situation in the Roman congregations—whether to eat meat, drink wine, observe certain days as holy—with Paul

ultimately answering, "Love one another." This theme of loving others has dominated Paul's discussion since 12:9. Moreover, significant differences between Romans 14:1–15:13 and 1 Corinthians 8:1–11:1 indicate that Paul has tailored his parenetic material in the latter to apply to a specific situation in the former. For instance, unlike 1 Corinthians 8:1–11:1, Romans 14:1–15:13 makes no mention of idolatry or eating meat dedicated to pagan deities in the temple, which are the key issues addressed in 1 Corinthians 8:1–11:1. It therefore seems clear that Romans 14:1–15:13 speaks to a specific issue in the Roman churches.

Romans 14:1–15:13, most commentators recognize, divides into four sections: 14:1–12; 14:13–23; 15:1–6; 15:7–13. Romans 14:1–12, as Douglas Moo observes, is chiastic in structure:[4]

    A The exhortation to unity (14:1–3)
      B The theology for unity (14:4–9)

A′ The exhortation to unity (14:10–12)

I will follow this division in the "Interpretive Insights" section below.

Historical and Cultural Background

The key background for Romans 14:1–15:13 is the identification of the strong and the weak in faith. Because this background dominates this entire section in Romans, here I must present an extended discussion of that identification.

Moo conveniently delineates six possible categories of identification of the weak and the strong:

1. The "weak" were mainly Gentile Christians who abstained from meat (and perhaps wine), particularly on certain "fast" days, under the influence of certain pagan religions.
2. The "weak" were Christians, perhaps both Jewish and Gentile, who practiced an ascetic lifestyle for reasons that we cannot determine.
3. The "weak" were mainly Jewish Christians who observed certain practices derived from the Mosaic law out of a concern to establish righteousness before God.
4. The "weak" were mainly Jewish Christians who followed a sectarian ascetic program as a means of expressing their piety. This

Remains of the two-story marketplace that was part of Trajan's forum in Rome (early second century AD). Administrative offices and shops would have occupied this area.

Key Themes of Romans 14:1–12

- Both weak and strong Christians at Rome are accepted in Christ, and therefore they should accept one another.
- Both weak and strong Christians at Rome are accountable to Christ.

program may have been the product of syncretistic tendencies.

5. The "weak" were mainly Jewish Christians who, like some of the Corinthians, believed that it was wrong to eat meat that was sold in the marketplace and probably was tainted by idolatry.
6. The "weak" were mainly Jewish Christians who refrained from certain kinds of food and observed certain days out of continuing loyalty to the Mosaic law.

Moo, following C. E. B. Cranfield,[5] opts for the sixth view, with which I agree. Moo adduces four pieces of evidence in support of that contention. First, the dispute between the weak in faith and the strong (14:1–15:13) corresponds to the differences between Jews and Gentiles (see Rom. 1:18–4:22; 9–11; 15:14–33). Second, a Jewish origin of the position of the weak can clearly be seen in the term *koinos* ("unclean" [14:14]), which had become a semitechnical way of proscribing certain foods under the Mosaic law (see Mark 7:2, 5; Acts 10:14).[6] It is probably in that light that we are to understand the references to the abstention from meat and wine (14:3, 6b, 14b, 21) along with the observance of special days (14:6) on the part of the weak in faith.[7] These considerations effectively eliminate the first, second, and fourth options above. Third, Paul's plea for both weak and strong to accept one another indicates that the weak were not propagating views antithetical to the gospel, such as was being done by the Judaizers, for whom Paul reserved his most scathing critique (see Rom. 1:18–3:31). This point refutes the third option above. Fourth, the lack of mention of "food sacrificed to idols" (cf. 1 Cor. 8:1) speaks against the fifth option above. Thus we arrive at the sixth option as the preferred identification. The weak in faith were largely Jewish Christians who felt obligated to keep the ritual aspects of the law,[8] while the strong in faith were mostly Gentiles (and Jewish Christians, like Paul) who felt no such compulsion, because they realized that the law's role ended at the cross.

Interpretive Insights

14:1–3 *Accept the one whose faith is weak . . . for God has accepted them.* In 14:1–3 Paul gives the first of two exhortations found in 14:1–12: Christians are to accept one another even as God has accepted them. Verses 1–3 unfold that exhortation in parallel statements:

The strong in faith (vv. 1–2)
The weak in faith (v. 2b)

The strong in faith (v. 3a)
The weak in faith (v. 3b)

To the strong in faith—those mostly Gentile Christians plus some Jewish Christians like Paul who ate meat—Paul offers the challenge to receive the weak in faith but not for the purpose of quarreling with them to belittle them (14:1–2a). In 14:3a Paul restates the exhortation: the strong in faith are not to despise or look down on those Christians who avoided nonkosher meat. Likewise, 14:2b and 14:3b admonish the weak in faith not to judge those who eat nonkosher food. Such a judgmental attitude brings to mind the condescending attitude of Jews toward Gentiles back in chapter 2. Instead, both groups are to fully and unconditionally accept each other because their faith, strong or weak, is in Christ, and therefore God accepts both parties.[9]

14:4–9 *Who are you to judge someone else's servant? . . . live or die, we belong to the Lord.* In these verses Paul supplies the theological rationale as to why the two groups in Rome should accept each other: both are accountable to God and Christ.[10] Verse 4 explicitly states the theological rationale: neither strong nor weak have the right to judge each other, since both are servants, with the Lord as their master. Only he has the prerogative to judge, and he will empower each group to stand accepted (implied) on judgment day.

Verses 5–6 specify the situation at Rome: each individual makes a personal decision in the matter of meat, special days, and wine, since both the strong and the weak take their respective stances as unto and in thanks to God.

Sarcophagus lid fragment showing a banquet scene from the Cemetery of Via Anapo, Rome (AD 280–300). In these passages Paul tells the believers in Rome that they are to love and accept each other regardless of their individual convictions of what is appropriate to eat and drink.

Verses 7–9 make the point that Christians neither live nor die to themselves alone. Rather, since Jesus Christ died and arose again, Christians live and die unto Christ their Lord.

14:10–12 *each of us will give an account of ourselves to God.* Verses 10–12 return to the exhortation given in 14:1–3: Paul rebukes the weak for judging their fellow believer (14:10a) and the strong for despising their fellow believer (14:10b). This should not be, because both will stand before the judgment seat of God.[11] Paul reinforces the fact that all will stand before God in judgment by quoting Isaiah 45:23 LXX: "Every knee will bow, and every tongue will confess to God" (cf. Phil. 2:11).[12] Paul concludes his exhortation with the reminder that all will give an account of their life to God. So two reasons emerge in 14:1–12 as to why weak and strong are to accept one another: first, God and Christ have accepted both; second, both are answerable to God and Christ.

Theological Insights

Romans 14:1–12 deals with "doubtful things" or "gray areas," things that are not bedrock issues of the Christian faith but rather are matters of Christian liberty. So to the weak and the strong in faith Paul gives two exhortations. First, because both are accepted by God, both should be welcomed as fellow believers. Second, because both are answerable to God, in nonessential matters neither side has the right to judge the other's viewpoint.

Teaching the Text

A good approach to communicating Romans 14:1–12 is to introduce some contemporary nonessential issues in an attempt to understand the situation Paul addressed in the Roman churches. (Nonessential issues are concerns that are important but do not directly relate to the fundamentals of the Christian faith; those fundamentals include justification by faith, the deity of Christ, the return of Christ, the virgin birth of Christ, and the inspiration of the Bible). Then show from 14:1–12 the two principles that Paul offers for Christians dealing with "doubtful things": because all Christians are acceptable and accountable to God, Christians ought to love fellow believers even when they differ on nonessential matters. Lutheran theologian Rupertus Meldenius (1582–1651) put the solution best: in essentials, let there be unity; in nonessentials, let there be liberty; in all things, let there be charity.

Here is a list of some of the nonessential issues that the church faces today: hair length for men, tattoos, alcoholic beverages, tobacco, appropriate forms of entertainment, types of music in worship services, ordination of women for pastoral ministry, tithing or proportionate giving, whether or not the more spectacular gifts of the Spirit are operative today, church governance, mode of baptism, whether or not the Lord's Supper and baptism are sacramental. In all of these Romans 14:1–12 should be brought to bear upon the discussion.

Yet a caveat must be added to this discussion. We are not talking about matters that the Bible clearly condemns. That is, some things being debated in the modern Western world cannot be condoned if we wish to live biblically based lives. Perhaps the most contentious matter debated today in some churches is homosexuality and, related to that, same-sex marriage. Often those who support the homosexual lifestyle say that the same Bible that condemns such a practice also supports slavery and discrimination against women. So, it is argued, to be consistent, one cannot have it both ways—appealing to the Bible against one cause (homosexuality) but ignoring its support for others (slavery and discrimination against women). William Webb has written a book explaining why Scripture forbids homosexual behavior but should not be used to condone slavery and deny the ordination of women.[13] Webb's answer is essentially that while the Bible clearly rejects homosexuality, it is ambiguous regarding slavery and the inequality of women. And it is the people of God who, following the trajectory of biblical teaching, discern that the seed was sown by Paul for the eventual overthrow of the latter two injustices.

Illustrating the Text

Both weak and strong Christians should be welcomed as fellow believers.

Literature: *The Pilgrim's Progress*, by John Bunyan. In part 1, section 8 of *The Pilgrim's Progress* (1678), Hopeful and Christian hear the story of a "good man" called Little-Faith who lives in the town of Sincere. He is much troubled by three brothers, Faint-Heart, Mistrust, and Guilt, who try to steal from him and even hit him on the head. Nevertheless, Great-Grace, from the city of Good-Confidence, helps him up. Clearly, Little-Faith will always feel his troubles deeply; nevertheless, he is not turned away from heaven. In his annotated version of this classic book, Warren Wiersbe comments, "This is one of our Lord's favorite names for his disciples. . . . See Matthew 8:26; 14:31;

16:8. . . . God honors even a little faith. Not all Christians are great victors."[14]

Quote: *Life Together*, **by Dietrich Bonhoeffer.** This small book is the account of Pastor Bonhoeffer's (1906–45) experience of Christian community, the story of the underground seminary conducted during the Nazi years, showing how life together in Christ can be carried on in families and in groups. Bonhoeffer writes,

> God does not will that I should fashion the other person according to the image that seems good to me, that is, in my own image; rather in his very freedom from me God made this person in His image. I can never know beforehand how God's image should appear in others. . . . Strong and weak, wise and foolish, gifted or ungifted, pious or impious, the diverse individuals in the community are no longer incentives for talking and judging and condemning, and thus excuses for self-justification. They are rather cause for rejoicing in one another and serving one another. Each member of the community is given his particular place. . . . In a Christian community everything depends upon whether each individual is an indispensable link in the chain unbreakable. . . . Every Christian community must realize that not only do the weak need the strong, but also that the strong cannot exist without the weak. The elimination of the weak is the death of fellowship.[15]

Christians must love one another, even when we have different perspectives.

Film: *Babette's Feast.* This Academy Award–winning Danish film (1987) is based on the story of the same title by Isak Dinesen (1885–1962). In this beautiful story, the theme of extravagant, sacrificial love is central. Babette, a prominent chef from Paris, arrives on the bleak coast of Jutland, escaping a political uprising in which her husband and son have been killed. She begs two sisters, Martine and Philippa, who preside over an aging, dwindling church, to hire her as a servant, and she gives everything to deliver these people from their spare, loveless religion, from living meagerly, bickering among themselves while claiming faith. After fourteen years as their cook, one day she wins a considerable sum of money in the lottery, and she chooses to spend it all on a sumptuous feast for the community. She invites this "frozen chosen" group to a lavish meal to taste the joy of the abundance of life. Babette woos them out of their darkness into a better way, of love for each other, one of joy.

Strong and Weak Christians:

The New and the Old Covenants

Big Idea *The Christians at Rome who are strong in faith should, by limiting their own liberty, love the Christians who are weak in faith. To put it another way, those Christians who are living in the new covenant should love those Christians who are living like they are in the old covenant.*

Understanding the Text

The Text in Context

Romans 14:13–23 continues Paul's instructions to the strong and the weak in faith at Rome by focusing on the need for the Christians strong in faith to love those Christians weak in faith. They should do this by limiting their own liberty in Christ and by not flaunting that liberty in the churches at Rome. Douglas Moo's outline of 14:13–23 is good, noting a chiastic structure reminiscent of 14:1–12:

A Exhortation to the strong in faith: Do not cause the weak to stumble (14:13–16)

B Basis of the exhortation: The kingdom of God is more than food and drink (14:17–18)

A′ Exhortation to the strong in faith: Do not cause the weak to stumble (14:19–23)[1]

Historical and Cultural Background

Three pieces of background information are vital to understanding Romans 14:13–23: the covenant language, the kingdom of God (and these first two are near synonyms), and the Jesus tradition. The first of these will require considerable discussion but will shed much light on this passage.

1. Several key terms in Romans 14:13–23 are rooted in Second Temple Judaism's convictions about the old covenant (for more on these terms, see the sidebar): "stumbling block" (the noun *proskomma* [vv. 13, 20]; the verb *proskoptō* [v. 21]) and "obstacle" (*skandalon* [v. 13]); "unclean" (*koinos* [v. 14]) versus "clean" (*katharos* [v. 20]); "destroy" (*apollymi* [v. 15]) and the related terms "cause grief" (*lypeō* [v. 15]) and "destroy" (*katalyō* [v. 20]); "blaspheme" (*blasphēmeō* [v. 16]) and "good" (*agathos* [v. 16]); "building up" (*oikodomē* [v. 19]); not to mention the ritual requirements to

avoid both nonkosher meat and wine devoted to pagan deities (v. 21). All of these words relate to ancient Judaism's adherence to the dietary law in order to be holy before God and to participate in his covenant. To eat unclean foods, conversely, was to break the stipulations of the covenant and to suffer its curses.

2. Paul refers to the kingdom of God in Romans 14:17 (elsewhere in 1 Cor. 4:20; Col. 1:13 [kingdom of God's son]; 1 Thess. 2:12 with reference to the "already" aspect, and in 1 Cor. 6:9, 10; 15:24, 50; Gal. 5:21; Eph. 5:5 [kingdom of Christ and God]; Col. 4:11; 1 Thess. 2:12; 2 Thess. 1:5; 2 Tim. 4:1, 18 with reference to the "not yet" aspect). Romans 14:17 describes the kingdom as righteousness, peace, and joy in the Holy Spirit, which are new-covenant blessings.

3. The Jesus tradition also undergirds Romans 14:13–23:

Romans 14:13–23	Synoptic Gospels
Do not judge (v. 13)	Matt. 7:1; Luke 6:37
Unclean (v. 14)	Mark 7:15
The kingdom of God (v. 17)	105 times in the Synoptic Gospels
The kingdom of God and eating/drinking (v. 17)	Luke 22:30; see also Matt. 6:25; 11:18–19; John 6:54
Joy (v. 17)	Matt. 5:12
All things clean (v. 20)	Mark 7:19

One of the animals sacrificed by the Romans for religious purposes was the pig. Pork was also one of the meats that they enjoyed eating. This bronze Roman relief from the first to second century AD shows a boar decorated for sacrifice with a wide ribbon around its belly. Under Jewish law the pig was considered "unclean" and would never be eaten or used for sacrifice.

Key Themes of Romans 14:13–23

- The Christians who are strong in faith are enjoying the blessings of the new covenant.
- Those Christians who are weak in faith are living like they are in the old covenant.
- The strong in faith should love the weak in faith by not flaunting their Christian liberty of eating meat, drinking wine, and not observing the Jewish days of celebration, including the Sabbath.

Interpretive Insights

14:13–16 *not to put any stumbling block . . . in the way of a brother or sister.* As I begin my interpretation of 14:13–23, it might be helpful to pull together in advance the argumentation of these verses, taking into consideration the "Historical and Cultural Background" section. I do so by making three statements. First, it is clear that Jesus and now Paul throw out the dietary laws as a means of keeping and staying in the covenant. Rather, the kingdom of God has dawned and, with it, the new covenant, which is entered into by faith in Christ alone. In terms of 14:13–23, it may be said, then, that believers strong in faith are in the new covenant and are living like it by enjoying the righteousness, peace, and joy of the kingdom of God. These persons enjoy the blessings of the new covenant (14:22). Second, the believers weak in faith are in the new covenant (Paul calls them "brothers and sisters" in 14:13, 15, 21), but their adherence to the dietary laws indicates that they are living like they are in the old covenant. Third, Paul nevertheless challenges the strong in faith to demonstrate the ethic of the new covenant—love—toward their weaker siblings.

Verse 13 has a play on the word "judge" (*krinō*).[2] Paul tells them not to "judge" one another to "judge" this: that they do not cause a fellow believer to stumble. The focus of 14:13, and indeed the whole section of 14:13–23, is on the believer who is strong in faith not using liberty regarding the dietary laws as a stumbling block to the weak believer who does feel compelled to observe the clean/unclean distinction. Even though Paul sides with the strong because Christ abolished the dietary laws (compare 14:14a with Mark 7:15; cf. Acts 10:15; 11:9; 15:9), he challenges the strong to consider the convictions of the weak in that matter (14:14b). Thus, the strong believers should not eat nonkosher meat in the presence of the weak in faith because this might adversely influence weak Christians to eat against their conscience. Indeed, as the majority of recent commentaries on this passage observe, the weak in faith may suffer loss of salvation at the judgment seat if they persist in disobeying their faith, even if their faith is immature. Such a tragedy, obviously, would not proceed from the strong's love for the weak, just as it is not based on Christ's sacrificial love for the weak (14:15). This would be to pervert the blessings of the covenant upon the strong in faith into the curses of the covenant upon the weak in faith (14:16).

14:17–18 *the kingdom of God is . . . righteousness, peace and joy in the Holy Spirit.* Verses 17–18 provide the theological rationale behind Paul's exhortation to the strong: what really matters before God is not whether or not one eats or drinks, but the kingdom of God. We saw earlier that Paul taps into the Jesus tradition to speak of the dawning of the kingdom of God. The kingdom of God is God's reign in the hearts of his people. He is their king, and they are his subjects. So the kingdom of God involves service to God and others, in this case service to the weak in faith by placing limits on one's own liberty. This is what pleases God and others (14:18).

Paul uses three nouns—"righteousness," "peace," and "joy"—to characterize the blessings of the kingdom of God, all of which proceed from the Holy Spirit (cf. Rom. 5:1–5). "Righteousness" is God's imputed righteousness to the sinner through faith in Christ, which brings peace with God and eschatological joy. The Spirit is the one who unites the believer to Christ

The lower-class residents of Rome, which would have included many in Paul's audience, lived in apartment houses that did not have indoor kitchens. Cooking would take place outdoors or, more often, food would be purchased from vendors. This thermopolium preserved in Pompeii operated in a similar way to our modern fast food restaurant. Jars to hold food or drink were part of the counter structure, and customers would buy their meal and stand to eat it. This might explain Paul's discussion of food choices, since eating in this manner would not be a private affair.

and his righteousness (cf. Rom. 8:1–16). Therefore, righteousness, peace, and joy in the Spirit are blessings of the new covenant (14:17).

14:19–23 *do what leads to peace and to mutual edification.* With 14:17–18 as the theological basis, Paul resumes his exhortation to the strong in faith in 14:19–23. Verses 19–20a challenge the strong to unify the church by making every effort to bring about peace and edification in their relationship with the weak in faith. Otherwise the strong's flaunting of their liberty before the weak will destroy the church over the issue of food, which is a spiritual nonessential.

Verses 20b–21 expand Paul's exhortation by stating that the liberty of eating meat and drinking wine can cause the weak to stumble and fall in their faith. Therefore, the strong should limit their liberty.

Verse 23, however, does encourage the strong in faith to enjoy their liberty in Christ, but to do so in private or at least not in the presence of weak believers. In practicing their liberty to eat meat and drink wine, the strong in faith can enjoy the approval and blessing of God and thereby the new covenant.

Verse 22 contains two principles, one regarding the weak in faith, and one regarding all believers. The weak in faith should not eat meat and drink wine if they believe that in doing so they break the dietary laws of the covenant. Going against their conscience condemns them now and ultimately on judgment day before God. To put it another way, it is better for the weak in faith not to presently enjoy the liberty of the new covenant than to fail to remain in that covenant. The second principle addresses

Covenant Terminology in Romans 14:13–23

Many of the key terms Paul uses in Romans 14:13–23 are rooted in the Old Testament covenant.[a] *Proskomma* ("stumbling block") is found in the Old Testament (LXX) and Second Temple Judaism in connection with ancient Israel's idolatry (Exod. 23:33; 34:12; Jer. 3:3), as is *skandalon* ("obstacle") (Judg. 2:3; 8:27; Ps. 106:36 [105:36 LXX]; Hos. 4:17; Wis. 14:11). *Skandalon* is specifically connected with the idolatry of eating Gentile food (Jdt. 12:2; *Pss. Sol.* 4.23).

Koinos ("unclean, profane") is used in the LXX to reflect the purity concerns of the dietary laws that accompanied the Maccabean and post-Maccabean stance against Hellenism. Thus, 1 Maccabees 1:47, 62 describe the faithful Israelites as those who refused to eat "unclean" (*koinos*) food. This concern is matched elsewhere in Judaism's concern to maintain the purity laws (Jdt. 12:1–2; *Jub.* 3.8–14; *Pss. Sol.* 8.12, 22; 1QS 3.5; CD 12.19–20), a concern held especially by the Pharisees and Essenes. Thus, "clean" (*katharos*) is the opposite of unclean (nonkosher) food (Gen. 7:2–3, 8; 8:20; Lev. 4:12; 6:11 [6:4 LXX]; 7:19; Ezra 6:20; Mal. 1:11; Jdt. 12:9; 1 Macc. 1:48; *Pss. Sol.* 8.12, 22; *Let. Aris.* 166; *T. Levi* 15.1; Philo, *Spec. Laws* 4.106; cf. Mark 7:19; Acts 10:15; 11:9).

James Dunn makes the point that "destroy" (*apollymi*) is rooted in Deuteronomy relative to the fate of the unfaithful Israelites, whose divine judgment removes them from the covenant with Yahweh. Dunn reads the related terms in Romans 14:13–21, "cause grief" (*lypeō*) and "destroy" (*katalyō*), in a similar light.

For the covenantal nuances of "blaspheme" (*blasphēmeō*) and "good" (*agathos*), we turn again to Dunn, who notes that the terms refer to covenantal curses and blessings, respectively.[b]

Finally, "building up" (*oikodomē*) is a favorite concept in the book of Jeremiah, where God's judgment on Israel in sending them into Babylonian captivity is described as "tearing down" and Israel's future restoration (in the new covenant) is described, using the related verb *oikodomeō*, as God's "building up" (Jer. 12:16; 31:4, 28 [38:4, 28 LXX]; 33:7 [40:7 LXX]; 42:10 [49:10 LXX]; 45:4 [51:34 LXX]).

[a] For discussion of these terms and references in relation to their covenantal setting, see Dunn, *Romans 9–16*, 817–29.
[b] Dunn, *Romans 9–16*, 821.

all believers: all of life should be lived by faith, for not to do so is sin. Indeed, faith is the means of justification, sanctification, and glorification.

Theological Insights

Several truths emerge from Romans 14:13–23. First, the more mature Christians may well need to limit their liberty in Christ for the sake of the weaker Christians and for the unity of the church. Second, although this is so, it need not mean that strong Christians should live in slavery to the whims of others. Limiting liberty does have reasonable boundaries. Third, either way—strong or weak in faith—the Christian life is a walk of faith.

Teaching the Text

There are two good ways to teach/preach Romans 14:13–23. One could follow the outline given above: exhortation to the strong (14:13–16); theological basis in the kingdom of God (14:17–18); exhortation to the strong (14:19–23). One could also follow a logical order in covering these verses: (1) The strong in faith enjoy the blessings of the new covenant. (2) The weak in faith are in the new covenant but live like they are in the old covenant. (3) The strong in faith should demonstrate toward the weak in faith the ethic of the new covenant: love. Either way, the title of this unit—"Strong and Weak Christians: The New and the Old Covenants"—could serve as the title of the lesson or sermon on this passage.

We might also compare the strong in faith today with those who feel comfortable with the responsible use of alcoholic beverages, or who feel free to wear to church whatever they want, or who prefer seeker-friendly worship. But when worshiping with believers who feel uncomfortable with the preceding matters, the strong may need to forgo having a glass of wine, or to dress differently, or to add a more traditional touch to worship. My father died because of alcoholism. Consequently, I do not drink any alcoholic beverages. Some of my ministerial colleagues, on the other hand, are comfortable with drinking responsibly. However, when they are with me they are considerate enough not to have a drink. In this case I would be the Christian weak in faith, and they would be the strong in faith, limiting their liberty in my presence.

An amphora from Italy used to transport and store wine (first century BC). This pottery design, with the pointed foot or base, allowed the jars to be stored upright by pushing them into soft soil or placing them into racks with holes. Wine was probably the most common drink in the Mediterranean region. It was also used by pagan cultures as a libation offering to the gods. In Romans 14:21 Paul says, "It is better not to eat meat or drink wine or to do anything else that will cause your brother or sister to fall."

Illustrating the Text

Mature Christians must limit their liberty for the weak and for church unity.

Quote: Martin Luther. In his beautiful piece "A Treatise on Christian Liberty," Luther writes the following:

> Although the Christian is thus free from all works, he ought in this liberty to empty himself, to take upon himself the form of a servant, to be made in the likeness of men, to be found in fashion as a man, and to serve, help, and in every way deal with his neighbor as he sees that God through Christ has dealt and still deals with himself. And this he should do freely, having regard to nothing except divine approval.[3]

Each Christian's conscience must be the guide for what is right or wrong.

Literature: *The Screwtape Letters*, by C. S. Lewis. In Letter XIII of this famous satiric piece (1941), Screwtape, a senior demon, counsels young Wormwood, a junior tempter, to make the Christian give up all "likings and dislikings" instead, of course, of thinking through what is right or wrong. He is to get the Christian to move away from personal preference, becoming neutral. Screwtape continues,

> I myself would carry this very far. I would make it a rule to eradicate from my patient any strong personal taste which is not actually a sin, even if it is something quite trivial such as a fondness for county cricket or collecting stamps or drinking cocoa. Such things, I grant you, have nothing of virtue in them; but there is a sort of innocence and humility and self-forgetfulness about them which I distrust. The man who truly and disinterestedly enjoys any one thing in the world, for its own sake, and without caring twopence what other people say about it, is by that very fact fore-armed against some of our subtlest modes of attack.[4]

This section could be done as a dramatic dialogue before the message.

Although Christians are called to sacrificially refrain from enjoying some things for the sake of our weaker brothers and sisters, this should not obscure the deeper truth that God has created these (and many other pleasurable things) as good (see Rom. 14:16).

The Unity of the Strong and the Weak and the New Covenant

Big Idea *Paul concludes his challenge to the strong and weak Christians at Rome that began in chapter 14. Here he challenges the strong and the weak to live in unity, thereby affirming the presence of the new covenant.*

Understanding the Text

The Text in Context

Romans 15:1–13 concludes Paul's challenge begun in 14:1 for the strong and weak Christians to be unified. The theme of the new covenant continues to dominate the discussion. Accordingly, I outline Romans 15:1–13 thus:

1. The unity of the strong and the weak as an illustration of the new covenant (15:1–6)
   a. The exhortation to the strong (15:1–2)
   b. The rationale for the exhortation (15:3–4)
      i. The sacrifice of Christ (15:3)
      ii. The witness of the Old Testament (15:4)
   c. The unity of the strong and weak (15:5–6)
2. Christ and the fulfillment of the Old Testament prophecies of Jew and Gentile in the new covenant (15:7–13)

   a. The exhortation to the strong and the weak (15:7a)
   b. The resulting glory to God (15:7b)
   c. The blessings of the new covenant (15:8–13)

Historical and Cultural Background

As many commentaries well recognize, the Old Testament prophecies of the coming new covenant are the key background informing Romans 15:1–13.[1] Such a background explains the following terms: "encouragement," "hope," "truth," "mercy," "promises" to the "patriarchs," "joy," and "peace," along with the catena of Old Testament texts that Paul quotes in 15:9–12. I now briefly comment on each of these.

First, "encouragement" (15:4, 5) is the word *paraklēsis*, the famous term in Isaiah 40 and following (LXX; in the form of the verb *parakaleō*) that refers to the future restoration of Israel and the new covenant.

Second, "hope" (*elpis*), as we saw in 5:1–5, also alludes to Israel's hope for restoration and the new covenant. But here in 15:1–13 "hope" is a possession of Gentiles because they too share in the new covenant of the people of God. This is in contrast to the Gentiles before Christ, who were outside the covenant with God and therefore had no hope (see Eph. 2:12–13).

Third, "truth" and "mercy" (15:8–9) combine to bring to mind *hesed*, God's faithfulness to his covenant with Israel in the Old Testament.

Fourth, the Old Testament "promises" to the "patriarchs" (15:8) consist of the same Abrahamic covenant / new covenant.[2]

Fifth, 15:9–12 draws on four Old Testament texts that predict that the new covenant (or the restoration of Israel) will unify Jew and Gentile in their praise to God (2 Sam. 22:50 // Ps. 18:49; Deut. 32:43; Ps. 117:1; Isa. 11:10). And this is now being fulfilled in Christ.

Sixth, "joy" and "peace" describe some of the blessings of the arrival of the new covenant (recall the comments on Rom. 14:17 for the former and on 5:1–5 for the latter regarding the these two terms).

Interpretive Insights

15:1–2 *We who are strong ought to bear with the failings of the weak*. Verses 1–6 have as their theme the unity of the strong and the weak as an illustration of the new covenant. We just noted the influence of the new covenant on 15:1–13 as a whole. Verses 1–2 provide the first step toward the unity of the strong and weak at Rome. The strong are to bear the weaknesses of those who are not strong. The strong (*hoi dynatoi*) are, as in Galatians 6:2, to bear (*bastazō*) the burdens (weaknesses) of the weak (*hoi adynatoi*), like Jesus bore (*bastazō*) our diseases (Matt.

Key Themes of Romans 15:1–13

- The Christians strong in faith at Rome are challenged by Paul to limit their liberty for the sake of their weaker siblings.
- Both strong and weak are challenged by Paul to accept one another.
- The unity of strong (Gentile Christian) and weak (Jewish Christian) is proof that the Old Testament promise of the new covenant is present in Christ.

8:17). In other words, the strong in faith (Paul includes himself in this category) are to be careful not to let their liberty regarding the ritual law hurt the weak in faith. In light of what Paul has said since 14:1 and what he will say until 15:13, we can summarize the two categories of the strong and the weak this way:

Strong in Faith	Weak in Faith
Gentiles	Jews
Do not observe ritual law	Observe ritual law

The strong should be sensitive to the weak (Paul calls them "our neighbors" [15:2]) as an act of selflessness that will build up Jewish believers whose scruples will not allow them to discard the ritual law.

15:3 *For even Christ did not please himself*. The rationale for such an exhortation to the strong is that Christ sacrificed himself for others. Quoting Psalm 69:9, Paul applies that text to Christ. Christ has embraced the reproaches heaped upon God by sinners. Psalm 69 is applied to the passion of Christ in the New Testament (Matt. 27:34, 48; Mark 15:23, 36; Luke 23:36; John 2:17; 15:25; 19:29; Acts 1:20; Rom. 11:9–10), so it is fitting that Paul would quote from it in this context. Just as Christ was willing to be scorned for God's honor, so also the strong should forsake their liberty for the weak.

15:4 *through the endurance taught in the Scriptures and the encouragement they provide we might have hope.* Paul further appeals to the Old Testament as a whole to motivate the strong to be sensitive to the weak. Paul believed that the Old Testament witnessed to Christ and his church (see, e.g., 1 Cor. 10:1–11). Here Paul says that the Scriptures produce "endurance" and "encouragement" (or "comfort") and thereby "hope" for believers. In light of the new-covenant theme that informs "encouragement" and "hope," I suggest that Paul has the story of Israel in mind here (cf. again 1 Cor. 10:1–11): Israel's sin and exile ("endurance," *hypomonē*) will give way to restoration ("encouragement, comfort," *paraklēsis*) and therefore hope (*elpis*). But this message of the restoration of Israel includes Gentiles (see 15:9–12 to follow). Recalling the lack of hope that Gentiles endured because they were outside of the covenant (see again Eph. 2:11–13), we may chart Romans 15:4 this way:

Before Christ	In Christ
Gentiles were in exile because they were outside the covenant and without hope.	Gentiles are in the new covenant and have hope.

We can thus summarize 15:3–4 by saying that since Christ's sacrificial death brought Gentiles into the new covenant, the least that the strong in faith at Rome (Gentiles) can do is to sacrifice for their weak Jewish Christian brothers and sisters there at Rome.

15:5–6 *May the God who gives endurance and encouragement give you the same attitude of mind.* Verses 5–6 exhort both the strong and the weak at Rome to be one with each other. Both were once in sin and exile but now are restored by Christ and made to be participants in the new covenant (notice again the terms "endurance" and "encouragement"). This unity will bring glory to God. And such unity of Jew and Gentile bringing glory to God, as 15:7–12 will make clear, will illustrate that God is faithful to his Old Testament covenant promises.

15:8–12 *that the promises made to the patriarchs might be confirmed . . . that the Gentiles might glorify God.* Verses 8–12 make the point that Christ has fulfilled the Old Testament prophecies that Jew and Gentile will share together in the new covenant. Paul states his thesis in 15:8–9a, while in 15:9b–12 he supplies the Old Testament proof. Verses 8–9a state that Christ has fulfilled God's covenant promises to the patriarchs, which included in their purview the conversion of the Gentiles.[3] According to 15:8, Jesus was a servant of the circumcised (the Jews) in that in him

Before Christ was sentenced to be crucified he was flogged and mocked by Roman soldiers. He endured these insults even though he was the Messiah. These fourteenth-century AD marble statuettes depict the flogging of Christ.

God has been faithful to his covenant with Abraham. In regard to the reference to the new covenant, recall my comments on 3:21–4:25 to the effect that Jesus' death and resurrection fulfilled God's covenant promise of salvation to Abraham by faith. Moreover, I also noted in that context that Paul aligns the Abrahamic covenant with the new covenant, and that in opposition to the Mosaic covenant. The terms "truth" (15:8) and "mercy" (15:9) recall *hesed*, the Old Testament term for God's faithfulness to his covenant with Abraham and Israel. According to 15:9, God's promise to Abraham, as well as the new covenant, includes the salvation of the Gentiles and consequently their praise of God.

Verses 9b–12 then supply the Old Testament proof that Christ is fulfilling God's promise to include both Jew and Gentile in the new covenant. Paul draws on five Old Testament verses:

Romans 15	Old Testament
Verse 9b	2 Samuel 22:50 // Psalm 18:49
Verse 10	Deuteronomy 32:43
Verse 11	Psalm 117:1
Verse 12	Isaiah 11:10

Here I will briefly comment on these Old Testament texts. The words of 2 Samuel 22:50 // Psalm 18:49 come from a psalm of David in praise of God for victory over the Gentiles. As Douglas Moo points out, Paul interprets the psalm typologically of Christ: Christ has conquered the Gentiles by converting them and including them in his messianic rule.[4]

As Thomas Schreiner observes, Deuteronomy 32:43 comes at the end of Moses' song against Israel containing the threat of the covenant curses. But these curses,

Moses predicts, will drive Israel and the Gentiles to God.[5]

Psalm 117:1 calls on Gentiles to praise the Lord. As Moo notes, the reason for such praise is that the Gentiles will also experience God's faithfulness to his covenant with Israel (Ps. 117:2).[6]

Isaiah 11:10 is the prophecy of the Messiah, the Davidic "branch" who will deliver Israel. Moreover, Isaiah is famous for his prediction that Gentiles will be converted to Yahweh at the end of time in connection with Israel's restoration (e.g., Isa. 2:1–4; 12:4–5; 17:7–8; 19:18–25). For Paul, Jesus is that messianic branch who is restoring Israel and converting the Gentiles.

These five verses that Paul quotes come from the Torah (Deut. 32:43), the Prophets (2 Sam. 22:50; Isa. 11:10), and the Writings (Pss. 18:49; 117:1), representing the three major divisions of the Hebrew Bible. And for Paul, these Old Testament prophecies of the inclusion of Jews and Gentiles in the new covenant are coming to fruition in Christ.

15:13 *May the God of hope fill you with all joy and peace . . . by the power of the Holy Spirit.* We met some of the key words in this verse back in 5:1–5. "Hope," "joy," "peace," and "the Holy Spirit" are all blessings of the new covenant.

There was much at stake, then, for Gentile Christians (the strong in faith) to get along with Jewish Christians (the weak in faith). In doing so, they illustrated that God was fulfilling his covenant in the Old Testament and now the new covenant.

Theological Insights

Romans 14:1–15:13 is often understood to be dealing with *adiaphora*, "indifferent things"—that is, things neither required of nor prohibited for Christians. Moo provides three helpful theological principles that emerge from these verses. First, Paul was a realist; he knew that we have to deal with people where they are (in the case of 14:1–15:13, Jewish scruples about ritual purity). Second, Christians who do not feel obligated by the scruples of their weaker brothers and sisters should nevertheless be willing to limit their liberty for the sake of fellow believers and for Christ's sake. Third, Paul's bottom line in *adiaphora* is the unity of the church.[7]

Teaching the Text

I would follow a somewhat different outline in preaching/teaching Romans 15:1–13 than the one noted above, making Christ the focal point of the two paragraphs: (1) Christ as the basis of unity (vv. 1–6); (2) Christ as the means to unity (vv. 7–13).

Many of the historic churches of Rome were built on the sites of house churches, homes where believing Jews and Gentiles gathered for teaching, fellowship, worship, and prayer, and where they could celebrate the unity that they had in Christ. The remains of second- and third-century Roman houses have been found beneath the church of Santi Giovanni e Paolo (shown here) on the Caelian Hill in Rome. The inset shows an area in the house decorated with Christian themes and thought to have been a confessional.

Verses 1–6 make the point that since Christ's sacrifice brought Gentiles into the arrangement of the new covenant, they need to be sensitive to their Jewish Christian siblings for the sake of Christ. Here I think that Gentile believers need to bear with their Jewish Christian brothers and sisters by affirming the latter's Jewish heritage. For example, for some time now in biblical scholarship Christian scholars have rightly focused on Jewish literature of the Second Temple period—the Apocrypha, Pseudepigrapha, Dead Sea Scrolls, and more. This literature is enormously important for a proper understanding of ancient (and modern) Judaism, not to mention the New Testament. For their part, Jewish scholars have made their own strides toward rapprochement with Christianity with their "reclamation of Jesus movement," one that appreciates Jesus' Jewishness. Also, in the worship setting of the church, Gentile believers would do well to celebrate the Passover Seder in connection with Good Friday services, since that was the background of the institution of the Lord's Supper. Or, at the very least, Gentile Christians could occasionally attend messianic congregations and support worship services held by their Jewish brothers and sisters. And Jewish believers can emulate the sacrifice of Christ by not imposing on their Gentile siblings Jewish culture.

Verses 7–13 root Christian unity in Christ. It is through Christ that both believing Jew and Gentile have access to God.

Ultimately, the catena of Old Testament prophecies concerning Jew and Gentile worshiping God together that Paul draws on in these verses finds its fulfillment in Christ. Here we may apply a truism lamenting the racial divide between blacks and whites in Christian worship: America is never so segregated as it is during Sunday morning worship. This point relates to the issue that Paul discusses here: Jewish and Gentile Christians are never so segregated as they are during worship (we cannot even say "Sunday," since messianic congregations worship on Saturday). But surely both of these people groups need to find a way to worship God together, if for no other reason than that they will do so before the heavenly throne one day.

Illustrating the Text

Christ is the basis for unity between weak and strong Christians.

Cultural Institution: Alcoholics Anonymous (AA) runs, writes Philip Yancey, "on two principles: radical honesty and radical dependence, the very same principles expressed in the Lord's Prayer, Jesus' capsule summary of living 'one day at a time.'" Many AA groups even recite the Lord's Prayer at their meetings. Members are not allowed to say that they are "cured." Even if they have not had a drink for many years, they must identify themselves as alcoholics, members of the same group based on the same principles and original weaknesses. "In AA," Yancey adds, "the ground is level." He then quotes Lewis Meyer, who puts it this way:

It is the only place I know where status means nothing. Nobody fools anybody else. Everyone is here because he or she made a slobbering mess of his or her life and is trying to put the pieces back together again. . . . I have attended thousands of church meetings, lodge meetings, brotherhood meetings—yet I have never found the kind of love I find at AA. For one small hour the high and mighty descend and the lowly rise. The leveling that results is what people mean when they use the word brotherhood.

The analogy is apt; just as AA members are united by their acknowledgment of weakness and need though they may be at different stages of growth and stability, so too Christians are united by their belief in Christ.[8]

Christ is the means for unity between weak and strong Christians.

Theological Book: *Life Together,* by Dietrich Bonhoeffer. Few books are better at describing what the life of the Christian community should be. In this book, referred to earlier (see the "Illustrating the Text" section in the unit on Rom. 14:1–12), Bonhoeffer notes,

The struggle we undergo with our brother in intercession may be a hard one, but that struggle has the promise that it will gain its goal. . . . Intercession means no more than to bring our brother into the presence of God, to see him under the Cross of Jesus as a poor human being and sinner in need of grace. . . . To make intercession means to grant our brother the same right that we have received, namely, to stand before Christ and share in his mercy.[9]

Paul the Apostle of the New Covenant to the Gentiles

Big Idea *Here Paul presents himself as the apostle of the new covenant to the Gentiles. Two ideas therefore inform this text. First, Romans 15:14–16:27 corresponds to the document clause of the covenant format. Second, Paul is the eschatological apostle to the Gentiles who offers them membership in the new covenant through faith in Christ.*

Understanding the Text

The Text in Context

Many commentators rightly argue that Romans 15:14–16:27 completes the epistolary frame of Romans. Thus, like the conclusions in Paul's other epistles, 15:14–16:27 contains, for example, Paul's travel plans (15:14–29; cf. 1 Cor. 16:1–9); his request for prayer (15:30–32; cf. Eph. 6:18–20); a prayer wish for peace (15:33; cf. 2 Cor. 13:11c); mention of his associates (16:1–2; cf. Col. 4:7–9); an exhortation to greet one another (16:3–15; cf. Phil. 4:21); the "holy kiss" (16:16a; cf. 1 Thess. 5:26); a warning/exhortation (16:17–19; cf. 2 Cor. 13:12a); an eschatological wish/promise (16:20; cf. 1 Thess. 5:24); concluding grace (16:20b; cf. 1 Tim. 6:21b); greetings from his associates (16:16b, 21–23; cf. Philem. 23–24); doxology (16:25–27; cf. Phil. 4:20).[1] Moreover, it has long been noted that

15:14–33 matches the contents of 1:1–15, especially 1:8–15, forming an *inclusio* for the whole letter (see table 1).[2]

My outline anticipates my findings in the "Historical and Cultural Background" section:

1. Romans is Paul's new-covenant letter; the document clause begins here (15:14–15a)
2. Paul's calling to be the eschatological apostle to the Gentiles (15:15b–21)
   a. The object of Paul's calling (15:15b–19a)
   b. The area of Paul's calling (15:19b)
   c. The principle of Paul's calling (15:20–21)

Most commentators view 15:14–21 as a self-contained paragraph. Thus, 15:14–21 focuses on Paul's past travel plans, while 15:22–23 focuses on Paul's future travel plans.

Table 1: The _Inclusio_ between Romans 1:8–15 and 15:14–33

Commendation of the Romans	15:14	1:8
Apostle to the Gentiles	15:15b–21	1:3, 13
Hindrance in visiting Rome	15:22	1:13a
Indebtedness	15:27	1:14
Desire to minister for mutual blessing	15:29	1:11–12
Prayer	15:30–32	1:9–10

Historical and Cultural Background

Two key ideas form the background to Romans 15:14–21 and, indeed, to 15:22–33 as well.

1. I suggest that 15:14–21 is a part of the document clause of the covenant formula (15:14–16:27). The document clause of the covenant (see Deut. 31:9, 24–26) required the document to be housed in a sacred place (Jerusalem's tabernacle or temple) where it would be safe. Deuteronomy 31:10–13 specified that that document be brought from the sacred place and be read every seven years before Israel renewed its commitment to the covenant of Yahweh. Joshua 8:30–35 and 24:1–27 declared that that the ceremony should be renewed with Israel (annually?). The foundational Dead Sea Scrolls documents (_Damascus Document_ [CD] and _Rule of the Community_ [1QS]) probably were read at the Essenes' annual (?) covenant renewal ceremony.

I think that Paul views his letter to Rome as a new-covenant document to be read to the Roman church by Phoebe (16:1–22). The purpose of the reading was to remind the Roman Christians (mostly Gentiles) of their obligation to the new covenant. Three details in 15:14–21 suggest this thesis.

Key Themes of Romans 15:14–21

- Romans 15:14–16:27 corresponds to the document clause of the covenant format.
- Paul is the eschatological apostle to the Gentiles. That is, his ministry is to bring about the end-time conversion of the Gentiles. This mission is well on its way to being fulfilled.

(a) The solemnity of the letter to the Romans is not mere protocol, but rather demonstrates that the letter is to be recognized for what it is: the authoritative word of God through Paul that is incumbent upon Paul's audience at Rome (15:14–15).

(b) Paul's metaphorical language of being an Old Testament priest whose evangelism of the Gentiles is a sacrificial offering to God (15:16)—that is, the obedience of the Gentiles (15:18)—is reminiscent of Israel's acceptance of the covenant with Yahweh. Recall how Moses sprinkled the blood of sacrifice upon Israel to enact the people's acceptance of the terms of that covenant (Exod. 24:1–8; cf. Rom. 12:1–2). Or, consider how the priests read the blessings and curses upon Israel at Mount Gerizim and Mount Ebal (Deut. 28–30).

(c) As Robert Funk long ago recognized, 15:14–16:27 is to be identified form-critically as Paul's "apostolic parousia." That is, Paul's letters were more than a substitute for his presence; they mystically conveyed his presence to the church—hence, apostolic "parousia" ("coming" or "presence").[3] For our purposes, Paul's letter to the Romans conveys his presence when it is read to the Roman Christians, which adds to the reading's solemnity.

Like Moses and the priests in the Old Testament, Paul "reads" his covenant letter to the Romans, reminding them of their obligations to the new covenant. This

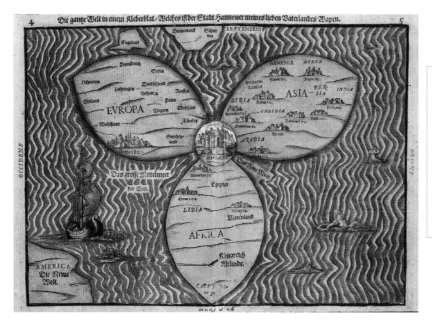

This is a map of the world with Jerusalem at its center created by Heinrich Bünting for his book, *Itinerarium Sacrae Scripturae*, first published in AD 1581. It provides an interesting visual to illustrate Paul's eschatological vision that in the last days Gentiles will go to Jerusalem as an acceptable offering to God.

functions as the document clause. These three details suggest that 15:14–16:27 corresponds with the document clause of the covenant formula.

2. The second piece of background information is the eschatological nature of Paul's apostleship; that is, Paul's ministry to the Gentiles is to bring about their end-time conversion. Seven details in 15:14–21 indicate this.

(a) Roger Aus has convincingly shown that 11:25 and 15:16 depict Paul's ministry as reflecting the eschatological pilgrimage motif, according to which Gentiles in the last days will go to Jerusalem to worship God (see also the "Interpretive Insights" section for Rom. 11:25–32). Aus argues that 11:25 and 15:16 are based on Isaiah 66:19–20, where God proclaims that in the last days he will send the Jewish remnant in the nations to declare to the Gentiles the glory of God. So Paul perceives that he, as a member of the Jewish Christian remnant, is called of God in the last days to summon the Gentiles to enter into Jerusalem to worship God.[4] As we will see in the next unit,

15:25–27 continues this theme. Paul's collection from the Gentile churches for the poor saints in Jerusalem will be the firstfruits of that pilgrimage.

(b) Paul's apostleship as the catalyst for bringing about the end-time conversion of the Gentiles informs his word "fulfill" (*plēroō* [NIV: "fully proclaim"]) in 15:19; he used a word of the same root in 11:25 for the "fullness" (*plērōma*) of the Gentiles.

(c) Paul's reference to the "obedience of the Gentiles" in 15:18 (cf. 1:5; 16:26) fits perfectly with the concept that Paul sees himself as a central figure in salvation history whose mission to the Gentiles will usher in the end time.

(d) Paul's language in 15:16 about Gentiles being a sacrificial offering to God represents, as Douglas Moo observes, the eschatological transformation of the Old Testament cultic ministry whereby animal sacrifices are replaced by obedient Christians (cf. Rom. 12:1) and the praise that they offer to God (Heb. 13:15) in the temple of new-covenant believers (1 Cor. 6:19; 1 Pet. 2:5).[5] Paul's ministry to Gentiles is effecting that transformation.

(e) The power for Paul to accomplish his mission is none other than the end-time gift of the Holy Spirit, who performs signs and wonders (miracles) through Paul to convert the Gentiles (compare Rom. 15:19 with Acts 2:22, 43; 4:30; 5:12; 14:3; 15:12; 2 Cor. 12:12; 2 Thess. 2:9; Heb. 2:4).

(f) As Robert Jewett has demonstrated, Paul's evangelism of Gentiles from Jerusalem to Illyricum (15:19) follows the arc on ancient strip maps dating back to at least AD 79 (see photo and discussion in the unit on Rom. 1:8–15 above). Those maps ran the arc from Jerusalem to Illyricum (northwest of Macedonia) to Rome, the halfway point in the arc, to Spain, the end of the arc. For Jewett, this means that Paul believed that he was called to evangelize Gentiles across the world: from Jerusalem to Rome, the center of the world, to Spain, the end of the world. When that was accomplished (see Rom. 15:25–29), Christ then would return.[6]

(g) All of this is reinforced by Paul's quotation of Isaiah 52:15 in Romans 15:21. Paul preaches Jesus, the Suffering Servant, to the Gentiles. Thus, Paul's pioneering planting of Gentile churches was fulfilling Isaiah's prophecy that in the end time Gentiles will come to the Lord.

These seven details make it likely that Paul believed God had called him to preach the gospel to the Gentiles in order to bring about the end-time conversion of the nations.

Interpretive Insights

15:14–15a *you yourselves are . . . competent to instruct one another. Yet I have written you quite boldly.* I argued above that 15:14–16:27 corresponds to the document clause of the covenant format. Verses 15:14–15a initiate that feature, combining Paul's tact and his authority as the apostle to the Gentiles. In 15:14 Paul compliments the Roman Christians for their spiritual knowledge of the gospel and their mutual encouragement, but in 15:15a he shows his authority in that he has written a bold letter to the Romans. To put it another way, the Roman Christians are members of the new-covenant community. Therefore, with language reminiscent of Israel's renewal of the covenant ceremony, Paul is admonishing the Roman Christians to accept afresh and anew the obligation of that covenant, which is holiness (see 15:16).

15:15b–21 *the grace God gave me to be a minister of Christ Jesus to the Gentiles.* Verses 15b–21 highlight Paul's call to be the apostle who is the catalyst for the end-time conversion of the Gentiles, as we observed above. Assuming that background, we see that Paul makes three points about his calling from God to be the apostle to the Gentiles: the object (15:15b–19a); the area (15:19b); and the principle (15:20–21).

The object of Paul's calling by the grace of God to be an apostle is the Gentiles (15:15b–19a). We noticed earlier that Paul compares himself to the Old Testament priest, with his evangelism of the Gentiles being like a sacrificial offering to God (15:16). Paul here refers to the Gentile churches that he has established during the course of his three missionary journeys. Those converted Gentiles now live lives set apart for God. Paul gives all glory to God for the power of the Spirit working through him to win the Gentiles to Christ (15:17). Indeed, Paul will take no glory for the results of his ministry; he will give all the glory to Christ for working through him to bring about the end-time conversion of the Gentiles—that is, the obedience of the Gentiles (15:18). The signs and wonders performed through Paul in the power of the Spirit constitute one of the end-time signs that the last days have dawned.

The area of Paul's ministry to the nations encompassed the world: from Jerusalem to Illyricum (15:19b) to (hopefully) Rome and then to Spain, the end of the then-known world (15:25–27). Although neither Paul's letters nor the book of Acts specifically refers to his ministry in Illyricum, his mission to Macedonia would have bordered that area. I mentioned earlier that the word "fulfill" (*plēroō*) in 15:19b (cf. 11:25) connotes the fullness of the Gentiles' conversion to Christ. Paul believed that his service from Jerusalem to Illyricum put him well on the road to converting the nations and thus hastening the parousia.

Verses 20–21 spell out the principle of Paul's calling. He was a pioneer for the gospel. He therefore did not duplicate the efforts of other apostles in areas already reached for Christ. It may be that we are to understand Paul to say here that he reached out to Gentiles while leaving Peter and the other apostles to reach out to Jews (see Gal. 2:7–8). Paul roots his call to the Gentiles in Isaiah 52:15. Like the Suffering Servant, Paul will proclaim the goodness of the gospel of spiritual restoration (see Isa. 52:7) to Gentiles (so Isa. 52:15).

Theological Insights

At least three striking truths emerge in Romans 15:14–21. First, only the grace of God could turn Paul the zealot for the Pharisaic tradition into the apostle to the Gentiles (cf. Gal. 1:13–16). It takes that same grace today to transform a religious bigot into a compassionate disciple of Jesus. Second, Paul well recognized that it was not his power that so effectively ministered to Gentiles, but rather it was the miraculous power of Christ by the Spirit that accomplished such signs and wonders through him. Third, the imminent expectation of the parousia motivated Paul to evangelize the nations. We today, undoubtedly closer to that event, should be all the more motivated to win the world to Christ.

Teaching the Text

I would preach/teach Romans 15:14–21 by first explaining the text using the outline followed above: Paul's opening remarks of the document clause (vv. 14–15a); Paul's calling (vv. 15b–21). And there is a connection between those two points. The more serious Christians are about being members of the new covenant, the more they will strive to evangelize the world. And this connection is even more striking because both Jesus and Paul believed that the sooner Christians evangelize the world, the sooner the parousia will occur (for Jesus, see Mark 13:10; for Paul, see Rom. 15:14–33). It would be effective for pastors to simulate the reading of Romans at its first hearing by reading Paul's letter in its entirety during a worship service and then asking the congregation to accept afresh and anew the stipulations of Paul's new-covenant letter. Those stipulations would include a renewal of commitment to justification by faith, holiness of lifestyle, service to others, love for fellow believers and a watching world, and evangelization of the lost. One of the greatest weekends I ever experienced was years ago when our church hosted a team skilled in training church members to share their faith with the lost. We spent Thursday and Friday nights being trained for that task, and then some three hundred of us blanketed our community all day Saturday, going door to door tactfully and graciously sharing the gospel with whoever would listen. Then that evening we had a celebration service at the church to report the results. It was heavenly. There was something exhilarating about making a commitment to go out and share the gospel. Door-to-door evangelism is not necessarily a method for all churches and for all times, but for us, the solemnity of commitment resulted in a joyous outpouring of the Spirit on his church. One wonders if Romans might not have a similar effect today.

Illustrating the Text

Only the miraculous power of God made Paul's ministry effective.

Film: *The Blind Side.* This film (2009) is based on the true story of Baltimore Ravens football player Michael Oher. Michael came from a troubled home. His father was frequently in prison and eventually was murdered there. His mother was a crack-cocaine addict. Michael was placed in foster care at the age of seven. Having attended eleven different schools during his first nine years as a student, alternating between foster homes and homelessness, he had no fixed address until he was sixteen. The Tuohys, a Christian family, took Michael in and cared for him, eventually adopting him. After hiring a tutor for him, later they sent him to Briarcrest Christian School. At the entrance of the campus is inscribed this statement: "With God, all things are possible." Michael's adoption and transformed life resulted from the power of God through the effective ministry of the Tuohy family.

Book: *To End All Wars,* **by Ernest Gordon.** This book, rereleased in conjunction with the film of the same name (2001), is a reprint of *Through the Valley of the Kwai* (1963), Gordon's narrative of his time in a Japanese POW camp during World War II. Fellow captives practicing John 15:13 began a chain reaction among the POWs forced to build the Burma-Thailand railroad. "Our regeneration, sparked by conspicuous acts of self-sacrifice, had begun. . . . It was dawning on us all—officers and other ranks alike—that the law of the jungle is not the law for man. . . . We were seeing for ourselves the sharp contrast between the forces that made for life and those that made for death. . . . Love, heroism, self-sacrifice, sympathy, mercy, integrity and creative faith . . . were the essence of life."[7] Later, Gordon says, "Through our readings and discussions we gradually came to know Jesus. He was one of us. . . . We understood that the love expressed so supremely in Jesus was . . . other-centred rather than self-centred, greater than all the laws of men."[8]

Expecting the imminent coming of Christ should motivate us to evangelism.

Christian Organization: Voice of the Martyrs. Giving aid to our Christian brothers and sisters suffering under totalitarian regimes, Voice of the Martyrs (VOM) brings hope to many. What may be surprising to the reader of VOM's website is the consistent calling that persecuted Christians feel to tell the good news of Jesus Christ to everyone, including their captors.[9]

Paul's Collection for Jerusalem and Mission to Spain

Big Idea *Paul likely believes that delivering the Gentiles' collection to the poor saints in Jerusalem and then evangelizing Spain will catalyze Christ's return.*

Understanding the Text

The Text in Context

Romans 15:22–29 finishes Paul's discussion of his travel plans. In 15:14–21 Paul discussed past missionary work, while in 15:22–29 he unveils future mission plans: to collect the offering from the Gentiles to be delivered to Jerusalem and then to travel to Spain to evangelize the Gentiles there. In 15:30–33 Paul asks the Roman congregation to pray that his collection from the Gentiles will meet with success. In this unit we examine 15:22–29 and its chiastic outline:

A Paul's plan to visit Spain (15:22–24)
 B Paul's collection for the Gentiles (15:25–27)
A′ Paul's plan to visit Spain (15:28–29)

Historical and Cultural Background

1. The first piece of background material is Paul's collection from the Gentile churches for Jewish Christians at Jerusalem. This collection was a major focus on Paul's third missionary journey (see 1 Cor. 16:1–2; 2 Cor. 8–9).[1] On that journey Paul took up a collection of money from the Roman provinces of Macedonia (modern northern Greece, Macedonia, and southern Albania/Macedonia) and Achaia (the bulk of modern Greece). Pauline churches in those provinces included the congregations at Philippi, Thessalonica, Berea, and Corinth. It is possible that the recipients of the collection—the poor Jewish Christians at Jerusalem—were poor for two reasons: the overly enthusiastic resourcing of the common fund in the beginning days of the church (Acts 2:44–45; 4:34–37), and the famine that engulfed Jerusalem in AD 48 (Acts 11:27–30). Three motivations drove Paul's collection for Jerusalem. First, Paul believed that Gentile Christians should help their Jewish Christian siblings in their time of need. After all, Jewish Christians first sent the spiritual blessings of the gospel to the Gentiles, and so Gentile Christians should now

reciprocate with material blessings (Rom. 15:25–27). Second, Paul earlier agreed with the Jerusalem apostles to be alert to the needs of the poor Jewish Christians (Gal. 2:10). Indeed, giving alms to the poor was an expression of one's faithfulness to the covenant with Yahweh (Sir. 29:12; 40:24; Tob. 4:10; 12:9; 14:10–11; Acts 10:4, 31; 24:17). Third, Paul calls this collection the *koinōnia* in Romans 15:26 (NIV: "contribution") and in 1 Corinthians 8:4; 9:13, which intimates the spiritual union of Jewish and Gentile Christians. And that is something that the strong and the weak in Rome needed to hear. Indeed, for Paul, the collection among the Gentile churches going to Jerusalem was the beginning fulfillment of the eschatological pilgrimage of the Gentiles to Jerusalem to worship God. In other words, the collection was a sign of the end-time conversion of the Gentiles, which Paul hoped would be the catalyst for the conversion of Israel to Jesus.

2. The second piece of background information is Paul's plan to evangelize Spain. Why Spain? For three reasons. First, Spain was the westernmost edge of the then-known world, completing the arc of evangelization for Paul beginning in Jerusalem, moving to Illyricum, and then, hopefully, going to Rome and on to Spain. Second, Spain, as Robert Jewett has suggested, was a place where Paul wanted to go in order to press on into territory unreached by either Jews or by the gospel itself.[2] Third, combining the previous two points, Roger Aus, tying together Romans 11:25–27; 15:16, 24, 25–27, maintains that Paul understood Spain to be the Tarshish of Isaiah 66:19. Only when Paul has brought Christian representatives from Spain (15:16, 24) to

Jerusalem as part of his collection enterprise (15:25–27) will the "full number" of the Gentiles come in (compare 11:25 with 15:19, 29) and the grand finale of 11:25–27 unfold.[3] Related to this is the probability that Paul views a collection from Gentiles spread from Jerusalem all the way to Spain, the end of the world, as fulfilling the Jewish expectation that the wealth of the nations would flow into Jerusalem at the end of history in association with Israel's restoration (Isa. 45:14; 60:5–17; 61:6; Mic. 4:13; Tob. 13:11; 1QM 12.13–15).[4] This, Paul hoped, would stir Israel to jealousy to accept Jesus as their Messiah (11:13–14) and thus trigger the parousia.[5]

In conclusion, although Paul's letters do not mention his visit to Spain, *1 Clement* 5.7 (late first century AD) says that he reached the "farthest limits of the west," which likely refers to this mission to Spain.

Interpretive Insights

15:22–23 *I have been longing for many years to visit you.* Verses 22–23 explain why Paul has been unable to visit Rome thus far: he was busy winning Gentiles to Christ and establishing churches from Jerusalem to Illyricum (recall my discussion of 15:14–21). Now that this pioneering work is complete, the apostle to the Gentiles turns his sights toward Rome, the capital of the world and the center of the world.

Key Themes of Romans 15:22–29

- Paul's collection of the Gentiles' offering for Jewish Christians was the beginning of the end-time pilgrimage of Gentiles to Jerusalem to worship God.
- Paul's evangelization of Spain marked the progress of the gospel to the end of the then-known world, which would precipitate the parousia.

Paul's Third Missionary Journey

← Paul's route

was part and parcel of Paul's challenge to the Christians at Rome.

15:25–26 *I am on my way to Jerusalem . . . to make a contribution for the poor among the Lord's people.* Verses 25–26 spell out Paul's intent to take the Gentiles' offering to Jerusalem. The phrase *ptōchous tōn hagiōn* can be taken either financially, indicating impoverished persons among the Lord's people in Jerusalem (so the NIV), or spiritually, indicating Jewish Christians as a whole, with "poor" referring to their lowliness and dependency on God (cf. Ps. 69:32; 72:2; Pss. Sol. 5.2, 11; 10.6; 15.1; 18.2; 1QpHab 12.3, 6, 10; 1QM 11.9, 13; 4Q171 2.10; CD 19.9; cf. also Acts 2:44–45; 4:34–37). However, both views may be at work here in 15:26. Many of the Jewish Christians (the saints, the poor) were economically poor because of the famine of AD 48.

15:27 *they owe it to the Jews.* Verse 27 reveals the impetus for the Gentile Christians' offering. Jewish Christians first ministered to them spiritually by sending them the gospel; now Gentile Christians need to reciprocate by supporting their Jewish Christian brothers and sisters financially. This verse also attests to the historical order mentioned in 1:16: the Jew first. As the Jews shared their salvation with the Gentiles, so the Gentile churches in Macedonia and Achaia (15:26) were pleased to give to the collection for the Jewish Christians.

15:28–29 *after I have completed this task and have made sure that they have received this contribution . . . I will come in the full*

15:24 *I hope to see you while passing through and to have you assist me on my journey.* Here Paul relates that he wants to visit Rome in order to garner the spiritual and financial support that it would take to evangelize the Gentiles in Spain. The verb *propempō* (NIV: "assist") was a technical term for missionary support (see Acts 15:3; 20:38; 21:5; 1 Cor. 6:6, 11; 2 Cor. 1:16; Titus 3:13; 3 John 6). Paul did not mention such support early on in his letter (1:10–13), probably because he wanted to explain his gospel and thereby build a relationship through the letter to a church that he did not establish. As I mentioned in an earlier note, I see no reason why a part of the financial support that Paul sought from the Roman congregation did not include both help for the journey to Spain and a Roman contribution to the Gentiles' offering for the Jewish Christians at Jerusalem. Such a display of unity of Jew and Gentile in Jerusalem and Rome

measure of the blessing of Christ. After safely delivering the Gentiles' offering to Jerusalem, Paul plans to sail for Rome and from there on to Spain. Two phrases here call for comment. The first, "sealed this fruit for them" (15:28 [NIV: "made sure that they have received this contribution"]), is drawn from the commercial world of Paul's day. Merchants often sealed their sack of goods to be traded by closing the sack at the top and placing the seal/impression of their ring in the wax on it. This practice ensured the safe delivery of the goods. Paul no doubt means by the phrase that he, along with appointed representatives of the churches, will accompany the offering to Jerusalem to ensure its safe arrival.

The second phrase, "the fullness of Christ's blessing" (15:29 [NIV: "the full measure of the blessing of Christ"]), indicates that the collection from the Gentiles from east of Rome and soon from west of Rome to Spain symbolizes that the "fullness of the Gentiles" has come into the kingdom of God and the gospel (see 11:25–27) and the blessings of the new covenant. And such an offering paraded into Jerusalem, Paul hopes, will trigger the conversion of Israel to Christ and the parousia. Thus, the Gentiles' offering from the Macedonians and Achaians will be the firstfruits of the rest to come from Rome and Spain.

Theological Insights

Three insights emerge from Romans 15:22–29 that apply to Christians today. First, Christians should join the other two Abrahamic faiths—Judaism and Islam—by giving alms to the poor in general. Second, more than that, Christians should honor their Jewish ancestry by giving to Jews who are hurting economically today—say, in Russia. Even though Paul's collection was primarily for Jewish Christians, Christianity owes its reception of the gospel to Jews in general and messianic Jews in particular. Third, as we noted in the last unit, Christians may well hasten the return of Christ by funding worldwide missions.

Teaching the Text

In teaching/preaching Romans 15:22–29, I would divide that text into its two constituent parts: Paul's trip to Rome/Spain (vv. 22–24, 28–29), and Paul's collection from Gentiles for the Jewish Christians in Jerusalem (vv. 25–27). The first point should motivate contemporary believers to strive to reach the world for Christ, by financially supporting missions, if not going themselves, at least for a short time. I have done the latter and was much the better for it. Second, Christians must always be sensitive to the

Shown here is a Greek signet ring from the second to third century BC. Rings like this and stamps were used to make impressions in clay to affirm the authenticity or authority behind items such as letters, proclamations, or commercial goods. Paul uses this imagery to communicate his personal delivery of the monetary collection to Jerusalem.

financial needs of others. Indeed, Christianity has a wonderful track record of giving to those who hurt, which may explain why the United States is one of the most humanitarian nations in the world. But can we be more specific concerning the second point and say that Gentile churches should make giving to Jewish Christian missions their top priority? Here we must exercise a reasonable balance. Thus, on the one hand, Gentile believers do owe their spiritual lives to the Jewish people and therefore should pray for the peace of Jerusalem. Moreover, I for one support Israel's right to be in their land. Furthermore, Jews certainly deserve any profound apologies that they have received and will continue to receive for

the Holocaust, perpetrated on them while many in the church turned a blind eye.

However, one can see how quickly spiritual appreciation for Israel can become political commitment to Israel. And where does the church draw the line in this matter? Thus, for example, some Christians are convinced that Jesus, at his return, will set up his millennial kingdom in Jerusalem, at which time the Old Testament sacrifices will be resumed and all nations will be made to bow before Israel. These same well-meaning believers no doubt are the ones who find no fault with Israel today in its dealings with Palestinians, not even in the continued and even flagrant building on the West Bank and beyond, which almost certainly will be the catalyst for the next war between Jews and Arabs.

To be sure, these are delicate matters to which there is no simple solution. The only point that I wish to make here is that the

There is not much information about the early church in Spain. One recorded incident is the martyrdom of Bishop Fructuosus and two deacons in Tarragona, Spain, during the reign of Emperor Valerian (AD 253–60). They were burned at the stake inside the Roman amphitheater (pictured here). In the sixth century a Christian basilica was built in the center of the amphitheater to honor their courageous stand for Christ. Its remains are also visible.

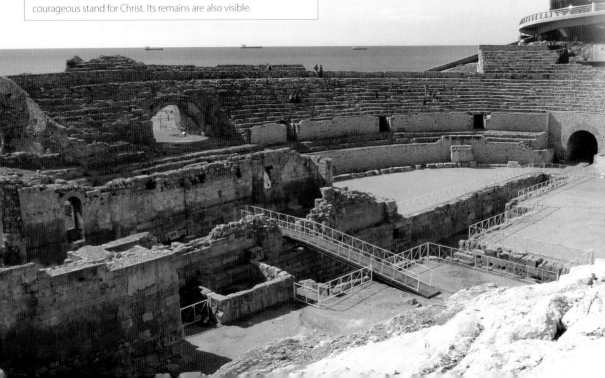

church needs to show some proper balance between showing appreciation and support for the Jewish people and loving all peoples of the world for Jesus' sake.

Illustrating the Text

We should go out to reach the world for Christ or provide support to send others.

Christian Ministries: Prison Fellowship has demonstrated successfully how Christian organizations can work in collaboration instead of competition, starting Operation Starting Line, an affiliation of thirty-seven ministries that work together in prison evangelism. After Prison Fellowship president Mark Earley reached an agreement with the Progressive National Baptist Convention (PNBC) leadership, Prison Fellowship began holding and funding training sessions at PNBC pastors' gatherings, also providing prison ministry teaching resources. In one instance, a chaplain at the Allegheny County jail in Pennsylvania described how Prison Fellowship had helped him set up a program with their materials. Recidivism declined significantly.[6]

True Story: During one of his early visits to London, Billy Graham was confronted by a local priest who casually dismissed the entire crusade effort. "Young man," said the priest, "I do not approve of your style of evangelism." "I'm sure that what I'm doing isn't perfect," replied Graham. "But I like the evangelism that I'm doing better than the evangelism that you're not doing."[7]

Christians must always be sensitive to the financial needs of others.

Christian Biography: **Thomas Traherne.** Traherne (1637–74) was an English religious writer and poet, known particularly for his *Centuries of Mediations.* In a contemporary version of his principles, *Waking Up in Heaven,* David Buresh writes that "The desire of riches was removed from himself pretty early. He often protested . . . he could not understand a farthing worth of benefit that he should receive . . . unless in giving it away." His principle was "sometimes it may so happen that to contemn the world in the whole lump was as acceptable to God as first to get it with solicitude and care, and then to retail it out in particular charities."[8]

Curses on Unbelievers, Blessings on Believers

Big Idea *Paul identifies two groups of Jews: disobedient Jews, upon whom fall the covenant curses, and believing Jews (and Gentiles), upon whom rest the covenant blessings. Paul hopes that believing Jews in Jerusalem will not allow their nonbelieving kin to adversely affect them concerning their reception of the Gentiles' offering.*

Understanding the Text

The Text in Context

Romans 15:30–33 concludes Paul's discussion of his travel plans (15:14–33) and contains two points:

1. Paul's prayer that the collection from Gentiles will be accepted by the Jerusalem church (15:30–31)
2. Paul's wish that peace will rest upon the Roman Christians (15:32–33)

Historical and Cultural Background

The key background information concerning Romans 15:30–33 relates to the nature of Paul's opposition, "the unbelievers in Judea" (15:31). Here I summarize four intertwining reasons as to why non-Christian Jews opposed Paul. We will see along the way that Paul prayed that such opposition would not jade the Jerusalem church's perspective against him and the collection from Gentiles. I rely on some of Paul's other letters besides Romans to compose a profile of his opponents.

First, non-Christian Jews were scandalized by Paul's message of the cross (1 Cor. 1:18–25; Gal. 6:12–16). To them, a crucified Messiah is cursed of God (Deut. 21:23). Related to this conviction, it does not seem that Second Temple Judaism expected a suffering Messiah. In Israel's mind, the Messiah and the Suffering Servant were not to be equated. The latter Israel identified with itself, but the former Israel equated with the Davidic Messiah who could deliver Israel from its enemies and then set up the kingdom of God in Jerusalem.

Second, the unbelieving Jews opposed Paul because they believed that he disparaged the law of Moses. Statements by Paul in Romans that the law stirs up sin (e.g., 3:20; 4:15; 5:12–14; 7:8–11) and that the Torah is finished (10:4) alarmed non-Christian Jews. Acts 21:20–21 relates how

Jews were disturbed by reports that Paul taught the Jews that they should "turn away from Moses, telling them not to circumcise their children or live according to [Jewish] customs."

Third, Paul's success among the God-fearers compounded the problem. The God-fearers were Gentiles who came to believe in God, lived by the Noahic summary of the Torah, and worshiped in the synagogues (see the "Historical and Cultural Background" section in the unit on Rom. 2:25–29). But Paul's law-free gospel greatly appealed to the God-fearers (cf. Acts 13:16, 26, 43, 50; 16:14; 17:4, 17; 18:7).[1] Moreover, as Irina Levinskaya has demonstrated, the mass conversion of the God-fearers to Paul's law-free gospel diminished Jewish support in the cities that Paul evangelized. Consequently, the Jews lost political clout in those cities when the God-fearers no longer aligned themselves with their Jewish counterparts.[2]

Fourth, Paul had good reason to be concerned that the unbelieving Jews in Judea (Rom. 15:21a) might adversely affect the Jerusalem church's reception of the Gentiles' offering (Rom. 15:31b) because, as Robert Jewett has demonstrated, Judaizers in the late 40s and early 50s had mounted a campaign to get Christian Gentiles circumcised so that the Jerusalem church would not be persecuted by the Zealot movement. The Zealot movement was one wing of Judaism that tried to purify the land of Israel from Gentile impurity, including the presence of its Roman occupiers. Indeed, the Zealot movement succeeded in stirring up the First Jewish Revolt against Rome in AD 66.[3] It is significant that Luke mentions the Gentiles' offering only once in Acts, in

Key Themes of Romans 15:30–33

- The Trinity is involved in the believer's prayer.
- Paul faced much opposition from unbelieving Jews, opposition that he feared would cause the Jerusalem Christians not to accept the Gentiles' offering.
- Paul looks forward to visiting the Roman congregation and prays God's peace on them.

Paul's defense before Felix, Roman governor of Judea (24:17). Luke's virtual silence about the Jerusalem church's acceptance of the Gentiles' offering does not bode well for a positive response. This suspicion is strengthened by the report from Josephus (*J.W.* 2.409–10) that what made the First Jewish Revolt inevitable was the Jerusalem priesthood's decision to no longer accept gifts or sacrifices from foreigners.

These four intertwining reasons build a profile of Paul's Jewish opponents. They were Palestinian Zealots pressuring Judaizers (professing Jewish Christians) to enforce the whole Torah on Jew and Gentile alike. This was bound to collide with Paul's

Up until the sixth century AD, images of Christ on the cross were very rare. This ivory plaque from around AD 425 is one of the earliest crucifixion scenes. For the Jews, "anyone who is hung on a pole is under God's curse" (Deut. 21:23).

law-free gospel. There would be much for the Jerusalem church leadership to ponder before accepting Paul's collection from the Gentiles—hence his solicitation of the Roman congregation to pray for him in his struggle (Rom. 15:30–31).

Interpretive Insights

15:30–31 *Pray . . . that the contribution I take to Jerusalem may be favorably received.* Two points emerge in 15:30–33: Paul's prayer that the collection from Gentiles will be accepted by the Jerusalem church (vv. 30–31); Paul's wish that peace will rest upon the Roman Christians (vv. 32–33). The first point taps into the covenant curses, especially Paul's label "the unbelievers in Judea." The second point draws on the covenant blessings, especially in Paul's statement "The God of peace be with you all. Amen." These two—covenant curses and blessings—will unfold in my ensuing comments.

I begin with three observations about 15:30. First, Paul urges (*parakaleō*) the Roman Christians to pray for him, a deep-seated plea from the apostle. Second, Paul needs intercessory prayer because he is in a struggle with unbelieving Jews (15:31). The Greek term behind "struggle" (*synagōnizomai*) is an athletic, even military one, signaling that Paul was in the fight of his life. Indeed, Acts 20:3 and 23:12–22 mention that the Jews twice failed in their attempts to assassinate Paul. Third,

the Trinity was involved in Paul's prayer: "by our Lord Jesus Christ" (the basis of Paul's prayer); "by the love of the Spirit" (the means of Paul's prayer); "to God" (the object of Paul's prayer).

I have already discussed the historical background to 15:31, so here I note that Paul's label for his opponents, "unbelievers in Judea" (literally, "the disobedient ones in Judea"), is tied into his description of Jews hostile to his message in 1 Thessalonians 2:14–16:

> For you, brothers and sisters, became imitators of God's churches in Judea, which are in Christ Jesus: You suffered from your own people the same things those churches suffered from the Jews who killed the Lord Jesus and the prophets and also drove us out. They displease God and are hostile to everyone in their effort to keep us from speaking to the Gentiles so that they may be saved. In this way they always heap up their sins to the limit. The wrath of God has come upon them at last.

This photo shows a portion of the Appian Way, or Via Appia, close to the city of Rome. It was one of the main thoroughfares into Rome and was the one on which Paul traveled when he finally visited the city. Construction was started in 312 BC, and when the road was completed it ran for over 360 miles to the port of Brundisium (Brindisi) on the Adriatic Sea.

It is commonly recognized by Pauline interpreters that 1 Thessalonians 2:14–16 conveys Paul's belief that unbelieving Jews were under the covenant curses because they rejected the gospel and tried to prevent Gentiles from accepting the gospel. So Paul's terse label in Romans 15:31, "the disobedient ones in Judea," is a short script for 1 Thessalonians 2:14–16 and its pronouncement of the covenant curses upon such individuals.

15:32–33 *The God of peace be with you all.* In 15:32 the tone of the paragraph changes. Paul now looks forward to visiting the Roman churches after his trip to Jerusalem to deliver the Gentiles' offering. And his visit there will be all the more joyous if the Jerusalem church does indeed accept that gift.

Paul then concludes 15:30–33 by offering a benediction over the Roman Christians: "The God of peace be with you all. Amen." Jewett insightfully catches the covenantal nuance of this blessing:

> The typical Jewish conclusion of a blessing or curse provides the final punctuation of this pericope. In Deut. 27:15–26, for instance, each of the twelve curses is followed by an "amen." The "amen" in Rom. 15:33 had a function similar to the use earlier in the letter (1:25), inviting the Romans audience to add its concurrence by a liturgical response to what Paul has just said.[4]

So it seems that Paul's benediction in 15:33 upon the Roman Christians hopes that God will pour out the blessings of the new covenant, including peace, upon his audience. And their "Amen" response confirms such a blessing, since they believe in Paul's law-free gospel.

Theological Insights

At least four truths from Romans 15:30–33 apply to believers in Christ today. First, the whole of the Trinity is involved in Christian prayer. Second, Christians should not be surprised if their message of a law-free gospel is met with opposition, especially in religious sectors. This is only to confirm that, as Paul would say, the covenant curses rest on such unbelievers. Third, the new-covenant blessing of the peace of God rests on Christians. Fourth, Christians need to pray for each other in their spiritual holy war against the enemies of the cross.

Teaching the Text

I can envision three lessons/sermons based on even such a brief unit as Romans 15:30–33. First, one could teach/preach on the topic "The Trinity and Prayer" by comparing 15:30 with 8:26–30 (the Trinity is there as well). Second, one could preach/teach a message entitled "Expect Opposition to the Gospel," based on 15:31. The "Historical and Cultural Background" section in this chapter could illuminate 15:31 in that task. Third, based on 15:32, one could teach/preach a message entitled "Say Amen to Your Blessings!" Here one could develop the concept of peace with God via 5:1.

I choose to focus in this section on the second possibility: opposition to the gospel. I do a class lecture in connection with Romans on the topic "The Top Five Heresies in the New Testament." First, there is the Judaizer. This individual taught that salvation is based on faith in Christ plus obedience to the law of Moses, especially as symbolized in submitting to the rite of circumcision (the sign of the Torah). As we have noted throughout this work on Romans, Paul refutes such a notion, arguing instead that justification before God is based solely on faith in Christ apart from the works of the law (chaps. 1–5). Second, there is the antinomian, also refuted by Paul in Romans (chaps. 6–8). Antinomian teaching distorted Paul's message of grace into licentious living. Its motto was "Let us sin so that grace may increase!" The false assumption driving such teaching was that it does not matter how Christians live their lives, something with which Paul would beg to differ. Third, the enthusiast taught that the age to come has completely arrived. Therefore, the believer has already been resurrected to heaven (spiritually) and now lives like the angels. Paul counters this naïve notion in 1–2 Corinthians. Fourth, gnostics (from *gnōsis*, "knowledge") viewed the spirit as good and the physical body as evil, in Platonic dualistic fashion. They denied the resurrection of the body, opting instead for the immortality only of the soul. Although a gnostic theology had not fully developed in the first century, incipient forms of such thinking can be discerned in Paul's opponents in 1 Corinthians 15. Fifth, another early form of gnosticism was doceticism, which denied that Jesus Christ was truly human. The epistles of John oppose that error, which denied the incarnation and atonement of Jesus.

Illustrating the Text

The whole of the Trinity is involved in the believer's prayer.

Christian Year: All Saints' Day, celebrated on November 1, is important on the Christian calendar. The climax of the Christian story is found here, best displayed in John 17:21: "That all of them may be one, Father, just as you are in me and I am in you." As James Houston says, "All true theological education results in community, a community expressive of the triune God of love, flowing naturally out of the state of being open to the mystery of the Trinity."[5]

The believer must be courageous in the face of opposition to the gospel.

Church History: Polycarp had been a disciple of the apostle John and was a revered elder of the early church. Offering Polycarp the opportunity to escape death, the Roman proconsul pleaded with him, "Curse Christ, and I will release you." Polycarp replied, "Eighty-six years I have served Him. He has never done me wrong. How then can I blaspheme my King who has saved me?" (*Mart. Pol.* 9.3). Likewise, Blandina, a young female slave, inspired others with her courage:

> After the scourging, after the wild beasts, after the roasting seat, she was finally enclosed in a net, and thrown before a bull. And having been tossed about by the animal, but feeling none of the things which were happening to her, on account of her hope and firm hold upon what had been entrusted to her and her communion with Christ, she also was sacrificed. (Eusebius, *Hist. eccl.* 5.1.56)[6]

Believers must pray for each other in the midst of spiritual war.

Quote: J. C. Ryle. Ryle (1816–1900), first Anglican bishop of Liverpool, was often described as a man who found prayer as natural as breathing. In his book *A Call to Prayer,* he writes,

SDEMITIER ✝SCS POLICARPVS✝SCSVINCENTIVS✝SCSPANCRATIVS✝SCSCRISOGONVS

I commend to you the importance of intercession in our prayers. We are all selfish by nature, and our selfishness is very apt to stick to us, even when we are converted. . . . We should stir ourselves up to name other names besides our own before the throne of grace. We should try to hear in our hearts the whole world . . . the heathen, the Jews, the Roman Catholics, the body of true believers . . . the country to which we belong, the household in which we sojourn, the friends and relations we are connected with.[7]

Quote: James Houston. James Houston (b. 1922), an original founder and the first

This is a reproduction of a portion of the *Procession of the Holy Martyrs* mosaic from the Basilica of Sant'Apollinare Nuovo in Ravenna, Italy. Created around AD 560, it represents twenty-five martyrs. Shown here from left to right are Demetrius, Polycarp, Vincent, Pancras, and Chrysogonus.

principal of Regent College, says, "Prayerfulness is the breath of relationship, an antidote to the godless poison of secular psychoanalysis. Prayer becomes intertwined with the desire to be indwelt by the Holy Spirit as we relate to others. . . . I have found it impossible to separate prayer from friendship."[8]

Paul, Phoebe, Patronage, and Spain

Big Idea *Phoebe, Paul's patron, will deliver Paul's covenant letter and have it read to the Roman Christians. Phoebe's authority as patron and deaconess will reinforce the reading's solemnity. The Roman Christians should respond to Paul's letter by providing hospitality for Phoebe and joining their resources with hers to launch Paul's mission to Spain.*

Understanding the Text

The Text in Context

Romans 16:1–2 continues the document clause of Paul's covenant letter to the Roman Christians (15:14–16:27). Romans 16:1–27 divides into five units:

1. Phoebe and Paul's mission to Spain (16:1–2)
2. Paul's greetings to some thirty-six Roman Christians (16:3–16)
3. Paul's warning about false teaching (16:17–20)
4. Greetings to the Roman Christians from Paul's coworkers (16:21–23)
5. Paul's concluding doxology (16:25–27)[1]

Historical and Cultural Background

1. Thomas Schreiner observes that letters of commendation were common in the ancient world because travelers often were unknown and needed hospitality and thereby support to carry on their business or ministry (cf. Acts 18:27; 2 Cor. 3:1; 4:2; 5:12; 10:12; 12:11; 3 John 9–10; 1 Macc. 12:43; 2 Macc. 9:25).[2] From the Greco-Roman literature, Robert Jewett supplies the following example:

> So-and-so, who is conveying this letter to you, has been tested by us and is loved on account of his trustworthiness. You will do well if you deem him worthy of approval both for my sake and his, and indeed for your own. For you will not be sorry if you entrust to him, in any manner you wish, either confidential words or matters. Indeed, you will also praise him to others when you notice how useful he can be in everything.[3]

Chan-Hie Kim shows that these letters of commendation include an introduction and a listing of credentials of the bearer, and the desired action on the part of the recipient.[4] These three components occur in Romans 16:1–2: introduction of Phoebe

(v. 1a); Phoebe's credentials (vv. 1b, 2b); Phoebe's (and Paul's) desired action on the part of the Roman Christian recipients of the letter (v. 2a). In my analysis of 16:1–2 to follow I will use this three-point outline.

2. It is widely agreed that the word *prostatis*, describing Phoebe's role in 16:2b, is a technical term for "patron."[5] A patron was a wealthy person from the upper class of Roman society who gave of his or her means to a cause for a city or people, including civic buildings, humanitarian efforts, and religious causes. In return, the recipients of such benefaction would dedicate, for example, a building to that patron in thanks for the contribution.[6] Both men and women functioned as patrons in the Roman world.[7] It is clear from this that Phoebe acted as patron for Paul and for others as well (16:2b). Most likely, Phoebe helped Paul at the very least by paying Tertius, Paul's professional scribe (16:22), to copy the letter to the Romans, travel to Rome, and read it to them, with Phoebe's presence at the reading as Paul's imprimatur on the occasion. More specifically, Phoebe's task of delivering the letter of Romans and having it read was intended to garner support from the Roman Christians for Paul's upcoming mission to Spain.

3. In 16:1 Phoebe is called a "deacon" (*diakonos*), which prompts me to discuss, quite briefly, the leadership structure of the early church.

Key Themes of Romans 16:1–2

- Phoebe, Paul's patron and a deaconess in the church of Cenchreae, will deliver the letter to Rome.
- Given this role, Phoebe's supervision of the reading of Paul's covenant letter to the Roman congregations will add solemnity to its presentation.
- The Roman Christians will need to respond in kind—by welcoming Phoebe and by committing themselves to Paul's mission to Spain.

Although some say that *diakonos* in 16:1 is simply the general term for "servant," most commentators see the term as indicating the office of deacon (cf. Phil. 1:1; 1 Tim. 3:8, 12; see also Ign. *Eph.* 2.1; Ign. *Magn.* 6.1). Schreiner lists three reasons for this: (a) 1 Timothy 3:11 probably identifies women as deacons; (b) the designation "deacon of the church in Cenchreae" (Rom. 16:1) indicates that an office is intended; as does (c) the usage of the masculine word *diakonos*.[8] Thus, the office of the deacon in the early church seems to have included both men and women. The latter came to be known later as deaconesses. The other leadership office in the

The fuller's guild in the city of Pompeii dedicated this statue to their patron, Eumachia. She was a wealthy woman who financed the construction of a large public building in the forum at Pompeii. To be a patron was a worthy activity for well-to-do Roman women, and many were involved in public projects. Personal patronage, like Phoebe provides for Paul, did occur but was less common.

Romans 16:1–2

EVMACHIAE·L·F
SACERD·PVBI
FVLLONES

early church was that of elder (see, e.g., 1 Tim. 3:1–7; 1 Pet. 5:1–4).

Philippians 1:1–2 mentions the offices of elder and deacon in the early church. Moreover, it is clear that the elder was also called "bishop/overseer" (Phil. 1:1; 1 Tim. 3:1), and that some elders were teaching elders/pastors (Acts 20:17–31; 1 Pet. 5:1–4). In other words, in the early church "elder," "bishop," and "pastor" were one and the same. It was not until the second century that the monarchial episcopate (a bishop presiding over several churches in a region) emerged in the later notion of apostolic succession. It is debated whether or not women served as elders in the early church, though Romans 16:7 may shed light on that subject, as we will see later.

4. In 16:1 Paul uses the word "church" for the first time in Romans. The New Testament word for "church" is *ekklēsia*, which means "gathering, congregation, assembly." In classical Greek the term was used almost exclusively for political gatherings. In particular, in Athens the word signified the assembling of the citizens for the purpose of conducting the affairs of the city. Moreover, *ekklēsia* referred only to the actual meeting, not to the citizens themselves. When the people were not assembled, they were not considered to be the *ekklēsia*. The New Testament records a couple of instances of this secular usage of the term (Acts 19:32, 41). The most important background of the term *ekklēsia* is the LXX, which uses the word in a religious sense about one hundred times, almost always as a translation of the Hebrew word *qahal*. In Deuteronomy, *qahal* especially refers to Israel's sacred meetings since it is linked with the covenant. Likewise,

ekklēsia, though carrying a secular connotation in Greek, has a strong religious sense in light of the LXX.

In the New Testament, *ekklēsia* is used to refer to the community of God's people 109 times (out of 114 occurrences of the term). Although the word occurs in only two Gospel passages (Matt. 16:18; 18:17), it is of special importance in Acts (23x) and the Pauline writings (46x). It is found twenty times in Revelation and in isolated instances in James and Hebrews. Three general conclusions can be drawn from this usage. First, *ekklēsia* (both in the singular and plural) applies predominantly to a local assembly of those who profess faith in and allegiance to Christ. Second, *ekklēsia* designates the universal church (Acts 8:3; 9:31; 1 Cor. 12:28; 15:9; especially in the later Pauline letters, Eph. 1:22–23; Col. 1:18). Third, the *ekklēsia* is *God's* congregation (e.g., 1 Cor. 1:2; 2 Cor. 1:1). We probably are to gather from these first two points that the universal church is manifested in the local congregation.

Interpretive Insights

16:1–2 *I commend to you our sister Phoebe, a deacon of the church . . . I ask you to receive her.* We follow the three components of an ancient letter of recommendation noted above: introduction, credentials, desired action. First, Paul introduces Phoebe (16:1a), the probable bearer of the letter to the Romans. Phoebe no doubt was a Gentile; her namesake is the Greek goddess Phoebe, grandmother of Apollo and Artemis. But, unlike the goddess, Phoebe is a sister in the Lord. Second, Paul provides Phoebe's credentials. She is a deacon (deaconess) in the church of Cenchreae (16:1b). Cenchreae was a port city for Corinth on the Saronic Gulf. This is an indication that Paul wrote the letter of Romans from Corinth. Also, this is the first time Paul uses the word "church" (*ekklēsia*) in Romans. Thus, Phoebe should be well received by the Roman Christians whom she serves in an authoritative office of the church. Phoebe also was a patron of Paul and others (16:2b). So she was a woman of the upper class who used her resources to benefit Paul and others. Third, the desired action that Paul and Phoebe intended was that the believers in Rome give her a gracious Christian welcome and provide her with whatever assistance she needed as she (and later Paul upon his arrival in Rome) ministered to the Roman church and prepared for Paul's future mission to Spain (16:2a).

Theological Insights

Two truths grip the reader of Romans 16:1–2. First, the gospel values women and men equally. Indeed, Jesus elevated the status of women compared to Greco-Roman society and even the Jewish religion. Second, every church should be involved with missions, both nationally and internationally.

Teaching the Text

If one is going to devote a whole lesson or sermon to such a short unit as Romans 16:1–2, the three-point outline given above could be used. One could also make use of the historical-background material to talk about letters of recommendation, patronage, and leadership structure of the early church. And I think the title of this unit, "Paul, Phoebe, Patronage, and

Cenchreae was the eastern seaport city for Corinth. Shown here are remains of an early Christian basilica (ca. fourth century AD) now under water. Further out archaeologists have also located the remains of the Sanctuary of Isis and foundations of warehouses that would have been in use during Paul's time.

Spain," works well. But here I offer some background material from the New Testament to help the reader get a grasp on the possible structure of leadership in the early church, since Phoebe served in such a capacity in the church at Cenchreae. As I mentioned before, we learn from Philippians 1:2 and the Pastoral Epistles that there were mainly two offices of leadership in the early church: elder and deacon. (Apostles apparently were not confined to one church.) Of the first position, one may gather from texts such as Acts 20:17, 28; 1 Peter 5:1–5 that "bishop," "pastor," and "elder" likely referred to the same person. The office of the monarchial episcopate (one bishop presiding over several churches) did not arise until early in the second century. According to the Pastoral Epistles, apparently several elders led a local church, and those elders seem to have been divided into "teaching" and "ruling" elders. We also learn from these texts that more than one deacon served in a local church. It is also possible that deaconesses (the deacons' wives?) assisted deacons as servant leaders in the church as well (besides Rom. 16:1, see 1 Tim. 3:8–13).

We might also note here the order of worship in the early church, especially since it seems to have borrowed the order of worship from the synagogue service. This is shown in table 1.[9]

Illustrating the Text

The gospel values men and women equally.

Church History: Catherine Booth (1829–90), cofounder of the Salvation Army, had a powerful preaching ministry in England

Table 1: The Order of Worship in the Synagogue and the Church

Jewish Synagogue Service	Christian Worship as Reflected in Ephesians
Shema (Deut. 6:4–5)	Shema/Creed (4:4–6)
Shemoneh Esreh (the Eighteen Blessings)	Blessings from the Trinity (1:3–14)
Singing	Singing (5:19)
Scripture reading, followed by the sermon	Scripture, followed by the sermon (5:18–20)
Benediction	Benediction (6:23)

at a time when women did not speak at adult meetings. She said, "If the Word of God forbids female ministry, we would ask how it happens that so many of the most devoted handmaidens of the Lord have felt constrained by the Holy Ghost to exercise it? . . . The Word and the Spirit cannot contradict each other." Booth's book *Female Ministry* is not merely a reflection of the feminist ideas of the time. Instead, she based her argument on what she believed the Bible said about the absolute equality of men and women before God.[10]

Church History: Catherine of Siena (1347–80), a Catholic nun, theologian, and philosopher, began an active ministry to the poor, the sick, and the imprisoned of Siena. When a wave of the plague struck her hometown in 1374, most people fled, but she and her followers stayed to care for the sick and bury the dead. She was said to work tirelessly day and night, healing all those whom the physicians considered hopeless; some even claimed that she raised the dead. Later she sought to root out corruption from the church, even writing to the pope to exhort him to return to Rome from France and address problems: "Respond to the Holy Spirit, who is calling you! I tell you: Come! Come! Come! Do not wait for time, because time is not waiting for you."[11]

Every church should be involved with missions, both national and international.

Church Missions: Here are some questions that churches should be asking: (1) Are mission resources used to maintain local churches or to plant new ones? (2) Does support create unhealthy dependence or encourage national church initiative? (3) Are national church leaders ethically, morally, and spiritually responsible to other national church leaders who understand their culture? (4) Are missionaries ethically, morally, and spiritually responsible to teammates on the field, national church leaders, and church leaders of their sending congregation or agency? (5) Do supported national leaders expect to be supported by their own people in the near future? (6) Are national leaders supported on a level consistent with the local economy or on the economic level of members of the supporting church?[12]

True Story: People have always tried to find a variety of ways in which to fulfill Jesus' command that we love our neighbors. One couple, Saji and Priya Mathi, dug toilets for HIV-infected patients, individuals who are seen as beyond hope in the city of Hyderabad, India, where the couple works. "We consider these actions of love as one of the best opportunities to show God's love to them," the husband said. He reported that in time the people want to know about the God he worships. "Some say it is a dirty job, but isn't it a wonderful dirty job." Toilets are an imperative because of HIV's relationship to the immune system; each one costs about $217 US to construct.[13]

The tomb of St. Catherine of Siena, shown here, lies under the high altar in the Basilica of Santa Maria sopra Minerva, Rome.

Romans 16:1–2

Paul's Greetings to the Roman Churches

Big Idea *Romans 16:3–16 is no anticlimactic conclusion to Paul's covenant letter to the Roman Christians. The thirty-six people whom Paul greets here reveal a treasure trove of information about early Christianity in Rome: socioeconomic levels, places of worship, egalitarianism, and unity in Christ. Thus, Paul's greetings in these verses are no small matter.*

Understanding the Text

The Text in Context

Romans 16:3–16 is similar to other greetings that conclude Paul's letters (see 1 Cor. 16:15–20; Phil. 4:21–22; Col. 4:10–17; Philem. 23–24), except that Romans contains the greatest number of personal names.

Romans 16:3–16 falls into three divisions: greetings to Paul's missional coworkers in the past who now reside in Rome (vv. 3–10a, 12–13); greetings to those Roman Christians whom Paul does not know (vv. 10b–11, 14–15); greetings with the holy kiss (v. 16).

Historical and Cultural Background

1. Classical scholars have worked to uncover the socioeconomic structure of Roman Christianity.[1] John Gager identified five levels of Roman socioeconomic structure, listed here from the lowest to the highest class: slaves, freedmen and freedwomen (those born slaves who later obtained freedom), plebians (freeborn Roman citizens), equestrian class (knights; Roman political figures, military leaders, etc.), and senators (the Roman aristocracy) (see table 1 below).[2] Drawing on Robert Jewett's superb analysis of the thirty-six names that Paul mentions in 16:3–16 (including himself), we can classify them this way: Paul was a nonwealthy, freeborn Roman citizen, as probably was Rufus; Phoebe and Priscilla probably were wealthy (patrons), freeborn Roman citizens; the rest were either slaves or freedmen and freedwomen, including Aquila. It seems difficult to distinguish whether these names were those of slaves or freedmen and freedwomen, but either way, they stood on the lower rungs of the ladder of Roman society.[3] This evidence does seem to confirm what New Testament scholars have said for years: early Christianity was a movement mainly of the lower classes of Roman society, though there were important exceptions.

2. Early Christians in Rome and throughout the empire met in house churches.[4] Those Christians who could afford houses opened their homes to worship. From the house church excavated at Dura-Europos, we learn that a typical house church could accommodate about fifty worshipers. So those hosts of house churches, such as Priscilla and Aquila, probably were wealthy patrons of the Christian movement. Jewett has provided a masterful analysis of the five congregations in first-century Rome to which Paul wrote, showing that only Priscilla and Aquila's worship place was located in the wealthier section of Rome; the other four were tenement churches located in the poorer sections. These were apartment complexes above businesses. According to Jewett, the five congregations met as follows: (1) in the house church of Priscilla and Aquila (16:5a) and in the tenement churches of (2) those among the slaves of Adronicus (16:10b), (3) those among the slaves of Narcissus (16:11b), (4) the brothers with Asyncritus (16:14b), and (5) the saints with Philologus (16:15b).[5] This too shows that Roman Christianity at the time of Paul was mostly of the lower classes.

3. Paul's greetings to women in the churches of Rome (Priscilla [Prisca], Mary [Miriam], Junia,[6] Tryphena and Tryphosa [sisters?], Persis, Rufus's mother, and

- Paul's greetings serve at least two purposes: (1) to convey Paul's fond affection to colleagues in ministry and to honor esteemed believers in Rome whom he has not met; and (2) to communicate to the Roman churches that do not know Paul that their leaders fully support his apostleship and so should their congregations.

- Paul provides a window that offers a fascinating look at first-century Christianity in Rome.

Julia) reveal that females were deeply involved in the ministry.

Interpretive Insights

16:3–5a *Greet Priscilla and Aquila . . . also the church that meets at their house.* Paul makes four comments about the husband-and-wife team of Priscilla and Aquila. (1) They are coworkers with Paul in Christ (16:3). "Coworker" (*synergos*) signifies that they were involved in the ministry with Paul. So the couple became Christians before meeting Paul, but they joined him in proclaiming the gospel. (2) They risked their lives for Paul (16:4). Paul never specifies how they did so, but perhaps they interceded for him when the riot broke out in Ephesus (see Acts 19:23–41; 1 Cor. 15:32; 2 Cor. 1:8–11). (3) Both Paul and his Gentile churches are indebted to the

These are the excavated remains of the house church at Dura-Europos, dated to AD 235. The room at the far right served as the meeting room. A baptistery room was also unearthed uncovering Christian artwork that currently is our earliest portrayal of Jesus. Christians all over the Roman Empire gathered together in small, local house churches for worship and prayer.

couple (16:4). This detail may have been due to the couple's resourcing Paul's ministry to the Gentiles. (4) They host a house church in Rome (16:5a).

16:5b *Greet my dear friend Epenetus.* Next, Paul greets Epenetus. Epenetus most likely was a freedman who was one of the first converted to Christ in Asia, perhaps in connection with the ministry of Priscilla, Aquila, and Paul in Ephesus (see Acts 18:18–19:20). Jewett contends that Epenetus became associated with the family of Priscilla and Aquila, moving to Rome with them and joining their house church.[7]

16:6–7 *Greet Mary . . . Andronicus and Junia . . . They are outstanding among the apostles.* The three people mentioned in these verses were Jewish: Mary (Miriam), Andronicus, and Junia(s). The last two Paul call his "relatives" (*syngenesis*), meaning "fellow Jews" (NIV) or "compatriots." "Mary/Miriam" (v. 6) was the name of Moses' sister (Exod. 15:20). Since the Jewish community in Rome began primarily as enslaved prisoners of war brought from Judea to Rome in 62 BC, Miriam was either a slave or freedwoman. The technical phase "labored [*kopiaō*] for you" indicates that she labored as a missionary.[8]

There has been a huge debate as to whether Junia(s) was a man or a woman. But the case for "Junia," a female name, is far stronger than that for "Junias," a male name. Those opting for the latter argue that "Junias" is a contraction of "Junianus." However, "Junias" as a contraction for "Junianus" is nowhere to be found in Greek literature, and until the thirteenth century the dominant view of the church was that the person in question was a woman. Thus, Junia and Adronicus most

likely were a husband-and-wife team for the gospel, who either were slaves or had obtained their freedom. These two Paul calls "outstanding among the apostles." Moreover, they had become Christians before Paul was converted.

The meaning of "apostles" is also much debated. Thomas Schreiner and Douglas Moo argue that the term is not the technical one for the twelve apostles.[9] James Dunn and Robert Jewett do not necessarily disagree, arguing that Paul, Andronicus, and Junia belonged to the group of apostles (larger than twelve disciples/apostles) who were appointed apostles by the risen Christ (see 1 Cor. 15:7). Therefore, this couple had a high spiritual status, as did Paul, in preaching the gospel.[10] Dunn and Jewett apparently are correct, for in Romans 16:7a Paul commends Andronicus and Junia for being imprisoned with him. This was likely so because they, like him, preached the gospel as eyewitnesses of the risen Jesus.

16:8–10a *Greet Ampliatus, my dear friend in the Lord . . . Greet Urbanus . . . Stachys . . . Apelles.* Here Paul greets additional persons at Rome. Ampliatus, most agree, is Ampliatus the slave of Domitilla whose name appears twice in the Domitilla catacombs in Rome. Domitilla came from a senatorial family but was exiled as a Christian during Domitian's reign (AD 81–96). Urbanus probably was a freedman of Roman origin who was also a coworker with Paul in the past. Stachys no doubt was of slave origin, perhaps now a freedman. His Greek name suggests this, since both Jews and Greeks first appeared in Rome as slaves. He too was dear to Paul in the ministry.

Apelles also has a Greek name, suggesting his status as a slave or freedman. The fact that Paul knows that Apelles is honored because he was obedient to the Lord during a time of testing suggests that the two men also served the Lord together in the past.

16:10b–11 *Greet . . . the household of Aristobulus . . . Herodion . . . the household of Narcissus.* In 16:10b Paul greets those in the house of Aristobulus. Aristobulus may well have been the grandson of Herod the Great (d. 4 BC). Aristobulus was brought as a hostage with his brother Herod Agrippa to Rome. This Aristobulus was trained with the future emperor Claudius. Aristobulus later protested the action of the then-emperor Caligula, who decreed that his statue should be placed in the Jerusalem temple (Josephus, *Ant.* 18.273–76). After Aristobulus's death (ca. AD 45), his household was absorbed into the household of his friend Claudius, now emperor. Thus, those of the household of Aristobulus probably were Christian slaves or freedmen who constituted a tenement church.[11]

Paul greets Herodion, a fellow Jewish Christian. If Aristobulus was of the Herodian family, so too was the man called "Herodion." It may be that Paul mentions him on the heels of his reference to the household of Aristobulus because Herodion is also a slave or freedman who worships in that same tenement church.

In 16:11b Paul greets those of the household of Narcissus who are in the Lord. Like Aristobulus, Narcissus is not said to be a

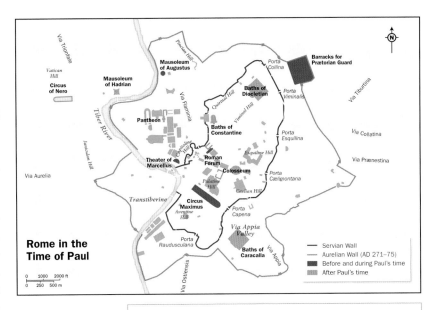

Rome in the Time of Paul

Christians in Rome were largely concentrated in the Transtiberine region (home to a large Jewish population) and along the Via Appia near the Porta Capena, two swampy areas where the poorest populations lived. The Aventine Hill, home to many aristocrats, was likely the location of the church of Priscilla and Aquila.

Christian; rather, those of their households are Christians. Narcissus may well have been the influential freedman of Emperor Claudius (Suetonius, *Claudius* 28). So those Christian slaves or freedmen and freedwomen of Narcissus seemed to constitute a third church in Rome, another tenement church. These Christians and other believers like them demonstrate that the gospel made deep inroads into Caesar's household (cf. Phil. 4:22).

16:12 *Greet Tryphena and Tryphosa . . . Persis.* In 16:12 Paul greets three Christian women. Tryphena and Tryphosa probably were sisters, given their similar names and the close union between them reflected in "and." They, along with Persis, another Christian woman, likely were of slave origin. Paul's praise for their work in the Lord probably stemmed from their ministry with him in the eastern provinces.

Romans 16:3–16

16:13 *Greet Rufus . . . and his mother.* Rufus and his mother were Jewish Christians. Long ago, J. B. Lightfoot defended the plausible theory that Rufus and his brother (see Mark 15:21) were sons of Simon of Cyrene, who was forced to carry Jesus' cross.[12] That Paul calls Rufus "chosen in the Lord" may be because his father helped Jesus carry the cross. This Rufus had a direct link to the historical Jesus. Moreover, Rufus's mother treated Paul as a son in the faith. For their faithful service to the Lord and to him, Paul honors them.

16:14–15 *Greet Asyncritus, Phlegon, Hermes, Patrobas, Hermas . . . Philologus, Julia, Nereus . . . Olympas.* Verses 14–15 contain greetings from Paul to the last two tenement churches. Paul greets five individuals who apparently were the leaders of another tenement church: Asyncritus, Phlegon, Hermes, Patrobas, Hermas, and the brothers with them. Paul does not greet these individuals personally. Jewett observes that all five of these men had slave names and may have become freedmen. This is because their names are Greek.[13] Therefore, it is likely that they led a congregation of slaves who met in a tenement apartment.

Verse 15 contains Paul's greeting to a fifth congregation in Rome (the fourth tenement church), the "saints" (*hagioi*) with Philologus and Julia (perhaps another husband-and-wife team) and Nereus and his sister. These individuals were presumably the leaders of the congregation and were undoubtedly slaves or freedmen and freedwomen.[14] Interestingly, two of these leaders were women—Julia and Nereus's sister—again showing the egalitarian nature of the early church. Even though Paul called Jewish Christians "saints" (*hagioi* [NIV: "the Lord's people"]) in Romans 15:25; 1 Corinthians 16:1; 2 Corinthians 8:4; and 9:12, the term can include Gentile Christians as well (as in Romans 1:7, a reference to all Christians, Gentile and Jew alike). The Greek names here in v. 15 might also point in that direction.

16:16 *Greet one another with a holy kiss.* Paul instructs the Roman Christians to greet one another with a holy kiss. Greeting others with a nonromantic kiss was customary in the Greco-Roman world (see, e.g., Euripides, *Andr.* 416–17; Pseudo-Lucian, *Asin.* 17) and in Judaism (see Gen. 27:26; Luke 7:45; Acts 20:37). But Jewett observes that nowhere in Greco-Roman tradition or Judaism is holiness connected with a kiss, as Paul states of the Christian kiss here.[15] The holy kiss among Christians was a sign of family affection and unity in Christ.

Theological Insights

Several theological insights surface in Romans 16:3–16. First, Paul's egalitarian principle—the equality of Christians because they are in Christ—so beautifully stated in Galatians 3:28 is displayed concretely here. In Christ, Jew and Gentile, slave and free, male and female are one. Second, Paul was no loner in his ministry. He had many coworkers in the spreading of the gospel. Third, Christians should honor and build up other Christians, as Paul did, because all are coworkers in the gospel.

Teaching the Text

In teaching this text, one could divide it according to the five Roman congregations, commenting on each of them. But perhaps a more detailed discussion of the five Roman

Table 1: The Five Roman Orders of Society

Name	Number	Description	Religion
Senator	Restricted to six hundred by Caesar	Upper class; ruling body; hereditary criterion of being freeborn and patricians	Conservative; Greco-Roman pantheon of gods
Equestrian (knights)	Unlimited; designated by Caesar; background of being military leaders and then administrators	Upper class; freeborn; controllers of Roman businesses, industry; nonhereditary	Mystery religions (from the army); Roman imperial cult
Plebeian	Many (several hundred thousand in Rome alone)	Lower/upper class; freeborn; financially depressed; slaves took over their jobs, leaving much unemployment in the plebeian rank	Mystery religions; open to new religions because of financial hardship and much free time; appeased by "bread and circuses"
Freedmen	80 percent of the Roman citizenry	Middle class; former slaves freed by manumission; some social mobility	Mystery religions and the Roman imperial cult
Slaves	Approximately 30 percent of the population of the Roman Empire (approx. sixteen million)	A thing / property; many obtained freedom and joined the work force; could be well educated	Open to Christianity, especially when compared to the first three levels of society, as the names in Romans 16 would suggest.

orders of society might be put to good use in teaching the background of these verses. These are displayed in table 1.

Illustrating the Text

Christians must affirm each other in the unity of Christ.

Culture: College culture, especially the worldviews held by professors, influences young minds. Kenneth Badley, professor at George Fox University, says,

> Students live in a vulnerable position. They must face the challenges of the world of thought while assuming no conflict exists between the truth therein and the truth of Scripture. Presumably they do so with God's help, but, as I have described it, they will do so without any supporting social structure. . . . We can aid our students by coming alongside them in the midst of their tensions. When we do, we shift the locus of integration by implicitly inviting them to continue their struggles, not alone, but within the relative safety of the faith community.[16]

The body metaphor used by Paul indicates a unity of community, and the church is one of the best places "to receive the kind of teaching that encourages and deepens faith."[17]

Christians should unite all ethnicities, genders, and socioeconomic groups.

Personal Testimony: I (Marvin) recently attended the funeral of the father of one of my student advisees. The service was both touching and triumphant. It was obvious that Jeff had lived a Christian life in view of the diversity of the body of Christ. Over five hundred people attended his memorial service. They represented different ethnic groups: men and women, haves and have nots, highly educated and not. During his life Jeff had touched each of those present at the service with his witness for the Lord. I felt like I was in heaven joining the worship of "every nation, tribe, people and language" (Rev. 7:9). I left that day thinking how much the church should emulate Jeff's example of reaching out to others.

Curses on the False Teachers, Blessings on the Roman Christians

Big Idea *As Paul nears the conclusion of his letter to the Romans, he both issues a warning about the false teachers who might invade the Roman congregations and praises the Roman Christians for their obedience to the gospel. To the former belong the covenant curses, but to the latter belong the covenant blessings.*

Understanding the Text

The Text in Context

Romans 16:17–20 abruptly punctuates Paul's warm greetings to the Roman churches. This has led some to theorize that these verses are a later interpolation added to Romans after Paul's death. Robert Jewett, for example, suggests that the school that produced the Pastoral Epistles (with their emphasis on strong doctrine as the remedy for false teaching) placed these verses in their present location.[1] Yet those of us who accept the Pauline authorship of the Pastoral Epistles have no problem with the emphasis in 16:17–20 on sound doctrine as the preventative to being tricked by false teaching.

Moreover, Paul issues similar abrupt warnings toward the end of some of his other letters (1 Cor. 16:22; Gal. 6:12–17; Phil. 3:2–4:1).[2] Furthermore, as we will see, 16:17–20 once again taps into the theme of the covenant curses and blessings that has

governed much of the letter to the Romans. The former applies to the Judaizers, and the latter to the Roman Christians.

Verses 17–20 easily divide into two points, both, I suggest, influenced by the covenant theme:

1. Covenant curses on the Judaizers (16:17–18)
2. Covenant blessings on the Roman Christians (16:19–20)

Historical and Cultural Background

1. Commentators identify the false teachers in 16:17–20 with either Gentile libertines or Judaizers. The key word in this discussion is *koilia* ("belly" [NIV: "appetites"]) in 16:18. A generation ago it was popular to point to the referent of this word as gnostic libertines whose loose morals and appetites governed their lifestyles. Gnosticism (from *gnōsis*, "knowledge") offered the "special insight" that the body is evil

and only the soul is good; one therefore can give one's body over to licentiousness because the physical does not impact the soul. Today, most scholars reject the claim that gnosticism had developed in the first century; rather, Pauline scholars today believe gnosticism did not arise as a fully developed religious system until the second century, long after the writing of Romans.

A much better case can be made that the false teachers' focus on their "belly" (*koilia*) is a reference to the Judaizers, those professing Christians who propagated the notion that salvation is based on faith in Christ plus works of the law. Indeed, this group dogged Paul's footsteps (see 2 Corinthians; Galatians; Phil. 3; cf. Acts 15:1–35). The "belly," then, is an allusion to the Judaizers' emphasis on the dietary laws as the means to be ritually clean before God. Indeed, we have met these Judaizers throughout Romans.[3] Thus, the false teachers whom Paul has in mind in 16:17–19 most likely are the Judaizers.

2. The Old Testament background to 16:20, "The God of peace will soon crush Satan under your feet," is Genesis 3:15, known as the *protoevangelion*—that is, the first occurrence of the gospel. There, God promises that the seed of the woman will crush the head of the serpent. Two comments are in order here. First, this promise of Genesis 3:15 becomes in Judaism and Christianity apocalyptic in orientation: the Messiah will come and crush Satan in the end time (see, e.g., *T. Levi* 18.12 for Judaism; Rev. 12:17 for Christi-

- False teachers are on their way to deceive the Roman congregations, so Paul warns the Roman Christians.

- But the Roman Christians are obedient to the Lord, and therefore they are blessed by him.

anity). For Paul, Jesus is the Messiah, and he will soon crush Satan at the parousia. Second, Genesis 3:15 is Deuteronomic in perspective. Thus, the covenant curses of Deuteronomy 28:15–68 inform Genesis 3:15. Just as God cursed the serpent and exiled Adam and Eve from the garden, so God will curse Israel for breaking their covenant and will send them into exile. (We assume here that the author of the Pentateuch [Moses] knew the end of the Pentateuch from its beginning and thus perceived that the earlier story of Genesis was influenced by the later story of Deuteronomy.)

So, for Paul, the false teachers, inspired by the serpent/Satan, are under the covenant curses. But, by way of contrast, the obedient Roman Christians are under the blessings of the new covenant of the Messiah. Indeed, the two diverse paths delineated in 16:17–20, the one of obedience and blessing (the "good") and the other of disobedience and curse (the "evil") (16:19), distinctly bring to mind the

The imagery Paul uses in Romans 16:20 of crushing adversaries under one's feet can be seen in this statue of Hadrian, Roman emperor from AD 117 to 138. Hadrian stands in victory (note the laurel wreath on his head) over an enemy of Rome with his foot on the back of a fallen barbarian.

"two ways" tradition beginning in Deuteronomy 30:15–20. The way of disobedience leads to the covenant curses; the way of obedience leads to the covenant blessings.

Interpretive Insights

16:17–18 *watch out for those who cause divisions and put obstacles in your way.* Paul "urges" (*parakaleō* [cf. 12:1]) the Roman Christians to "watch out" (*skopeō*) for the false teachers (the Judaizers). Paul then offers four characteristics of these individuals. First, they cause divisions (a work of the flesh [see Gal. 5:20]) in the church (16:17a). Second, the false teachers put "obstacles" (*skandalon* [cf. 9:33; 11:9; 14:13]) in the way of the teaching that the Roman Christians have learned. The "teaching" (*didachē*) is the truth of the gospel that the Roman believers had received long before Paul wrote his letter to them (16:17b). Third, the false teachers serve not Jesus the Lord, but rather their own appetites (16:18a). We noted above that *koilia* ("appetites" or "belly") probably alludes to the Judaizers' message that Christians should keep the whole law of Moses, including the dietary laws (cf. Col. 2:16–17, 20–23; Phil. 3:18–19). Fourth, the Judaizers persuade the unsuspecting by smooth speech and flattery (16:18b). Such "deceit" (*exapataō* is an intensive form of the word used of Satan in Gen. 3:13 LXX [cf. Rom. 7:11]) is inspired by Satan.

16:19–20 *The God of peace will soon crush Satan under your feet.* By way of contrast to the false teachers, Paul asserts in 16:19 that the Roman Christians are well known for their obedience to the gospel (cf. 1:5; 16:26). And Paul wants them to persist in such obedience to the gospel (the "good") and not be hoodwinked by the false teachers (the "evil"). Indeed, God will soon conquer Satan's emissaries at the parousia of Christ, and the Roman Christians will share in that victory. Verse 20

Paul describes false teachers as using "smooth talk and flattery" to deceive (Rom. 16:18). The residents of Rome were used to hearing smooth words. The study and performance of oratory was taken very seriously, and schools of rhetoric existed for training. The *contio*, or public meeting, was an important opportunity for speakers to address the general public. Most often these meetings were called prior to or after a vote was taken in the senate building, or Curia, which was located in the Roman Forum. Adjacent to the Curia was the Rostra, or speaker's platform, around which crowds could gather and where orators could be seen and heard as they gave their usually well-prepared speeches. This photo from the Roman Forum shows the reconstructed Rostra with the Curia just visible on the right side of the picture.

summarizes 16:17–20: the Roman believers enjoy peace now and victory later (covenant blessings) because they are obedient to the gospel; but the false teachers, who disobey the stipulation of faith by adding the law to salvation, are under the curses of the covenant.

Theological Insights

Two truths confront the reader of Romans 16:17–20. First, false teaching is an ever-present reality. Satan is a master at "tweaking" the truth of the gospel, adding the law here, subtracting holiness there. But such "adjustment" corrupts the gospel. Therefore, Christians must be vigilant to resist any inroad of false doctrine into the church. Second, the best way for Christians to resist false teaching is to know well the truth of the gospel.

Teaching the Text

A sermon or lesson based on Romans 16:17–20 could be entitled "Stay the Course" and make reference to being faithful to the truth of the gospel. The twofold outline above could be followed using these two captions: (1) Distortion of the gospel by false teachers (vv. 17–18); (2) Faithfulness to the gospel by true Christians (vv. 19–20).

Regarding the first point, a poem and two powerful illustrations come to mind regarding the distortion of the gospel that false teachers bring about. The first, a rhyme:

> Johnny was a chemist's son, but
>   Johnny is no more.
> What Johnny thought was H_2O was
> H_2SO_4!

Covenant and the Mindset of the Ancient Jew

Here I explore a thought that I have long considered about the Judaizers and Second Temple Judaism as a whole. Although this idea is psychological in orientation, I believe it can help us moderns, especially those of us who are Gentiles, to better understand the motivation behind the attitude toward the law that Paul critiques. Actually, if this theory is correct, it will also help the modern reader to better appreciate what motivated Paul's critique of the law itself.

Let us put ourselves in the place of the typical Jew around the first century AD. Such a person will have repeatedly heard from the Hebrew Bible the story of Israel: sin, exile, and restoration. God promised that if Israel obeyed the Torah, he would pour out the covenantal blessings on them, including plentiful harvest, protection from enemies, and long life in the land. But if Israel disobeyed God's law, the covenantal curses would be their lot—drought and famine, defeat at the hands of enemies, and exile. And so it was that Israel sinned against the law and consequently was defeated by the Assyrians, Babylonians, Syrians, Egyptians, and now the Romans.

It is not hard to understand the mindset of ancient Jews in all this: God said that if they returned to him by seriously obeying his law, he would restore them to their land and to their God. If I were a Jew living in those circumstances, then certainly I, like most other Jews, would have reasoned something like this: I might have failed to follow the Torah in the past, but you can be sure that this will not happen again, because this time I am going to obey the law to the nth degree! And this, I think, is what ancient Jews did. They tried to obey the law to its fullest degree to ensure God's favor.

The reader will now see the possible psychological dynamic at work in Second Temple Judaism: some Jews, understandably, became obsessive-compulsive in their perspective toward the Torah. They felt that they had to get it right, rituals and all, to once again experience God's blessings. Looking at ancient Judaism in this light should elicit much compassion and sensitivity from modern readers. Paul's part in all of this, like a good therapist shocking his patient into reality, was to point to the grace of God as the liberating factor from such an obsessive mindset.

Johnny thought he was drinking water, when in fact he drank sulfuric acid, a deadly chemical! Johnny was sincerely wrong. One thinks here of the followers of Jim Jones in the late 1970s, who were led astray by the distortion of the gospel preached by that minister. Jones's followers—about one thousand of them—relocated from California with the dynamic speaker to the jungles of Guyana, where they drank deadly poison at his command rather than face the authorities. That congregation was sincerely wrong, being deceived by a false teacher.

The second point of the lesson would be to encourage listeners to be true to the gospel. As Paul put it, we should fight the good fight, finish the race, and keep the faith (2 Tim. 4:7). The result for Paul, and for all believers who are faithful to sound biblical doctrine, is a crown of righteousness at the Lord's return (2 Tim. 4:8). When I think of modern faithful preachers of the gospel, the late W. A. Criswell comes to mind. Criswell will always be remembered as a faithful preacher of the gospel and the Bible. He did expository preaching when biblical exposition was not in vogue, as it is in many evangelical circles today. When Criswell started his ministry at the First Baptist Church of Dallas, he decided to preach through books of the Bible. It took him many years (1948–63), but Criswell finished "the Book" cover to cover. He loved telling people that the members of his church could refer to the time that they joined the church not by the date but by the book of the Bible Criswell was preaching at the time.

Criswell's scholarship was pounded out in his preaching ministry. He gave the best efforts of his intellectual capacities to making a thorough study and presentation of the text of Scripture to his people for over seventy years. Criswell always counseled young pastors to do what he did: to reserve their mornings for deep study of God's Word. He used the afternoons and evenings to do the work of the church, but his mornings were always reserved for time with God. Criswell studied Scripture in the original languages and utilized a vast library that included theological works, biblical commentaries, theological dictionaries, volumes of word studies, biographies and historical books, works of poetry and well-known literature, dissertations and theses, and much more. Preachers and teachers of this generation could learn much from Dr. Criswell's faithfulness to the gospel.

Illustrating the Text

False teaching is an ever-present reality.

Quote: George Orwell. In his unpublished preface to *Animal Farm* (1945) Orwell wrote,

> At any given moment there is an orthodoxy, a body of ideas which it is assumed that all right-thinking people will accept without question. It is not exactly forbidden to say this, that, or the other, but it is 'not done' to say it. . . . Anyone who challenges the prevailing orthodoxy finds himself silenced with surprising effectiveness. A genuinely unfashionable opinion is almost never given a fair hearing, either in the popular press or in the high-brow periodicals.[4]

This little novel is a satiric parable that shows the subtle way in which people are deceived and then deceive others.

Quote: Irenaeus. The church father Irenaeus (ca. AD 115–202?) wrote, "Error, indeed, is never set forth in its naked deformity, lest, being thus exposed, it should at once be detected. But it is craftily decked out in an attractive dress, so as, by its outward form, to make it appear to the inexperienced . . . more true than truth itself" (*Haer.* 1.2).[5]

The best way to resist false teaching is to know well the truth of the gospel.

Quote: Franz Kafka. Essayist and educator George Steiner (b. 1929) wants to read books that operate on his affections: "To read great literature as if it did not have upon us an urgent design . . . is to do little more than make entries in a librarian's catalog." He then quotes from a letter that the renowned novelist Franz Kafka (1883–1924) wrote at twenty years of age:

> If the book we are reading does not wake us, as with a fist hammering on our skull, why then do we read it? . . . What we must have are those books which come upon us like ill-fortune, and distress us deeply, like the death of one we love. . . . A book must be an ice-axe to break the sea frozen inside us.[6]

Kafka was not writing about the Bible, but this certainly is a powerful description of how the Word of God operates on us when we know it.

Quote: Michel de Montaigne. A highly influential Renaissance essayist, Montaigne (1533–92) wrote, "To hunt after truth is properly our business, and we are inexcusable if we carry on the chase impertinently and ill; to fail of catching it is another thing, for we are born to inquire after truth:

it belongs to a greater power to possess it; it is not, as Democritus said, hid in the bottom of the deeps, but rather elevated to an infinite height in the divine knowledge."[7]

Roman Christians would have had their beliefs challenged on many fronts. Besides a myriad of Roman gods and their ritual worship supported by the state, several mystery religions were springing up and attracting converts. The cult of Serapis (the Roman twist on the cult of Isis), the cult of Cybele (the goddess pictured here), and the cult of Mithras were all gaining popularity during this time. It may have been easier, however, for the Christians of Rome to reject these false religions than to resist the more subtle false teachers within the church. Paul warns believers against such troublemakers. The statue of Cybele is from Nicaea, second century AD.

Greetings to Roman Christians from Paul's Coworkers in Corinth

Big Idea *Paul concludes the greetings section of his letter by sending warm regards from his coworkers in Corinth to the Roman congregations. No doubt some of those coworkers had gathered in Corinth to accompany Paul as he took the collection from Gentiles to the Jerusalem church. Moreover, their greetings to Rome constituted their approval of the upcoming Pauline mission to Rome and Spain.*

Understanding the Text

The Text in Context

Romans 16:21–23 resumes Paul's greetings after the warning issued in 16:17–20. Therefore, these verses form the closing of the letter to the Romans. My summary of these verses will look at Paul's coworkers who send greetings to the Roman Christians, beginning with Timothy, then Lucius, Jason, and Sosipater, and finally Tertius, Gaius, Erastus, and Quartus.

Historical and Cultural Background

1. The proverb "All roads lead to Rome" was no exaggeration. The Romans built roads (called *viae* [plural of *via*]) that have lasted to this very day, roads that greatly facilitated the spreading of the gospel. At its peak, the Roman road system spanned fifty-three thousand miles and contained approximately 372 links. These roads served

Rome's military, commercial, and political purposes. The roads, built by Roman engineers, consisted of rubble, gravel, and stone as the bottom layer (designed to allow water to pass through without turning into mud), another layer of stone, and then concrete as the surface layer. Milestones were placed every 1,620 yards. Way stations dotted the Roman roads every fifteen to eighteen miles. Augustus founded the postal system. The mail was delivered by cart and horse, but also by horse and rider for special delivery. Maps were hard to come by, so travelers followed an itinerary listing the cities on a given road. But such roads were not free. Tolls and import and export taxes helped to fund the construction and maintenance of Roman roads. Paul would have traveled one of the most famous thoroughfares in the empire, the Via Egnatia, the road that connected Asia Minor, Europe, and Italy. Paul utilized that road in his trips to Macedonia and Achaia. On his journey to Rome, when he arrived in Italy, Paul took another famous road, the Via Appia.

2. Romans 16:22 records that Paul used a secretary—an amanuensis—to write down the letter to the Romans. Tertius was a professional scribe (probably paid by Phoebe). One author writes of the ancient secretary,

> Evidently, secretaries were used up and down the spectrum of public life, from royal secretaries to the marketplace secretaries. They were a vital part of the administrative structure of the Greco-Roman world, as can be seen by the bureaucracy in Roman Egypt. From the "central office" in Alexandria, with its hordes of secretaries who kept the main accounting and recordkeeping, there was a hierarchical structure of secretaries that reached all the way down to the local village secre-

Key Themes of Romans 16:21–23

- Paul was well networked with Christians east of Rome.
- The cooperation of Jewish Christians and Gentile Christians as Paul's coworkers and in his collection for the parent church in Jerusalem modeled the unity Paul desired for the Roman believers.
- Paul's coworkers also supported his gospel and his plans to visit Rome and Spain.

tary. Secretaries were critical to the functioning of the Roman government. They were the record keepers for the massive bureaucracy.[1]

E. Randolph Richards's study of ancient letter writing shows that there was a continuum of how much input amanuenses had in the composition of a letter, moving from little control (dictation), to some control (shorthand), to complete control (composer).[2] Given the importance of Paul's letter to the Romans, no doubt he dictated it, leaving Tertius very little control over its composition.

What materials were utilized in ancient letters? Pen and ink were staples of ancient writing. Pens often were cut from a small reed plant that flourished on the banks of the Nile River. One end of the reed was cut to a point. The point was cut with a small split, resembling a quill pen of more recent times. Ink was basically standardized by the first century AD. There were two types of ink: red and black. Red ink was prepared by mixing ochre with gelatin, gum, and

> This Roman milestone from the Gallikos River on the Via Egnatia has inscriptions in Latin and Greek that give the mileage from Dyrrachium, on the western coast of Macedonia, to the Gallikos River, near Thessaloniki, as 260 miles. Since Dyrrachium was across the Adriatic Sea from Brundisium, travelers could go from Rome to Byzantium (now Istanbul, Turkey) using the Via Appia, a sea crossing, and the Via Egnatia.

321   Romans 16:21–23

beeswax. Black ink was prepared from lamp black or ground charcoal mixed with gum arabic. The weakness of black ink was that it was not waterproof. Consequently, writing in black ink could be erased by contact with water.

Various writing materials were used by the ancients: ostraca (broken pottery), clay, wooden tablets, parchment (animal skin), and papyrus (made from reed plants, the inner pith of which was extracted and cut into strips, which were layered side by side and then at right angles), rolls or scrolls (individual parchment or papyrus sheets sewn together).[3]

Richards provides three intriguing details about Paul's letter to the Romans: it would have cost approximately $2,275 (in modern currency); the travel time to deliver a letter from Corinth to Rome by sea would have been about ten days; the same letter would have taken about two months to travel by land from Corinth to Rome.[4]

3. The last occurrence in Romans of the word "church" (*ekklēsia*), in 16:23, gives us the opportunity for a glance at the trinitarian content of worship in the early church:

1. Messianic—the Son
   a. Jesus is the Messiah (2 Sam. 7; Ps. 110; Isa. 53)
   b. Jesus is God (christological hymns, Rom. 1:3–4; Phil. 2:5–11; Col. 1:15–20; 1 Tim. 3:16; Rev. 5, probably sung to Jesus in worship)
2. Charismatic—the Holy Spirit
   a. The Spirit as eschatological gift (Acts 2)
   b. Worship led by Spirit (1 Cor. 14; 1 Thess. 5:16–20)
3. Prophetic—the Father

a. Worship in response to God's saving act in Christ's death and resurrection (Rom. 1:3–4)
b. Worship as the anticipation of heaven (Rev. 1)

Interpretive Insights

16:21–23 *Timothy . . . Lucius, Jason and Sosipater . . . Tertius . . . Gaius . . . Erastus . . . Quartus send you their greetings.*[5] Paul sends greetings to the Roman churches from some eight of his coworkers who have gathered at Corinth. Timothy became part of Paul's mission team on his second journey (Acts 16:1–3) and was Paul's closest colleague (cf. Acts 19:22; 1 Cor. 4:17; 16:10; 2 Cor. 1:1, 19; Phil. 1:1; 2:19–24; Col. 1:1; 1 Thess. 1:1; 3:2, 6; 2 Thess. 1:1; 1 Tim. 1:2, 18; 6:20; 2 Tim. 1:2; Philem. 1). Timothy's mother was Jewish, but his father was Greek (Acts 16:1).

Lucius, Jason, and Sosipater were Jewish Christians who served with Paul (he calls them his "relatives" [*syngenesis*], meaning "fellow Jews" [NIV] or "compatriots"). Lucius (*Loukios*) does not seem to be Lucius of Cyrene (Acts 13:1), nor is he Luke (whose name Paul spells as *Loukas*; and Luke was a Gentile [see Col. 4:10–14]). Jason probably is the man named in Acts 17:5–7, 9, and Sosipater is probably the Sopater of Berea mentioned in Acts 20:4. No doubt these three coworkers rendezvoused at Corinth to assist Paul in taking the collection of the Gentiles to Jerusalem.

Tertius was the secretary to whom Paul dictated Romans, and probably he was Phoebe's amanuensis. Moreover, Tertius's greeting, "I, Tertius, . . . greet you in the Lord," indicates that he was a Christian.

Gaius may well have been the Gaius of 1 Corinthians 1:14. Gaius provided hospitality to Paul and many other Christian itinerant missionaries. Some think that Gaius hosted the church of Corinth in his home.

Erastus may well be the one mentioned in Acts 19:22 and 2 Timothy 4:20. Here, Paul identifies him as the director of public works in Corinth. An inscription found in Corinth by archaeologists in 1929 reads, "Erastus, in return for the aedileship, laid the pavement at his own expense" (see photo). This inscription reflects the ancient custom of an elected public official expressing his appreciation to the citizens of his city by contributing something back to that town, in this case paving a street. An aedile was a public director who was in charge of the city's building projects. The Greek *oikonomos* was an equivalent of the Latin *aediles*.[6]

Robert Jewett plausibly argues that Quartus was Erastus's brother (most translations render *Kouartos ho adelphos* as "our brother Quartus" or "Quartus, a brother"). If so, Paul will have started and concluded his greetings to the Roman Christians with the names of high-society people (Phoebe [16:1], and Erastus and Quartus [16:23]).[7]

Three key themes, as we noted above, govern Romans 16:21–23. First, Paul was well networked in his ministry, as the eight names in these verses indicate (not to mention the thirty-six he named earlier). Second, some of the eight men no doubt were in Corinth for the purpose of assisting Paul as he took the offering from the Gentiles to Jerusalem. This gesture of Jewish Christians taking the Gentiles' offering to Jerusalem was a symbol of Christian unity that Paul wanted the Romans to emulate. Third, Paul's coworkers from the east supported him in his plans to visit Rome and to evangelize Spain. Their social clout and spiritual authority, Paul hoped, would add weight to his request to the Roman congregations to also support his preaching of the gospel there and abroad. And if Clement of Rome (*1 Clem.* 5), *Actus Petri Vercellenses* (chaps. 1–3), and the Muratorian Canon (lines 34–39) are correct, Paul did indeed realize his dream to preach the gospel in Spain.

Theological Insights

Two simple truths are striking concerning Romans 16:21–23. First, the gospel was cross-cultural. It encompassed Jew and Gentile, Roman and Greek, barbarian and civilized. It does the same today in our pluralistic world, regardless of the culture. Second, the gospel was countercultural. It unified slaves and free, rich and poor, male and female, powerful and weak.

The Erastus Inscription

Roman culture, in which birth determined status and left very little room for social mobility, was no match for the egalitarian gospel of Jesus Christ.

Teaching the Text

Perhaps the best way to teach/preach Romans 16:21–23 is simply to expound upon each of the eight names that Paul mentions and then conclude with the two theological insights that I just presented. But here I think that it might be illuminating to provide an itinerary of Paul's mission after his first captivity in Rome. Those who assume Pauline authorship in some measure for the Pastoral Epistles (1–2 Timothy and Titus) typically envision the following scenario. After his house arrest in Rome (Acts 28), Paul was released (AD 62). After that, he most likely began a fourth missionary journey, which looked something like the following:

Years	Location	Scripture	Comments
62–64	Spain	Rom. 15:24, 28 (cf. *1 Clem.* 5; Eusebius, *Hist. eccl.* 2.22.1–3; Muratorian Canon, lines 34–39)	
64–65	Crete	Titus 1:5	Paul left Titus here as his representative at the church.
65	Miletus	2 Tim. 4:20	
66	Colossae	Philem. 22	
66	Ephesus	1 Tim. 1:3	Paul put Timothy in charge of the church here.

Years	Location	Scripture	Comments
66	Philippi	Phil. 2:23–24; 1 Tim. 1:3	Paul wrote 1 Timothy and Titus here.
66–67	Nicopolis	Titus 3:12	
67–68	Rome		Here Paul was imprisoned in 67 and martyred in 67/68, before which he wrote 2 Timothy. Luke may have helped Paul to write 2 Timothy (see 2 Tim. 4:11), since the apostle was confined in prison.

Illustrating the Text

The gospel was and is cross-cultural.

Quote: **Tom Cruise.** Film star Tom Cruise discussed human unity in what he learned while filming *The Last Samurai*, an ode to Japan's ancient class of warriors. He said,

> One of the great things about being an actor and what I do is that I get to travel to all these places. I get to learn about the people, and that is the most enjoyable thing for me, to learn the history of other people and how they live in their daily lives. Also, you find a common ground, even though the language is different and their culture is different. You find that common ground of joy, happiness, pain. And it's the humanity that really gives you a sense of—Whoa, we're all in this thing together.[8]

Theological Book: *Cross-Cultural Servanthood*, **by Elmer.** In this book, missionary Duane Elmer notes the differences between countries and emphasizes for Christians that cross-cultural communication and contextualization need to find common ground. He writes, "Many missionaries may be like me: well intentioned, dedicated and wanting to serve, but also naïve and in some denial about what it means to serve in *another culture*. The reality is that many of us want to serve from our own cultural context. That is, we believe that servanthood everywhere else probably looks like it does in our own culture."[9]

The gospel was and is countercultural.

Theological Book: *Same Kind of Different as Me*, **by Ron Hall and Denver Moore, with Lynn Vincent.** This book can make one laugh and cry, rekindling the fire for serving others in Christ's name. It tells the stories of a most unlikely friendship between Ron Hall, a wealthy art dealer, and Denver Moore, an impoverished homeless man, and Debbie Hall, who brought them together. The two men become friends through the message of the gospel, helping one another to help others. In a follow-up volume, *What Difference Do It Make?*, the two men tell more stories about Christians bringing hope and healing as they make a difference in their world for Christ.

Quote: Timothy Keller. In his book *Counterfeit Gods*, pastor and author Keller says,

> Religion [in the ancient Near Eastern world] was a form of social control. The operating principle of religion is: If you live

a good life, then the gods or God will have to bless you and give you prosperity. It was natural, then, to assume that the most successful people in society were those closest to God. They would be the ones who could get whatever they wanted from God. That is why traditional religion always expects that the gods will be working through the successful, not through the outsider and the failures.[10]

Literature: *The Idiot*, **by Fyodor Dostoevsky.** Ranked as one of Dostoevsky's brilliant achievements in Russia's golden age of literature, this novel (1869) presents us with Prince Myshkin, intended to be a picture of a good man, having a Christlikeness seen in his utter humility and goodness to people. He is countercultural, an irony and paradox to modern society so twisted that acts of simple goodness are looked down upon as acts of idiocy. In Myshkin's willingness to suffer for the sake of others, he is literally a "fool for Christ." In one particularly evocative scene from the novel, the story of Marie, Prince Myshkin quietly accepts the ridicule that he is an idiot. Myshkin dominates the novel, showing a desire to offer people an alternative to the violent passions and conflicts of nineteenth-century Russia. The novel has been adapted into films, operas, and stage plays, and the book itself also has appeared in movies throughout the years on coffee tables, referred to and being read by various characters in the films.

The Doxology

Big Idea *This doxology concludes Paul's new-covenant letter to the Roman churches. Paul praises God for giving him the gospel of Jesus Christ, which proclaims the mystery of the end-time conversion of the nations.*

Understanding the Text

The Text in Context

Many scholars believe that Romans 16:25–27 was not written by Paul but rather was added to Romans after Paul's death. They point to four major reasons for this interpolation theory.[1] First, Paul nowhere else closes his letters with a doxology. Second, there are words in 16:25–27 that Paul does not use elsewhere: "proclamation of Jesus Christ" and "command of the eternal God." Third, the doxology in 16:25–27 seems to be supersessionist. Only the Gentiles are mentioned, indicating that Israel is no longer in God's plan of salvation. Fourth, the doxology occurs in some Greek manuscripts after 14:23, in others after 15:32, and in still others after 16:23.

However, these arguments can be answered in favor of the authenticity of the doxology. To the first and fourth arguments it can be said that the manuscripts containing this doxology at this point are very strong (Papyrus 46, Codex Sinaiticus, Codex Vaticanus). To the second argument it may be said that the supposedly non-Pauline language of the Romans doxology is similar to Ephesians, Colossians, and the Pastoral Epistles. To the third argument it can be said that 16:25–27 forms an *inclusio* with 1:1–7; both of them focus on Paul's ministry to the Gentiles but need not exclude God's future plans for the salvation of Israel. Therefore, I believe that the doxology was placed in its present location by Paul.

As we just noted, 16:25–27 forms an *inclusio* with 1:1–7, centering on three themes:

1. The gospel is about Jesus Christ (compare 16:25a with 1:1–4).
2. This gospel is proclaimed in the Old Testament Scriptures (compare 16:25b–26 with 1:2).
3. This gospel given to Paul reveals the mystery of the end-time conversion of the Gentiles (compare 1:5–7 with 16:26b).

Historical and Cultural Background

The following pieces of background information for interpreting 16:25–27 could also be applied to the letter as a whole.

1. The latest research on Romans reveals that Paul's letter contains an anti-imperial message. Of the numerous things that could be said about this, I mention three. First, the term "gospel" early on was applied to Caesar Augustus as the savior of the world. Thus, the famous Priene inscription (dated ca. 9 BC) about Augustus reads,

> Providence . . . created . . . the most perfect good for our lives . . . filling him [Augustus] with virtue for the benefit of mankind, sending us and those after us a saviour who put an end to war and established all things . . . and whereas the birthday of the god [i.e., Augustus] marked for the world the beginning of good tidings [*euangelion*] through his coming . . .[2]

Paul counters with the assertion that the true gospel concerns Jesus Christ.

Second, imperial worship (confessing that Caesar is a god) was on the rise in the Roman provinces in the first century due to Gaius (AD 37–41), Nero (AD 54–68), and later Domitian (AD 81–96). But Paul challenges the Roman Christians to confess that Jesus, not Caesar, is Lord (Rom. 10:9).

Third, Paul is, after all, writing to the churches in Rome, the capital of the empire. And Paul could hope that his letter to the Romans would ultimately spell the demise of the anti-Christian sentiment of the Roman Empire, in an ironic way. The

Key Themes of Romans 16:25–27

- The gospel is the proclamation of Jesus Christ.
- This gospel is revealed in the Scripture and given to Paul.
- This gospel contains the mystery of the end-time conversion of the Gentiles.

support that Paul needed from the Roman Christians to launch his mission to Spain would bring about the conversion of the full number of the Gentiles, the restoration of Israel, and the parousia. The actual impact

The front of this altar dedicated to the sun portrays Nero's head surrounded by rays of the sun. From the time of Julius Caesar, Roman emperors linked themselves to the gods and accepted worship of themselves as gods. In ancient Roman writings we have examples of emperors being labeled "lord," "savior," "benefactor," and "god." Statues and temples were erected in their honor. When Nero came to power he deified Claudius, the emperor before him. During his reign, Nero identified himself with Apollo and the sun.

Romans 16:25–27

of Paul's letter to Rome no doubt contributed to Emperor Constantine's decision to adopt Christianity.[3]

2. Paul's language in 16:25–27 about the mystery of old being revealed to him in the prophetic writings is very similar to the *pesher* method of interpretation used in the Dead Sea Scrolls. The *pesharim* (e.g., *Pesher Isaiah, Pesher Hosea, Pesher Habakkuk*) claim that God revealed the mystery of the Old Testament Scripture to the Teacher of Righteousness, who then founded the Essene Community, the new-covenant community of the end time.

3. Speaking of the new covenant, the liturgical closing to Paul's doxology in 16:25–27 requires the audience hearing the reading of Romans to respond "Amen." That is, "We agree and we accept the terms of the new covenant."[4]

Interpretive Insights

16:25–27 *Now to him . . . the only wise God be glory forever through Jesus Christ! Amen.* Paul makes three points in 16:25–27, which correspond with the three points made in 1:1–7.

First, the content of the gospel is Jesus Christ (taking *Iēsou Christou* as an objective genitive). Paul defines this gospel as the "proclamation" (*kērygma*) of Jesus Christ (compare 16:25a with 1:1–4). C. H. Dodd long ago identified the components of the *kērygma* from the book of Acts. He noted that there were at least five end-time aspects of Jesus' life, death, and resurrection: (1) in Jesus the messianic age has dawned (Acts 2:16; 3:18, 24), in his ministry, death, and resurrection (Acts 2:23); (2) by his resurrection, Jesus has been exalted to the right hand of God as the messianic head of the

new people of God (Acts 2:33–36; 3:13); (3) the Holy Spirit is the sign of the presence of the eschaton as well as the proof that Jesus currently reigns in heaven in power and glory (Acts 2:33); (4) the messianic age will shortly reach its consummation in the return of Christ (Acts 3:21); (5) an invitation is always extended for people to receive Christ and the life of the age to come (Acts. 2:38–39).[5] Paul no doubt knew and concurred with these components, but, as we will see, he added one more item to the *kērygma* as revealed to him by God.

Second, this gospel of Jesus Christ was proclaimed in the Old Testament ("the prophetic writings" [compare 16:25b–26a with 1:2). As I mentioned above, Paul saw himself as an apocalyptic seer to whom God had revealed the mysteries in the Old Testament heretofore unknown. Indeed, "revelation" (*apokalypsis*) and "mystery" (*mystērion*) are eschatological terms. Mysteries of the end time couched in Old Testament prophecies were now being brought to light by God through the apocalyptic seer, in this case Paul. Recall the *pesher* hermeneutic employed by the Teacher of Righteousness in the Dead Sea Scrolls. Two similar words are used by Paul: "reveal" (*phaneroō*) and "make known" (*gnōrizō*). This spiritual illumination came from God.

Third, 16:26b spells out the content of the mystery God revealed to Paul. Gentiles, through Christ, are a part of the people of God. This truth was not clear in the Old Testament (cf. Eph. 3:3–6, 9; Col. 1:26–27). But two Old Testament prophecies envisioned in some sense the end-time conversion of the Gentiles. These are the Abrahamic covenant (Gen. 12:1–3) and the prophets' predictions of the nations streaming into Jerusalem to worship God (e.g., Isa. 45:15; 60:15–17; Mic. 4:13). Paul began Romans with exactly that hope (1:5–7). This is the added detail to the *kērygma* that Paul contributes to the gospel of Jesus Christ. With this, Paul has come full circle in his letter to the Romans. He is the apostle of grace whose eschatological mission was to win the Gentile world to Christ and thereby be the catalyst for the parousia. For this reason, Paul exclaims, "To the only wise God be glory forever through Jesus Christ!" We, like the Roman Christians, should respond, "Amen!"

This silver plaque with the chi-rho monogram is part of the Water Newton treasure dated to the fourth century AD. Water Newton was the ancient Roman town of Durobrivae in Britain. The discovery of many silver items with this early Christian symbol shows that Paul's gospel reached Gentiles not only in Spain, the western end of the Roman Empire, but in Britain, the northern frontier of Rome's conquests.

the Messiah and thus bring about the second coming of Christ.

Teaching the Text

A good way to approach Romans 16:25–27 is to cover the three points that I identified therein, comparing them with Romans 1:1–7. This can be done by way of a chart, as shown in table 1, and a summary of that material. This will bring a sense of closure to this marvelous message of Paul's letter to the Romans.

Theological Insights

Several truths meet us in Romans 16:25–27. First, history is "his story." God's plan of salvation can be traced in the Old Testament; it piqued the interest of Jews in Second Temple Judaism and was fully revealed in the New Testament in the gospel of Jesus Christ. And that plan will culminate in Christ's return. Second, the gospel is for all—Jew and Gentile alike. Where would we be in the West without Paul's message of the gospel? There is a strong possibility that without Paul's mission to Gentiles, the gospel could have been largely restricted to Jews in Palestine. Third, on the one hand, Paul's timetable of reaching Spain (which, I believe, he did) and winning the Gentiles to precipitate the parousia was not met; but, on the other hand, Paul's gospel reached Gentiles far beyond Spain, and one day that will stir the Jews to accept Jesus as

Table 1: A Comparison between Romans 16:25–27 and 1:1–7

My gospel = preaching of gospel (16:25)	The gospel of God concerning Jesus Christ (1:1–4)
Revelation of the mystery now manifested in Scripture/prophets (16:26)	Promised in the prophets of the Scriptures (1:1–4)
Obedience of faith of the nations (16:26)	Obedience of faith of the Gentiles (1:5)

First, Paul preached the good news (gospel) of the true restoration of Israel, which is that Jesus the Messiah provides the correct way to being at peace with God—justification by faith. Such a restoration is not restricted to the land of Israel or to the Jewish people but is open to the whole world and to all people groups. In other words, God through Christ reigns in the hearts of his people. Second, this good news of restoration was predicted in the Old Testament but has now become clear in Paul's proclamation of Christ. One finds here the tie that binds together the Old and New Testaments. That is, the new covenant promised in the former is fulfilled in the latter. Third, Gentiles especially have accepted the gospel. Their commitment to Christ is the end-time obedience of the nations hoped for in the Old Testament. Together with Jewish Christians they form the one people of God based on faith.

Illustrating the Text

History is his story.

Church History: Because of his desire to see the Bible translated into the language of his people, John Wycliffe is generally considered the first great English Reformer. This, and his denunciation of the Catholic Church of his day, led to his expulsion from his post at Oxford in 1381. He died after a stroke in 1384 and was buried, but not for long. At the Council of Constance in 1415, Wycliffe was condemned by Pope Martin V, and it was ordered that Wycliffe's

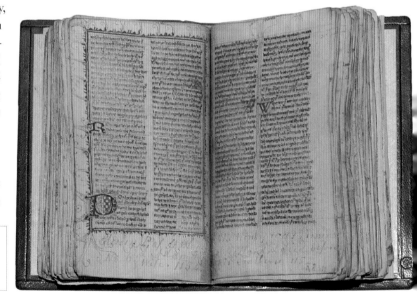

Copy of John Wycliffe's translation of the Bible from the Latin Vulgate into English, late fourteenth century AD

remains be exhumed and burned. But it was Wycliffe who had the last laugh. Church historian Thomas Fuller wrote, "To city of Lutterworth they come, . . . take what was left out of the grave, and burnt them to ashes, and cast them into the Swift, a neighbouring brook running hard by. Thus this brook hath conveyed his ashes into Avon, Avon into Severn, Severn into the narrow seas, they into the main ocean; and thus the ashes of Wicliffe are the emblem of his doctrine, which now is dispersed all the world over."[6]

The gospel is for all—Jew, Gentile, anyone.

Quote: John Stott.

It is he who opens the eyes of our hearts and those eyes and hearts belong to young and old, Latin and Anglo-Saxon, African, Asian and American, male and female, poetic and prosaic. It is this "magnificent and intricate mosaic of mankind" (to borrow a phrase of Dr. Donald McGavran's) which the Holy Spirit uses to disclose from

Scripture ever more of the many-coloured wisdom of God.[7]

The gospel reached far beyond Spain, Paul's specific interest.

Biography: James Yen (1893–1990) came to know the Lord in rural China through the influence of China Inland Mission. He was discipled by a Christian YMCA worker and profoundly affected by the plight of the poor, illiterate Chinese people. Yen got his undergraduate degree at Yale then his Master's at Princeton. Upon his return to China in 1921, Yen became a leader of the Mass Education Movement, in which thousands of Chinese intellectuals, many of them Christians, taught literacy to the masses in rural areas. He founded the International Institute of Rural Reconstruction, and in 1950 *Life Magazine* listed him as one of the ten most significant people in the world at the time. He died in 1990 in New York City, having affected the lives of 50 million Chinese and millions around the world, though he was virtually unknown in other parts of the world.[8]

Notes

Introduction to Romans

1. For more on these individuals, see below under "The Importance of Romans in Church History." For further discussion of the Old and New Perspectives on Paul, see the commentary on Romans 3:9–20.

2. On the issue of what Paul's experience on the road to Damascus should be called, see the commentary on Romans 1:1–7.

3. See the discussion below under "The Purpose of Romans."

4. For documentation and bibliography dealing with these three arguments and the traditional counterarguments, see the introduction in Pate, *End of the Age*, 34–40.

5. F. C. Baur's key works are *Paul, the Apostle of Jesus Christ* and *The Church History of the First Three Centuries*.

6. The reader can pursue these theories in the introduction to Pate, *End of the Age*. The Greek mystery religions were secret religious cults that claimed that rites such as baptism and sacred meals unified the worshiper with Isis, Cybele, or other Greek deities. Hellenistic mysticism, whereby the worshiper was thought to be deified, was a more general phenomenon that pervaded Greco-Roman spirituality. Gnosticism was a second- to third-century aberration of Christianity that, in good Platonic fashion, disparaged the body but extolled the soul. One can see Plato's anthropological dualism in this: matter is evil, and spirit/soul alone is good. An incipient form of gnosticism known as docetism (Christ was divine but only appeared to be human) is refuted by the Johannine Epistles. It would fall to early church fathers such as Irenaeus and Tertullian in the second century to refute the full-blown gnosticism that threatened the church of their day.

7. The classic work on the subject is Martin Hengel's *Judaism and Hellenism*.

8. For thorough documentation of this point, see Pate, *End of the Age*, and the works cited there.

9. The classic defense of this approach is George Ladd's *A Theology of the New Testament* (1974), updated by Donald A. Hagner (1993).

10. "Preface to the Latin Writings," 336–37.

11. Wesley's journal, May 24, 1738.

12. See Moo, *Epistle to the Romans*, 4.

13. See Acts 10:2, 22; 13:6, 26; 16:14; 17:17; 18:7; for further discussion, see Pate, *Reverse of the Curse*, 326–30.

14. The work of N. T. Wright, especially *The New Testament and the People of God* and *Jesus and the Victory of God*, has alerted biblical scholars that the story of Israel is pervasive in the literature of Second Temple Judaism and in the New Testament. Commentaries on Romans by Douglas Moo (*Epistle to the Romans*) and Thomas Schreiner (*Romans*) have broached this subject relative to Romans 1:16–17. Much more could be said, however, about how the story of Israel affects Romans 1:16–17 and indeed the entire book of Romans; see my theory below under "The Genre/Outline of Romans."

15. Robert Jewett (*Romans*) has shown convincingly that the mission to Spain was uppermost in Paul's mind when he wrote Romans. I agree with Jewett for the most part, except that in my view he has focused too little on the eschatological status of Paul's mission to Spain via Rome; see my remarks in the commentary on Romans 15:22–29.

16. Moo, *Romans*, 22. It should be noted, however, that contrary to what I am arguing here, Moo does not see Paul's mission to Spain as the all-encompassing purpose for the writing of Romans.

17. Quoted in Boadt, *Reading the Old Testament*, 179. For studies on the relationship between the suzerain-vassal treaties and the Old Testament, see Mendenhall, "Covenant Forms in Israelite Tradition"; Kline, *Treaty of the Great King*.

Romans 1:1–7

1. The revised NIV (2011) rightly translates *horisthentos* as "appointed" instead of "declared" (NIV 1984); on this

point, see Moo, *Epistle to the Romans*, 47–48, and the bibliography there; cf. Schreiner, *Romans*, 41–42.

2. On the fourth point, see the convincing discussion in Wright, *New Testament and the People of God*, 320–34.

3. Brooks, "What Life Asks of Us."

4. Spurgeon, *All of Grace*, 54.

5. Quoted in Barclay, *Letter to the Romans*, 23.

Romans 1:8–15

1. The phrase "the obedience of faith" is quite positive in that it taps into the Old Testament promise of the end-time conversion of the Gentiles, except that, according to Paul, the Gentile nations will be saved through faith in Christ alone. However, some commentators hold that the phrase is negative, in that Paul is critiquing covenantal nomism (see the sidebar for Rom. 2:17–24), or that the phrase refers to the Noahic laws.

2. Jewett, *Romans*, 130.

3. Jewett, *Romans*, 130–32; cf. 74–79.

4. Dowley, *Eerdmans' Handbook to the History of Christianity*, 364.

5. Wangerin, *Ragman and Other Cries of Faith*, 57.

6. Wangerin, *Ragman and Other Cries of Faith*, 62.

Romans 1:16–17

1. Schreiner, *Romans*, 58–59.

2. For the drawing and discussion, see below under "Illustrating the Text"; see also Ferguson, *Backgrounds of Early Christianity*, 476.

3. See Moo, *Epistle to the Romans*, 63–89; Schreiner, *Romans*, 66–69; Wright, *What Saint Paul Really Said*, 95–107. I seem to be the first author to root "not ashamed" and "revealed" in Isaiah's promise of the restoration of Israel.

4. See the discussions and bibliographies in Moo, *Epistle to the Romans*, 70–75, 79–91; Schreiner, *Romans*, 63–70; Dunn, *Romans 1–8*, 40–43; Jewett, *Romans*, 141–44.

5. E. P. Sanders famously called this "covenantal nomism" in his book *Paul and Palestinian Judaism*. In doing so, Sanders initiated the movement now known as the New Perspective on Paul. I will interact with this school of thought later in the commentary; see particularly comments on Romans 3:9–20.

Romans 1:18–32

1. For documentation of this point, see Wright, "Adam in Pauline Christology."

2. See Dunn, *Romans 1–8*, 172–73.

3. Dunn, *Romans 1–8*, 64.

4. For further documentation, see Dunn, *Romans 1–8*, 67.

5. See Moo, *Epistle to the Romans*, 118–19.

Romans 2:1–11

1. See Dunn, *Romans 1–8*, 82.

2. Dunn, *Romans 1–8*, 84. How Paul reconciles the ideas in Romans 2:1–11 that works are the basis for God's evaluation of where a person spends eternity and that attempting to find merit before God brings judgment will be discussed below.

3. N. T. Wright's works, which argue that Israel knew that even though they had been restored to their land since 536 BC, they were still in "exile," as evidenced by Syrian, Egyptian, and now Roman occupation of that land, have convinced many (see Wright, *The New Testament and the People of God* and *Jesus and the Victory of God*).

4. Most commentators pick up on this chiasm; here I am following the arrangement in Moo, *Epistle to the Romans*, 135.

Romans 2:12–16

1. See Stowers, *Diatribe and Paul's Letter to the Romans*.

2. See Augustine, *Julian* 4.3.25; *Spir. Let.* 26.43; Barth, *Romans*, 136; Cranfield, *Romans*, 1:156–63.

Romans 2:17–24

1. See Stowers, *Diatribe and Paul's Letter to the Romans*, 112.

2. See Pate, *Reverse of the Curse*, part 1.

3. The recent majority of Pauline interpreters agree that in Romans Paul is counteracting covenantal nomism, though individuals disagree on whether or not covenantal nomism is legalistic. James Dunn and others tend to think not, and they claim that Paul is not criticizing the law per se but the use of the law as a national marker to exclude Gentiles from the covenant. Others, like Douglas Moo, think that Paul is criticizing covenantal nomism as being legalistic and further argue that "works of the law" refers to the law of Moses. I agree with Moo. See my discussion of Romans 3:20 and "the works of the law" to follow.

4. The word *kauchaomai* ("boast") can be positive if one's boast is in God (Rom. 5:2, 3, 11).

5. See Garlington, "ΙΕΡΟΣΥΛΕΙΝ and the Idolatry of Israel," 39–40. Garlington bases his view on two pieces of evidence. First, *hierosyleō* can be translated in general as "commit sacrilege." Second, Paul accuses the Jew of boasting in the law of Moses. Even if Garlington's view does not stand, my suggestion below in the last of the six ironies is viable: the continued adherence of the Jew to the law since the coming of Christ is idolatrous. Moo discusses the above three possibilities, opting for the first (*Epistle to the Romans*, 164).

6. See, for example, Moo, *Epistle to the Romans*, 164–65; Schreiner, *Romans*, 133–34.

Romans 2:25–29

1. See the documentation in Moore, *Judaism in the First Centuries*, 1:323–35.

2. For argument that the covenant blessings and curses of Deuteronomy 27–30 undergird Romans 2:25–29, and even the whole of Romans 2, see Ito, "Romans 2."

3. Lloyd Gaston (*Paul and the Torah*) first popularized this view among some Pauline scholars.

Romans 3:1–8

1. Moo, *Epistle to the Romans*, 182–83 (though Moo does not mention the cursing/blessing scenario of the Balaam oracle that I am noting here).

Romans 3:9–20

1. For a sampling of work by these authors devoted to the defense of the New Perspective on Paul, see Sanders, *Paul and Palestinian Judaism*; Dunn, *Romans 1–8*; Wright, *What Saint Paul Really Said*. For rebuttals, see Moo, "Excursus: Paul, 'Works of the Law,' and First-Century Judaism," in *Epistle to the Romans*, 211–17; Pate, *Reverse of the Curse*; Gathercole, *Where Is Boasting?*

2. Moo, *Epistle to the Romans*, 212.

3. Moo, *Epistle to the Romans*, 206.

Romans 3:21–26

1. The Writings might not yet have been clearly delineated at the time of the New Testament. This is a debated question.

2. For two works focused on this teaching in Paul's letters, see Pate, *Adam Christology* and *Glory of Adam*.

3. For additional discussion, see "Additional Insights" following this unit.

Additional Insights

1. *Hilastērion* is the Greek translation of the Hebrew *kapporet*, which literally means "performance of atonement" but traditionally is rendered as "mercy seat" (NIV: "atonement cover"). In the Old Testament the Day of Atonement is *yom hakkippurim*, and today the Jewish feast is Yom Kippur.

2. Dodd, *Bible and the Greeks*; Morris, *Apostolic Preaching*.

3. Morris, *Apostolic Preaching*, 144–213.

4. See Schreiner, *Romans*, 189.

5. Schreiner, *Romans*, 189–91.

6. For excellent discussion of this issue, see Jewett, *Romans*, 270, 286, 289.

Romans 3:27–31

1. See Gathercole, *Where Is Boasting?*, 216–51. Gathercole did this work/dissertation under the supervision of James D. G. Dunn and came to disagree with the New Perspective on Paul that Dunn espouses.

2. My translation of 3:27–28 is slightly different from the NIV here, intending to bring out better the two nuances of the usage of *nomos* therein: "Where, then, is boasting? It is excluded. On what principle [nomos]? Of works? No, but on the principle [nomos] of faith. . . . a person is justified by faith apart from works of the law [nomos]."

3. See the defense by Dunn (*Romans 1–8*, 185–86) of this position, which usually is the position of the New Perspective on Paul.

4. See the defense by Moo (*Epistle to the Romans*, 249–50) of this position, which usually is the position of the traditional perspective on Paul.

5. Paul begins 3:29 with a contrastive Greek particle (*ē*) to show that he is offering a new contrast between the law and faith.

6. Thielicke, *Exercise for Young Theologians*, 16–17.

Additional Insights

1. For discussion of these constructs, see Pate, *End of the Age* and *Reverse of the Curse*.

Romans 4:1–8

1. For Gen. 15:6; 17, see, e.g., Sir. 44:19–20; *m. Ned.* 3.11; for Gen. 15:6; 22, see, e.g., 1 Macc. 2:52; compare *Jub.* 23.10 with *Jub.* 17.15–18.19; 19.8; see *m. 'Abot* 5.3; Philo, *Abraham* 191–99; Josephus, *Ant.* 1.223–25; 1.233–336; *L.A.B.* 40.2; 4 Macc. 14:20; CD 3.2–4; James 2:21–24. These references are cited in Schreiner, *Romans*, 215–16. There is much debate as to whether or not Paul and James (2:21–24) are divided on this issue.

2. See the discussion of Romans 4 along this line of interpretation in Sanders, *Paul, the Law, and the Jewish People*, 33–35; Dunn, *Romans 1–8*, 204; Wright, *New Testament and the People of God*, 192.

3. These references are cited in Dunn, *Romans 1–8*, 204–5.

4. Protestants, on the basis of Romans 4 and other Pauline texts, contend (rightly, I believe) that faith is not a work.

5. Barclay, *Letter to the Romans*, 75–76.

Romans 4:9–17a

1. See Jewett, *Romans*, 324.

2. See Str-B 3:211; cf. Dunn, *Romans 1–8*, 210.

3. For a helpful discussion of this perspective of the Old Testament prophets, see Pate et al., *Story of Israel*, 102.

4. See Dunn, *Romans 1–8*, 213.

5. See Cranfield, *Romans*, 1:234; Käsemann, *Romans*, 114.

6. See Str-B 3:203; see also Moo, *Epistle to the Romans*, 268, where he observes that Paul reinterprets Genesis 17:11—circumcision as the sign of the covenant—in Romans 4:10–11 to say that circumcision is a "sign," thus avoiding the tendency of Paul's Jewish contemporaries to identify this covenant with the Mosaic law; cf. Dunn, *Romans 1–8*, 232.

7. Romans 4:12 is referring to Jewish Christians. They also walk in the footsteps of Abraham's faith, having placed their trust in Christ. Compare Romans 4:11b–12 with Galatians 3:6–9.

8. For this approach to 4:13–15, see Dunn, *Romans 1–8*, 214–15.

9. "John Wesley (1703–1791)," in Kerr and Mulder, *Famous Conversions*, 54–60.

Romans 4:17b–25

1. Many commentators debate how 4:17b is related to its context. Most likely, it is a transitional statement in that it links the fatherhood of Abraham (4:16b–17a) to the faith of Abraham (4:18–22).

2. Genesis 17:17, which says that Abraham laughed at the notion that he and Sarah could have a child, appears to contradict Paul's statement in Romans 4:19–20 that Abraham's faith did not weaken. But although Abraham did have lapses along the way, the overall tenor of his life was one of belief in the promises of God. Another tension between the Abrahamic story and Paul's telling of it here in Romans 4:17b–22 is that Abraham had six more sons by Keturah (Gen. 25:1–2). How could this be if Abraham was impotent? The answer probably is that the procreative power that God granted Abraham carried on after Sarah's death.

3. Moo (*Epistle to the Romans*, 285n83) and Schreiner (*Romans*, 238) take *enedynamōthē* as active (Abraham "grew strong in faith") rather than as a true passive ("was strengthened"), as do Cranfield (*Romans*, 1:248) and Morris (*Romans*, 212). I agree that the verb is to be translated as a passive.

4. The words *hois mellei logizesthai* ("to whom [righteousness] will be credited [by God]") in 4:24 present three possible interpretations: (1) Paul is speaking of future justification before God on the final day (so Dunn, *Romans 1–8*, 223); (2) Paul is declaring that the believer is justified in the present (compare 4:25 with 5:1) (so Moo, *Epistle to the Romans*, 295); (3) Paul is saying that Genesis 15:6 was written with both Abraham and the Christian in view (4:23–24a), so that in the future (from the perspective of Gen. 15:6) the Christian will be justified (so Schreiner, *Romans*, 242). Schreiner seems to have the better argument, though the third view can also include the second, as Schreiner himself suggests.

5. Note that in 4:25 Paul may well be quoting an early Christian creed, as he did in 1:3–4 and perhaps in 3:25–26. There is a grammatical discussion about the preposition *dia*, used twice in 4:25 to create parallel statements: "who was handed over *dia* [because] of our sins" and "who was raised *dia* [?] our justification." The issue is whether the second *dia* should also be translated "because" (causal sense) or as "with a view to" (final sense). It appears that the causal sense is Paul's meaning for both uses of *dia* here. This rendering, however, need not mean that the resurrection is the sole cause of our justification, since in 5:9 Paul can say that we are "justified by [Jesus'] blood." Rather, Paul is assuring his reader in 4:25 that the proof of our justification is the resurrection of Jesus.

6. Quoted in Moo, *Epistle to the Romans*, 284.

Romans 5:1–4

1. See the surveys in Dunn, *Romans 1–8*, 242–44; Moo, *Epistle to the Romans*, 290–95; Schreiner, *Romans*, 245–49.

2. See Moo, *Epistle to the Romans*, 292.

3. See Pate, *Glory of Adam*.

4. Pate, *Glory of Adam*.

5. It is debated whether in 5:1 the text should be read as "we have" (*echomen*, an indicative) or as "let us have" (*echōmen*, a subjunctive). Although the manuscript evidence is much stronger for the latter reading, most commentators argue that the context—assurance before God—supports the former reading.

6. For this point, see Dunn, *Romans 1–8*, 248.

Romans 5:5–11

1. Dunn, *Romans 1–8*, 255.

2. I have tried to word this point here and above so as not to become embroiled (yet) in the controversy between Calvinism and Arminianism. The former holds to the perseverance of the saints (once saved, always saved), whereas the latter believes that Christians can lose their salvation through willful sin. But both sides agree that in Christ the believer is eternally secure. We will have occasion to enter into this controversy a little more when we examine Romans 9 and the issue of divine election.

Romans 5:12–14

1. H. Wheeler Robinson championed this approach that ancient Hebrew thinking focused on corporate solidarity, not on the individual as in modern Western culture. African culture likewise thinks in terms of the solidarity of humans. I had an American professor who earlier had lived in Africa for a time. He told our class that it was not until he moved to Africa and imbibed the sense of community promoted there that he first felt truly human, for Western culture, with its individualism, had drained the life out of him. J. W. Rogerson ("Hebrew Conception of Corporate Personality") has criticized the concept of corporate personality, arguing that it implies that there is only one personality between the individual and the group represented. This critique is helpful, but one need not therefore reject the concept itself. Both the individual and the members of the group have their respective personalities, but that does not negate the reality that the representative's action impacts the group. One has only to think here of any society that has a representative system of governance.

2. The NIV places a dash at the end of 5:12 because Paul most likely interrupts his sentence at that point only to resume it at 5:18. The interruption, 5:13–17, serves to expand on the nature of Adam's transgression as contrasted to Christ's obedience.

3. Dunn, *Romans 1–8*, 379. We should also note in this regard that Genesis foreshadows the story of Israel: sin, exile, restoration. Thus, Adam sinned against the Torah in the garden, the result of which was exile and death. But the promise to Abraham that he would be the father of Israel was viewed as the restoration. See "The Pentateuch," in Pate et al., *Story of Israel*, 29–49.

4. So Wright, "Adam in Pauline Christology," 372. Wright shows that this concept is latent already in Genesis itself.

5. Pate, *Reverse of the Curse*, 304.

6. In Romans 7:7 Paul affirms that the law is holy and good, but it is sin that is the ultimate problem. But 5:13–14 seems to be in some tension with that perspective.

7. The title "last Adam" comes from 1 Corinthians 15:45, where Paul calls Christ the "last [*eschatos*] Adam."

8. The "coming one" was a messianic title applied to Jesus (see Matt. 11:3; Luke 7:20; John 4:25).

Romans 5:15–21

1. The word "type" (*typos*) denotes those Old Testament persons, institutions, or events that have a divinely intended function of prefiguring the eschatological age inaugurated by Christ; hence the word "typology."

2. To my knowledge, many commentators have not picked up on this *inclusio* and the pattern that it projects onto 5:15–19.

3. Jewett, *Romans*, 381.

4. Here we see the interplay between the individual choice of each human to sin (5:16) and humanity's corporate solidarity with Adam's sin (5:12–14, 17–21).

5. For documentation, see Wright, "Adam in Pauline Christology."

6. There is a debate whether the verb *kathistēmi* in 5:19 means "make" or "appoint." The first has ethical connotations, while the second is legal in nuance: does Christ make us righteous or declare us so? In light of the context of 5:15–19, "make" is to be preferred, for just as Paul thinks that the old humanity is sinful (not just declared sinful), so also is the new humanity righteous (not just declared righteous).

Romans 6:1–7

1. The Greek word for "sanctification" is *hagiasmos* (the adjective *hagios* means "holy"). The term originated in Exodus 19:5–6, where Israel is labeled God's "holy people." Later Judaism used the term to refer to the inheritance of the messianic kingdom by the elect people of God (Dan. 7:18–19; *Pss. Sol.* 17). Thus, the nomenclature applied to the New Testament refers to the church as the new people of God who are set apart for divine holy purposes.

2. Paul's question in 6:1, "Shall we go on sinning so that grace may increase?" in essence is asking, "Does sanctification necessarily flow from justification?"

3. Although themes of Christ's/Christians' death and life are present in both 6:3–5 and 6:6–10, death receives a little more attention than life in the former, while life receives a little more attention than death in the latter.

4. It is much debated as to whether Paul felt that baptism by immersion symbolizes the believer's death, burial, and resurrection with Christ. I tend to think that Paul did have this in mind here.

5. Burial is the seal of death.

6. In New Testament times, because baptism happened right on the heels of a person's conversion to Christ by faith, the two—faith and baptism—went together (see Acts 2:38; 8:31–38; Titus 3:5; 1 Pet. 3:20–21), but faith preceded baptism.

7. Dunn, *Romans 1–8*, 316. See, for example, Exodus 16:4; Leviticus 18:3–4; Deuteronomy 28:9; Joshua 22:5; Jeremiah 44:23; Ezekiel 5:6–7; Daniel 9:10; Micah 4:2, where *halak* ("walk") is used.

8. On this point, see Moo, *Epistle to the Romans*, 366n71. For *kainotēs* and related terms as a reference for the new covenant in Paul's writings, see Romans 7:6; 1 Corinthians 11:25; 2 Corinthians 3:6.

9. The majority of commentators take *dedikaiōtai*, a perfect tense of the verb *dikaioō*, as meaning "delivered" rather than having the strictly forensic meaning that it has conveyed up to this point in Romans.

Additional Insights

1. Though the matter is debated, most scholars of the Dead Sea Scrolls think that the Essenes authored them. For further discussion about the Essenes and their religious community, see Pate, *Communities of the Last Days*.

2. For defense of this statement, see Pate, *Communities of the Last Days*, 81–82.

3. Reitzenstein, *Hellenistic Mystery-Religions*; Bousset, *Kyrios Christos*.

4. For further discussion of these criticisms as well as bibliography on the issue, see Pate, *End of the Age*, 27–28.

Romans 6:8–14

1. Once again, the New Perspective on Paul would reduce the "law" here to Jewish social markers (Dunn, *Romans 1–8*, 340), but it is clear that Paul has in mind the entirety of the Mosaic code.

Romans 6:15–23

1. For further discussion, see Pate, *End of the Age*, 198–203; Gager, "Religion and Social Class."

2. Jewett, *Romans*, 415. Both of these Old Testament verses record Israel gathering at the foot of Mount Sinai to receive the law while the divine thunder and fire swirled above at the top of the mountain.

3. Schreiner, *Romans*, 334.

4. Gagnon, "Heart of Wax"; cf. Schreiner, *Romans*, 336.

5. See Gagnon, "Heart of Wax"; Käsemann, *Romans*, 181; cf. Schreiner, *Romans*, 336.

6. For a helpful discussion of 6:19a, see Moo, *Epistle to the Romans*, 403–4.

7. Some commentators place the question mark in 6:21 after *tote* ("then"), which yields the following wording: "What fruit, then, were you reaping from those things? You are now ashamed of those things, for the outcome of those things is death" (e.g., Moo, *Epistle to the Romans*, 423). I think that Schreiner (*Romans*, 338–39) has a better argument, however, opting for the punctuation followed in the NIV, for the former translation would imply that the Roman Christians are ashamed now of their former sin because its outcome is death. It seems odd that present shame is based on future death.

8. Jewett, *Romans*, 426.

9. Note that Paul has not forgotten that believers' victory over sin and rule in the new dominion is based on the fact that they are united to Christ's death and resurrection. They are "in Christ" (6:23).

10. Luther, *Bondage of the Will*, 245.

Romans 7:1–12

1. For further discussion and documentation, see Dunn, *Romans 1–8*, 360.

Romans 7:13–25

1. For an excellent defense of this view, see Dunn, *Romans 1–8*, 387–99; Cranfield, *Romans*, 1:342–47, 355–70.

2. See Deissmann, *Paul*, 92; W. D. Davies, *Paul and Rabbinic Judaism*, 498.

3. This understanding of Romans 7:13–15 was popularized by Kümmel, *Römer 7*; this approach is also taken by Jewett, *Romans*, 459–73.

4. Moo, *Epistle to the Romans*, 447–48.

5. Dunn, *Romans 1–8*, 387–99. It should be noted that not all who see *nomos* here as the Mosaic law take the New Perspective on Paul.

6. John Donne, "Holy Sonnet XIV," in Eitel, *Treasury of Christian Poetry*, 152.

Romans 8:1–17

1. See Cranfield, *Romans*, 1:397.

2. The 1984 edition of the NIV has "set me free" in 8:2, but the better reading is "set you free" (so Codex Sinaiticus and Codex Vaticanus), which the NIV revision uses.

3. See Dunn, *Romans 1–8*, 416–17; Schreiner, *Romans*, 399.

4. In 8:10 an alternate translation to "the Spirit gives life" is "your spirit is alive" (NIV mg.). Most commentators concur that the "spirit" here is the Holy Spirit.

5. Scott, *Adoption as Sons of God*.

6. I have heard small children in the streets of Jerusalem call their father "Abba."

7. Thorpe, *Ringing Ballads*, 22.

Romans 8:18–30

1. See Pate, *End of the Age*, 113.

2. See Pate, *End of the Age*, 114–15.

3. The one who subjected creation to the curse was God, on account of Adam's sin.

4. Genesis 3:15 is thought to be the first promise of a Messiah in the Bible, hence the title *protoevangelion* ("first gospel"). Paul certainly applies Genesis 3:15 to Christ, the seed of the woman who crushed the head of the serpent/Satan (see Rom. 16:20).

5. The adoption of believers has already begun (8:15), but it is not yet complete (8:23).

6. There are various ways to translate 8:28 (see the NIV mg.), and there is also a variant reading in the Greek manuscripts. The debate basically involves whether "God works" or "all things work." But the issue is moot, since either way it is God who is causing things to work for the benefit of believers.

Romans 8:31–39

1. See the discussion in Moo, *Epistle to the Romans*, 541.

2. Moo, *Epistle to the Romans*, 541n29.

3. For further discussion, see Pate, *Glory of Adam*.

4. Schreiner, *Romans*, 466–67.

Romans 9:1–5

1. Dunn, *Romans 9–16*, 519. I have added the covenantal blessings and curses to Dunn's outline and also delineated the verses.

2. The last two references were suggested by my colleague Douglas Nikolaishen.

3. Dunn, *Romans 9–16*, 526.

4. These references are cited in Dunn, *Romans 9–16*, 526.

Romans 9:6–29

1. The Greek text is even more specific: *henos koitēn* (= one conception). Moo (*Epistle to the Romans*, 570) translates it as "one act of intercourse."

2. Some commentators take this description to reflect Semitic parlance whereby one quality is described in terms of its opposite.

3. There is a debate regarding 9:22. Is it concessive (*even though* God waited patiently for Israel to repent they did not,

and therefore he judged that nation) or causal (God waited for Israel's sins to become ripe *so that* he could unleash his wrath on them)? I opt for the concessive nuance, but the causal translation still confirms my contention that the metaphor of creator/potter and creation/clay occurs in the context of Israel's sin and judgment (covenantal curses).

4. Ironside, *Acts*, 80–81.

5. Sproul, *Holiness of God*, 124–26.

Romans 9:30–10:5

1. Romans 9:33 applies Isaiah 8:14; 28:16 to Christ. The Jews tried to attain righteousness through the law instead of trusting Christ. In doing so, they stumbled over Christ and faith righteousness. See also Romans 10:11; 1 Peter 2:6–8.

2. Dunn, *Romans 9–16*, 581–83, 587–88, 593–95; cf. Howard, "Christ the End of the Law," 333–37; Badenas, *Christ the End of the Law*.

3. Schreiner, *Law and Its Fulfillment*, 106.

4. Schreiner, *Law and Its Fulfillment*, 106–9.

5. See, for example, Howard, "Christ the End of the Law," 335–37; Badenas, *Christ the End of the Law*, 118–25; G. N. Davies, *Faith and Obedience in Romans*, 189–200.

6. Schreiner, *Law and Its Fulfillment*, 109–12.

7. The attempt by Cranfield (*Romans*, 2:521–22) to interpret Romans 10:5 as referring to Christ as the one who does the law and lives is unconvincing.

8. Rydelnik, "Jewish People and Salvation," 447.

9. Rydelnik, "Jewish People and Salvation," 448, 451.

10. Dostoevshy, *The Brothers Karavazov*, 255.

Additional Insights

1. Scott, "Paul's Use of Deuteronomic Tradition," 659–65; compare Bell, *Provoked to Jealousy*. See also Steck, *Israel und das gewaltsame Geschick der Propheten*.

2. Examples include Simeon and Levi (Jdt. 9:2–4; *Jub.* 30.5–20, referring to Gen. 34), Phinehas (Num. 25:10–13; Sir. 45:23–24; 1 Macc. 2:54; 4 Macc. 18:12), Elijah (Sir. 48:1–2; 1 Macc. 2:58), Mattathias (1 Macc. 2:19–26; Josephus, *Ant.* 12.271), and, once upon a time, Saul/Paul (Acts 9:1–4; Gal. 1:13–14; Phil. 3:4b–6).

3. For further discussion, see Dunn, *Romans 9–16*, 586–87.

4. On the meaning "termination," see Schreiner, *Law and Its Fulfillment*, 134–36; Bruce, "Paul and the Law of Moses." For a defense of the meaning "goal," with appeal to the church fathers in support, see Cranfield, *Romans*, 2:515–20; see also Badenas, *Christ the End of the Law*; Rhyne, *Faith Establishes the Law*, 103–4. For a hybrid view, see, for example, Dunn, *Romans 9–16*, 589; Leenhardt, *Romans*, 266.

5. For a treatment of the lexical evidence leading to this conclusion, see Badenas, *Christ the End of the Law*, 38–80.

6. Compare this with a similar understanding of the verb *katalambanō* in 1 Corinthians 9:24; Philippians 3:12.

7. So Badenas, *Christ the End of the Law*, 114–15; now also Thielman, *Paul and the Law*, 207–8.

8. See Schreiner, *Law and Its Fulfillment*, 134–36; cf. 133n26; see also, rather surprisingly, Dunn, *Romans 9–16*,

589–91, 597. The only text where the meaning indisputably is "goal" is 1 Timothy 1:5.

Romans 10:6–21

1. For discussion and documentation, see Pate, *Reverse of the Curse*.

2. For further documentation and discussion, see Pate, *Communities of the Last Days*, 85–106.

3. Romans 10:9 puts the confession by the mouth before believing in the heart only because that is the order in Deuteronomy 30:14 ("the word . . . is in your mouth and in your heart"). But Romans 10:10 provides the correct theological order of salvation: believe then confess.

4. Colson, "From Every Tribe, Tongue, and Nation."

5. Tucker, *From Jerusalem to Irian Jaya*, 80–84.

6. Mattingly, "Hitchens, Hitchens and God, Too."

Romans 11:1–10

1. It is unclear here whether Paul thinks that Gentiles are a part of the remnant, although certainly they are a part of the true restoration of Israel.

2. Paul draws upon the threefold division of the Old Testament to show the completeness of Israel's judgment. Moreover, Paul draws on the three Old Testament texts—Deuteronomy 29:4; Isaiah 29:10; Psalm 69:22–23—apparently because they make reference to not being able to see.

3. The references to the entrapping table and the bent backs in Psalm 69:22–23 probably should not be pressed to mean anything more than that Israel will experience judgment.

4. Feinberg, *Israel in the Spotlight*, 184–85.

Romans 11:11–24

1. See Ramsay, "The Olive-Tree and the Wild-Olive." The ancient texts cited are Columella, *Rust.* 5.9.16; Palladius, *Insit.* 53–54.

2. Paul never states why it took Israel to reject Christ before the Gentiles would come to Christ, but perhaps he felt that if Israel had accepted Jesus as their Messiah when he was on earth, then salvation would center in Jerusalem instead of going to the Gentile world. But this is only hypothetical because, obviously, Israel rejected the historical Jesus.

3. Dunn, *Romans 9–16*, 658–59.

4. There is no room here for the older dispensationalist view that the Bible speaks of two peoples of God: Israel in the Old Testament and the church in the New Testament. Rather, there is only one people of God—one tree—Jews and Gentiles whose lives are based on faith. See my further discussion of dispensationalism and covenantalism relative to 11:25–27.

5. Does Paul mean here that a genuine Christian can lose salvation? Calvinists say no; Arminians say yes. Either way, Paul's warning in 11:21 is not to be trifled with.

6. It seems clear from all of this that Paul believed that only the remnant in the Old Testament and believing Jews in the New Testament era were saved.

7. Plantinga, *Not The Way It's Supposed to Be*, 165n22.

Romans 11:25–32

1. See Cranfield, *Romans*, 2:576–77; Dunn, *Romans 9–16*, 681. Most modern commentators agree with this interpretation.

2. Bruce, *Romans*, 222; Barrett, *Romans*, 223.

3. Typical of this interpretation is the exegesis by Berkouwer, *Return of Christ*, 335–49.

4. See Sanday and Headlam, *Romans*, 335.

5. Longenecker, "Different Answers to Different Issues," 97.

6. The modern analogy of the reunification of Germany after the fall of the Berlin Wall might be useful to help us grasp the sense of Paul's concept of a unified Israel.

7. Some Greek manuscripts lack the word "now" (*nyn*) here; others replace it with "later" (*hysteron*).

8. It is clear from this that the *Sonderweg* (separate path) view of Israel's salvation is misguided. That is, Paul knows nothing here of two covenants: the old covenant of the law for Israel and the new covenant of the gospel for Gentiles. Rather, Jew and Gentile are saved in the same way: faith in Christ alone.

9. O'Connor, *Mystery and Manners*, 40–42.

Romans 11:33–36

1. For the first two influences, see Johnson, *Apocalyptic and Wisdom Traditions*, 166–73; Pate, *Reverse of the Curse*, 252–60.

2. Hanson, *Interpretation of Scripture*, 85.

3. Pate, *Reverse of the Curse*, 252–60.

4. Many commentators think that Paul's doxology in Romans 11:36 is only to God, but others have argued that Paul includes Christ in the doxology (see Pate, *Reverse of the Curse*, 253–55) for at least two reasons. First, the language of 11:36 is applied to Christ in other texts by Paul: "riches" (Phil. 4:19; Col. 1:27); "wisdom" (1 Cor. 1:21–24, 30); "knowledge" (1 Cor. 8:3; Gal. 4:9); "from him, through him, and to him" (1 Cor. 8:6; Col. 1:16–17). Second, the context of 11:36 is Christ. All of this is to say that the doxology to God in 11:36 involves Christ as the means to culminating the divine plan of salvation history.

5. Quote in Kotulak, "Seriously Weird Science."

Romans 12:1–2

1. Dunn, *Romans 9–16*, 715.

2. Moo, *Epistle to the Romans*, 758.

3. Commentators regularly note the connection between 12:1–2 and 1:21–25 but without specifying the Adam theology that undergirds 12:1–2.

4. For Greek philosophy, especially Stoicism, see, for example, Epictetus, *Disc.* 1.6.20–21; for Hellenistic Judaism, see especially *T. Levi* 3.6; Philo, *Spec. Laws* 1.277.

Romans 12:3–8

1. Some understand *metron* as the standard of faith—that is, the gospel. But "measure" or "quantity" is the preferred translation.

2. *Analogian pisteōs* ("proportion of faith" [12:6]) is parallel to *metron pisteōs* ("measure of faith" [12:3]).

Notes

3. See Schreiner, *Romans*, 658.

4. Wangerin, *Ragman and Other Cries of Faith*, 29–31.

5. Dickinson, *Selected Poems*, 9–10.

Additional Insights

1. Schweizer, "σῶμα," 1024–44.

2. See Dunn, *Romans 9–16*, 723.

3. Knox, *St. Paul*, 161.

4. Best, *One Body in Christ*, 83.

5. Cerfaux, *Theology of St. Paul*, 263–65.

6. For a critique of the theory that Paul was influenced by the mystery religions, see Best, *One Body in Christ*, 87–89; Wagner, *Pauline Baptism*; see especially the devastating critique by Wedderburn, *Baptism and Resurrection*.

7. Bultmann, *Theology of the New Testament*, 1:178–79.

8. Dunn, *Romans 9–16*, 723–24.

9. W. D. Davies, *Paul and Rabbinic Judaism*, 53–57.

10. W. D. Davies, *Paul and Rabbinic Judaism*, 57.

11. Wedderburn, *Baptism and Resurrection*, 350–56. Wedderburn also convincingly responds to criticisms of the Hebrew corporate personality theory. For more discussion, see Pate, *End of the Age*, 170–72.

Romans 12:9–21

1. See Sirach 7:34 (Rom. 12:15); Proverbs 3:7 and Isaiah 5:21 (v. 16); Proverbs 3:4 and 5:8 (v. 17); Leviticus 19:18 and Deuteronomy 32:35 (v. 19); Proverbs 25:21–22 (v. 20); and *Testament of Benjamin* 4.3 (v. 21). See also Dunn, *Romans 9–16*, 738.

2. See Matthew 5:44 and Luke 6:27–28 (Rom. 12:14); Luke 6:27–36 (v. 17); and Luke 6:27–36 (v. 21).

3. The assumed verb in 12:9 is the command to "let love be sincere." Other times in 12:9–21 the participle and the infinitive are used to express commands, while still other times an imperative is used. This use of participles, infinitives, and imperatives creates a rapid-fire chain of admonitions in 12:9–21.

4. The *phil-* root is used in this way by both the New Testament and other ancient writers (1 Thess. 4:9; Heb. 13:1; 1 Pet. 1:22; 2 Pet. 1:7; *1 Clem.* 47.5; 48.1; Philo, *Abraham* 168, 198; *Moses* 1.150; *Spec. Laws* 2.240).

5. Dunn, *Romans 9–16*, 744.

6. *NPNF¹*, 11:507.

7. In 12:16a Paul uses the verb *phroneō* twice ("think" the same toward one another), and then in 12:16b the adjective *phronimos* (do not "think" haughtily or conceitedly of yourself).

8. Some translate *tapeinois* as neuter (= "menial tasks"). But the fact that *tapeinois* is masculine (= "lowly people") everywhere else in the New Testament (Matt. 11:29; Luke 1:52; 2 Cor. 7:6; 10:1; James 1:9; 4:6; 1 Pet. 5:5) tips the scales toward the masculine form. See Schreiner, *Romans*, 668.

9. The context of 12:19 suggests that it is *God's* wrath that is being considered.

10. Harnack, *Mission and Expansion of Christianity*, 181–249.

Romans 13:1–7

1. The traditional translation of *psychē* is "soul," but by this term Paul means the whole person.

2. Cullmann, *State in the New Testament*, 55–70; cf. Wink, *Naming the Powers*, 45–47.

3. See Sherwin-White, *Roman Society and Roman Law*, 8–11.

Romans 13:8–14

1. See the bibliography in Dunn, *Romans 9–16*, 790–91.

2. Lövestam, *Spiritual Wakefulness*, 10–27, 34–35.

3. In addition, Lövestam cites *1 Enoch* 10.5; 92.4–5; 108.11; 1QS 1.9; 2.16; 3.13; 1QM 1.1; *2 Baruch* 18.2; 48.50. These texts also evidence an apocalyptic reading of the Deuteronomistic tradition.

4. Moo, *Epistle to the Romans*, 817.

5. For this view, see Schreiner, *Romans*, 690–95.

6. See Dunn, *Romans 9–16*, 775, 781.

7. See Pate, *End of the Age*, 117–18.

Romans 14:1–12

1. See, most notably, Sanday and Headlam, *Romans*, 399–403.

2. Sanday and Headlam, *Romans*, 399–403.

3. See the list of similarities in Schreiner, *Romans*, 704–5.

4. See Moo, *Epistle to the Romans*, 827–28.

5. Moo, *Romans*, 829–30; Cranfield, *Romans*, 2:694–97.

6. Moo (*Romans*, 852n14) notes the parallelism between *koinos* (unclean) and *akathartos* (impure) in Mark 7:2, 5; Acts 10:14 (cf. Acts 10:15, 28; 11:8, 9; Heb. 10:29). The cognate verb *koinoō* connotes the same nuance consistently in the New Testament (Matt. 15:11, 18, 20; Mark 7:15, 18, 20, 23; Acts 10:15; 11:19; 21:28; Heb. 9:13).

7. Regarding the abstention from meat and wine, scrupulous Jews sometimes avoided all meat in environments where they could not be sure of its kosher purity (see Dan. 1:8; 10:3; Tob. 1:10–12; Jdt. 12:2, 19; Add. Esth. 14:17; *Jos. Asen.* 7.1; 8.5; Josephus, *Life* 14), while wine was avoided because it was offered as a libation to the gods (see Dan. 1:3–16; 10:3; Add. Esth. 14:17; *T. Reub.* 1.10; *T. Jud.* 15.4; *Jos. Asen.* 8.5; *m. 'Abod. Zar.* 2.3; 5). Concerning the observance of special days, obviously the Mosaic law stipulated observing the weekly Sabbath as well as the major religious festivals.

8. The weak may also have included Gentile God-fearers. Roman writers noted the popularity of both the Sabbath and Jewish food laws even among the Gentiles (see Juvenal, *Sat.* 14.9b–10b; Horace, *Sat.* 1.9.67–72; Ovid, *Cure* 219–20). It is also possible that some of the God-fearers belonged to the "strong" in faith.

9. *Krinō* ("to judge") and words derived from it play a central role in Romans 14: *diakrisis* (v. 1); *krinō* (vv. 3, 4, 5 [2x], 10, 13 [2x], 22); *diakrinō* (v. 23); *katakrinō* (v. 23). Paul also includes himself in the "strong in faith" category, another indication that he believed that the law was no longer incumbent on Christians.

10. *Kyrios* is another key word in 14:1–12: sometimes it indicates God (vv. 4, 6 [3x], 11), and other times Christ (vv. 8 [3x], 9 [*kyrieuō*]), though scholars debate which verses

refer to which. This indicates that Paul places Christ on par with God.

11. Moo (*Epistle to the Romans*, 846n104) notes that *bēma* denotes a secular scene of judgment (Matt. 27:19; John 19:13; Acts 7:5; 12:21; 18:12, 16, 17), and that Paul is the only New Testament author who uses the term theologically of God's judgment seat (in 2 Cor. 5:10 it is Christ's judgment seat).

12. "As surely as I live" does not occur in the Isaiah passage, but it does occur twenty-two times in the LXX, so Paul may not have had any particular Old Testament text in mind for that phrase.

13. Webb, *Slaves, Women and Homosexuals*.

14. Wiersbe, Annotated *"Pilgrim's Progress"*, 142.

15. Bonhoeffer, *Life Together*, 93–94.

Romans 14:13–23

1. Moo, *Epistle to the Romans*, 849–50.

2. *Krinō* and cognate words occur five times in these verses (14:13 [2x], 22, 23 [2x]).

3. Luther, "Treatise on Christian Liberty," 251.

4. Lewis, *The Screwtape Letters*, 69.

Romans 15:1–13

1. See, for example, Moo, *Epistle to the Romans*, 869, 874, 878; Schreiner, *Romans*, 745, 755–56, 758; Dunn, *Romans 9–16*, 840, 845, 847, 850.

2. Recall my earlier observation from Romans 3–4 that Paul positively connects the Abrahamic and the new covenants but distances them from the Mosaic covenant.

3. For a defense of the view that 15:8a introduces these two parallel statements, see Moo, *Epistle to the Romans*, 876.

4. Moo, *Epistle to the Romans*, 878–79.

5. Schreiner, *Romans*, 758.

6. Moo, *Epistle to the Romans*, 879.

7. Moo, *Epistle to the Romans*, 881–84.

8. Yancey, *What's So Amazing about Grace?*, 275–76.

9. Bonhoeffer, *Life Together*, 86.

Romans 15:14–21

1. Moo, *Epistle to the Romans*, 884.

2. See Moo, *Epistle to the Romans*, 886. These parallels were already noted by John Chrysostom, *Hom. Rom.* 29.

3. Funk, "Apostolic *Parousia*," 251.

4. Aus, "Paul's Travel Plans," 251–52.

5. Moo, *Epistle to the Romans*, 891.

6. Jewett, *Romans*, 912–15.

7. Gordon, *To End All Wars*, 103–6.

8. Gordon, *To End All Wars*, 117–18.

9. http://www.persecution.com.

Romans 15:22–29

1. For an excellent study on the subject, see Nickle, *The Collection*.

2. Jewett, *Romans*, 74–77.

3. Aus, "Paul's Travel Plans."

4. See Dunn, *Romans 9–16*, 874.

5. It is splitting hairs to object to Aus's eschatological reading of Paul's collection from the Gentiles by saying that the offering of the Gentiles is not the Gentiles themselves, for the one (the collection) was the extension of the other (the Gentiles). Furthermore, although Paul does not make it explicit, he seems to imply that the Roman Christians and soon the newly evangelized Gentiles in Spain should also contribute to the Gentiles' offering to the saints in Jerusalem.

6. Colson, "A Perfect (Cultural) Storm."

7. Mattingly, "Memory Eternal."

8. Traherne, *Waking Up in Heaven*, 228.

Romans 15:30–33

1. Acts uses two similar terms for these Gentiles: "God-fearer" and "God-worshiper."

2. Levinskaya, *Book of Acts*.

3. Jewett, "Agitators and the Galatian Congregation"; cf. Jewett, *Romans*, 936–37.

4. Jewett, *Romans*, 939–40.

5. Houston, *Joyful Exiles*, 175.

6. See Trafton, "Dying to Be Faithful."

7. Ryle, *A Call to Prayer*, 73.

8. Houston, *Joyful Exiles*, 135.

Romans 16:1–2

1. Verse 24 is most likely a later addition to the test of Romans, for two reasons: (1) the only Greek manuscripts that contain this benediction are poor witnesses (e.g., D, F, G); (2) since the doxology in vv. 25–27 is most likely a part of the original, the secondary nature of the benediction in v. 24 would thereby be confirmed.

2. Schreiner, *Romans*, 786.

3. Jewett, *Romans*, 943.

4. Kim, *Form and Structure*, 126.

5. For this discussion on patronage, see Jewett, *Romans*, 89–91.

6. For extensive documentation of the Roman patronage system, see Winter, *Seek the Welfare of the City*.

7. For support of this from the archaeological evidence, see the bibliography in Jewett, *Romans*, 947.

8. Schreiner, *Romans*, 787.

9. See the excellent study on this and much more of the Jewish heritage of the early church in Skarsaune, *Shadow of the Temple*. The references to Ephesians are my own suggestions.

10. Christian History, "Catherine Booth."

11. Christian History, "Catherine of Siena."

12. Van Rheenen, "Money and Mi$$ion$ (Revisited)."

13. Olmsted, "A Wonderful Dirty Job."

Romans 16:3–16

1. Peter Lampe's studies have been invaluable to this research. See Lampe, "Roman Christians"; *From Paul to Valentinus*.

2. Gager, "Religion and Social Class."

3. Jewett, *Romans*, 954–74.

4. For the groundbreaking study highlighting the significance of worship in house churches among early Christians, see Filson, "Significance of Early House Churches."

5. Jewett, *Romans*, 953; see also 62–69.

6. See the discussion of the name "Junia" below.

7. Jewett, *Romans*, 959–60.

8. See Harnack, "*Kopos.*"

9. Schreiner, *Romans*, 796; Moo, *Epistle to the Romans*, 924.

10. Dunn, *Romans 9–16*, 894–95; Jewett, *Romans*, 961–62.

11. So Jewett, *Romans*, 966.

12. Lightfoot, "Caesar's Household," 174.

13. Jewett, *Romans*, 969–71.

14. Jewett, *Romans*, 971–72.

15. Jewett, *Romans*, 973.

16. Badley, "Community of Faith," 292–93.

17. Eckel, "I Love Those Guys." Quote from Hart, *Student's Guide*, 48.

Romans 16:17–20

1. Jewett, *Romans*, 981–88.

2. Concerning Philippians, it looks like Paul is about to end the letter at 3:1, but then he immediately launches into a diatribe against false teachers.

3. The Judaizers' emphasis on the dietary laws differs from that of the weak Jewish Christians in 14:1–15:13, for the latter did not prescribe the dietary laws as the means of salvation, whereas the former did.

4. Orwell, "The Freedom of the Press."

5. *ANF* 1:315.

6. Steiner, *Reader*, 36.

7. Montaigne, *Essays*, 4:41.

Romans 16:21–23

1. Richards, *Paul and First-Century Letter Writing*, 60.

2. Richards, *Paul and First-Century Letter Writing*, 64–80.

3. Richards, *Paul and First-Century Letter Writing*, 47–58.

4. Richards, *Paul and First-Century Letter Writing*, 165, 169, 199.

5. Some Western Greek texts (a family of texts that exhibit quite a bit of freedom in making changes, omissions, and insertions), such as D, F, and G, include 16:24, which is a benediction similar to the one in 16:20, "the grace of our Lord Jesus Christ be with all of you." But the earliest and best textual witnesses omit it, as do the vast majority of text critics. I agree with the majority opinion here.

6. See Jewett, *Romans*, 981.

7. Jewett, *Romans*, 983–84.

8. Smithey, "The Last Samurai."

9. Elmer, *Cross-Cultural Servanthood*, 16–17.

10. Keller, *Counterfeit Gods*, 84.

Romans 16:25–27

1. For a defense of the interpolation theory, see Jewett, *Romans*, 997–1002.

2. Translation from Lewis and Reinhold, *Roman Civilization*, 2:64.

3. For a recent anti-imperialist reading of Romans, see Wright, *Paul*, 25–27.

4. Dunn, *Romans 9–16*, 913.

5. Dodd, *Apostolic Preaching*, 38–45.

6. Fuller, *Church History of Britain*, 424.

7. Stott, *Authentic Christianity*, 132.

8. Wilberforce Academy, "Students Making a Difference."

Bibliography

Recommended Resources

Cranfield, C. E. B. *A Critical and Exegetical Commentary on the Epistle to the Romans*. 2 vols. International Critical Commentary. Edinburgh: T&T Clark, 1975–77.

Dunn, James D. G. *Romans 1–8*. Word Biblical Commentary 38A. Dallas: Word, 1988.

———. *Romans 9–16*. Word Biblical Commentary 38B. Dallas: Word, 1988.

Jewett, Robert. *Romans*. Hermeneia. Minneapolis: Fortress, 2007.

Moo, Douglas J. *The Epistle to the Romans*. New International Commentary on the New Testament. Grand Rapids: Eerdmans, 1996.

Pate, C. Marvin. *The End of the Age Has Come: The Theology of Paul*. Grand Rapids: Zondervan, 1995.

———. *The Reverse of the Curse: Paul, Wisdom, and the Law*. Wissenschaftliche Untersuchungen zum Neuen Testament 114/2. Tübingen: Mohr Siebeck, 2000.

Schreiner, Thomas R. *Romans*. Baker Exegetical Commentary on the New Testament. Grand Rapids: Baker Academic, 2008.

Other Works

Aus, Roger D. "Paul's Travel Plans to Spain and the 'Full Number of the Gentiles' of Rom. XI 25." *Novum Testamentum* 21 (1979): 232–62.

Badenas, R. *Christ the End of the Law: Romans 10:4 in Pauline Perspective*. Journal for the Study of the New Testament: Supplement Series 10. Sheffield: JSOT Press, 1985.

Badley, Kenneth R. "The Community of Faith as the Locus of Faith-Learning Integration." In *Alive to God: Studies in Spirituality Presented to James Houston*, edited by J. I. Packer and Loren Wilkinson, 286–95. Downers Grove, IL: InterVarsity, 1992.

Barclay, William. *The Letter to the Romans*. 3rd ed. New Daily Study Bible. Louisville: Westminster John Knox, 2002.

Barrett, C. K. *A Commentary on the Epistle to the Romans*. Harper's New Testament Commentaries. New York: Harper & Row, 1957.

Barth, Karl. *The Epistle to the Romans*. Translated by Edwyn C. Hoskins. London: Oxford University Press, 1933.

Baur, F. C. *The Church History of the First Three Centuries*. Translated by Allan Menzies. 2 vols. 3rd ed. London: Williams & Norgate, 1878–79.

———. *Paul, the Apostle of Jesus Christ: His Life and Works, His Epistles and Teachings*. Edited by Eduard Zeller. Translated by Allan Menzies et al. 2 vols. 2nd ed. London: Williams & Norgate, 1873–75.

Beale, G. K. *The Erosion of Inerrancy in Evangelicalism: Responding to New Challenges to Biblical Authority*. Wheaton, IL: Crossway, 2008.

Bell, Richard H. *Provoked to Jealousy: The Origin and Purpose of the Jealousy Motif in Romans 9–11*. Wissenschaftliche Untersuchungen zum Neuen Testament 2/63. Tübingen: Mohr Siebeck, 1994.

Berkouwer, G. C. *The Return of Christ*. Edited by Marlin J. Van Elderen. Translated by James Van Oosterom. Grand Rapids: Eerdmans, 1972.

Best, Ernest. *One Body in Christ: A Study in the Relationship of the Church to Christ in the Epistles of the Apostle Paul*. London: SPCK, 1955.

Boadt, Lawrence T. *Reading the Old Testament: An Introduction*. New York: Paulist Press, 1984.

Bonhoeffer, Dietrich. *Life Together*. Translated by John W. Doberstein. New York: Harper, 1954.

Bousset, Wilhelm. *Kyrios Christos: A History of the Belief in Christ from the Beginnings of Christianity to Irenaeus.* Translated by John E. Steely. Nashville: Abingdon, 1970.

Bowker, John. *The Targums and Rabbinic Literature: An Introduction to Jewish Interpretations of Scripture.* London: Cambridge University Press, 1969.

Brooks, David. "What Life Asks of Us." *New York Times,* January 26, 2009. http://www.nytimes.com/2009/01/27/opinion/27brooks.html.

Bruce, F. F. *The Epistle of Paul to the Romans: An Introduction and Commentary.* Tyndale New Testament Commentaries. Grand Rapids: Eerdmans, 1963.

———. "Paul and the Law of Moses." *Bulletin of the John Rylands Library* 57 (1975): 259–79.

Bultmann, Rudolf. *Theology of the New Testament.* Translated by Kendrick Grobel. 2 vols. New York: Scribner, 1951–55.

Cerfaux, Lucien. *The Church in the Theology of St. Paul.* Translated by Geoffrey Webb and Adrian Walker. New York: Herder & Herder, 1959.

Christian History. "Catherine Booth: Compelling Preacher and Cofounder of the Salvation Army." http://www.christianitytoday.com/ch/131christians/activists/catherinebooth.html.

———. "Catherine of Siena: Mystic and Political Activist." http://www.ctlibrary.com/ch/131christians/innertravelers/catherinesiena.html.

Colson, Chuck. "From Every Tribe, Tongue, and Nation: Ralph Winter's Legacy." *Breakpoint Commentary,* June 1, 2009. http://www.breakpoint.org/commentaries/1801-from-every-tribe-tongue-and-nation.

———. "A Perfect (Cultural) Storm: How the Church Should Respond." *Breakpoint Commentary,* May 8, 2009. http://www.breakpoint.org/commentaries/1819-a-perfect-cultural-storm.

Cullmann, Oscar. *The State in the New Testament.* New York: Harper & Row, 1956.

Davies, Glenn N. *Faith and Obedience in Romans: A Study in Romans 1–4.* Journal for the Study of the New Testament: Supplement Series 39. Sheffield: JSOT Press, 1990.

Davies, W. D. *Paul and Rabbinic Judaism: Some Rabbinic Elements in Pauline Theology.* London: SPCK, 1948.

Deissmann, Adolf. *Paul: A Study in Social and Religious History.* Translated by William E. Wilson. Reprint, New York: Harper, 1972.

Dibelius, Martin. *A Fresh Approach to the New Testament and Early Christian Literature.* New York: Scribner, 1936.

———. *James.* Revised by Heinrich Greeven. Edited by Helmut Koester. Translated by Michael A. Williams. Hermeneia. Philadelphia: Fortress, 1976.

Dickinson, Emily. *Selected Poems.* New York: Dover, 1990.

Dodd, C. H. *The Apostolic Preaching and Its Developments.* New York: Harper, 1944.

———. *The Bible and the Greeks.* London: Hodder & Stoughton, 1935.

Dostoevsky, Fyodor. *The Brothers Karamozov.* Translated by Richard Pevear and Larissa Volokhonsky. New York: Farrar, Straus & Giraux, 1990.

Dowley, Tim, ed. *Eerdmans' Handbook to the History of Christianity.* Grand Rapids, Eerdmans, 1977.

Dunn, James D. G. "Once More, *Pistis Christou.*" In *Society of Biblical Literature 1991 Seminar Papers,* edited by Eugene H. Lovering Jr., 730–44. Atlanta: Scholars Press, 1991.

Eckel, Mark. "I Love These Guys." *Warp and Woof* (blog), March 31, 2009. http://warpandwoof.org/uncategorized/474/.

Eitel, Lorraine, et al., eds. *The Treasury of Christian Poetry.* Old Tappan, NJ: Fleming H. Revell, 1982.

Elmer, Duane. *Cross-Cultural Servanthood: Serving the World in Christlike Humility.* Downers Grove, IL: InterVarsity, 2006.

Feinberg, Charles Lee. *Israel in the Spotlight.* Chicago: Moody, 1975.

Ferguson, Everett. *Backgrounds of Early Christianity.* Grand Rapids: Eerdmans, 1990.

Filson, F. V. "The Significance of Early House Churches." *Journal of Biblical Literature* 58 (1939): 105–12.

Fuller, Thomas. *The Church History of Britain: From the Birth of Jesus Christ until the Year 1648.* Vol. 2. Oxford: Oxford University Press, 1845.

Funk, Robert. "The Apostolic *Parousia:* Form and Significance." In *Christian History and Interpretation: Studies Presented to John Knox,* edited by W. R. Farmer, C. F. D. Moule, and R. R. Niebuhr, 249–68. Cambridge: Cambridge University Press, 1967.

Gager, John. "Religion and Social Class in the Early Roman Empire." In *The Catacombs and the Colosseum: The Roman Empire as the Setting of Primitive Christianity,* edited by Stephen Benko and John J. O'Rourke, 99–120. Valley Forge, PA: Judson, 1971.

Gagnon, R. A. J. "Heart of Wax and a Teaching That Stamps: ΤΥΠΟΣ ΔΙΔΑΧΗΣ (Rom. 6:17b) Once More." *Journal of Biblical Literature* 112 (1993): 667–87.

Garlington, Don B. "ΙΕΡΟΣΥΛΕΙΝ and the Idolatry of Israel (Romans 2:22)." *New Testament Studies* 36 (1990): 142–51.

Gaston, Lloyd. *Paul and the Torah.* Vancouver: University of British Columbia Press, 1987.

Gathercole, Simon J. *Where Is Boasting? Early Jewish Soteriology and Paul's Response in Romans 1–5.* Grand Rapids: Eerdmans, 2002.

Gordon, Ernest. *To End All Wars.* Grand Rapids: Zondervan, 2002.

Guernsey, Lisa. "Rewards under a Microscope." *New York Times,* March 2, 2009. http://www.nytimes

.com/2009/03/03/health/03rewa
.html?pagewanted=all.

Hall, Ron, and Denver Moore, with Lynn Vincent. *Same Kind of Different as Me: A Modern-Day Slave, an International Art Dealer, and the Unlikely Woman Who Bound Them Together*. Nashville: Thomas Nelson, 2006.

———. *What Difference Do It Make? Stories of Hope and Healing*. Nashville: Thomas Nelson, 2009.

Hanson, A. T. *The New Testament Interpretation of Scripture*. London: SPCK, 1980.

Harnack, Adolf von. "*Kopos (kopian, hoi kopiōntes)* im frühchristlichen Sprachgebrauch." *Zeitschrift für die neutestamentliche Wissenschaft* 27 (1928): 1–10.

———. *The Mission and Expansion of Christianity in the First Three Centuries*. Vol. 1. Translated and edited by James Moffatt. New York: Putnam, 1904.

Hart, Darryl G. *A Student's Guide to Religious Studies*. Wilmington, DE: ISI Books, 2005.

Hays, Richard B. *Echoes of Scripture in the Letters of Paul*. New Haven: Yale University Press, 1989.

———. *The Faith of Jesus Christ: An Investigation of the Narrative Substructure of Galatians 3:1–4:11*. Society of Biblical Literature Dissertation Series 56. Chico, CA: Scholars Press, 1983.

Hengel, Martin. *Judaism and Hellenism: Studies in Their Encounter in Palestine during the Early Hellenistic Period*. Translated by John Bowden. 2 vols. Philadelphia: Fortress, 1974.

———. *The Son of God: The Origin of Christology and the History of Jewish-Hellenistic Religion*. Translated by John Bowden. Philadelphia: Fortress, 1979.

Houston, James. *Joyful Exiles: Life in Christ on the Dangerous Edge of Things*. Downers Grove, IL: InterVarsity, 2006.

Howard, G. E. "Christ the End of the Law: The Meaning of Romans 10:4ff." *Journal of Biblical Literature* 88 (1969): 331–37.

Ironside, H. A. *Acts*. Ironside Expository Commentary. Grand Rapids: Kregel, 2007.

Ito, Akio. "Romans 2: A Deuteronomistic Reading." *Journal for the Study of the New Testament* 59 (1995): 21–37.

Jewett, Robert. "The Agitators and the Galatian Congregation." *New Testament Studies* 17 (1971): 198–212.

Johnson, E. Elizabeth. *The Function of Apocalyptic and Wisdom Traditions in Romans 9–11*. Society of Biblical Literature Dissertation Series 109. Atlanta: Scholars Press, 1989.

Käsemann, Ernst. *Commentary on Romans*. Translated and edited by Geoffrey W. Bromiley. Grand Rapids: Eerdmans, 1980.

Keller, Timothy. *Counterfeit Gods: The Empty Promises of Money, Sex, and Power, and the Only Hope That Matters*. New York: Dutton, 2009.

Kennard, Douglas W. *Messiah Jesus: Christology in His Day and Ours*. New York: Peter Lang, 2007.

Kerr, Hugh T., and John M. Mulder, eds. *Famous Conversions: The Christian Experience*. Grand Rapids: Eerdmans, 1983.

Kim, Chan-Hie. *Form and Structure of the Familiar Greek Letter of Recommendation*. Society of Biblical Literature Dissertation Series 4. Missoula, MT: Scholars Press, 1972.

Klauck, Josef. *Ancient Letters and the New Testament: A Guide to Context and Exegesis*. Translated and edited by Daniel P. Bailey. Waco: Baylor University Press, 2006.

Kline, Meredith G. *Treaty of the Great King: The Covenant Structure of Deuteronomy*. Grand Rapids: Eerdmans, 1963.

Knox, Wilfred L. *St. Paul and the Church of the Gentiles*. Cambridge: University Press, 1939.

Kotulak, Ronald. "Seriously Weird Science: Hidden Dimensions, Phantom Particles—Even Time Travel—Are among Fermilab's High-Energy Pursuits. *Chicago Tribune Magazine*, January 11, 2004. http://articles.chicagotri bune.com/2004-01-11/features /0401110472_1_extra-dimensions -tevatron-cern.

Kümmel, Werner Georg. *Römer 7 und die Bekehrung des Paulus*. Untersuchungen zum Neuen Testament. Leipzig: J. C. Hinrichs, 1929.

Ladd, George. *A Theology of the New Testament*. Revised by Donald A. Hagner. Grand Rapids: Eerdmans, 1993.

Lampe, Peter. *From Paul to Valentinus: Christians at Rome in the First Two Centuries*. Edited by Marshall D. Johnson. Translated by Michael Steinhauser. Minneapolis: Fortress, 2003.

———. "The Roman Christians of Romans 16." In *The Romans Debate*, edited by Karl P. Donfried, 216–330. Rev. ed. Peabody, MA: Hendrickson, 1991.

Leenhardt, Franz J. *Epistle to the Romans: A Commentary*. Translated by Harold Knight. London: Lutterworth, 1961.

Levinskaya, Irina. *The Book of Acts in Its Diaspora Setting*. Grand Rapids: Eerdmans, 1996.

Lewis, C. S. *The Screwtape Letters*. Uhrichsville, OH: Barbour, 1990.

Lewis, Naphtali, and Meyer Reinhold, eds. *Roman Civilization: Selected Readings*. 2 vols. New York: Harper & Row, 1955–66.

Lightfoot, J. B. "Caesar's Household." In *Saint Paul's Epistle to the Philippians*, 169–76. 2nd ed. London: Macmillan, 1869.

Longenecker, Bruce W. "Different Answers to Different Issues: Israel, the Gentiles and Salvation History in Romans 9–11." *Journal for the Study of the New Testament* 36 (1989): 95–123.

Lövestam, Evald. *Spiritual Wakefulness in the New Testament*. Translated by W. F. Salisbury. Lunds universitets årsskrift 55/3. Lund: Gleerup, 1963.

Luther, Martin. *The Bondage of the Will*. Vol. 33 of *Luther's Works*. Edited by Philip S. Watson. Translated by Philip S. Watson in collaboration with Benjamin Drewery. Philadelphia: Fortress, 1972.

———. "Preface to the Complete Edition of Luther's Latin Writings." In vol. 34 of *Luther's Works*, translated by Lewis W. Spitz Jr., edited by Lewis W. Spitz, 323–38. Philadelphia: Muhlenberg, 1960.

———. "A Treatise on Christian Liberty." In *Three Treatises*, translated by C. M. Jacobs, A. T. W. Steinhaeuser, and W. A. Lambert, 251–90. Philadelphia: Muhlenberg, 1947.

Mattingly, Terry. "Hitchens, Hitchens and God, Too." http://www.tmatt.net/2010/03/29/hitchens-hitchens-and-god-too.

———. "Memory Eternal, Robert E. Webber." http://www.tmatt.net/2007/05/02/memory-eternal-robert-e-webber.

Mendenhall, G. E. "Covenant Forms in Israelite Tradition." *Biblical Archaeologist* 17 (1954): 3, 50–76.

Montaigne, Michel de. *Essays of Montaigne*. Edited by William Carew Hazlitt. Translated by Charles Cotton. 4 vols. New York: Scribner, 1902.

Moo, Douglas J. *Romans*. NIV Application Commentary. Grand Rapids: Zondervan, 2000.

Moore, George F. *Judaism in the First Centuries of the Christian Era: The Age of the Tannaim*. 2 vols. Reprint, New York: Schocken, 1971.

Morris, Leon. *The Apostolic Preaching of the Cross*. Grand Rapids: Eerdmans, 1965.

———. *The Epistle to the Romans*. Pillar New Testament Commentary. Grand Rapids: Eerdmans, 1988.

Nanos, Mark D. *The Mystery of Romans: The Jewish Context of Paul's Letter*. Minneapolis: Fortress, 1996.

Nickle, Keith F. *The Collection: A Study in Paul's Strategy*. Studies in Biblical Theology 48. London: SCM, 1966.

O'Connor, Flannery. *Mystery and Manners: Occasional Prose*. Edited by Sally and Robert Fitzgerald. New York: Farrar, Straus & Giroux, 1969.

Olmsted, Elizabeth. "A Wonderful Dirty Job." http://www.ywam.org/News-Stories/news/A-Wonderful-Dirty-Job.

Orwell, George. "The Freedom of the Press." Online at "Orwell's Preface to *Animal Farm*." http://home.iprimus.com.au/korob/orwell.html.

Pate, C. Marvin. *Adam Christology as the Exegetical and Theological Substructure of 2 Corinthians 4:7–5:21*. Lanham, MD: University Press of America, 1991.

———. *Communities of the Last Days: The Dead Sea Scrolls, the New Testament, and the Restoration of Israel*. Downers Grove, IL: InterVarsity, 2000.

———. *The Glory of Adam and the Afflictions of the Righteous: Pauline Suffering in Context*. Lewiston, NY: Mellen Biblical Press, 1993.

Pate, C. Marvin, J. Scott Duvall, J. Daniel Hays, E. Randolph Richards, W. Dennis Tucker Jr., and Preben Vang. *The Story of Israel: A Biblical Theology*. Downers Grove, IL: InterVarsity, 2004.

Plantinga, Cornelius, Jr. *Not the Way It's Supposed to Be: A Breviary of Sin*. Grand Rapids: Eerdmans, 1995.

Ramsay, W. M. "The Olive-Tree and the Wild-Olive." Pages 219–50 in *Pauline and Other Studies in Early Christian History*. London: Hodder & Stoughton, 1908.

Reitzenstein, Richard. *Hellenistic Mystery-Religions: Their Basic Ideas and Significance*. Translated by John E. Steely. Pittsburgh: Pickwick, 1978.

Rhyne, C. Thomas. *Faith Establishes the Law*. Society of Biblical Literature Dissertation Series 55. Chico, CA: Scholars Press, 1981.

Richards, E. Randolph. *Paul and First-Century Letter Writing: Secretaries, Composition, and Collection*. Downers Grove, IL: InterVarsity, 2004.

Ripley, Amanda. "Should Kids Be Bribed to Do Well in School?" *Time*, April 8, 2010. http://www.time.com/time/nation/article/0,8599,1978589,00.html.

Rogerson, J. W. "The Hebrew Conception of Corporate Personality: A Reexamination." *Journal of Theological Studies* 21 (1970): 1–16.

Rydelnik, Michael. "The Jewish People and Salvation." *Bibliotheca sacra* 166 (2008): 447–62.

Ryle, J. C. *A Call to Prayer*. Grand Rapids: Baker Books, 1976.

Sanday, William, and Arthur C. Headlam. *A Critical and Exegetical Commentary on the Epistle to the Romans*. 5th ed. International Critical Commentary. Edinburgh: T&T Clark, 1899.

Sanders, E. P. *Paul, the Law, and the Jewish People*. Philadelphia: Fortress, 1983.

———. *Paul and Palestinian Judaism: A Comparison of Patterns of Religion*. Philadelphia: Fortress, 1977.

Schreiner, Thomas R. *The Law and Its Fulfillment. A Pauline Theology of Law*. Grand Rapids: Baker Academic, 1993.

Schweizer, Eduard. "σῶμα." In vol. 7 of *Theological Dictionary of the New Testament*, edited by Gerhard Kittel and Gerhard Friedrich, translated by Geoffrey W. Bromiley, 1024–94. Grand Rapids: Eerdmans, 1979.

Scott, James M. *Adoption as Sons of God: An Exegetical Investigation into the Background of ΥΙΟΘΕΣΙΑ in the Pauline Corpus*. Wissenschaftliche Untersuchungen zum Neuen Testament 2/48. Tübingen: Mohr Siebeck, 1992.

———. "Paul's Use of Deuteronomic Tradition." *Journal of Biblical Literature* 112 (1993): 645–65.

Sherwin-White, A. N. *Roman Society and Roman Law in the New Testament*. Oxford: Clarendon, 1963.

Skarsaune, Oskar. *In the Shadow of the Temple: Jewish Influences on Early*

Christianity. Downers Grove, IL: InterVarsity, 2002.

Smithey, Cole. "The Last Samurai: An Exclusive Interview with Tom Cruise." http://www.review-mag .com/archive/560-569/562/Ncruise .htm.

Sproul, R. C. *The Holiness of God*. Rev. ed. Carol Stream, IL: Tyndale, 1998.

Spurgeon, Charles Haddon. *All of Grace*. Chicago: Moody, 2010.

Steck, Odil Hannes. *Israel und das gewaltsame Geschick der Propheten: Untersuchungen zur Überlieferung des deuteronomistischen Geschichtsbildes im Alten Testament, Spätjudentum und Urchristentum*. Wissenschaftliche Monographien zum Alten und Neuen Testament 23. Neukirchen-Vluyn: Neukirchener Verlag, 1967.

Steiner, George. *George Steiner: A Reader*. New York: Oxford University Press, 1984.

Stendahl, Krister. "The Apostle Paul and the Introspective Conscience of the West." *Harvard Theological Review* 56 (1963): 199–215.

Stott, John. *Authentic Christianity: From the Writings of John Stott*. Edited by Timothy Dudley-Smith. Downers Grove, IL: InterVarstiy, 1995.

Stowers, Stanley K. *The Diatribe and Paul's Letter to the Romans*. Society of Biblical Literature Dissertation Series 57. Chico, CA: Scholars Press, 1981.

Thielicke, Helmut. *A Little Exercise for Young Theologians*. Translated by Charles L. Taylor. Reprint, Grand Rapids: Eerdmans, 1997.

Thielman, Frank. *Paul and the Law: A Contextual Approach*. Downers Grove, IL: InterVarsity, 1994.

Thorpe, Rose Hartwick. *Ringing Ballads, including "Curfew Must Not Ring To-night."* Boston: D. Lothrop, 1887.

Trafton, Jennifer. "Dying to Be Faithful: Persecution Brought Out the Best and Worst in the Early Christians." http://www.christianitytoday.com /ch/news/2008/jan10.html.

Traherne, Thomas. *Waking Up in Heaven*. Edited by David Buresh. Spencerville, MD: Hesed, 2002.

Tucker, Ruth. *From Jerusalem to Irian Jaya: A Biographical History of Christian Missions*. Grand Rapids: Zondervan, 1983.

Van Rheenen, Gailyn. "MR #13: Money and Mi$$ion$ (Revisited): Combating Paternalism." *Missiology. org* (blog), January 12, 2001. http:// missiology.org/?p=247.

Wagner, Gunter. *Pauline Baptism and the Pagan Mysteries: The Problem of the Pauline Doctrine of Baptism in Romans VI.1–11, in the Light of Its Religio-Historical "Parallels."* Translated by J. P. Smith. Edinburgh: Oliver & Boyd, 1967.

Wangerin, Walter, Jr. *Ragman and Other Cries of Faith*. San Francisco: Harper & Row, 1984.

Webb, William J. *Slaves, Women and Homosexuals: Exploring the Hermeneutics of Cultural Analysis*. Downers Grove, IL: InterVarsity, 2001.

Wedderburn, A. J. M. *Baptism and Resurrection: Studies in Pauline Theology against Its Greco-Roman Background*. Wissenschaftliche Untersuchungen zum Neuen Testament 44. Tübingen: Mohr Siebeck, 1987.

White, E. B. *The Trumpet of the Swan*. New York: Harper Trophy, 1970.

Wiersbe, Warren. *The Annotated "Pilgrim's Progress."* Chicago: Moody, 1980.

Wilberforce Academy. "Students Making a Difference." http://www .wilberforceacademy.org/differ ence.html.

Wink, Walter. *Naming the Powers: The Language of Power in the New Testament*. Philadelphia: Fortress, 1984.

Winter, Bruce. *Seek the Welfare of the City: Christians as Benefactors and Citizens*. Carlisle: Paternoster, 1994.

Wright, N. T. "Adam in Pauline Christology." In *The Climax of the Covenant: Christ and the Law in Pauline Theology*, 18–40. Minneapolis: Fortress, 1991.

———. *Jesus and the Victory of God*. Vol. 2 of *Christian Origins and the Question of God*. Minneapolis: Fortress, 1996.

———. *The New Testament and the People of God*. Vol. 1 of *Christian Origins and the Question of God*. Minneapolis: Fortress, 1992.

———. *Paul: In Fresh Perspective*. Minneapolis: Fortress, 2005.

———. *What Saint Paul Really Said: Was Paul of Tarsus the Real Founder of Christianity?* Grand Rapids: Eerdmans, 1997.

Yancey, Philip. *What's So Amazing about Grace?* Grand Rapids: Zondervan, 1997.

Image Credits

Unless otherwise indicated, photos, illustrations, and maps are copyright © Baker Photo Archive.

The Baker Photo Archive acknowledges the permission of the following institutions and individuals.

Photo on page 117 © Baker Photo Archive. Courtesy of the Altes Museum, Berlin, Germany.

Photos on 35, 276 © Baker Photo Archive. Courtesy of the Antikensammlung, Berlin, Germany.

Photos on pages 5, 8 (2×), 17, 29, 38, 54, 112, 152, 169, 213, 258, 273, 329 © Baker Photo Archive. Courtesy of the British Museum, London, England.

Photo on page 87 © Baker Photo Archive. Courtesy of the Collection of Classical Antiquities, Berlin, Germany.

Photo on page 255 © Baker Photo Archive. Courtesy of the Eretz Museum, Tel Aviv, Israel.

Photo on page 248 © Baker Photo Archive. Courtesy of the Greek Ministry of Antiquities and the Archaeological Museum of Ancient Corinth, Greece.

Photos on pages 24, 78, 164, 321 © Baker Photo Archive. Courtesy of the Greek Ministry of Antiquities and the Archeological Museum of Thessaloniki, Greece.

Photo on page 60 © Baker Photo Archive. Courtesy of the Holyland Hotel. Reproduction of the City of Jerusalem at the time of the Second Temple, located on the grounds of the Holyland Hotel, Jerusalem, 2001. Present location: The Israel Museum, Jerusalem.

Photo on page 227 © Baker Photo Archive. Courtesy of the Jordanian Ministry of Antiquities and the Amman Archaeological Museum.

Photos on pages 229, 280 © Baker Photo Archive. Courtesy of the Musée du Louvre; Autorisation de photographer et de filmer. Louvre, Paris, France.

Photo on page 53 © Baker Photo Archive. Courtesy of the National Archaeological Museum of Spain, Madrid.

Photos on pages 42, 118 © Baker Photo Archive. Courtesy of the Pergamon Museum, Berlin.

Photo on page 330 © Baker Photo Archive. Courtesy of Sola Scriptura: the Van Kampen Collection on display at the Holy Land Experience, Orlando, Florida.

Photo on page 80 © Baker Photo Archive / Timothy Ladwig.

Photo on page 2 © Baker Photo Archive. Courtesy of the Turkish Ministry of Antiquities and the Antalya Museum, Turkey.

Photos on pages 14, 105, 201, 319 are © Baker Photo Archive. Courtesy of the Turkish Ministry of Antiquities and the Istanbul Archaeological Museum.

Photos on pages 10, 74, 124, 155, 176, 269 © Baker Photo Archive. Courtesy of the Vatican Museum.

Additional image credits

Photo on page 135 © AJ Alfieri-Crispin, CC-by-sa-2.0.

Photo on page 307 © Anthony Majanlahti, CC-by-2.0.

Photo on page 230 © Arnold Dekker / Wikimedia Commons, CC-by-sa-3.0.

Photo on page 294 © Bernard Gagnon / Wikimedia Commons, CC-by-sa-3.0.

Photo on page 21 © Calidius / Wikimedia Commons, CC-by-sa-3.0, courtesy of the Antikensammlung, Berlin.

Photo on page 108 © Cappella della Sacra Sindone, Duomo, Turin, Italy / The Bridgeman Art Library.

Photo on page 218 © Chixoy / Wikimedia Commons, CC-by-sa-3.0.

Photo on page 233 courtesy of NASA.

Photo on page 303 © Dennis Taylor, CC-by-2.0.

Photo on page 36 © Dr. James C. Martin and the Israel Museum. Collection of the Israel Museum, Jerusalem, and courtesy of the Israel Antiquities Authority, exhibited at the Israel Museum, Jerusalem.

Photos on page 41 © Dr. James C. Martin and the Israel Museum (Rockefeller Museum). Collection of the Israel Museum, Jerusalem, and courtesy of the Israel Antiquities Authority, exhibited at the Rockefeller Museum, Jerusalem.

Photo on page 262 © Dr. James C. Martin and the Israel Museum (Shrine of the Book). Collection of the Israel Museum, Jeruslaem, and courtesy of the Israel Antiquities Authority, exhibited at the Shrine of the Book, the Israel Museum, Jerusalem.

Photo on page 315 © G.dallorto / Wikimedia Commons, courtesy of the Istanbul Archaeology Museum.

Photo on page 161 © Ijon / Wikimedia Commons, CC-by-sa-3.0.

Photo on page 194 © Itzhak Baum / Wikimedia Commons, CC-by-sa-3.0.

Photo on page 215 © Jaimrsilva / Wikimedia Commons, CC-by-sa-3.0.

Photo on page 130 © Jebulon / Wikimedia Commons.

Photos on pages 256, 274 © Jensens / Wikimedia Commons.

Photo on page 244 © Jürgen Howaldt / Wikimedia Commons, CC-by-sa-2.0, courtesy of the Bremen Cathedral Museum, Germany.

Photos on pages 47, 62, 68, 133, 138, 144, 206, 256, 261, 305 © Kim Walton.

Photo on page 8 © Kim Walton. Courtesy of the British Museum, London, England.

Photo on page 220 © Kim Walton. Courtesy of the Chora Museum.

Photo on page 327 © Kim Walton. Courtesy of the National Archaeological Museum of Florence, exhibited on the Palatine Hill, Rome.

Photo on page 127 © Konrad Kurzacz / Wikimedia Commons, CC-by-sa 3.0.

Photo on page 162 © Kurt Wichmann / Wikimedia Commons, CC-by-3.0.

Photo on page 282 © Lalupa / Wikimedia Commons, CC-by-sa-3.0.

Photos on pages 96, 235, 250 © Marie-Lan Nguyen / Wikimedia Commons. Courtesy of the Musée du Louvre; Autorisation de photographer et de filmer. Louvre, Paris, France.

Photos on pages 105, 156 © Marie-Lan Nguyen / Wikimedia Commons, courtesy of the Musée National du Moyen Âge.

Photo on page 179 © Marie-Lan Nguyen / Wikimedia Commons. Courtesy of the Vatican Museum.

Photo on page 293 © Marie-Lan Nguyen / Wikimedia Commons, CC-by-3.0.

Photo on page 309 © Marsyas / Wikimedia Commons, CC-by-3.0.

Photo on page 23 © Osterreichische Nationalbibliothek, Vienna, Austria / The Bridgeman Art Library.

Photo on page 51 © Roland zh / Wikimedia Commons, CC-by-sa-3.0,

courtesy of the Kunsthaus Zürich, Switzerland.

Photo on page 316 © Sailko / Wikimedia Commons, CC-by-sa-3.0.

Photo on page 297 © Sailko / Wikimedia Commons, CC-by-sa-3.0, courtesy of the British Museum, London, England.

Photo on page 120 © Sailko / Wikimedia Commons, CC-by-sa-3.0, courtesy of the Museum der Bildenden Kuenste, Leipzig, Germany.

Photo on page 94 © San Vitale, Ravenna, Italy / The Bridgeman Art Library.

Photo on page 241 © Shakko / Wikimedia Commons, CC-by-sa-3.0, courtesy of the Pushkin Museum, Moscow.

Photo on page 141 © Teqoah / Wikimedia Commons, CC-by-sa-3.0.

Photo on page 158 © TheLeopards / Wikimedia Commons.

Photo on page 209 © U.S. Center for World Mission.

Photo on page 115 © William Brigham / Hawaii State Archives.

Photo on page 282 © www.RomeCabs.com, CC-by-sa 2.0.

Photos on pages 170, 173, 242, 265, 301 © The Yorck Project / Wikimedia Commons.

Photos on pages 33, 103, 143, 180, 192, 286 © Zev Radovan / www.BibleLandPictures.com.

Contributors

General Editors
Mark L. Strauss
John H. Walton

Associate Editor, Illustrating the Text
Rosalie de Rosset (with Mark Eckel)

Series Development
Jack Kuhatschek
Brian Vos

Project Editor
James Korsmo

Interior Design
Brian Brunsting

Visual Content
Kim Walton

Cover Direction
Paula Gibson
Michael Cook

Subject Index

prophets (*continued*)
193, 202, 205, 212–13, 222, 226, 232, 240, 278, 280, 281, 283, 287, 328–29, 335
Psalms, 65–66, 70, 72, 73, 92, 95–96, 99–100, 102, 179, 180, 212, 279, 281, 339

qal wahomer, 73, 93, 95, 116, 119, 129–31, 179, 217–19
Qumran, 135, 140, 202, 227, 262–63, 337
  and the covenant, 112, 141, 205, 275, 285, 328

rabbinic Judaism, 55, 92–93, 95, 99, 100, 116, 135, 137, 140, 150, 155, 157, 228, 246
remnant. *See* Jews: remnant of
resurrection, 166–69, 218, 300
  of believers, 111, 114, 137, 142, 168, 170, 173–74, 176, 181
  of Israel, 19, 111, 168, 181
  of Jesus Christ, 5, 18–19, 28, 32, 104–9, 118, 132, 134, 136–38, 141–45, 148, 153, 156, 168, 169, 172, 181, 206, 208, 231, 265, 281, 322, 328, 336, 337
revelation, 32, 36, 46, 49, 65–66, 73, 81, 172, 214, 231–32, 243, 328–29
  natural, 37–38, 47, 207, 208
  special, 47, 48, 72, 208
righteousness, 5, 6, 74, 76–81, 83, 94–96, 100–102, 107, 109, 112–13, 130, 134, 139, 145, 146, 148–53, 156, 174, 196–99, 204–9, 263, 273–75, 318. *See also* faith: and righteousness
  of God, 7, 11, 26, 28, 30–32, 34, 56, 66, 67, 72, 73, 76–80, 86–88, 96, 102, 131, 197–99, 205, 206
  of Jesus Christ, 50, 67, 96, 129, 137, 168, 274–75
  and the law, 196–97, 199, 205, 206, 267, 338
  and life, 128–29, 131, 132, 143, 148–52, 156
  and works, 1, 101, 158, 198, 199
Roman Christians, 7, 9, 10, 23–25, 150–51, 248, 255, 256, 266, 285, 287, 296, 298, 299, 305, 308–9, 312, 314–19, 329, 337. *See also* Rome: Gentile Christians in; Rome: Jewish Christians in

Paul's ethical challenge to, 234, 236, 260, 292, 327
Paul's greetings to, 16, 302, 308, 310, 320–25
and support for Paul's ministry, 11–12, 17, 22, 26, 303, 327, 341
weak and strong, 267–69, 272, 278–80, 291
Roman Empire, 1–2, 12, 17, 22, 29, 32, 112, 149–50, 202, 207, 248, 255, 258, 287, 297–98, 313, 320–22, 327, 329
Rome, 47, 112, 113, 152, 179, 197, 236, 253, 256, 261, 267, 282, 298, 311, 316
  churches in, 7, 10–13, 19, 20, 59, 254, 255, 258, 266, 270, 272, 285, 299, 305, 308–14, 322, 326–27
  destination of Romans, 1, 8, 9, 16, 20, 285, 303, 327
  Gentile Christians in, 10, 12, 13, 20, 23, 24, 59, 219, 280–83, 285, 292
  Jewish Christians in, 10, 12–13, 19, 24, 34, 37, 47, 67, 87, 219, 250–51, 280, 311
  Jews in, 9, 10, 180, 310, 311
  Paul's visit to, 8, 10–12, 24, 28, 285, 291–93, 305, 320–21, 323, 324

sacrifice, 5, 94, 234–40, 248, 254, 255, 268, 273
  of Jesus Christ, 76–80, 116, 118–19, 153, 167, 171, 178–79, 235, 278–80, 282
  Old Testament, 76, 77, 79, 82–83, 116, 167, 235–36, 285–87, 294
salvation, 7, 11, 21, 28–32, 53, 118, 135, 141, 151–52, 173, 179, 186, 193–94, 197–99, 204–8, 220, 226, 261–63, 274, 336, 339, 342
  by faith, 4, 13, 31, 32, 90, 102, 108, 199, 281, 299, 315
  God's plan of, 56, 88, 213, 228–33, 326, 329
  by grace, 80, 96–97, 107, 211–14
  and the law, 17, 32, 77, 80, 101, 317
  and works, 55, 88–91, 96–97, 101, 206, 315
salvation history, 28, 56, 164, 190, 191, 226, 228–32, 237, 286, 339

sanctification, 96, 149, 151–52, 235, 337
  and justification, 21, 26, 134–35, 138–39, 143, 234, 237, 238, 275
Sanders, E. P., 55, 72, 74, 334
Sarah. *See* Abraham: and Sarah
Schreiner, Thomas, 28, 82, 150, 181, 198, 199, 281, 302, 303, 310, 333, 336, 337
second coming. *See* Jesus Christ: second coming of; parousia
Second Temple Judaism, 41–42, 61, 71, 72, 74–76, 92, 93, 98, 99, 112, 122, 124, 130, 157, 166, 169, 196, 204, 272, 275, 296, 317, 329
  literature of, 5, 19, 36, 52, 84, 282, 333
sin, 5–6, 37–38, 51, 54–55, 57, 73, 77, 82–83, 95–96, 125–26, 134–39, 142–43, 145, 146, 154, 178, 181, 185–86, 194, 264, 275
  and death, 122–23, 128, 132, 134, 135, 143, 148–52, 156, 157, 160, 162–64, 167–68, 337
  and exile, 42, 54, 58, 61–62, 65–66, 99, 111, 150, 193, 261, 280, 317, 336
  forgiveness of, 79, 81, 96, 99–100, 150
  of the Gentiles, 35, 41, 43–49, 79, 226
  and grace, 13, 64, 66, 131, 134–35, 149–51, 300, 337
  of Israel, 11, 28, 34–35, 40–44, 49, 54–56, 61–62, 65–66, 70–71, 79, 81, 82, 98–99, 111, 116, 123, 131, 150, 186, 193, 205, 217–18, 226, 235, 240, 261, 280, 317, 338
  Jesus Christ died for, 20, 32, 82, 104, 107, 116–20, 137, 142, 152–53, 165, 167
  and judgment, 34, 36, 42, 50, 66–67
  and the law, 32, 49, 55–56, 70–71, 73–74, 87, 102, 122–25, 128–29, 132, 134, 143, 148–49, 151–52, 156, 160–64, 167–68, 199, 226, 261, 296
  power of, 71–72, 75, 136, 161, 163
  and righteousness, 143, 148, 150, 151

sinful nature, 56, 74, 123–24, 129, 158, 160–62, 167, 168, 261, 265
slavery, 18, 24, 78, 148–51, 164, 252, 270, 308–13, 323
  to the law, 62, 149, 154–60
  to sin, 70, 111, 134, 135, 149–51, 160, 164
sovereignty, divine, 108, 190–95, 200, 212
Spain, 3, 11–12, 17, 22–25, 53, 287–88, 290–95, 302–7, 320–21, 323–24, 327, 329, 333, 341. *See also* Paul: mission to Spain
spiritual gifts. *See* Holy Spirit: gifts of
Stoicism, 2, 35–37, 47, 52, 181, 229, 246, 339
suffering, 107, 110–14, 174–75, 180, 296
  and glory, 112, 166, 172–76, 181
  of Jesus Christ, 32, 116, 165, 169, 173
Suffering Servant, 17–18, 107, 131, 207, 287, 288, 296
synagogue, 10, 59, 71, 88, 135–36, 155, 197, 297, 306

temple, 13, 14, 53, 55, 111, 286
  Jerusalem, 5, 54, 56, 60, 71, 167, 186–88, 201, 218, 224, 255, 257, 285, 311
  pagan, 9, 54, 62, 112, 231, 236, 266, 327
Ten Commandments, 15, 55, 57, 67, 262
Torah. *See* law of Moses
total depravity of humanity, 70–73, 152, 194
Trajan, 12, 144, 253, 267
"two ways" tradition, 15, 43, 129, 248–49, 315–16

wisdom, 228, 243, 248, 339
  of God, 32, 204–6, 210, 228–32, 242
  and the law, 54, 198, 204, 206, 229, 231
  preexistent, 206, 228, 229, 231
works of the law, 4, 6, 11, 55, 61, 63, 70–72, 74–75, 84–86, 90–91, 99–101, 149, 151, 197, 230, 300, 315, 334
Wright, N. T., 72, 75, 333, 334, 336